THE MYTH
OF LIBERATION

THE
MYTH
OF
LIBERATION

**East-Central Europe in
U.S. Diplomacy and Politics
since 1941**

BENNETT KOVRIG

THE JOHNS HOPKINS UNIVERSITY PRESS
Baltimore and London

The Johns Hopkins University Press, Baltimore, Maryland 21218
The Johns Hopkins University Press Ltd., London

Library of Congress Catalog Number 72-4028
ISBN 0-8018-1361-1
Manufactured in the United States of America

Library of Congress Cataloging in Publication data will
be found on the last printed page of this book.

232045

To My Mother
and to the Memory
of My Father

CONTENTS

PREFACE

East-Central Europe is a geopolitical term that normally designates those countries which passed into the Soviet sphere of influence in the aftermath of World War II—to wit, Albania, Bulgaria, Czechoslovakia, East Germany, Hungary, Poland, Rumania, and, for a briefer period, Yugoslavia. This study attempts to trace the course of American foreign policy and its domestic sources and repercussions from the moment the United States entered the war and proclaimed as one of its war aims the restoration of the sovereignty of the various nations of East-Central Europe. To single out one area in a foreign policy that reflects global responsibilities incurs the risk of imputing to that area an unwarranted significance. Yet it is undeniable that East-Central Europe has played a catalytic role in the recent history of conflicts on that continent; for instance, if Poland was at least symbolically the *casus belli* that impelled Britain and France to declare war on Hitler, it also served as the first of many contentious issues that drove the erstwhile Allies into the rigid postures of the cold war. Since the United States appears to have acknowledged its inability to influence the political evolution of East-Central Europe, the moment is opportune for an analytical account of the sources and implementation of the various American policies which, from the Atlantic Charter onward, have had as a common denominator an interest in, if not necessarily a commitment to, the liberation of East Europeans from the hegemonic rule of their more powerful neighbors.

Analysis of the foreign policy process presents a formidable challenge to the scholar by virtue of both the scale and the complexity of the subject; in the case of the United States, the peculiarities of the division of powers, the relative but deceptive absence of secrecy, and a unique amalgam of *Realpolitik* and official and popular idealism only accentuate this complexity. For an overview spanning some thirty years, a rigid analytical framework clearly was not suitable. Nevertheless, certain implicit questions guided the progress of this work, the most fundamental being, what real and perceived confluence of forces influenced the policy-making elites? This question naturally subsumes a plethora of subsidiary lines of enquiry regarding objectives, priorities, capabilities, and outcomes, all of which receive attention within the limitations of length and historical data.

This is a retrospective study, and, beyond noting certain sins of omission or commission on the part of American statesmen, it offers no grand prescription for future policies toward East-Central Europe. Through much of the period observed, the principal failure of these statesmen was their inability—intellectual or political—to reconcile the operational and declaratory facets of their policies, and the resulting confusion did much harm to the prestige of the United States. That such a dichotomy may be one of the burdens of democracy is suggested by A. J. P. Taylor's observation that a democratic foreign policy must be idealistic, "or at the very least it has to be justified in terms of great general principles." Yet the reader will find few villains and even fewer heroes, for seldom in the history of America's foreign relations have good intentions reaped such a bitter harvest.

The sources for this work encompass a wide range of published documents, memoirs, press files, secondary studies, as well as the Dulles papers and private communications, but one servitude of students of international politics is that they must be content with data which, *raison d'état* prevailing, remain fragmentary. As the eminent British historian Sir Lewis Namier once noted, *definitive* means "until superseded by something better." Nevertheless, the necessity remains of throwing light on recent history in order to provide a more thorough understanding of policies and political processes, as well as a basis for the constructive criticism of current orientations. Such, then, are the limitations and pretensions of the study at hand.

Finally, some acknowledgments are in order. To Professors W. T. Easterbrook and Alexander Brady of the University of Toronto I owe a great debt for their many years of encouragement and support. Dr. F. S. Northedge of the London School of Economics and Political Science at one stage provided invaluable guidance. Richard Gregor and James Barros, colleagues and friends, helped in ways sometimes unknown to themselves. Financial support came from the Mackenzie King Trust, the Canada Council, and the International Studies Programme of the University of Toronto. Mrs. Elinor Foden of Erindale College contributed essential stenographic and editorial skills.

THE MYTH
OF LIBERATION

I

TOWARD SPHERES
OF INFLUENCE

*Responsibility for political conditions
thousands of miles overseas can no longer
be avoided by this great nation.*

*Perfectionism, no less than isolationism
or imperialism, or power politics, may
obstruct the paths to international peace.*
FRANKLIN D. ROOSEVELT

When on December 7, 1941, the pride of America's Pacific Fleet settled
under the quiet waters of Pearl Harbor, the dominant and enduring principle of that nation's foreign policy, isolationism, lost the last shreds of
popular as well as strategic legitimacy. The United States thereupon found
itself at war not only with Japan, Germany, and Italy, but with three
smaller and more reluctant members of the Axis, Bulgaria, Hungary, and
Rumania, which issued their own declarations of war five days after
Japan's crippling surprise attack. At the same time, two other East European countries, Poland and Czechoslovakia, acquired a powerful champion, as did Yugoslavia, where royalist and leftist partisans vied with each
other in harassing the occupiers. Thus, for the second time in twenty-five
years, that much oppressed, oft-conquered, quarrelsome region known as

East-Central Europe involved the distant United States in the determination of its fate.

Nevertheless, such involvement was granted only grudgingly in Washington, for it was evident that Hitler's minor allies had acted largely under duress and that in any event little opportunity for direct hostilities was likely to materialize. Led by its pro-Nazi dictator General Antonescu, Rumania had declared war on the Soviet Union on June 22, 1941, and was playing host to sizable German forces, as was Bulgaria, whose King Boris had by 1940 aligned himself with Hitler, without, however, taking hostile action against Russia. The reasons for Hungary's membership in the Axis were equally compelling; irredentism stemming from the ill-conceived Treaty of Trianon, by which Hungary in 1920 lost two-thirds of its territory and more than three million ethnic Hungarians, had aroused a calculated sympathy only in Rome and Berlin, and, when the Vienna Awards of 1938 and 1940, engineered by Ciano and Ribbentrop, restored to Hungary parts of Slovakia and Transylvania, support for the Axis became a foregone conclusion. Unlike the Bulgarians, Hungarians and Rumanians had historical grievances against Russia which were skillfully exploited by Hitler, as were the divisions among the East Europeans themselves. Hungarian, Bulgaro-Macedonian, and Croatian revisionism was pitted against Czechoslovakia, Rumania, and Yugoslavia, whose regimes all favored the interwar *status quo*. In the final analysis, their own weakness and the lack of any countervailing force to Germany's economic and military preponderance—demonstrated first at Munich and then in the invasion of Poland—left little alternative to these three nations. Conservative, nationalistic, and more authoritarian than democratic, their regimes responded to Hitler's lure with little enthusiasm and some foreboding, but the specter of bolshevism, which haunted not only their ruling classes but also an overwhelming majority of their peoples, proved at least as effective as German threats in overcoming their hesitation. The United States, remote and fascinating, had seldom in history aroused any popular animosity in the area, and its positive influence necessarily waned with the onset of isolationism. In Hungary, which retained a modicum of independence longer than any of its neighbors, the last American minister perceived the essence of their dilemma: "It is . . . surprising that the Hungarians sympathized with the cause of the Allies to such a great extent as they did. It is undeniable that they did not receive encouragement from the democracies. We did not promise anything—we only threatened." "I was asked many times if we could help Hungary if she followed our policy, and how, but I was compelled to say that we would not and I did not know how we could."[1] America's reluctance to acknowledge the enmity of Hitler's minor allies was finally overcome by the Soviet Union, which admittedly had more tangible evidence of their belligerence. It is likely that, as Senator Vandenberg suggests, Molotov's secret presence in Washington was instrumental in persuading President Roosevelt to respond; in recommending the declarations of war, ratified by Congress on June 5, 1942, the president observed that the Bulgarian, Hungarian, and Rumanian governments had declared war on the United States, "not upon their own initiative or in response to the wishes of their own peoples but as instruments of Hitler."[2] Understandably, the undertone of leniency found no echo in Moscow.

Even prior to its official entry into the war, however, the United States had indicated that it did not consider the dismemberment and occupation of Poland, Czechoslovakia, and Yugoslavia legitimate. Washington never accepted the validity of the Molotov-Ribbentrop Pact of 1939, and it subsequently recognized the London-based government headed by General Sikorski. The Czechoslovak National Committee had created a provisional government, also in London, and led by President Beneš, to which the United States extended formal recognition on July 30, 1941, a few days after Foreign Minister Jan Masaryk and Soviet Ambassador Ivan Maisky had endorsed a Soviet-Czechoslovak agreement on mutual assistance. In the final months of 1940, Washington had urged Yugoslavia's regent to resist Hitler's blandishments (protested Prince Paul to the U.S. minister, Arthur Bliss Lane, "You big nations are hard. You talk of our honor but you are far away."),[3] but could not prevent his capitulation and the German occupation that followed a palace coup; diplomatic relations were thereafter maintained with King Peter's exile regime in London. By mid-1942, then, Washington's relations with East-Central Europe testified to a clear-cut rejection of the Hitlerian status quo through the recognition of three exile governments and the existence of a nominal state of war with the three satellite regimes.

POLITICAL PROMISES AND MILITARY STRATEGY

America's emergence from isolationism proved to be a painfully slow process, for the domestic economic crisis, the dismal record of the League of Nations as conciliator and peacekeeper, and the predominance of virulent isolationist-neutralist sentiments in Congress all induced in Roosevelt an extreme caution in responding to the international upheavals of the 1930s. In August 1940, after the fall of France, he provided by executive agreement some destroyers for beleaguered Britain, an act that, at least in Churchill's eyes, symbolized the passage of the United States from neutrality to nonbelligerence. The president tried to follow a middle course, on the one hand promising in the 1940 campaign not to send American boys to die in foreign wars, and on the other hand successfully guiding the

Lend-Lease program through Congress the following spring; once the Germans had launched their attack on the Soviet Union in June 1941, he sent his close adviser Harry Hopkins to sound out Stalin on the Russians' need for American aid. These gestures remained within the confines of non-belligerence, as were the embargoes imposed on Japan in retaliation for the latter's sweeping expansion through the Far East. While it is true that, as John J. McCloy, assistant secretary of war during the period of hostilities, later observed, isolationism had produced a vacuum of political objectives, American concern for the future of East-Central Europe can be traced back to the summer of 1941, when principles were proclaimed which formed the basis for the first myth of liberation.[4] In their secret meetings aboard the U.S.S. *Augusta* and the H.M.S. *Prince of Wales*, anchored off Argentia, Newfoundland, the British prime minister and the president conferred over a set of broadly phrased objectives, suffused with Wilsonian idealism, which became known as the Atlantic Charter.

Churchill had come to Placentia Bay in the hope that the Americans might be induced to issue a strong policy statement opposing Japanese expansion in the Far East. This expectation proved to be premature, for Pearl Harbor was still some four months off, and Roosevelt manifested an acute consciousness of the persistence of isolationism in Congress and within his electorate. These same pressures made the president reluctant to allow any direct reference to a postwar international organization in the proposed Charter, and the two leaders compromised on a circumlocution that referred to a wider and permanent system of general security. The Americans were concerned that the British had already made secret commitments to the Soviet Union and others on territorial questions, but these fears were put to rest by categorical denials, notably from Cadogan to Sumner Welles.[5] The final document, issued on August 14, informed the world of a joint Anglo-American commitment to "respect the right of all peoples to choose the form of government under which they will live."[6] The British, as original proponents of the Charter, viewed it more as a propaganda piece than as a blueprint for future action, and Roosevelt himself took pains to emphasize that it could not be construed as a formal treaty. The Charter did not explicitly commit the two powers to direct intervention in pursuit of its terms; neither, for that matter, did it differentiate between Hitler's allies and his victims. In fact, the vague terminology proved to be of some embarrassment to Churchill, who clearly did not intend for the Charter's principles to be applied to British dependencies; he subsequently explained that the Charter was aimed primarily at the "restoration of the sovereignty, self-government, and national life of the States and nations of Europe now under the Nazi yoke, and the principles governing any alterations in their territorial boundaries which may have to be made."[7] Such alterations, according to the Charter, would not be made without the freely expressed wishes of the people concerned. When in September the Soviet government endorsed the Atlantic Charter, it did so with the rather ambiguous reservation that "the practical application of these principles will necessarily adapt itself to the circumstances, needs, and historic peculiarities of particular countries"; at the time, this qualification passed virtually unnoticed, but according to Churchill the Russians intended to use it to legitimize their claim to Polish territories annexed as a result of the Molotov-Ribbentrop Pact.[8]

Despite the public or private reservations of its signatories, the Atlantic Charter was taken by East Europeans of all origins, at home and in exile, as a genuine commitment to an equitable and popularly based settlement of Europe's postwar configuration. This conviction was only strengthened once the Grand Alliance came into being. The twenty-six signatories of the United Nations Declaration, issued in Washington on January 1, 1942, undertook to respect the principles first enunciated in the Atlantic Charter; similar sentiments were expressed in the Four Nation Declaration on General Security, signed by the United States, Great Britain, the Soviet Union, and China in Moscow on October 30, 1943. Thus the Allies' declaratory policy at least boded well for the future of East-Central Europe.

It has become a historical truism that profound differences in the realms of ideology, national interest, and diplomatic style made the Grand Alliance a fragile aberration, and that a euphoric unawareness of this weakness, particularly on the part of American leaders, destroyed the chances for a satisfactory and enduring conclusion of Europe's agony. For many years after the war, charges of betrayal and of willful sacrifice of East-Central Europe's rights to self-determination filled the political atmosphere; as late as 1968, President de Gaulle asserted that at Yalta the United States had sanctioned Soviet hegemony over that area. Yet, in order to do any justice to the West's wartime diplomacy, it is essential to evaluate it in its proper historical and psychological context. Undeniably the members of the Grand Alliance made strange bedfellows. The Soviet Union had been a pariah in the international state system up to the moment of Hitler's attack upon it. The Western powers had materially hindered the consolidation of the regime that issued from the Bolshevik revolution, and, although in the 1930s diplomatic contacts were intensified and the Depression made Marxism less distasteful an ideology to many in the West, Stalin's draconian methods for dealing with internal opposition, the activities of the Comintern, the Russo-Finnish War, and, finally, the Molotov-Ribbentrop Pact of 1939 contributed to a lingering hostility in the chancelleries of the West. For Britain, it was a matter of survival that the Soviet Union join in the crusade against Germany, and, while Churchill had few illusions regarding Stalin's ambitions, he recognized that British power was scarcely sufficient to stave off national disaster, let alone guarantee that the Soviet Union behave like a docile and predictable ally. Stalin, for his part, took pains in the early years of the war not to offend the sensibilities of the democracies; for this reason, and also to galvanize his people, he relegated contentious ideological principles to the background, ostensibly dissolved the Comintern, made his peace with the Orthodox church, and stressed patriotism as the dynamic ideal of the Russian war effort.

Public opinion in the United States responded slowly to this new image, but the Roosevelt administration threw itself wholeheartedly into the task of convincing Americans that a miraculous metamorphosis had indeed occurred, and that the pitiless dictator was little worse than a misguided reformer who was now behaving as an honorable and invaluable ally in the struggle against Nazi tyranny. The elemental politician in Roosevelt saw Stalin as a reasonable man who could be maneuvered into sharing Western goals by the undeniable personal charm and acumen of the American president. Particularly in the two years during which Russia stood alone on the Continent against the onslaught of Hitler's *Wehrmacht*, its allies shared a legitimate moral reluctance to seek specific commitments from the Soviet Union with respect to the future of East-Central Europe. In official Washington, this attitude took the form of an unwillingness to go beyond the commendable but vague principles of the Atlantic Charter in planning for a postwar political settlement. The inclination to present a definitive solution to the age-old problem of interstate conflict and to assess such conflict in terms of inadequate institutions and venal leadership had long been inherent in the American approach to world politics, and had surfaced most dramatically in the missionary zeal of President Wilson. Remembering Wilson's humiliation at the hands of an isolationist Congress, Roosevelt initially advocated that the Allies act after the war as the benevolent "Four Policemen," and only later, when the domestic political atmosphere appeared favorable, did he espouse the cause of a universal organization so dear to the heart of Secretary of State Cordell Hull. The lesser political issues were to be postponed pending victory on the battlefield. It was in this spirit that the Advisory Committee on Postwar Foreign Policy, created in 1942, devoted itself almost exclusively to the problem of creating a successor to the hapless League of Nations. Meanwhile, under Roosevelt's direction, American policy regarding the political future of Europe evolved as an elusive amalgam of high moral purpose and devastating pragmatism.

The wartime conferences serve well to illustrate Washington's posture of principled postponement—"no predetermination"—as well as the ultimately divergent goals of Britain and the Soviet Union, whose leaders never lost sight of the possible and desirable political consequences of victory over the Axis. Stalin's profound distrust of the West and his determination to secure a protective and therefore ideologically compatible sphere of influence became more evident when the tide began to turn against Germany after Stalingrad, but even in the darkest days of the war he would find occasion to press his case. By the time of Eden's visit to Moscow in December 1941, Stalin was already complaining that the Atlantic Charter appeared to be directed against the Soviet Union; he proceeded to present specific proposals for a postwar settlement that included the incorporation of Estonia, Latvia, Lithuania, and parts of Finland, Poland, and Rumania into the Soviet Union as well as the annexation of East Prussia to Poland and of the Sudetenland to Czechoslovakia.[9] Nor did these demands represent the sum total of Soviet interests; this war, observed Stalin to the Yugoslav partisan leader Milovan Djilas, had the novel characteristic that "whoever occupies a territory also imposes on it his own social system."[10] Therefore, even though the Soviet leader was too pragmatic to adopt a rigid blueprint and would press simply for the maximum advantage, it is clear that he anticipated in order of priority certain territorial annexations, the imposition of the Soviet political system on areas under his ultimate military control, and the political penetration of the rest of Europe by the intermediation of local communist movements. His policy's general thrust was the expansion of Soviet influence to the fullest extent allowed by the eventual configuration of power on the Continent and by the determination of his allies to pursue their own interests.

If Britain's leaders seldom lost sight of these potentially divisive stakes, their counterparts in Washington wallowed in ambivalence. In a reference document on Russia's position which he brought to the Quebec conference of August 1943, Harry Hopkins noted that, "since without question she will dominate Europe on the defeat of the Axis, it is . . . essential to develop and maintain the most friendly relations with Russia."[11] Both these views were shared by the president—the first privately and rather inconsistently, the second with the full fanfare of wartime propaganda. When in September of the same year he was questioned by Archbishop Spellman regarding the future of certain predominantly Catholic areas in East-Central Europe, Roosevelt conceded that Austria, Hungary, and Croatia were likely to fall under Soviet protectorate and voiced the hope that in ten or twenty years European influences would encourage the Russians to become less barbarous. Even more startling was Roosevelt's disclosure of a plan to divide the world into spheres of influence, with China getting the Far East, the United States getting the Pacific, and

Britain and Russia getting Europe and Africa; and, since Britain's interests were mainly colonial, observed the president, it could be assumed that Russia would predominate in Europe. According to Spellman's record, Roosevelt went on to argue that in view of Stalin's power it would be realistic to gracefully grant him Finland, the Baltic states, the Eastern half of Poland, and Bessarabia.[12] The unsurpassed and rather premature *Realpolitik* of Roosevelt's remarks certainly cast his "Four Policemen" proposal in a less favorable light than did his public utterances. However genuine the fears that he expressed to Spellman might have been, his confidence that he could manipulate Stalin appears in retrospect to have been more a characteristic of the president's personality. "I have just a hunch," he told his first ambassador to Moscow, William C. Bullitt, "that Stalin . . . doesn't want anything but security for his country, and I think that if I give him everything I possibly can and ask nothing from him in return, *noblesse oblige*, he won't try to annex anything and will work with me for a world of democracy and peace."[13] These contradictions might lead one to the conclusion that the president, convinced of the inevitability of Soviet predominance in Europe, wilfully misled friend and foe alike in the interest of Allied unity in proclaiming war aims that were patently incompatible with his expectations. A perhaps more accurate assessment would be that in the face of uncertainty Roosevelt's self-confidence and his belief in the inherent validity of the Atlantic Charter's Wilsonian principles generally took precedence over his occasional perception that the Soviet dictator was cast in a different mold and that the ultimate implementation of those principles might require a costly confrontation with his Russian ally. While Roosevelt was neither as treacherous nor as naïve as various critics have claimed, his undeniable political skills on the domestic scene simply proved to be inadequate in the vastly more complex world arena.

With America's entry into the war and the growing dependence of the Allies on its material assistance, the alliance took on a different complexion. Roosevelt became the crusaders' conscience, and Stalin opted for a tactical deference to the president's proclaimed ideals. Thus, in his refusal to undertake specific political commitments regarding the future of Europe, Roosevelt was ostensibly vindicated by Russian assurances of good intent. This apparent consensus cast Churchill in the role of an anachronistic practitioner of *Realpolitik*. When in October 1943, at the Moscow Conference of Foreign Ministers, the British came forward with a proposal for a Danubian confederation, Molotov charged with righteous indignation that this was a devilish plot to create a *cordon sanitaire* containing the Soviet Union, and professed that his country had no intention of dividing Europe into spheres of influence. The final outcome of the conference was a four-nation declaration on general security which, *inter alia*, committed the signatories not to use their military forces on foreign territory except in the war effort against the Axis or after joint consultation. To Cordell Hull, this declaration meant that "there will be no longer need for spheres of influence, for alliances, for balance of power, or any other of the special security arrangements through which, in the unhappy past, the nations strove to safeguard their security or to promote their interests."[14] While the secretary of state was never as close to Roosevelt as his office warranted and was by far the more idealistic of the two, there is no evidence that the latter's "plan" for spheres of influence, as divulged to Spellman, came up for serious consideration at this or subsequent wartime conferences. However, to the extent that Stalin perceived ambivalence on this question in Roosevelt's councils and a recognition of his need for "friendly" neighbors, he must have been reinforced in his belief that the Atlantic Charter and other joint proclamations would not be pressed by Washington where they might prove incompatible with the long-term security interests of the Soviet Union.

Washington's inclination to postpone political issues was also reflected in a military strategy that excluded any political considerations other than the need to retain Soviet cooperation. In the context of military strategy, East-Central Europe became a source of discord not so much between the West and Stalin as between the British and the Americans. Despite the Americans' occasional accusations that Churchill was harboring traditional British imperialist schemes to preserve influence in the Balkans, the prime minister repeatedly attempted to reorient Anglo-American strategy toward that region. Initially, he and his military advisers were motivated more by a desire to relieve the pressure on the Russians, who momentarily stood alone against the *Wehrmacht* on the Continent, than by expectations of political gain. His recommendation to Roosevelt, prior to the Casablanca conference of January 1943, for a "strike at the under-belly of the Axis in effective strength and in the shortest time" did not, however, gain the support of the American Joint Chiefs of Staff, who showed a definite preference for a single, massive invasion over a piecemeal approach involving the Balkans.[15] Nevertheless, the successful campaigns in North Africa and Sicily induced Churchill to press again for an intensification of operations in the Mediterranean theater, even at the expense of the forthcoming Overlord invasion of northern France. On October 7, the prime minister wrote to Roosevelt to argue that the political collapse of the Mussolini regime foreshadowed a "similar and even greater landslide" in Greece, Yugoslavia, Hungary, Bulgaria, and Rumania in the event military pressure was increased by the Allies, but his proposal did not accord with American and Soviet strategic priorities.[16] The Joint Chiefs of Staff urged that operations in the Balkans be limited to bombing raids and assistance to local insurgent movements. For their part, the Russians viewed with alarm the prospect of a spearhead by their allies into what they considered was their exclusive sphere of operations, and Eden and Hull agreed that, in view of the fact that Soviet forces were the only ones directly confronting the Rumanians and the Hungarians, Stalin was entitled to have the decisive voice.[17]

Coordination of Soviet and Anglo-American military strategy at the Teheran conference resulted in the dismissal of Churchill's alternative. The attitudes of the three allied leaders were aptly sketched by an American eyewitness.

> Stalin appeared to know exactly what he wanted at the Conference—this was also true of Churchill, but not so of Roosevelt.... His apparent indecision was probably the direct result of our obscure foreign policy. President Roosevelt was thinking of winning the war; the others were thinking of their relative positions when the war was won. Stalin wanted the Anglo-American forces in western, not southern Europe; Churchill thought our post-war position improved and British interest served best if the Anglo-Americans as well as the Russians participated in the occupation of the Balkans.[18]

When Churchill suggested that Operation Overlord be delayed for a few months to allow for Turkey's entry into the war and for combined Allied operations in the Balkans, all of which might induce the regimes in Hungary and Rumania to change sides, he ran into the joint opposition of Stalin and Roosevelt. The latter agreed that nothing should compromise the success of Overlord, and the president remarked that he saw "no reason for putting the lives of American soldiers in jeopardy in order to protect real or fancied British interests on the European continent."[19] The conference ended on the understanding that Overlord would be postponed for one month so as to allow the Western Allies to advance to the Pisa-Rimini line and prepare for Operation Anvil, the diversionary invasion of southern France. Stalin's exclusive jurisdiction over the eastern front was reaffirmed.

Although Teheran ended on a note of unanimity, Churchill left the conference with grave misgivings and decided to consult with General Alexander, supreme commander in the Mediterranean theater, observing that "we've got to do something with these bloody Russians."[20] In the event, the Allies met unexpected resistance in their march to Rome, and that city fell only two days before the launching of the Normandy invasion; as a result, Anvil was postponed and lost its original function of splitting the German forces in France prior to Overlord. The British thereupon revived their case for a Balkan strategy. In June, following the initial success of Overlord, General Alexander put forward a plan for a spearhead through Trieste and the Ljubljana Gap into Austria and asked Harold Macmillan to recommend this course of action to the prime minister; Vienna, observed Alexander, was an "object of great political and psychological value." Churchill proved amenable to this proposal, being, as he put it, "very anxious to forestall the Russians in certain areas of Central Europe"; he was also influenced by the knowledge that the Hungarians were prepared to surrender to a British force.[21] In a letter to the prime minister, Roosevelt made it clear that his priorities lay elsewhere: "I agree that the political considerations you mention are important factors, but military operations based thereon must be definitely secondary to the primary operations of striking at the heart of Germany"; he concluded by noting that, "for purely political considerations over here, I should never survive even a slight setback to 'Overlord' if it were known that fairly large forces had been diverted to the Balkans." When, at the second Quebec conference, Churchill returned to the attack, the president stuck to his argument that at Teheran Stalin had been assured of Operation Anvil and that the Joint Chiefs of Staff continued to support his preference.[22] Eden recalls that both he and Churchill were "unhappy about the reluctance of our American ally to exploit victory in Italy and so enable us to play a more influential part in Central Europe. Though the United States argued that this was for strategic reasons, we were not convinced that political inhibitions about becoming 'involved in the Balkans' did not play a part."[23] Other factors came into play; German resistance on the western front was believed to be nearing collapse, and, more than ever before, Stalin needed reassurance that his allies would make no separate peace with Germany, despite the earlier agreement on unconditional surrender. To Roosevelt and his advisers the unity of the alliance took precedence over any British predilections for forestalling the Russians in the Balkans. The conference dashed Churchill's last hopes for establishing an Anglo-American military presence in East-Central Europe. The final approval of Anvil meant that no forces would be available for any operations in the Balkans.

These abortive attempts to implement a "Mediterranean strategy" prompted extensive debate among armchair strategists after the war. Many of them, including Chester Wilmot and Hanson Baldwin, argued that Churchill's proposals arose from an accurate perception of Soviet intentions and would have produced a more advantageous negotiating position for the West at war's end.[24] Others, notably Michael Howard, observed that by the end of 1944 the Red Army had advanced well into Bulgaria, Rumania, and Hungary, while difficult terrain and logistical difficulties would have made an Anglo-American spearhead through the Ljubljana

Gap extremely costly and, in political terms, probably futile.[25] On the other hand, it is more than idle speculation to suppose that, had the Western Allies opted for a Balkan strategy at an earlier date, the fate of East-Central Europe would have been drastically altered. Before the German coup in October 1944, the Hungarian government had made repeated attempts to negotiate with the British and the Americans and had expressed its willingness to surrender the moment their forces set foot in Hungary. It was to forestall such an eventuality that the Russians concentrated on their southern front and willingly relaxed their drive toward the heart of Germany. For Stalin and Churchill, military strategy went hand in hand with political considerations.[26] For Roosevelt and his top military advisers, the two were distinct entities; first, the war was to be won with the greatest expediency, and only afterwards would the victorious Allies come to grips with nonmilitary issues. It is therefore not surprising that, intent upon the defeat of Germany, Roosevelt agreed to Stalin's demand at Teheran for a clear East-West division of the spheres of operation, despite Churchill's misgivings. Only later did it become evident that this decision had in effect predetermined the political future of East-Central Europe.

Nevertheless, if Allied military strategy relegated East-Central Europe to the Soviet sphere of operations, it did not imply at the time Western acquiescence in ultimate Soviet hegemony over that area. The postwar status of Hitler's satellites and subject states and the eventual application of the principles first enunciated in the Atlantic Charter received increasing attention at successive conferences from Teheran to Potsdam. As a result of Roosevelt's chronic reluctance to broach political issues, responsibility for East-Central Europe devolved, almost by default, upon the British government until very nearly the cessation of hostilities. Britain had given refuge to the Polish, Czech, and Yugoslav exile governments and had, through its longstanding involvement, a far greater expertise in East European affairs than did the Americans (at one point Stettinius had asserted that Bessarabia was part of Hungary); the British also provided logistical assistance to the royalist—and, after Teheran, to the leftist—partisans in Yugoslavia. On the broader question of a postwar settlement, however, Churchill found himself caught in the middle between Stalin's explicit requests and the Americans' almost doctrinal posture of postponement. Beyond the issue of territorial adjustments there lay a disturbing uncertainty regarding the role the Russians expected to play in determining the political future of East-Central Europe and the advisability of trying to extract specific commitments from them as long as the outcome of the war depended in large measure on the Red Army. When Roosevelt and Eden met in March 1943, they agreed that both

Hungary and Austria should become fully independent states, but they also recognized that the Soviets were not too well disposed toward the Hungarians; Stalin had demanded that the latter be punished, and Eden had interpreted this to signify Hungarian territorial concessions to Rumania, perhaps as compensation for the latter's loss of Bessarabia.[27] Understandably, neither of the Western Allies was prepared to rise to the defense of an enemy state. In the end, the status of a minor ally came to serve as the most telling barometer of Soviet and Western intentions regarding East-Central Europe.

THE POLISH DILEMMA

Poland, observed Churchill, was the "first of the great causes which led to the breakdown of the Grand Alliance."[28] As the country whose invasion finally impelled Britain to declare war on Hitler's Germany, Poland (and the restoration of her freedom) had particular symbolic significance; as a nation historically at odds with Russia, however, it was destined to play a divisive role within the alliance. For much of the war the question of boundaries predominated in Allied discussions concerning Poland, and it proved to be a problem which for historical reasons did not bear equitable resolution. When Poland was re-established as a sovereign state at the Paris peace conference of 1919, the entente powers proposed that her eastern borders follow the so-called Curzon line, but the Poles chose to lay claim to further territories, and, after a period of hostilities with the Soviet Union, agreement was reached in the Treaty of Riga of 1921 to extend those borders by some 150 miles. In terms of ethnic self-determination the new boundaries were no great improvement over the Curzon line, for they incorporated a majority of Ukrainians and White Russians while still leaving about one million Poles under Soviet rule; as in the rest of East-Central Europe, the ethnic mosaic simply did not lend itself to the application of Wilsonian principles. The Molotov-Ribbentrop Pact of August 23, 1939, produced yet another partition, and in October of that year the Russians proceeded to hold elections in the areas under their occupation and to deport eastward some 1.6 million Poles.[29] These measures contributed to the profound Russophobia of the Polish government-in-exile, which, after Germany's attack on the Soviet Union in June 1941, found itself implicitly allied with one of Poland's traditional enemies. Churchill thereupon advised Premier Sikorski to reach an agreement with Stalin, if only in the interest of Allied unity, but in the course of negotiations the Russian ambassador in London, Ivan Maisky, refused to promise the restoration of the prewar frontiers. The Russo-Polish Pact of July 30, 1941, merely noted that the Molotov-Ribbentrop agreements had lost their validity, while, concurrently, Moscow advised the British government that it favored the ultimate restoration of the 1939 partition line, which corresponded roughly to the earlier Curzon proposals. Had the Poles been less intransigent, it is conceivable that they might have negotiated a compromise at a time when German armies were threatening Moscow itself; in the course of his meeting with Sikorski in December 1941, Stalin hinted at only marginal changes in the prewar boundaries, without, however, eliciting a positive response.[30]

Churchill, who had more sympathy than did the adamant Poles for the Soviet Union's desperate struggle against the common enemy, adopted a conciliatory approach in arguing that, in view of the Russians' mounting sacrifices, the momentarily inactive Allies could scarcely object to their claim to territories gained by the Molotov-Ribbentrop Pact. "This was the basis," he observed to Roosevelt on April 23, 1942, "on which Russia acceded to the Charter."[31] By the time of Eden's conference with Roosevelt in March 1943, the argument that agreement on the Curzon line, combined with compensation for Poland in the form of German territory, might dissuade Stalin from intervening in the political life of the country had acquired currency and added a new dimension to Churchill's recommendations.[32] In contrast, relations between Moscow and the Sikorski regime continued to deteriorate. One scheme that the London Poles assiduously advocated throughout the war concerned a Central European confederation (including even Turkey) oriented ostensibly against a recurrence of German expansionism, but designed in reality to contain that of the Soviet Union. The latter dismissed the scheme out of hand; the Americans simply ignored it. Churchill spoke favorably of a confederation upon occasion, but its essentially anti-Soviet purpose ruled out serious consideration by the Allies. Although the London Poles represented, for better or for worse, the vast majority of their beleaguered compatriots, such initiatives could not help but alienate the Russians. Newly confident of ultimate victory after Stalingrad, the latter established in March 1943 a "Union of Polish Patriots" free of any allegiance to the London government. The following month, when Sikorski demanded that the International Red Cross investigate the Katyn massacre of some ten thousand Polish officers—implying that the Russians had been responsible for the outrage—Stalin severed all relations with the government-in-exile. Churchill had advised against any provocation of the Russians—"If they are dead nothing you can do will bring them back," he told Sikorski—but the Poles failed to share his pragmatism.[33] For his part, Roosevelt had sent a message to Stalin deploring Sikorski's initiative and mentioning that a break in Soviet-Polish relations would have harmful side-effects among his Polish constituents.[34]

In October, Cordell Hull traveled to Moscow, hoping to effect a reconciliation and carrying Roosevelt's recommendation that the new frontier run somewhat east of the Curzon line; he returned with the impression that Stalin would recognize the London government once again if the latter agreed to cede the bulk of the territories in dispute.[35] The exiles, headed by Peasant party leader Stanislaw Mikolajczyk following Sikorski's untimely death, refused to budge and demanded instead a guarantee of Polish independence and the eventual stationing of Anglo-American forces in Poland "to prevent Polish-Soviet friction." To bolster these demands, they issued veiled threats that the Home Army might clash with the Russians and they mobilized the sizable Polish-American community to put pressure on its government.[36] Roosevelt, loath to relinquish their electoral support, shared his concern with Stalin at the Teheran conference; the Russian leader advised him to do some propaganda work among the Polish-Americans.[37] That first meeting of the Big Three in effect disposed of the issue of Poland's boundaries with a notable disregard for the wishes of the government-in-exile. For reasons that are still unclear, Churchill took the initiative in proposing to Stalin that the Allies agree in principle to the restoration of the Curzon frontier. Perhaps he still feared a last-minute Soviet accommodation with Hitler; more likely he acted in the hope of gaining Stalin's guarantee of Polish independence and recognition of the London government. Roosevelt played an essentially supporting role in the discussions at Teheran concerning Poland, but he did voice certain reservations over the appropriateness of the entire Curzon line, urging that it be modified so as to allow Poland to retain Lwow and the Galician oil fields. The ultimate agreement, tentative and informal though it was, envisaged the annexation to Poland of East Prussia, Danzig, and Upper Silesia to the Oder in compensation for the loss of Poland's eastern territories. Whatever the merits of various eastern boundaries might have been, the unilateral decision by the Allies to redraw the map of Central Europe paid tribute to the requirements of wartime unity and expediency. Even the ruffled feelings of the London Poles paled in significance compared to the long-term implications of the agreement, for it imposed on a liberated Poland the burden of German revanchism and the necessity to seek the protection of the only other proximate Great Power, the Soviet Union. If, with the wisdom of historical hindsight, one were to seek the origins of the cold war, the decisions at Teheran over Poland and the military spheres would emerge as the first steps in the fateful and futile appeasement of Stalin.

On January 11, 1944, exactly one week after the Red Army crossed the Riga frontier, Moscow issued an official statement referring to the Curzon line as the legitimate Soviet-Polish boundary. Shortly thereafter a State Department memorandum informed the alarmed Poles of the limited nature of American support: "The basic position of the United States Government that general discussion of the many European frontier questions during the period of active hostilities against the Axis will run the risk of creating confusion and diverting concentration from the over-all objective of defeating Germany is well known. This attitude, however, does not preclude the possibility of any 2 countries having mutual territorial problems from seeking a direct settlement by mutual accord." Although a *pro forma* offer of good offices was made, there could be "no question of guarantees as far as the United States is concerned."[38] The London Poles grew more desperate by the hour, but the Americans kept delaying a proposed visit by Mikolajczyk, who finally arrived in Washington in June to plead his country's case with the president. The latter, under strong pressure from the Polish-American Congress in that election year, avoided the brutal frankness exhibited by Churchill, but he pointed out to Mikolajczyk that the Soviet Union could swallow up Poland and that the government-in-exile had best come to terms with the Russians; concurrently, the president reassured Stalin (who had earlier reminded him of the Teheran agreement on the Curzon line) that his meeting with Mikolajczyk ought not to be interpreted as American interference in the "discords" between Moscow and the London Poles. The date of the Normandy landings was near, and, as Cordell Hull noted, the United States "could not afford to become partisan in the Polish question to the extent of alienating Russia at that crucial moment."[39]

Faced by the reluctance of the Western Allies to champion Poland's cause, Mikolajczyk set out to meet Stalin, but, while in transit, he learned that the Russians' price had escalated beyond acceptance of the Curzon line and minor modifications in the composition of the government-in-exile. On July 22 the Soviet-sponsored Polish Committee of National Liberation materialized as a rival administration in the newly liberated town of Lublin, giving clear indication that Stalin now envisaged little compromise on the pro-Soviet sympathies of an eventual Polish government. Upon his arrival in Moscow, Mikolajczyk was urged by the Russians to come to an understanding with the ad hoc regime, and this he proceeded to attempt in the forlorn hope that, despite the absence of firm Western support, a broadly based and autonomous compromise government might yet be engineered with Stalin's blessing.

The unfortunate premier was still in the Soviet capital when one of the most tragic episodes in his country's history began to unfold. For months the commander of the underground Home Army, General Bor-Komorowski, had been preparing plans to take control of Warsaw immediately prior to the entry of the Red Army so as to create a beachhead for the London government and rally the masses around it; he also aimed to forestall the local communists from taking a similar initiative, the Moscow-based Union of Polish Patriots having multiplied its broadcast calls to battle. The exile cabinet endorsed the scheme reluctantly and with qualifications, leaving him, in effect, with full responsibility for the consequences of his actions.[40] On August 1, aroused by the sound of Russian artillery some seven miles across the Vistula, Bor-Komorowski's forces rose against the Germans, but the latter, far from bowing to the inevitable, rushed in reinforcements to crush the uprising. Although Stalin had assured Mikolajczyk that the Red Army would enter Warsaw on August 6, it soon became evident that the Russians had seized the opportunity to eliminate—with German assistance—the powerful and well-organized, but predominantly anticommunist, underground and to discredit the London regime. For the Western Allies, who had retained certain illusions regarding Stalin's political and strategic designs, the moment was one of painful reappraisal, for he now disclaimed any responsibility to aid the insurgents and on August 22 wrote to Roosevelt and Churchill, "Sooner or later the truth about the group of criminals who have unleashed the Warsaw adventure will become known to everybody."[41] The American posture remained one of equivocation. Washington and London dispatched pleas for Russian intervention, but Marshal Rokossovsky's forces remained on their side of the Vistula, and, when Ambassador Harriman and General John Deane met with Stalin and Molotov to request the use of bases in the Ukraine for American planes to drop supplies to the rebels, they were rebuffed and left, as George Kennan recalls, "shattered by the experience."[42] Yet, even at this critical moment, the U.S. State Department advised restraint, in the interest of preserving existing facilities provided by the Russians for the shuttle-bombing of Germany.[43] The gallant Poles fought on for two months, but all that their fugue achieved in the end was the total devastation of Warsaw.

Stalin subsequently took pains to explain that his reasons for not intervening were strategic and logistical rather than political, but, even if Rokossovsky's forces had been overextended at the beginning of the uprising, the tenacity of the insurgents provided ample time for the mounting of a supportive operation. Had Bor-Komorowski prevailed in Warsaw with Soviet assistance, it is still doubtful whether Stalin would have allowed the repatriation of the London regime, but at least the latter would have retained the considerable power base of a victorious Home Army. In the event, Washington's policy of accommodating Stalin once again overrode all other considerations, and there appeared to be no dissent with this policy on the part of Churchill.[44] Changes since Teheran in the strategic balance—the successful establishment of a second front and the liberation of all Soviet territory—failed to induce Roosevelt to reconsider his unquestioning loyalty to his Soviet ally in terms of political objectives. At least in retrospect, it is difficult not to agree with Kennan that "this was the moment when, if ever, there should have been a full-fledged and realistic showdown with the Soviet leaders: when they should have been confronted with the choice between changing their policy completely and agreeing to collaborate in the establishment of truly independent countries in Eastern Europe or forfeiting Western-Allied support and sponsorship for the remaining phases of their war effort."[45] Stalin still feared a last-minute unholy alliance between the Western powers and Hitler, and it is conceivable that this fear could have led him to compromise on his political goals in the face of concerted Anglo-American pressure.

LIBERATING THE SATELLITES

The possible fruitfulness of such pressure was illustrated by the case of Finland, which was officially at war with the Soviet Union and Britain but which retained diplomatic relations with the United States until the end of June 1944. At Teheran, Churchill and Roosevelt had strongly advocated lenient armistice terms consistent with the maintenance of Finnish independence, and Stalin for once had complied by proposing relatively modest reparations and minor territorial adjustments. When the Finns finally capitulated in September 1944, the Russians kept their word, for the armistice made no provision for military occupation and thus allowed the Finns to pursue a cautiously independent course. Stalin's generous treatment of Finland could also be attributed to that nation's marginal position and the momentary requirements of the war effort against Germany, factors which were not likely to influence Soviet policies regarding the nations of East-Central Europe. With the steady advance of the Red Army, the East-Central Europeans reluctantly came to grips with the prospect that the Hitlerian order might be superseded by an equally unpalatable hegemony from the east. Satellite regimes and governments-in-exile alike manifested an increasing awareness of Stalin's politico-strategic ambitions and of the Western Allies' unwillingness to challenge them in the aftermath of Teheran.

The Czechs, unimpeded by any historical enmity toward the Russians, and officially free of the stigma of collaboration (despite the pro-Nazi regime of Father Tiso in Slovakia), were the first to draw what appeared to be realistic conclusions. After preliminary discussions in London with Soviet ambassador A. Y. Bogomolov had produced agreement in principle on a draft Soviet-Czechoslovak treaty, President Beneš traveled to the United States and Canada in May–June 1943 to win support for a policy of accommodation to eventual Soviet predominance in East-Central Europe. He told Roosevelt that the proximity of the Soviet Union was bound to "exercise a certain influence on our internal policy in connection with our future social and economic development," and in his memoirs claims that the American response was favorable. Above all, Beneš feared another Munich, and this he calculated could be avoided only by a "firm and *permanent* agreement between the Anglo-Saxons and the Soviet Union"; he considered his draft treaty to be a major step in the direction of such an agreement. Back in London, he ran into stiff opposition from the exiled Poles and from Eden, who considered the timing of the treaty inopportune—presumably because the Big Three's policies on postwar problems remained to be elaborated and coordinated. Undeterred by the lukewarm, if not outright hostile, attitude of the West, and pressed by the Russians for an early conclusion of the proposed treaty of friendship and alliance, Beneš waited until the Moscow conference had taken place, then in December made the trip to the Soviet capital. The Czech president was delighted with the bargain he struck; he agreed to include some communists in the postwar government and tacitly accepted Soviet claims over Ruthenia, while Stalin undertook to support the restoration of the other prewar frontiers (including Teschen, which Poland had annexed in 1938), the expulsion of the German and Hungarian minorities, and the principle of noninterference in the country's political life.[46]

The United States and Britain reacted to the treaty with a notable lack of enthusiasm, construing its bilateral negotiation, if not its actual terms, as a premature extension of Soviet influence.[47] The treaty also administered a setback to the London Poles' efforts to achieve a Central European confederation, but Beneš had consistently opposed their scheme as being essentially (and unrealistically) anti-Soviet and unlikely to advance the political and territorial interests of Czechoslovakia. Taking Stalin's promises at face value, the Czech president could reasonably argue that the former's guarantee of sovereignty and territorial integrity outweighed the momentary displeasure of the other Allies. The subsequent rising in Slovakia, launched by the predominantly communist-led underground in August 1944, partially vindicated Beneš' decision to deal with the Soviet Union. After some procrastination, the Russians responded to Masaryk's appeals for assistance to the insurgents by dispatching supplies and advisers, while the Americans and British demurred, on the grounds that Slovakia belonged to the Soviet military sphere.[48] Admittedly, even the Russians might have been more forthcoming with their aid, for advance units of the Red Army were as close as eighty miles, but in view of the uprising's leftish tinge its ultimate failure could scarcely be attributed to Stalin's political designs. Frustration with Washington's passive policy, the dismal example of Soviet-Polish relations, and apprehension that Anglo-American power would be outweighed in Central Europe by that of the Soviets logically led to Beneš' independent diplomatic forays, but in retrospect his choice of Stalin's embrace was strategically futile and tactically counterproductive; in the long run it failed to safeguard his country's sovereignty, while in the context of wartime politics it only weakened the Western Allies' resolve to forestall the creation of a Soviet sphere of influence in East-Central Europe.

The satellite regimes, on the other hand, followed the Polish pattern in their distaste for any accommodation with the Soviet Union and chose to look to the West for their salvation. In the early months of 1944, the Hungarians, Bulgarians, and Rumanians all made secret approaches to the Western Allies in the hope of saving their countries from Russian occupation by effecting a separate peace, and sporadic negotiations ensued in the various neutral capitals of Europe. Hungarian premier Nicholas Kállay created within the foreign ministry a special section charged with exploring the possibility of striking a bargain whereby Hungary would leave the Axis the moment the airborne Anglo-American forces landed on Hungarian soil; similarly qualified peace feelers were advanced in Cairo by Rumania's Prince Barbu Stirbey. Although there existed in London and Washington a certain sympathy for these regimes' abhorrence of communism, neither the British nor the Americans were prepared to renege on the explicit Allied policy of unconditional surrender in order to ensure the survival of what were, after all, enemy governments; in any case, pre-emptive occupation was a criterion that the Western Allies would not and could not meet. Apprised of this position, the Hungarians nevertheless invited further discussions, and, under the supervision of the OSS chief in Bern, Allen Dulles, a three-man team was dispatched to Budapest with a personal message from Roosevelt to the regent, Admiral Horthy. In the meantime, however, Hitler had lost patience with the Hungarians' defeatism and had ordered the country's "protective" occupation. This followed closely the arrival of the U.S. mission in Budapest on March 18 and led to the prompt incarceration of the Americans.[49]

On May 12, 1944, the three Great Powers issued a declaration warning the governments of Bulgaria, Hungary, Rumania, and Finland to cease their collaboration with the Axis or face harsh terms of surrender; through more private channels the Hungarians and Rumanians were told to seek an armistice with the Soviet Union, to whose sphere of military responsibility they belonged. Not being officially at war with the Soviet Union, Bulgaria could legitimately sue for peace with Britain and the United States, and inter-Allied discussions did follow the initial peace feelers in February, but the Bulgarians shrank from turning on the Axis, even after the Regency

Council appointed a more moderate cabinet on September 2. When a few days later the Soviet Union issued its belated declaration of war, a pro-communist "Fatherland Front" seized power and requested an armistice from the Russians.[50]

In April the Red Army entered Rumania, and four months later, unable to secure a separate peace with the West, King Michael ousted the pro-Nazi regime of General Antonescu in favor of General Sanatescu, who headed the National Democratic Bloc, a broadly representative coalition of the Communist, National Peasant, National Liberal, and Social Democratic parties. The armistice, signed by this administration on September 12, committed Rumania to declare war on Germany and to pay reparations in the amount of $300 million, promised the return of all or the larger part of Transylvania, and stipulated that its terms be executed by the "Allied (Soviet) High Command, acting on behalf of the Allied Powers."[51] In October, Hungary's turn came to bow to the inevitable, and Regent Nicholas Horthy dispatched his envoys to Moscow to negotiate an armistice, but his belated initiative was aborted by a German coup which replaced him with the short-lived puppet regime of the Arrow Cross (Nazi) leader Ferenc Szálasi. It befell the delegation of a rival, relatively representative ad hoc administration, established at Debrecen in Soviet-occupied territory and headed by General Béla Miklós, to sign the armistice in Moscow on January 20, 1945.

In the view of the United States, all of these armistices represented interim arrangements, negotiated by the ally which had exclusive military responsibility for the East European theater, and would ultimately be superseded by formal peace treaties. The Americans themselves had somewhat injudiciously set the precedent the previous March, when the Joint Chiefs of Staff had ruled that Soviet participation in the Italian surrender would not be practicable.[52] Even so, Cordell Hull records that Washington protested in numerous diplomatic communications over the armistice terms for the three ex-satellites.[53] The United States viewed as premature the actual fixing of the amount of reparations in the case of Rumania, and, when the harsh treatment of Hungary promised by Stalin materialized in a Soviet request for $400 million (later reduced by one quarter, to be divided in the proportion of 50:25:25 between the Soviet Union, Czechoslovakia, and Yugoslavia), Hull charged that the sum was "clearly excessive, from the point of view both of Hungarian capacity to pay and of legitimate Russian claims on Hungary."[54] Allied representation in the liberated areas provided an even greater bone of contention than the question of reparations. The Rumanian armistice had not spelled out the nature of the Allied Control Commission for that country, and, when, on September 6, Harriman and the British ambassador, Sir Archibald Clark

Kerr, broached this subject with Molotov, the latter indicated that the ACC in Rumania would operate much as its counterpart in Italy, that is, *mutatis mutandis*, with only token Western participation.[55] The Russians did agree to admit American and British political representatives not attached to the ACC, again as in Italy. The initial experience of the Western Allies with the operation of the ACC in Rumania had a sobering effect on them, and they attempted to improve their position in the course of the negotiations on the Hungarian instrument. When Harriman and Clark Kerr brought up the matter of equal participation in the projected Hungarian ACC, however, Molotov bluntly reminded them that it was "not necessary for the Soviet Union to conclude an armistice with Hungary since the Red Army was practically the master of that country [and] could do what it wished"; his interlocutors conceded the point, but reserved the right to review the terms after the defeat of Germany.[56] (Arguing from different premises, the counselor at the Moscow embassy, George Kennan, advised against *any* American participation, pointing out that it would only saddle the U.S. "with moral responsibility for an armistice regime, the operation of which we have no means of influencing.")[57] In the final armistice document, Article 18 outlined the *modus operandi* of the ACC.[58]

> For the whole period of the armistice there will be established in Hungary an Allied Control Commission which will regulate and supervise the execution of the armistice terms under the chairmanship of the Allied (Soviet) High Command and with the participation of the representatives of the United Kingdom and the United States. During the period between the coming into force of the armistice and the conclusion of hostilities against Germany, the Allied Control Commission will be under the general direction of the Allied (Soviet) High Command.

Thus, despite Western pressures, their own Italian model prevailed once again. Views also diverged on the Hungarian territorial clause. Although the earlier Rumanian armistice had specified that Transylvania, "or the greater part thereof," be given to Rumania, Washington continued to favor a more equitable settlement based on ethnic distribution. These American reservations notwithstanding, the Hungarian instrument reaffirmed that the two Vienna Awards were null and void. On this and other issues, the United States limited itself to objections of principle while reserving the right to reopen discussions at the peace settlement; the Russians, on the other hand, considered such objections to be largely *pro forma*, pointed repeatedly to the Italian precedent, and proceeded to treat East-Central Europe as their exclusive preserve.

The situation in Yugoslavia differed in most respects from that in the satellites, or indeed in Poland, and in the early years of the war the Western Allies showed little interest beyond maintaining diplomatic relations with King Peter's government in London and contact with General Draža Mihailović, the latter's minister of war, who was heading the predominantly Serbian Chetnik guerrilla movement against the Germans. As the war progressed, it became increasingly clear that the rival partisan army led by Tito and other communists not only was more effective in harassing the occupiers but also enjoyed wider popular and ethnic support than did the Chetniks, whose hostility toward the Partisans drove them into compromising understandings with the Italians. Impelled by the logic of his Balkan strategy, Churchill realistically sought to improve relations with the more effective of the two insurgent movements. Having sent Fitzroy Maclean in July 1943 to liaise with Tito, he proceeded to shift British logistical support to the latter, viewing him as more of a nationalist than a communist. Washington saw no reason to follow suit, having already ruled out a Balkan strategy and harboring deep-rooted suspicions not only of Tito's communist politics but also of British, as well as Russian, designs on Yugoslavia, and persisted in its material support for Mihailović.[59] When Tito suffered a military setback in the spring of 1944, Churchill seized the occasion to engineer a tentative reconciliation between him and the London government; on July 7, agreement was reached to postpone divisive domestic political issues such as the monarchy and to form a new Yugoslav government under the exile prime minister, Ivan Šubašić. The Americans remained aloof and disapproving, Hull having correctly interpreted the compromise as a Churchill-Tito pact favoring the Partisans.[60] The Russians, suspicious of Tito's independent stance and of his plans for a southern Slav federation, also kept him at arm's length for much of the war and urged him to make his peace with the royalists; when Tito, apprehensive about the approaching Red Army, visited Stalin in the fall of 1944, the latter even favored the return of King Peter, then agreed to Soviet noninvolvement in Yugoslavia's domestic affairs after the end of hostilities.[61] By this time Churchill himself was having second thoughts about the postwar suitability of Tito, who in one way or another baffled and irritated all three major Allies. American goals regarding Yugoslavia were, as for the rest of East-Central Europe, ill-defined and uncertainly implemented. Thus, King Peter, encouraged by American hostility to the Tito-Šubašić agreement, would dismiss the Šubašić government on January 23, 1945, but then would find himself in such isolation that he was forced to transfer his powers to a Regency Council. The Americans, aloof and out of touch with the real course of Yugoslav affairs, would take another three years to come to terms with Tito.

SPHERES OF INFLUENCE

Meanwhile, Churchill was contemplating with growing apprehension the rapid advance of the Red Army into East-Central Europe and the potential spread of communism into Greece and the rest of the continent. Thwarted in his advocacy of a noncommunist Central European federation and of a Balkan military strategy, he shifted his energies to the diplomatic arena in order to salvage what he could of British (and Western) influence in that area. If his military proposals had run counter to American strategic preconceptions, his new tack encountered equally unfriendly winds in Washington, where, despite the Teheran understandings, the myth endured that at war's end the victors could make *tabula rasa* and construct in disinterested fashion a lasting and equitable settlement. On May 31, 1944, he wrote to Roosevelt suggesting an agreement with the Russians over the distribution of influence in the Balkans, his main concern being the safety of Greece. The proposal was coolly received, Hull in particular being "flatly opposed to any division of Europe or sections of Europe into spheres of influence."[62] Roosevelt also was unconvinced of the necessity for such an agreement, intended to cover military predominance in Rumania, Bulgaria, and Greece, but he eventually gave in to Churchill and, without consulting Hull or the State Department, sanctioned the initiative for a three-month trial period.[63] The agreement, reported the prime minister to his war cabinet, represented "only an interim guide for the immediate war-time future."[64]

The matter of spheres of influence did not rest there. Observing with heavy irony that "Russia was the deliverer, and Communism the Gospel she brought," and noting that Roosevelt was steadfast in his attitude of postponement, Churchill decided to travel to Moscow for a decisive face-to-face bargaining session with Stalin.[65] The meetings, which lasted from October 9 to 18, resulted in an Anglo-Soviet agreement that reflected with striking accuracy the prevailing distribution of power in East-Central Europe. Although Ambassador Harriman participated as an observer, he had been instructed by the president not to commit the United States government, a stance that could only have confirmed Stalin's belief that East-Central Europe was a matter of marginal concern to the Americans.[66] Churchill initially presented Stalin with a percentage proposal specifying a division of influence in the order of 10-90 over Greece (in favor of Britain), 50-50 over Yugoslavia and Hungary, 75-25 over Bulgaria, and 90-10 over Rumania.[67] In the ensuing negotiations, notes Eden, Soviet Foreign Minister Molotov "showed a disposition to haggle over the percentages for [Bulgaria and Hungary]. Finally I told him that I was not interested in figures. All I wanted was to be sure that we had more voice in Bulgaria and Hungary than we had accepted in Rumania"; in fact, one American diplomat commented that Eden had had "his pants traded off" on the three satellites.[68] When the haggling was over and done with, the Russians came away with an overwhelming predominance over the satellites, but Churchill achieved his original goal of preserving British influence in Greece and to a lesser extent over Yugoslavia. The prime minister was subject to certain moral qualms, for he asked Stalin, "Might it not be thought rather cynical if it seemed we had disposed of these issues, so fateful to millions of people, in such an offhand manner? Let us burn the paper." Stalin told him to keep it, and, with commendable respect for historical accuracy, Churchill recorded it in his war memoirs.[69]

One issue that did not bear such simple mathematical resolution was Poland. Mikolajczyk, who had been brought to Moscow for the occasion, finally succumbed to the merciless harangues of Churchill—"You are callous people who want to wreck Europe," the latter told him[70]—as well as of Stalin over the border question, which he was now told had in effect been settled among the Allies at Teheran. Half-convinced, he returned to London, only to resign when a majority of the exile cabinet, clinging to the illusion that Roosevelt's posture of postponement would lead to a better bargain at war's end, refused to ratify any compromise. The new government headed by Arciszewski found itself increasingly ignored by the Allies in the months preceding Yalta, although Mikolajczyk himself continued to serve as a possible figure of compromise.

If the October meetings served to momentarily improve Anglo-Soviet relations, they did little to strengthen the prospects of genuine self-determination in East-Central Europe. Churchill insisted on the purely provisional nature of the agreement, noting that it "is not intended to be more than a guide, and of course in no way commits the United States, nor does it attempt to set up a rigid system of spheres of interest. It may however help the United States to see how their two principal Allies feel about these regions"; he added that it was natural for the Soviet Union to exercise predominant influence in areas under its military control.[71] In an address to the Commons which touched on the Polish question, however, he could not refrain from deploring the unwillingness of the United States to formulate a clear-cut policy. Stalin drew his own and more far-reaching conclusions, figuring that the agreement and Washington's ostensible noninvolvement added up to a permanent *carte blanche* for his activities in East-Central Europe.

The Roosevelt administration remained aloof from the percentage deal, which merely provided some stimulus to the State Department to review American policies; when Hull handed over his office to Edward Stettinius on November 21, he recorded that "the question of our future relations with the satellite countries was still under discussion."[72] That question remained subordinated to Washington's primary commitment, the successful launching of an international organization, and for some months the American public was to receive little intimation that all was not well among the Allies. From his vantage point in Moscow, Kennan could analyze Russian aims more realistically. In a memorandum to Harriman dated December 16, he pointed out that "as far as border states are concerned the Soviet Government has never ceased to think in terms of spheres of interest. They expect us to support them in whatever action they wish to take in those regions, regardless of whether that action seems to us or to the rest of the world to be right or wrong." His recommendation, which in the event aroused no response, was to warn the Russians that the American people might have to be apprised of the Soviet Union's reluctance to submit all potential conflicts of interest, even those concerning East-Central Europe, to the judgment of the United Nations.[73] Although Harriman relayed similar estimates of Soviet policy, the illusion of a unity of purpose among the Allies continued to prevail in Washington.[74]

The posture of postponement also affected planning for Germany's future, and here again the British were left to take initiatives which necessarily had a bearing on postwar developments. Their proposal for a European Advisory Commission had been coolly received by Roosevelt, who was as reluctant as ever to dilute his style of personal diplomacy, and, when it was finally adopted at the foreign ministers' conference in October 1943, its terms of reference were restricted, at America's insistence, to the technical aspects of Germany's eventual surrender and occupation. The U.S. ambassador in London, John G. Winant, was designated as the American representative on the commission, but, from the outset, he operated in an embarrassing policy vacuum, for Washington, in Kennan's words, "appeared to have a total absence of thoughts" regarding the questions at hand. At the commission's first working session, in January 1944, the British came forward with a blueprint for the division of Germany into zones of occupation, and shortly afterward the Russians voiced their concurrence. Almost two months elapsed before an ambiguous note arrived from Washington; it had apparently originated with the Joint Chiefs of Staff and suggested, without explanation, a more easterly delimitation of the Soviet zone. When Kennan, who at the time served as adviser to Ambassador Winant, journeyed home to seek elucidation, he was told by Roosevelt that the note had arisen from "just something I once drew on the back of an envelope";[75] Winant was thereupon instructed to endorse the original British draft, which had the Russian zone extend to the Elbe. While it is not likely that, at the time, the Russians would have accepted a smaller zone, the episode provided a striking illustration of both the State Department's unpreparedness and the War Department's self-arrogated and obstructive meddling in negotiations that carried immense political implications. Austria provided another case in point. The Joint Chiefs of Staff had ruled in late 1943 that the United States should assume no responsibilities in the area of the Balkans, including Austria. In June 1944, the Chiefs agreed to American participation only after Winant had protested to Roosevelt that their ruling conflicted with the spirit of the three-power declaration on Austria of November 1, 1943, and would relegate that country to Soviet and British occupation and influence.

By the end of 1944, with victory approaching, preparations for the postwar settlement could be delayed no longer, and the Big Three made plans for a new summit meeting. In Washington, where East-Central Europe was now receiving belated attention, the principles of the Atlantic Charter continued to serve as a general policy orientation, but, as Churchill observed to Roosevelt at Yalta, that declaration represented not "a law but a star," not a firm commitment but an expendable ideal.[76] The necessity of accommodating Stalin even at this late stage in the war was strengthened by real or perceived military factors. On December 16 the Germans had launched their Ardennes offensive, and the initial setback suffered by American forces prompted an appeal to Stalin to attack in the east. By the time of the Yalta conference, most of Hungary was in Russian hands, and, in the north, advance units of the Red Army stood within 100 miles of Berlin.[77] Thus, Stalin could claim to be not only the sole liberator of East-Central Europe but also the prime contributor to the defeat of Germany itself. In the Far East, an early Allied victory appeared less likely. Although an operational atomic bomb had been promised for mid-1945, this new weapon remained an unknown quantity; the Joint Chiefs of Staff therefore advised Roosevelt prior to Yalta that the war against Japan might last another eighteen months and that its successful conclusion made Russian participation imperative.

In the months preceding Yalta, Poland continued to be the most irritating thorn in the flesh of Allied unity. When Churchill reported to Roosevelt his failure to settle the issue in Moscow in October, the president cabled Stalin, urging that the contentious matter of Poland's boundaries be postponed. Stalin replied on December 27 that agents of the Arciszewski government were sabotaging Soviet military activities (and, indeed, the noncommunist underground in Poland was rapidly shifting its sights from the Germans to the Russians and their indigenous supporters), and advised that he was about to recognize the Committee of National Liberation as Poland's provisional government. Although he had been comfortably re-elected, Roosevelt remained sensitive to the pressure of the Polish-Americans, most of whom supported the inflexible policies of the London regime; "disturbed and deeply disappointed," he entreated Stalin to delay recognition at least until Yalta and warned that the United States was not prepared to legitimize the Lublin group.[78] Nevertheless, six days later, on January 5, Moscow officially recognized the committee, which then proceeded to establish itself in Warsaw; in order to lend further legitimacy to this unilateral act, Stalin persuaded Beneš to follow suit in the name of Czechoslovakia.

Political developments in Bulgaria and Rumania also gave little cause for optimism in Washington and London. The Bulgarian Fatherland Front governed with some effectiveness and contributed to the war effort, but, despite membership in the ACC, Western influence was nil; in early 1945 the official persecution of non-communists was intensified, but neither the United States nor Britain felt that their limited interest in Bulgaria warranted any determined challenge to the activities of the Soviet-dominated, but popular, regime at that time.[79] American economic interests in Rumania were more substantial, notably in oil, while the popular appeal of the local communists appeared to be far weaker than that in Bulgaria; the State Department therefore voiced concern over what it considered to be unreasonable Soviet economic demands upon Rumania.[80] On the political front, Moscow seemed momentarily willing to tolerate the predominantly noncommunist coalition, and, although Soviet-inspired strikes and demonstrations prompted King Michael to appoint on December 6 a new prime minister, General Radescu, the king was reassured by Vyshinsky that the Soviet Union merely wanted a friendly neighbor.[81] This tolerance did not extend to the Western representatives on the Rumanian ACC, for they had no direct access to the government and followed the agitation of the communist front organizations—notably, the Plowmen's Front, led by the landowner Petru Groza—with powerless apprehension.

"WE MET IN THE CRIMEA..."

In Washington, interest in the future of East-Central Europe waxed amid an incipient pessimism regarding Soviet designs on the area. Warnings that their traditional quest for power and security would make the Russians inclined to dominate East-Central Europe, and that their universalist and revolutionary ideology, held in abeyance for much of the war, would reappear and be imposed upon their new buffer zone, began to issue from various, but as yet isolated, sources—notably, Senator Vandenberg in Congress and Navy Secretary James Forrestal in the administration. From Moscow, Ambassador Harriman dispatched increasingly gloomy assessments of the Russians' tactics of paving the ground for communization by extracting crippling reparations and eliminating potential political opposition through indiscriminate use of the pro-Nazi epithet.[82] At a time when Churchill was reflecting fatalistically that "the end of this war may well prove to be more disappointing than was the last," Roosevelt clung to the illusory principles of the Atlantic Charter, telling Congress in January:

"We and our allies have a duty which we cannot ignore to use our influence to the end that no temporary or provisional authority in the liberated countries block the eventual exercise of the people's right freely to choose the government and institutions under which, as free men, they are to live."[83] At least outwardly he remained confident that Stalin was not an imperialist, and that each of his own goals—a world organization, Allied unity in war and peace, and a settlement based on neo-Wilsonian principles—could be realized without prejudice to the others.[84] In November, in the wake of the Churchill-Stalin percentage agreement, Secretary of State Stettinius summed up for the president what he considered to be the major American interests in East-Central Europe. They encompassed a free choice of political, social, and economic systems; nonrestrictive trade and communications policies; freedom of access for American philanthropic and educational organizations; the protection of American citizens' rights and property; and the settlement of territorial disputes only after the cessation of hostilities.[85] These interests were in harmony not only with previous Allied declarations of principle but also with the predominant popular sentiments throughout East-Central Europe, and, to the extent that it favored self-determination, the American position necessarily anticipated noncommunist regimes, for in no East European country, not even Yugoslavia, did that ideology or the derivative Soviet model arouse anywhere near majority support. Stettinius' draft did not presuppose a return to the *status quo ante*, with its militant hostility to the Soviet Union in the case of Poland, Hungary, and Rumania; nor did the American position, as it developed, preclude social and economic reforms, particularly in the agricultural sector. Thus, the arguments of certain "revisionist" historians who equate Anglo-American (anti-Left) interests and influence in Western Europe with Soviet (pro-Left) influence in Eastern Europe overlook the limited popularity of the communist Left in both areas and amount to rationalizations of the Soviet Union's desire to create a servile buffer zone.[86]

A briefing book, the result of comprehensive groundwork at the State Department, was presented to Roosevelt on January 18 as he was about to sail for Malta and preliminary discussions with the British. It offered realistic estimates of local conditions as well as of Soviet objectives in East-Central Europe, and it outlined possible policy options for the United States. One paper, drafted by John D. Hickerson, deputy director of the Office of European Affairs, recommended that, since the United States was not in a position to influence Soviet decisions regarding the Baltic states, Bessarabia, part of East Prussia, and territories east of the Curzon line, it might as well accept their incorporation as a *fait accompli*. Another paper, noting that the "general mood of the people of Europe is to the left and strongly in favor of far-reaching economic and social reforms," proposed that the United States pursue a "middle course" between the British and the Russians in negotiations over the liberated areas' provisional governments and assess those regimes in terms of their performance in the spheres of civil liberties and social and economic policy. Yet another warned against allowing the Anglo-Soviet percentage agreements to become permanent. With respect to Poland, the briefing book recommended that only a widely representative government be recognized, one which would subsequently be legitimized by UN-supervised elections; that the Curzon line be modified to allow Poland to retain Lwow and the Galician oil fields; and that only parts of East Prussia and Pomerania (rather than all territories east of the Oder-Neisse line) be awarded to Poland in compensation.[87]

The briefing paper "Principal Hungarian Problems" reflected the prevailing asymmetry between theoretically desirable outcomes and practical commitments. The possibility was noted at the outset that Soviet and American policies "may not be in harmony if the Soviet Union uses its position as the power in actual control of the execution of the armistice to intervene in Hungarian domestic affairs, to dominate Hungary, or to pursue a severe policy on the reparation question which would cripple the Hungarian economy." Listed as policy objectives were maximum Western participation in the Allied Control Commission, a level of reparations which was compatible with economic recovery, and a settlement of Hungary's border disputes which would take into account Hungarian ethnic claims. The paper expressed American interest in territorial settlements which would rectify the pre-Vienna Award frontier with Rumania in favor of Hungary and transfer to the latter some of the predominantly Magyar-populated districts of southern Slovakia. The ambivalence underlying these recommendations was revealed by the paper's assertion that in the armistice period the United States "would not, of course, take the position of supporting Hungary against the Soviet Union . . . The United States government recognizes that the Soviet Union's interest in Hungary is more direct than ours. . . . We do not, however, consider that the Soviet Union has any special or dominant position in Hungary."[88]

Another initiative of the State Department was a draft proposal for a four-power declaration of policy regarding provisional administrations, the arranging of early elections to establish popular and stable governments, and assistance in economic reconstruction in the liberated areas, together with an emergency high commission to supervise its implementation. In the course of the preliminary discussions on Malta, Stettinius told Eden that the president "had misgivings that the proposed Emergency high commission might prejudice the prospects of world organization." At the preconference briefing at Yalta on February 4, which was attended by Stettinius, Harriman, and Soviet and East European experts Charles Bohlen and H. Freeman Matthews, Roosevelt finally rejected the idea of an emergency high commission, saying that he did not want "another organization," that the existing European Advisory Commission had a poor record, and that he preferred to leave the problems of the liberated areas to subsequent meetings of foreign ministers; a more substantive objection was that the United States "would be loath to assume the responsibilities in regard to the internal problems of the liberated countries that such a standing high commission would unavoidably entail."[89] As the matter rested, Roosevelt rather disingenuously retained that part of the State Department's proposal which proclaimed a principle and discarded the corollary provision for a supervisory organ. Stettinius later observed regretfully that his department "had worked hard preparing this proposal, and the establishment of such a commission . . . might have forestalled some of the difficulties which arose in eastern Europe."[90] Indeed, although the operation of the ACCs in Bulgaria and Rumania gave little cause for optimism, an Allied body with wider authority and less dependence than the ACCs upon the whims of the local Soviet high commands might well have moderated Moscow's influence in the liberated areas.

In fact, the ailing president had paid scant attention to the State Department studies, characteristically preferring to play things by ear; he did not waver in his faith that Soviet-American cooperation could be prolonged through his personal rapport with Stalin. His perception of American priorities relegated the problems of East-Central Europe to a secondary position, behind the primary goal of Soviet participation in the United Nations and in the final struggle against Japan. Stalin, on the other hand, was most concerned about consolidating his control over the western approaches to the Soviet Union, and, with victory in Europe a foregone conclusion, was no longer dependent upon his allies beyond the economic aid that they might offer for reconstruction. The balance of forces and interests at Yalta therefore militated against any outright challenge to the Soviet *Gleichschaltung* that was already in progress throughout much of East-Central Europe. Paradoxically, as the Americans' vocal commitment to the principles of the Atlantic Charter grew louder, their bargaining strength declined, in consequence not only of external factors but also of national policy; thus at the outset of the Yalta Conference, Roosevelt announced candidly that American forces would remain in Europe for a maximum of two years after the cessation of hostilities—a piece of news which must have delighted Stalin, since it promised the removal of the one conceivable obstacle to the predominance of Soviet power on the Continent. Roosevelt and his principal advisers had not yet fully perceived the existing and potential inconsistencies and incompatibilities among American interests, influence, and stated or implicit principles and objectives regarding East-Central Europe.

Meeting at Livadia Palace, Nicholas II's summer retreat near Yalta, the Big Three grappled with the entire gamut of issues arising from the war, from Germany to the United Nations. Upon Stalin's request, Germany was the first topic discussed, but these talks were postponed when disagreements arose over various proposals for dismemberment, deindustrialization, and reparations. Protracted negotiations ensued, however, over Poland's future government and boundaries. At the preliminary talks on Malta, the two Western Allies had agreed to attempt to limit Poland's expansion at Germany's expense, as well as to modify the Curzon line in Poland's favor. Repeatedly alluding to the pressures exerted on him by Polish-American organizations, the president presented Stalin with suggestions for a widely based government and the retention by Poland of Lwow and the Galician oil fields; he assured Stalin that he, Roosevelt, also viewed as essential a Poland friendly to the Soviet Union. For Britain, added Churchill, the maintenance of Polish sovereignty was a matter of honor. To these entreaties Stalin retorted that for the Soviet Union the matter was one of security as well as of honor, and he pointed out that, since the Curzon line had been a foreign idea, he could not be "less Russian than Curzon and Clemenceau."[91] The final compromise entailed only a marginal alteration in that line in favor of Poland, which was to get "substantial accessions of territory in the North and West," to be specified at the eventual peace conference. Uneasy about the impact on domestic opinion of the possible expulsion of some seven to eight million Germans, Roosevelt and Churchill approved the Oder, but balked at the western Neisse, as Poland's new boundary.[92] No consultations with the government-in-exile preceded this agreement, as if to emphasize the fading operational relevance of the Atlantic Charter. Indeed, the issue of Poland's government proved to be even more contentious than that of its boundaries. Bohlen later testified that the West had faced three choices: accept the *fait accompli* of an exclusively Soviet-sponsored regime already on the spot, stand by the London government and thereby probably ensure its permanent exile, or compromise on some reorganization and amalgamation of the two.[93] The last option, given appropriate safeguards for its representativeness, was clearly the most attractive one, but it led to interminable debates over the respective merits of the Russian version, which envisaged an "enlargement" of the provisional (Lublin) government, and that of the West, which stressed "reorganization." In the end, it was agreed that Molotov, Harriman, and the British ambassador, Sir Archibald Clark Kerr, would be charged with the responsibility of holding consultations with the various Polish factions with a view to establishing a Polish Provisional Government of National Unity, which would then be recognized simultaneously by the Allies. The Soviet version had in effect carried the day, for the agreement made no reference to the London regime, but spoke of merely reorganizing the existing provisional government "on a more democratic basis."[94] Molotov had promised free elections within a month's time, but the president, still conscious of the ethnic vote, sought further reassurance from Stalin: "I want the election in Poland to be beyond question, like Caesar's wife. I did not know Caesar's wife, but she was believed to have been pure." Rejoined the Soviet leader, "It was said so about Caesar's wife, but, in fact, she had certain sins." When Roosevelt's chief of staff, Admiral Leahy, warned that the vagueness of the agreement allowed the Russians wide latitude in its interpretation, the president replied with a touch of fatalism: "I know, Bill—I know it. But it's the best I can do for Poland at this time."[95]

Resolution of the various other issues at Yalta entailed even fewer Soviet concessions. In exchange for eventual Soviet participation in the war against Japan, Roosevelt promised Stalin territorial accessions in Japanese-occupied China, as well as the Kuriles and southern Sakhalin. The Western allies agreed to UN membership for the Ukraine and Byelorussia, a dubious compromise on the principle of one state–one vote, even considering the original request that all sixteen "republics" be admitted. Stalin was persuaded to allow the inclusion in the new Yugoslav Assembly of some exile politicians and to subject its legislative actions to ratification by a constituent assembly, but in reality none of the Allies could claim to exercise significant influence over developments in that country.[96] The rather inconclusive outcome of the debates over Poland did not bode well for the rest of East-Central Europe, which indeed received scant attention at Yalta. It was almost as an afterthought that the Americans proposed a joint declaration on Allied policy regarding the liberated areas. Much to their surprise, the Russians raised virtually no objections. "This struck me suspiciously," recalls Bohlen; "I thought Stalin would offer all sorts of arguments, but he just quietly played his hand."[97] The Soviet leader could well afford this gesture as a sop to the sensibilities of Western public opinion. The withdrawal of U.S. forces from Europe promised by Roosevelt, as well as his decision to omit the supervisory organ suggested by the State Department, left the Yalta Declaration on Liberated Europe an essentially hortatory—and, to Stalin, harmless—reiteration of the principles already enunciated in the Atlantic Charter. Although the declaration asserted the determination of the Allies to assist in the democratic and economic regeneration of East-Central

Europe, its enforcement was described in terms which later were interpreted by some to require unanimity: "When, in the opinion of the three governments, conditions in any European liberated state or any former Axis satellite state in Europe make such action necessary, they will immediately consult together on the measures necessary to discharge the joint responsibilities set forth in this declaration."[98]

It was later argued by some historians that the Americans, aware of Stalin's hegemonic designs but unable to contain them, had put forward the declaration as potential testimony to his duplicity, in which case the Soviet endorsement of the document could be viewed as a victory for the West. In fact, while some participants at Yalta—notably, Harriman—did not share Roosevelt's optimism, the president had not admitted, even to himself, that the inevitable outcome of his military strategy and of his policies would be to leave East-Central Europe as Stalin's exclusive preserve, and in his message of March 1 he attempted to reassure Congress.

> We met in the Crimea, determined to settle this matter of liberated areas. I am happy to confirm . . . that we did arrive at a settlement—a unanimous settlement. . . . [The Allies] will join together, during the temporary period of instability after hostilities, to help the people of any liberated area, or of any former satellite state, to solve their own problems through firmly established democratic processes.[99]

Even the usually skeptical Churchill rose to the occasion by claiming in the House of Commons that he knew of "no Government which stands to its obligations . . . more solidly than the Russian Soviet Government," an astonishing testimony which, he explained subsequently, had been prompted by the need to "proclaim my confidence in Soviet good faith in the hope of procuring it."[100] Sustained by such high-powered propaganda, the Declaration on Liberated Europe was received with popular enthusiasm in the West. Response to the Polish compromise—an "outstanding example of joint action by the three major Allied powers," in Roosevelt's view—was rather less positive. The Poles and many others were appalled at its implications. On February 14, the Arciszewski government denounced the Yalta decisions as being in violation of the Atlantic Charter; a few days later, Senator Vandenberg also expressed his "deep disappointment in respect to the Polish settlement (symbolic of the general treatment to be accorded to the smaller liberated nations)."[101] But, if the Western champions of Poland's sovereignty had failed Poland at Yalta, it was largely because of earlier and perhaps irreversible strategies. The issues of peace, as distinct from the requisites of war, should perhaps have received more concentrated attention from the United States by the time of the Yalta conference. These issues were, in descending order of urgency, elimination of the power of the Axis to threaten the peace again; implementation of the Atlantic Charter through equitable peace settlements; economic reconstruction of friend and foe alike; and an international organization to provide continuity in the resolution of these and future problems. Instead, Roosevelt chose to focus on the Far East, where Allied victory was inevitable, even without Stalin's assistance, and on the United Nations, whose effectiveness was predicated upon the full cooperation of an increasingly intractable ally. Between the short perspective of victory over Japan and the long perspective of an effective international organization lay the more practical problems of the postwar balance of power and the creation of a just and stable *status quo* in Europe. By his premature announcement of American withdrawal and by his refusal to countenance an emergency high commission, Roosevelt implicitly sanctioned the entrenchment of Soviet power and influence in the heart of Europe. While the Western powers had, in the Atlantic Charter and other pronouncements, waived the traditional claim to the spoils of victory in the interests of a lasting peace, Stalin, unimpeded by such altruism, intent upon securing ideological as well as strategic security, and fundamentally hostile to the West, proceeded to profit from the flux of history and to consolidate his gains. Thus, in retrospect, Yalta was less a betrayal of principles by America than the final act in the ill-conceived strategy of U.S. leaders to view the states of war and peace in isolation and to ignore the fact that, in either state, principles, without the judicious application of power, will give way to expediency. In the public eye, however, and notwithstanding the Polish compromise, the first myth of liberation, conceived in the Atlantic Charter, survived, and was even enhanced by the meeting of the Big Three in the Crimea.

II
THE PRICE
OF PEACE

The eagle should permit the small birds
to sing and care not wherefore they sang.
CHURCHILL TO STALIN

Everyone imposes his own system as far as
his army can reach. It cannot be otherwise.
STALIN TO DJILAS

Yalta proved to be the swan song of Allied solidarity. Bonds born of wartime necessity weakened as victory loomed near, and positions hardened on contentious but hitherto secondary issues. No more would the leaders of the Great Powers leave the conference table with ringing declarations of unity of purpose. In the new confrontation that arose from the ashes of the old, East-Central Europe played a key, divisive role which owed as much to a mutual misreading of intentions on the part of the Allies as to a reassertion of their traditional interests. The success of Roosevelt's strategy of postponement was contingent upon the continued collaboration of the Great Powers within the United Nations, which he hoped would give substance to the Yalta undertakings. Stalin, whose attitude regarding the United Nations implied that Soviet interests were likely to conflict with those of the other Great Powers and could never be

subordinated to the will of an international body, viewed those undertakings as propaganda for Western domestic consumption, as mere words,
not as an attempt, even by Western leaders, to present a tangible obstacle
to the incorporation of East-Central Europe into a Soviet sphere of influence or dominance.

Developments in the liberated areas soon testified to this new confidence on the part of the Russians. In Rumania, the Radescu regime came
under attack from the local communists, who were led by Ana Pauker and
Gheorghe Gheorgiu-Dej and abetted by the Soviet High Command. Fearing that the communist-inspired riots and demonstrations were the
preamble to a coup, the Roosevelt administration instructed Harriman to
request Allied consultations regarding the "orderly development" of the
Rumanian situation, which the ambassador did on February 24;[1] simultaneously, in Bucharest, the British and American members of the Allied
Control Commission pressed the Soviet chairman to call a meeting. The
Russians' schedule was not to be delayed by such consultations. Following
an official Soviet request that he restore order (which allegedly had been
disturbed by fascist elements), Radescu attempted to bring the army back
from the front, but, on February 27, Deputy Foreign Minister Andrei
Vyshinsky arrived to confront the king with an ultimatum that Radescu
be dismissed for his failure to suppress the fascists—a term which already
encompassed almost all who actively opposed the communists. In the next
few days the king attempted to create an alternative government that
would not be communist-dominated, but Vyshinsky made it clear that he
favored Petru Groza, and, when Michael attempted to reject Groza's first
cabinet as unrepresentative, he was told that the Soviet Union would
consider this a hostile act which imperiled Rumania's independence.
Under duress, the king approved the Groza government on March 6;[2] the
following day, Harriman was advised by Molotov that his earlier requests
were no longer relevant, for the crisis had passed. Throughout the crisis,
the U.S. representative, Burton Y. Berry, had not been consulted or
allowed access to the key figures. After the event, the president told
Harriman to propose that a joint committee be set up in Bucharest to
supervise the implementation of the Yalta Declaration. The Soviet Union
had been defending its actions in Rumania on the grounds that its military
lines of communication needed protection and that the Western powers
had taken similarly unilateral actions in Italy;[3] thus, Molotov rejected the
new proposal, asserting that the ACC sufficed. Conceding that the Soviet
army had to protect its rear and was already in effective control of the
country, Roosevelt concluded that Rumania was not a good test case of
the Yalta Declaration.[4] In the Moscow embassy, the lone voice of George
Kennan gloomily observed that the protests would be "fruitless polemic"

unless the United States withdrew from the ACC, an act that, in itself, might not alter the course of Rumanian politics, but that would at least eliminate the pretense of joint responsibility.[5]

The Yalta agreement on Poland struck Kennan as the "shabbiest sort of equivocation," and, indeed, it proved to be only one in a series of compromises which served the interests of the Soviet Union. The initial negotiations of the Moscow commission (comprised of Molotov, Harriman, and Clark Kerr) had ended in stalemate over a number of issues—principally, how many, and which, of the London Poles could participate in the consultations, and whether the regime *in situ* could veto any of them. Stalin himself maintained that only those Poles who unreservedly accepted the Yalta political and boundary decisions were eligible, a qualification that excluded most of the émigrés, who had retrenched themselves into a position of immutable hostility to any tampering with their country's territorial integrity. In Poland itself, the political situation in the early months of 1945 was uncertain. Land reform had been effected, and the popular mood was inimical to a return to the authoritarian prewar system. Neither Bierut's communist regime nor the Soviet liberators managed to arouse much enthusiasm; a few politicians had returned from exile, however, including Mikolajczyk, who had been persuaded by Churchill to openly accept the Yalta decisions, and noncommunist parties were being activated once again. While the Russians continued to advocate only token enlargement of the Warsaw regime, the Western powers, having sanctioned the territorial shift of a country across the face of Europe, appeared reluctant to make political concessions of equal magnitude. At the end of March, Churchill cabled Roosevelt, "Surely we must not be maneuvered into becoming parties to imposing on Poland—and on how much more of Eastern Europe—the Russian version of democracy?"[6] Roosevelt was more conscious of the emphasis placed on the Lublin regime in the Yalta agreement, but he joined Churchill in urging Stalin to accept in good faith those Polish candidates for consultations who had been recommended by the Western ambassadors, and warned that a Polish solution that "would result in a thinly disguised continuance of the Warsaw regime would be unacceptable and would cause the people of the United States to regard the Yalta agreement as having failed."[7] These entreaties caught Stalin at his most unreceptive, however, for he had apparently convinced himself that his allies had reached a secret agreement with the German commander in Italy, General Kesselring, who would "open the front to the Anglo-American forces and let them move east."[8] Meanwhile, Harriman's reports from Moscow had acquired a tone of urgency: "It may be difficult for us to believe, but it still may be true that Stalin and Molotov considered at Yalta that by our willingness to accept a general wording of the declaration on Poland and liberated Europe, by our recognition of the need of the Red Army for security behind its lines, and of the predominant interest of Russia in Poland as a friendly neighbor and as a corridor to Germany, we understood and were ready to accept Soviet policies already known to us." Warning that America's "generous and considerate attitude" was regarded in Moscow as a sign of weakness, he urged that a tougher line be taken with the Russians.[9]

TRUMAN AND THE NEW BALANCE OF POWER

The Moscow discussions were still in a state of stalemate when, on April 12, President Roosevelt died and the reins of power passed to Harry Truman. The change of leadership also brought a change in style. Supremely confident in his personal diplomacy, idealistic to a fault when it came to grand designs, but very much the pragmatic politician in matters of detail, Roosevelt had to some extent fallen victim to his own propaganda of extolling the virtues and solidarity of America's Soviet ally. Cast in a less-Olympian mold, his successor proved less susceptible to nostalgic feelings of comradeship-in-arms. Although in his last days Roosevelt had grown increasingly disillusioned with the Russians, it fell upon Truman to draw the appropriate conclusions. Stalin's latest proposal (April 7) regarding Poland had referred to the Yugoslav pattern (Tito and Šubašić having nominated twenty-one and six cabinet members respectively), and the Soviet leader continued to insist that the Moscow commission "as a whole" approve the proposal and issue the invitations to the Poles;[10] meanwhile, the Arciszewski government announced the disappearance of fifteen underground leaders who had been invited to meet with the Russians and had been guaranteed safe-conduct. In his first full day in office, President Truman was presented with a State Department briefing paper which noted that, since Yalta, the Soviets had "taken a firm and uncompromising position on nearly every major question that has arisen in our relations," and concluded that, in terms of American public opinion and U.S.-Soviet relations, Poland stood out as a critical test case.[11] Truman and Churchill's response to Stalin's proposal was to reject the Yugoslav model and suggest the alternative—equally loaded but favorable to the West—of allowing three representatives from each of the Warsaw and London regimes and two noncommunists from Poland to participate in the deliberations of the Moscow commission.[12] Such Western proposals and protests appeared to carry little weight in the Kremlin, however, where the more pressing problems of strengthening the Warsaw regime and eliminating the Polish opposition took top priority; one symbolic measure, taken unilaterally, was the conclusion of a treaty of mutual assistance with the Warsaw provisional government.

When Molotov arrived in Washington in mid-April, on his way to the San Francisco conference, he was accompanied by Ambassador Harriman, who lost no time in imparting to the president his views regarding the Russians' tactics of implanting police states and their concurrent, desperate need for economic aid.[13] The administration's new hard line was reinforced the following day, April 23, when Truman convened his top advisers for a meeting in the White House.[14] Taking part in this crucial conference were Secretary of State Stettinius, Secretary of War Stimson, Navy Secretary James Forrestal, General Marshall, Admiral King, Admiral Leahy, General John R. Deane (head of the military mission in Moscow), Assistant Secretary of State James Dunn, Harriman, and Charles Bohlen—an assembly which encompassed a wide range of opinion. The old bias of the military establishment against political involvement was reflected by Stimson, who, perhaps alone among the participants, failed to perceive the long-range political significance of the Polish crisis; he argued that "the Balkans and their troubles were beyond the sphere of proper United States action," and he cautioned the president against making too great an issue out of the Soviets' disregard for the Yalta Declaration, arguing that the Russian requirement for security in the west was a realistic one. Marshall reiterated the need for Soviet cooperation in the Far East, while Leahy pointed out that he had never expected the Russians to agree with the American interpretation of the declaration. In contrast to the isolationism of Stimson's implied acquiescence in a Soviet sphere of influence, Stettinius, Harriman, Forrestal, and Deane advocated firmness in defense of American interests, which they understood to include implementation of the Yalta promises. The secretary of the navy observed that, if the Russians' proprietary attitude toward East-Central Europe did not change, he for one would favor an early and decisive showdown.

Already attuned to the hard-liners, Truman emerged from the meeting in a belligerent mood and proceeded to berate Molotov and to insist on an adequately representative Polish government, adding a veiled threat to the effect that Soviet intransigence might compromise the prospects of American economic assistance. Protested a stunned Molotov, "I have never been talked to like that in my life."[15] The harsh words failed to budge Stalin, however, who in his message of April 24 asserted that at Yalta the Allies had agreed the Warsaw regime would serve as the core of a new government, that a friendly Poland was as essential to Soviet security as were Belgium and Greece to Britain, and that he, Stalin, had never claimed the right to determine the nature of the governments of those two countries.[16] The debate over Poland, fruitless and increasingly acrimonious, continued at the San Francisco Conference. Molotov's proposal that the Warsaw provisional government be invited to participate was opposed by

Eden and Stettinius and was voted down, and, when the Soviet foreign minister admitted that the missing Polish underground leaders had been arrested on charges of subversion, the negotiations were broken off. Already the Big Three, supposed guarantors of peace and security within the fledgling United Nations, stood in hostile confrontation.

Meanwhile, the war in Europe was coming to an end, but the new posture of toughness that materialized in Washington in the early days of the Truman administration did not extend to the military sphere, where loyal collaboration with Russia remained the order of the day. The occupation zones in Germany (as well as the sectors of Berlin) had been delineated by the European Advisory Commission at a time when the Anglo-Americans appeared unlikely to reach even the Elbe before the Russians.[17] In the event, and despite the setback in the Ardennes, by April 12, advance units had crossed the Elbe and penetrated to within fifty miles of Berlin, whereas the Russians had encountered unexpectedly stiff resistance, and were to take another eighteen days before finally capturing the capital. Ever conscious of the political advantage that accrues from physical control over territory, Churchill warned Roosevelt on April 3 that the Russians might be that much more difficult to deal with if they occupied Berlin as well as Vienna (which they in fact reached four days later), and supported the British Chiefs of Staff in their recommendation that Montgomery's forces press on and take Berlin, whose defenders were in any case more likely to surrender to the British and the Americans than to the Russians. The Joint Chiefs of Staff rejected such politically motivated departures from established strategy, as did Truman, who informed Churchill that existing agreements with the Russians would be respected; the latter did not reach the Elbe until April 25, the opening day of the San Francisco conference.[18] Churchill pinned his hopes on effecting a binding settlement with the Soviet Union "before the armies of democracy melted," arguing in a memorandum to Eden, dated May 4, that the Allies "ought not to retreat from their present positions to the occupational lines until we are satisfied about Poland, and also about the temporary character of the Soviet occupation of Germany, and the conditions to be established in the Russianized or Russian-controlled countries in the Danube valley . . . and the Balkans."[19] He felt that the Yalta Declaration had to a large extent invalidated the earlier percentage agreement with Stalin (a view the latter never came to share) and saw no reason to hold back the Anglo-American advance and thereby forego an even marginal improvement in the bargaining position of the West.

With Berlin already in Russian hands, Churchill set his sights on Prague and urged that at least the Czech capital be liberated by Western forces. Logistically this would have been much easier than pre-empting the Russians in Berlin earlier that month, but once again the military prevailed. Marshall advised Eisenhower that he "would be loath to hazard American lives for purely political purposes," a view the supreme commander shared all the more readily since he was preoccupied with a two-pronged thrust, north toward Lübeck and southwest into the Nazis' "National Redoubt." When Patton's Third Army crossed the border into Czechoslovakia in the first days of May, the British and the Czechs in London redoubled their urgings that he press on to Prague. Despite the favorable disposition of Secretary of State Stettinius, Truman ruled that political considerations were not to interfere with military plans.[20] The Russians, equally covetous of the honor of liberating the city, but in no position to reach it before Patton, requested that the latter's forces remain west of the Budejovice-Pilsen-Karlsbad line; Eisenhower agreed and issued appropriate orders on May 5. The matter did not rest there, however, for that same day Partisans in Prague rose up in arms (with the local communists playing only a supporting role) against the German occupier and sent appeals for assistance to Patton's headquarters near Pilsen. Word of the uprising reached Allied Headquarters in Reims as German emissaries were negotiating the final instrument of surrender on May 7, and the requests for help were merely transmitted to the Soviet military authorities. Meanwhile, oblivious to the surrender, the SS division in Prague persisted in its efforts to put down the rising. In the midst of this confusion, Churchill wired Eisenhower suggesting that American units, if available, should come to the rebels' assistance in case Marshal Koniev's forces had not yet reached Prague; the following day, the Czechs sent a desperate plea for air support, but to no avail. The May 5 line prevailed, Patton was not unleashed (although one of his patrols made a tentative foray into the outskirts of Prague), and all appeals to Allied Headquarters were relayed to the Russians. The latter entered Prague on May 9 as the city's official liberators, an event of some symbolic and political significance in a country which ostensibly had nothing to fear from the Soviet Union; only three weeks later were Czech units from Bradley's army group permitted by the Russians to follow suit. Apart from the unnecessary casualties in Prague caused by the delayed assistance of the Allies, the significance of the episode lay less in the West's missed opportunity to regain some prestige among the Czechs than in the hiatus it revealed between the tentative tough line in the White House and a military strategy that still assumed unity of purpose among the Allies.

By the time of the German surrender, Churchill had no doubts that first priority had to be given to dealing with the Soviet menace and he deplored the fact that "no comradeship against it existed." On May 12 he dispatched a message to Truman in which he contrasted the predicted withdrawal of American forces from Europe with the Soviets' consolidation, and pressed again for a settlement "before our strength is gone."[21] The prime minister's urgings went unheeded, however, and on June 21 all Western forces began withdrawing from an area 400 miles long and up to 120 miles deep to the previously set zonal demarcation lines; only in Czechoslovakia did a similar Soviet withdrawal eventually take place. In the United States, demobilization was an immensely popular prospect that few politicians wished to oppose, and, although certain advisers—notably, Forrestal and Harriman—protested, it was only some years later that Truman admitted what a fundamental error it had been to precipitously deplete American strength on the Continent before securing a satisfactory peace settlement.[22] Between June 1945 and March 1946, U.S. land forces in Europe were reduced in strength from 3.5 million to 400,000; Soviet demobilization left 2.9 million men in arms out of a pre-armistice total of some twelve million. By 1948, 40 Soviet divisions in Eastern Europe (and a readily accessible reserve of 250 more) faced a grand total of two American and nine British, French, and Belgian divisions on the Continent. Such was the balance of forces in Europe during the crucial years when the modalities of peace were hammered out by the erstwhile Allies. The atomic bomb, utilized only twice in anger, in August 1945, loomed as a potential but scarcely envisaged equalizer.

The only other potential bargaining counter held by the United States was that of credits and economic aid, but the story of their use, or rather nonuse, is riddled with a curious blend of negligence and procrastination.[23] The Lend-Lease program, without which the Soviet war effort would have been severely handicapped, particularly in the early years, provided that country with an aggregate of $9.5 billion in military material and industrial machinery. Early in 1944, however, with the end of the war in sight, U.S. congressional opposition mounted against using Lend-Lease for postwar reconstruction, the case in point being a much-increased Soviet request for industrial equipment within the framework of the Fourth Russian Supply Protocol then under negotiation, and the Lend-Lease Act, which passed in April, contained such a limiting amendment. Moreover, in subsequent discussions regarding the alternative fulfillment of the Soviet request by special credits, the two governments' positions on appropriate interest rates could not be reconciled. The following year, on the very day the war in Europe came to an end, all Lend-Lease shipments were abruptly curtailed, and even those in transit were recalled to American ports. The stoppage was in keeping with the terms of the Lend-Lease Act, but President Truman soon confessed that he had signed the document without reading it, and he rescinded the order in favor of a more gradual and orderly phasing out of the program. The damage had been done, however, for Stalin immediately concluded that the stoppage was a clumsy American attempt to extract political concessions from the Soviet Union; instead, it was an administrative oversight that produced exactly the opposite effect and nullified whatever good will had been engendered by the program to that date.

The previously noted request had been only one manifestation of the Soviet Union's concern with postwar reconstruction. In January 1945 the United States received another proposal, independent of Lend-Lease, for a credit of $6 billion at 2¼ percent interest, to be utilized for Russian purchases of manufactured goods and industrial equipment. Ambassador Harriman understood the request to be very much in earnest and recommended that its granting be made contingent upon acceptable Soviet "behaviour in international matters"; in a Yalta briefing paper for the president, the State Department, noting that the Soviet Union was in a position to service such a loan, observed that postwar credits could "serve as a useful instrument in our overall relations with the U.S.S.R."[24] Although Roosevelt expressed some interest and indicated he would take it up in the discussions at Yalta, the matter of credits sank into oblivion. Despite the obvious need of the Soviet Union for aid in reconstruction, and of the United States for moderating the Russian positions on the various peace settlements, neither at Yalta nor afterward did the requested credits come up for negotiation. There is no record of any American decision to reject the idea. At Yalta, Roosevelt presumably did not feel that the time had come yet for crass bargaining over a *quid pro quo* involving credits; in the succeeding months, as Soviet-American relations worsened over Poland and other issues, the prospect of granting advantageous credits to an increasingly recalcitrant ally lost whatever support it may have had in Washington, notwithstanding Truman's passing remark to Molotov. A final bit of bureaucratic bungling—the misplacement for six months of a further Soviet request, received in August 1945, for credits amounting to $1 billion—provided a fitting epilogue to the story of economic aid. It is difficult to escape the conclusion that, in view of the Russians' palpable and oft-expressed need for economic assistance in reconstructing their shattered industries, the United States could have handled the question of loans with far greater sophistication and possibly to useful political effect; a more positive approach to this problem might also have forestalled the patently excessive Soviet demand for German reparations totaling $20 billion and the resulting discord among the Allies.

This may be the appropriate place to consider the arguments, inspired mainly by economic determinism, that at war's end the United States willfully reoriented its world strategy into one of implacable hostility to the Soviet Union—arguments that incidentally form a counterpoint to an earlier revisionist orthodoxy which postulated the betrayal of American principles regarding East-Central Europe by a naïve and myopically Russophilist leadership. The record shows that, Alger Hiss *et al.* notwithstanding, no conspiracy of the Left could have been responsible for the failures of U.S. foreign policy. Assertions that a capitalistic-imperialistic establishment, motivated by a search for markets, or alternatively desirous of fostering the American armaments industry and of seeking an appropriately despicable enemy, willfully revived the old bogey of bolshevism and attempted to deprive the Soviet Union of its rightful *cordon sanitaire* at a time when Stalin was pursuing a policy of peace and friendship bears even less resemblance to reality.

Viewed in historical perspective, the wartime collaboration of the two Great Powers, one the fountainhead of a collectivistic and totalitarian, intrinsically revolutionary ideology, and the other equally committed to a rather less programmatic system of *laissez-faire* and pluralistic democracy, was hardly more than an expedient and symbiotic alliance born of necessity. The fundamental divergence of the two systems engendered a mutual mistrust that momentarily subsided, and then only through official manipulation, in the face of a common threat. Its reappearance cannot, however, be attributed to some new crusading spirit on the part of the United States. Despite its earlier lapses into crypto-imperialism in Latin America and the Far East, American foreign policy remained subject to an idealistic world view, incorporating the values of political self-determination and collective security, which found expression in numerous wartime pronouncements. It was the Soviet Union that, by professing concurrence in these principles, departed from its dogmatic preconceptions, and then, with victory in hand, allowed the latter to be reasserted. The success of Roosevelt's policies hinged upon an effective system of collective security, whose success in turn depended upon Great Power cooperation. When the time came to construct the new world organization, however, the Soviet Union indicated that it did not view the UN as an adequate safeguard for its security, and that the existence of such an organization did not invalidate its claim to a protective sphere of influence. It might have been foreseen that the prospect of a numerically Western-dominated UN would do nothing to mitigate the Russians' ideologically based mistrust of the capitalistic world, and that the Anglo-American insistence upon unfettered self-determination for East-Central Europe—which in the best of circumstances would still have led to noncommunist regimes—would reinforce the Russians' perception of Western hostility. In the months following Yalta, what one historian summed up as "the intransigence of Leninist ideology, the sinister dynamics of a totalitarian society and the madness of Stalin" served only to accentuate these differences.[25]

In contrast, American policy during the war had remained consistent in its doctrinal opposition to the concept of spheres of influence, and none of the Yalta agreements can be interpreted as having explicitly reversed this principle. The British themselves would later maintain that their 1944 percentage deal had been superseded by the Declaration on Liberated Europe, but Stalin understandably chose to ignore this argument, protesting that he had kept his part of the bargain by not interfering in the Greek civil war, whereas the British and the Americans had reneged on their earlier tacit acceptance of a Soviet sphere of influence in the rest of East-Central Europe. To the extent that this arose from a misperception of American intentions, the fault lay with Roosevelt for failing to oppose with sufficient vigor Churchill's ill-conceived bargain and to impress upon the Russians both its transitory nature and its inconsistency with the prevailing American view on spheres of influence. In sum, the percentage agreement represented for Stalin a gratuitous but welcome legitimization of his plans to create, by fair means or foul, a subservient buffer zone—plans which remained a constant factor amid the misperceptions and bitter recriminations that characterized Allied negotiations after Yalta. Having for years relied upon occasional declarations of principle, leaving the tactically weaker Churchill to cope with operational necessities, the American policy makers realized only gradually and belatedly that Stalin had never ceased to think in terms of power politics and that he expected them to make the same distinction between idealistic propaganda and the firm reality of national interest. By its very traditions, American foreign policy was lacking in such pragmatic flexibility, and consequently the eventual concessions to the reality of Soviet power and intransigence over East-Central Europe were made only in grudging admission of momentary impotence and amid indignant reassertions of principles that could not be implemented. American hostility, far from precipitating the procommunist coups in East-Central Europe (and, indeed, Bulgaria, Rumania, and Poland were already saddled with definitive or interim communist regimes by the time a hard line had materialized in the White House), was activated by tangible evidence of the Soviet Union's hegemonic designs.

Washington's persistence in preaching the principles of the Atlantic Charter and the Yalta Declaration has struck some who view Soviet dominance in East-Central Europe in terms of historical inevitability as an unrealistically rigid stance that forfeited any hope of future Soviet-American cooperation and led indirectly to Russian integrative policies that were harsher than originally planned. The validity of such criticism rests upon a number of questionable assumptions. The first, that nothing the United States might have done after Teheran could have altered the postwar balance in Europe, is the most difficult to refute conclusively, but the foregoing discussion of Balkan strategies, percentage agreements, the emergency high commission, occupation zones and demobilization, and economic aid has provided at least some points of doubt regarding the inevitability of Soviet hegemony. The second, that despite its stated principles regarding self-determination a democracy such as the United States could have executed a *volte-face* in foreign policy and suddenly condoned Stalin's East European *Gleichschaltung*, is even less realistic. The administration had to contend with a bipartisan commitment—one that rested on the broadest popular base (excluding only Henry Wallace's rather inconsequential faction)—to a position well expressed by a Republican policy statement released on December 5, 1945: "We believe in fulfilling to the greatest possible degree our war pledges to small nations that they shall have the right to choose the form of government under which they will live and that sovereign rights and self-government shall be restored to those who have been forcibly deprived of them. We deplore any desertion of these principles."[26] A third assumption, that Stalin desired no more than friendly neighbors and therefore presented no threat to American interests, conflicts both with the explicitly universalistic Leninist guidelines and with the reality of an immensely powerful Soviet Union already engaged in extending its ideology and influence to areas beyond East-Central Europe.

A corollary thesis advanced by some historians holds that American aggressiveness in the postwar era was motivated by some capitalistic-imperialistic inclination to keep "an open door to the Eastern European economies."[27] Throughout the protracted negotiations over the peace settlements, the United States stood in favor of (1) the right of the East Europeans to determine their own economic systems (assuming correctly that this would lead to necessary reforms, particularly in land tenure, but not to any wholesale application of the Soviet model), (2) nondiscriminatory trade policies and international administration of the Danubian waterways, (3) the protection of American property, and (4) a level of reparations that was compatible with economic recovery. In addition to being in harmony with the aspirations of most East Europeans, these *desiderata* were fully in keeping with previous Allied declarations of principle; they did clash, however, with a Russian disposition in the immediate aftermath of victory to extract crippling reparations and to impose exclusive and exploitative commercial and developmental arrangements. In light of America's hitherto modest commercial interest and level of investments in East-Central Europe, and of the rather limited prospects for future markets (secular limitations that, as will be noted in Chapter VI, continue to prevail), the argument that the economic factor lay at the root of U.S. policies regarding that area appears oddly contrived. In reality, it represented merely one of several important and interrelated elements in a policy that consistently opposed any unilateral predetermination of the fate of East-Central Europe.

To return to the Polish impasse, it has already been noted that the San Francisco conference brought it no nearer to satisfactory resolution, but rather added to the suspicion among the Western powers that Stalin was willfully holding up progress on a number of other issues—notably, the voting formula in the Security Council and the administration of occupied Austria—in order to win his case over Poland. Whereas at Yalta he had excluded from any future negotiations those Poles who refused to support the decisions reached at that conference, in a letter to Churchill dated May 4 Stalin posited even stiffer criteria, insisting that "only people who have demonstrated by deeds their friendly attitude to the Soviet Union, who are willing honestly and sincerely to cooperate with the Soviet state, should be consulted on the formation of a future Polish Government."[28] In desperation, Harriman suggested to the president that Roosevelt's confidant and adviser, Harry Hopkins, accompany him back to Moscow for a last-ditch attempt to break the deadlock—"to see," recalls George Kennan, "what could be salvaged from the wreckage of FDR's policy with relation to Russia and Poland."[29] Deploring the continued pretense of a united Allied policy at the expense of a consolidation of the democracies in Western Europe, Kennan advised Hopkins, upon the latter's arrival, not to agree to Stalin's terms, but the pressures in favor of a compromise prevailed. With the conclusion of the hostilities in Europe, continued concealment from the public of the discords tearing at the alliance became less and less feasible, and Hopkins warned Stalin that the preceding six weeks had seen a drastic deterioration of American public opinion regarding the Soviet Union, that many minority groups were clearly unsympathetic to that country, and that Poland provided the focal point for all this concern. Hopkins further remarked that American interests were world-wide, that Poland had become a symbol of Soviet-American ability to resolve problems, and that, far from encouraging anti-Soviet Poles, the United States would accept "any government in Poland which was desired by the Polish people and was at the same time friendly to the Soviet Union." Stalin, in turn, observed that twice in twenty-five years German invading armies had taken the Polish route, argued that his unilateral action in signing a treaty with the Warsaw regime when the latter had not yet been recognized by the other allies had been dictated by the Red Army's urgent need for a secure rear, and concluded that, far from wanting to Sovietize Poland—talk of which he derided as stupid, since the Soviet system was neither exportable nor desired by the Poles—he sought a strong and democratic neighbor that would not open the gates to Germany again.

When the discussion shifted to specifics, however, it became clear that the Soviet position had not altered. To Hopkins' request for assurances that certain fundamental rights, including free access by all democratic parties to the communications media, would be respected in Poland, Stalin replied by agreeing in principle, but with the proviso that during wartime these political freedoms could not be enjoyed to the full extent nor be applied without reservations to fascist parties trying to overthrow the government, qualifications whose definition and application rested implicitly with the Warsaw government and its sponsor. The final agreement between Hopkins and Stalin—not so much a compromise as a surrender to the latter's wishes—specified consultations with four representatives of the Warsaw regime, three London Poles not connected with the government-in-exile (which was thus summarily discarded by all concerned), and five others from Poland.[30] The majority of these being either communists or communist sympathizers, it was a foregone conclusion that the consultations with the Moscow commission would produce an overwhelmingly communist "Provisional Government of National Unity"; although Mikolajczyk was named deputy premier, the key ministries and the dominant voice in the cabinet belonged to the Lublin faction. Upon receiving assurances that the new government would respect the Yalta decisions regarding the holding of free elections, the United States and Great Britain extended their recognition to it on July 5. Having thus conceded the core of their demands, the Western powers nevertheless persisted in the pretense that the eventual elections would restore parliamentary democracy and representative government to Poland. There remained some hope in Washington that, despite the pro-Soviet orientation of the provisional government, Western loans and economic aid through the United Nations Relief and Rehabilitation Administration (UNRRA), as well as revived commercial links, would keep the country from being wholly absorbed into the Russian orbit. In fact, the immense task of reconstruction did create a momentary spirit of cooperation in Warsaw, both within the government and vis-à-vis the West, but the overwhelmingly anticommunist bias of the population left little doubt about the outcome of genuinely free elections, and, accordingly, all democratic parties were subjected to increasingly severe and ultimately fatal official discrimination. After centuries of abuse at the hands of its more powerful neighbors, the Polish nation was sacrificed once again, this time on the altar of an already defunct Allied unity.

The inconsistency between the Hopkins-Stalin formula and the hard line pursued concurrently by Truman and Churchill was to some extent mitigated by the corollary assurance of free elections; although by mid-1945 most Western leaders viewed such promises with skepticism, their public utterances gave little indication that any betrayal of the Poles' right to self-determination had occurred. Gratified by the outcome of Hopkins' visit, Stalin mellowed momentarily and allowed the satisfactory resolution of a number of pending issues regarding the UN and the interim administration of Germany and Austria, issues which he apparently considered to be less important than the consolidation of Soviet influence in East-Central Europe. Yet the old pattern whereby the United States and Britain made operational concessions and then reverted to a strident advocacy of contradictory principles continued to prevail. In insisting upon free and representative regimes, Truman's rhetoric was more vigorous than that of his predecessor. On the other hand, he also inherited Roosevelt's reluctance to commit American power in pursuit of these principles, observing in his memoirs: "I did not want to become involved in the Balkans in a way that could lead us into another world conflict. In any case, I was anxious to get the Russians into the war against Japan as soon as possible, thus saving the lives of countless Americans."[31] While Churchill saw the problems in terms of the European balance of power, Truman and most of his advisers appeared to be only dimly aware of the strategic implications of Soviet hegemony in East-Central Europe and did not regard the fate of democracy in that area as, by itself, a *casus belli*. Perceiving American interests primarily in quasimoral terms, terms that were rooted in wartime declarations, Truman felt no compunction about accepting the prearranged occupation zones and ordering demobilization after Germany's surrender. It is no idle speculation to suppose that, if the British and the Americans had concentrated their efforts on occupying as much of Germany as was physically possible, they would have gained a major bargaining counter vis-à-vis Stalin and might well have induced the latter, as one historian suggests, to grant a less qualified independence to the nations of East-Central Europe in exchange for the neutralization and demilitarization of Germany.[32] Being implicitly committed to the maintenance of friendly and democratic regimes in Western Europe, the United States clearly had a strategic interest in their security, which in turn would have been significantly enhanced by a withdrawal of the Red Army from East-Central Europe. The return to the Elbe line and the precipitous demobilization of American forces testify to the absence of such calculations in Washington, an absence that is usually attributed to the constraints of domestic politics. While there is no question that most American leaders perceived such constraints, it is less certain whether they were, in fact, all that prevalent or immutable. War-weary and latently isolationist, the American public was nevertheless sensitive to the news of Soviet depredations in liberated Europe—its mounting resentment was accurately related to Stalin by Hopkins—and would in all likelihood have responded positively to a clear-cut appeal by the administration which made explicit Stalin's disregard for the wartime declarations and the consequent necessity for maintaining American strength in Europe;[33] gains made by the Republicans in the 1946 congressional elections were due in no small part to their strong anticommunist stance. In the event, Truman chose to preach democratic theory to the Russians but refrained from taking those steps in the domestic political arena and in regard to the disposition of American power which might have brought that theory closer to reality in East-Central Europe, where the promise of liberation from foreign oppression was rapidly losing its credibility.

MAKING THE PEACE, FROM POTSDAM TO PARIS

In the period between the Hopkins mission and the Potsdam conference, when America's strength in Europe was already ebbing away, the tone of Truman's messages to Stalin only grew in reproachfulness. Urged by Stalin to extend diplomatic recognition to the Bulgarian and Rumanian (in addition to the Finnish) regimes, the president demurred, on the grounds that the governments in question were "neither representative of nor responsive to the will of the people."[34] In Washington's view, such recognition was contingent upon a reorganization and broadening of the two regimes (as well as that of Hungary, "should it become necessary") and a guarantee of free elections, although in retrospect it is difficult to comprehend how Stalin could have been expected to grant to these ex-enemy states political freedoms that he was withholding from Poland.[35]

The administration may have been prey to wishful thinking about the future, but it harbored few illusions regarding existing conditions in East-Central Europe. The briefing book that Truman took to Potsdam summed up the mounting evidence of Soviet unilateralism, including the conclusion of bilateral treaties with the Lublin Poles, Yugoslavia, and Czechoslovakia; the extension of Soviet control over much of Rumania's industry and trade through an exclusive economic agreement; and systematic interference in domestic politics.[36] Eastern Europe, noted the briefing paper, "is, in fact, a Soviet sphere of influence." Potsdam coincided with the departure of a key protagonist; Churchill, who claims he had been planning a definitive showdown with the Russians, learned of his defeat at the polls halfway through the conference and was replaced by Attlee and Foreign Secretary Ernest Bevin. The conference also marked the appearance of Truman's new secretary of state, James Byrnes, who was to play a far more prominent role than either Hull or Stettinius, for Truman, unlike Roosevelt, did not assume the day-to-day responsibilities of foreign affairs. Although an expert administrator, Byrnes manifested an inclination to expediency and compromise, in the interests of a politically palatable peace settlement and at the expense of a fundamental reappraisal of American interests within the alliance and in Europe. He subsequently confessed that he had been overly optimistic about the peacetime intentions of the Soviet Union, invoking in justification that country's "deposit of goodwill" in the United States.[37] By the time of the Potsdam conference, in July 1945, such optimism seemed grotesquely naïve.

The relatively congenial atmosphere that had prevailed at Yalta was no longer in evidence, but the new frankness led only to acrimony and stalemate. Charging that the obligations incurred by the Soviet Union in the Declaration on Liberated Europe had not been carried out, the United States tabled proposals for the reorganization of the Bulgarian and Rumanian governments, supervised free elections, and an unfettered press.[38] Putting it as tactfully as possible, Byrnes told Molotov that the Americans would "not wish to become involved in the elections of any country, but, because of the postwar situation, . . . would join with others in observing the elections in Italy, Greece, Hungary, Rumania and Bulgaria."[39] Churchill, despite Stalin's reminder that the Russians were keeping to the letter their earlier agreement with respect to Greece, supported the American proposal, whereupon Molotov retaliated with an attack on the political situation in that country and complained that the Soviet representative on the Italian ACC had been ignored; Churchill's parallel complaint, that an "iron fence" had descended around the British mission in Bucharest, was dismissed by Stalin as "fairy tales."[40] That international supervision of elections was inconsistent with Soviet interests was made clear by Stalin's brutally candid comment that a freely elected government in these countries would be anti-Soviet, "and that we cannot allow," though he did assure Churchill once again that he had no intention of Sovietizing the liberated countries.[41] While the Western powers argued for supervised elections, the Russians insisted on immediate diplomatic recognition of the regimes in the three ex-satellites. The outcome, noted an American participant, was "a complete impasse and might be said to have been the beginning of the cold war."[42] A face-saving compromise, introduced by Byrnes, was agreed upon on July 31: "The three Governments agree to examine, each separately in the near future, in the light of conditions then prevailing, the establishment of diplomatic relations with Bulgaria, Finland, Hungary and Rumania, to the extent possible prior to the conclusion of peace treaties with those countries."[43] Stalin had failed to gain immediate recognition for his wards, but, particularly in the case of Hungary, the delay was to be short.

Hostilities with Germany having been concluded, the need arose to revise the terms of reference of the ACCs in the satellites. The revision that was accepted by the Allies had as its basis Soviet proposals which were annexed to the general Potsdam agreement in the form of a letter. This letter, sent in the first instance to the American and British representatives on the Hungarian ACC on July 12, showed little willingness on the part of the Russians to relax their dominant role. It proposed that the (Soviet) chairman should "regularly call conferences with the British and American representatives for the purpose of discussing the most important questions relating to the work of the ACC," that free movement of the Western members be "permitted provided that the ACC is previously informed of the time and route of the journeys," and that ACC directives to local authorities *on questions of principle* be transmitted by the chairman only after "agreement" with the other representatives.[44] (It is worth noting that, when the time came to create an Allied Council for Japan, the Americans argued that the Soviet Union had consistently interpreted "agreement" as signifying "consultation" and that, therefore, this was the operative precedent!)[45] Byrnes concluded that the revision met, "in part, some of the requests" of the United States.[46] It is an open question whether Western acquiescence in greater Russian participation in the Italian ACC would have facilitated a tougher and more effective stand on this issue at Potsdam; at the time, it was considered that the risks of such participation, taken in conjunction with the rising influence of the local communists, would only create new problems.

At Potsdam, Poland surfaced one last time as a bone of contention among the Allies. Some weeks before the conference, the Soviet Union had unilaterally transferred to Polish administration all of the German territories east of the Neisse River; Stalin now explained that there had been an urgent need for some government in the area to protect his armies' rear lines, claimed (inaccurately) that all of the German population had fled, and noted that this was merely a temporary expedient. Faced with yet another *fait accompli*, President Truman could do little more than withhold his approval and insist that new boundaries could be established only at a full-fledged peace conference.[47] In August, the Soviet Union guaranteed Poland's rights to the territories in question, and, over the years, as the prospects of a German peace settlement dimmed, the Oder-Neisse frontier came to acquire its present *de facto* legitimacy. Only marginal progress was made at Potsdam in resolving the complex problem of Germany, but it nevertheless dominated the conference. Soviet claims to parts of East Prussia met little opposition; even Königsberg changed hands, ostensibly to give the Russians an ice-free port (which, in fact, they already possessed in the Baltic states). It was further decided that Germany would be treated as a single economic unit for all purposes, including reparations; that external German assets would be awarded to the Soviet Union in its zone in Austria and in Hungary, Bulgaria, and Rumania; and that ethnic Germans would be expelled from Hungary and Czechoslovakia.[48] Owing to the multiplicity of contentious issues, the conferees finally decided to establish a Council of Foreign Ministers and charged it with the task of drafting the various peace treaties. The American position regarding East-Central Europe appeared to be unchanged; upon his return from Potsdam, Truman reported that the three governments still recognized the Yalta Declaration as one of joint responsibility and declared that Bulgaria, Hungary, and Rumania were not to be spheres of influence of any one power.[49]

The first meeting of the Council, held in September at Lancaster House in London, ended in absolute stalemate. Byrnes recalls that "instead of issuing more I.O.U.s, I wanted to collect some we held. One of these I felt was the Yalta pledge on the treatment of the liberated states."[50] His promise to recognize the Hungarian provisional government upon receipt of a pledge of free elections did lead to a normalization of relations with Hungary shortly after the London conference, but no progress was made on the recognition of the Rumanian and Bulgarian regimes. Assuring Molotov that the United States desired a Rumanian regime that was both friendly to the Soviet Union and representative of all democratic elements, Byrnes warned that, "because of the manner in which the Groza government has been established and because of its subsequent actions, any elections held under its auspices would be suspect in the eyes of the American people," and he urged a reorganization of the government prior to elections. This Molotov rejected on the specious grounds that such a "Polish" solution would in Rumania lead to civil war; he then proceeded to complain about Western support for the anticommunists in Greece. To Byrnes's objection that in Rumania the Western press was unreasonably hampered, Molotov retorted, "Apparently in Greece the correspondents are happy but the people are not; whereas in Rumania the people are happy but the correspondents are not. The Soviet Government attaches more importance to the feeling of the people."[51] After further similar exchanges, typical of the emerging style of East-West negotiations, the meeting broke up over the issue of French and Chinese participation in the drafting of the peace treaties.

Back in Washington, Byrnes publicly blamed the Russians for the impasse, but he persisted in seeking some compromise that would seal the peace in Europe and give the new world organization a chance to show its mettle. In two countries his willingness to compromise appeared to bear fruit. The Moscow Declaration of November 1, 1943, had called Austria the first victim of nazism and had undertaken to restore its sovereignty;[52] the European Advisory Commission subsequently engaged in lengthy deliberations over the modalities of occupation and restoration, agreement finally being reached in July 1945. The Western powers objected, however, to what they considered to be over-representation of communists in the provisional government, headed by Dr. Karl Renner, which had been established under the aegis of the Soviet Union. Nevertheless, in a show of good will, the United States recognized this regime on October 20, an act that found justification in an overwhelmingly anticommunist vote at the general elections the following month. Although the zones of occupation remained, pending a peace treaty, the new federal republic of Austria was recognized by the great powers on January 7, 1946. In the case of Hungary, Byrnes's offer at Potsdam elicited the required guarantee of free elections from Foreign Minister Gyöngyösi, and formal recognition was extended to the provisional government on November 2, two days before the general elections (an action duplicated by the Soviet Union, both powers presumably hoping to influence the voters). The outcome could scarcely have been more satisfactory to the United States, for, despite numerous irregularities and Soviet support for the communists, the election was the most unfettered held in occupied East-Central Europe. It gave the communist party a scant 16.9 percent of the popular vote, while the Smallholder party emerged with an absolute majority, both in votes and in parliamentary seats. Although the coalition government was maintained in keeping with a pre-election agreement, and the communists retained the key interior portfolio, the political situation in Hungary momentarily caused little concern in Western capitals.[53]

Viewing the recognition of the Bulgarian and Rumanian regimes as the main stumbling block to progress on the peace settlements, Byrnes announced on October 10 the appointment of Mark Ethridge, a Louisville publisher, as the head of a fact-finding mission to those two countries. In Bulgaria the official persecution of anticommunists—and, indeed, of noncommunists—had been intensified in the first half of 1945, leading the Agrarian Union (whose secretary-general, G. M. Dimitrov, had sought asylum at the U.S. legation in May) and the Social Democrats to withdraw their support from the coalition Fatherland Front government. Their exit placed in question the democratic nature of the elections scheduled for August 26, since on the assumption that the Fatherland Front parties would run on a single list with a prearranged allocation of seats, their modalities made no provision for opposition parties. The American political representative in Sofia therefore advised the government on August 18 that the United States was not satisfied that the impending elections would be free and requested a postponement and new electoral procedures, whereupon the date was duly set back to November 18.[54] The firm stand taken by the Americans and British at Potsdam over the question of representative governments encouraged the opposition elements in

Bulgaria (and Rumania) in their defiance, but their freedom of action was progressively curtailed, and, in view of the upcoming elections, the Ethridge mission gave first priority to the Bulgarian situation. Their meetings with the communist leaders gave little cause for optimism; when the secretary-general of the Communist party, Traicho Kostov, was confronted with the fact that opposition parties were being denied access to the broadcasting media, he replied, "Allow us one fault!"[55] (Some months earlier the Americans had intercepted a message relating an exchange between the Bulgarian ambassador and the Russians; when queried whether the British and the Americans might impose a Mikolajczyk on Bulgaria, the latter answered reassuringly, "What if they do? It did not do them much good in Poland, did it?"[56]) After meeting with Gheorghe Dimitrov, the new head of the Communist party, who had returned two days earlier after twenty-two years of exile in the Soviet Union, Ethridge became convinced that local concessions would be meaningless, since all political directives originated in Moscow, and he decided to take his mission to that capital. Meanwhile, the Bulgarian opposition parties concluded that, in view of police terrorism, the elections would be a fraud, and they refused to register their candidates. Ethridge met with Andrei Vyshinsky on November 13 and urged a further postponement of the elections, a broadening of the interim government, and the registration of all opposition candidates, but his protests were dismissed out of hand, Vyshinsky suggesting that only the Bulgarian government could request a postponement.[57] In what was essentially a *pro forma* gesture, the American government dispatched a request to this effect to Sofia; the Ethridge mission was already on its way to Bucharest when the elections, held on schedule, produced the predictable communist victory.[58]

In Bucharest, as in Sofia, the mission was received with great fanfare, in keeping with the myth that both governing "fronts" were fully representative within the terms of the Yalta Declaration, but the political situation appeared equally unpromising. The Soviet Union was actively bolstering the position of the communists, having unilaterally transferred all of Transylvania to Rumanian administration four days after the accession to power of Groza's National Democratic Front in March, but the opposition parties continued their struggle against mounting odds, and on August 21 the king, after unsuccessfully demanding Groza's resignation and encouraged by the apparently tougher attitude of the West at Potsdam, asked the three Great Powers to assist in the formation of a new and more representative government. Washington agreed that the regime was not sufficiently representative of all democratic elements and promised to consult with the other Allies.[59] The Ethridge mission found ample evidence to support this stand, being told by Ana Pauker that the Liberal and Peasant parties were pursuing an unacceptably anti-Soviet and anticommunist policy, and by Groza himself that as long as a common border existed he would remain the most loyal ally of the Soviet Union.[60] Meanwhile, at the end of October, James Byrnes declared in a speech in New York that the United States did not wish to support groups hostile to the Soviet Union, but that "the best neighbors do not deny their neighbors the right to be friends with others."[61] Unfortunately for most East Europeans, the Soviet Union was uniquely empowered to determine the criteria of hostility and friendship.

Upon its return to Washington on December 3, the Ethridge mission presented Byrnes with a report which characterized the Rumanian and Bulgarian regimes as authoritarian and insufficiently representative and recommended elections at least as free as those recently held in Austria and Hungary.[62] The secretary of state, who was shortly to leave for Moscow for yet another round of negotiations, chose not to make the report public, in order to maintain a façade of optimism regarding the possibility of compromise. In the event, the Moscow meeting only confirmed the Russians' exclusive right to dictate political solutions in their sphere. When presented with a copy of the Ethridge report, Molotov dismissed its allegations out of hand, and the Western negotiators had to content themselves with extracting concessions that were little more than face-saving palliatives. With regard to the Rumanian question, Byrnes and Bevin persuaded Stalin to agree to a tripartite commission, composed of Vyshinsky and the British and American ambassadors, which was to confer with the king in Bucharest with a view to broadening the government by including one representative each from the Liberal and National Peasant parties. In exchange for this and a promise of free elections, Byrnes undertook to recognize the Rumanian regime. With regard to Bulgaria, where elections had already been held, Stalin agreed to "advise" the government to bring within its ranks two representatives from the two principal opposition parties and thereby earn Western recognition. Even this concession was granted only after an attempt was made to subvert its democratic intent; a Russian draft had stipulated the inclusion of only those politicians who were loyal to the regime. Byrnes and Bevin rejected this qualification as being implicitly exclusive of all those not already participating in the incumbent administration, but, as the conference drew to a close, Molotov told Byrnes that by mistake this unacceptable draft had been included in the Russian language text of the already signed protocol. For once the secretary of state remained adamant, and Molotov had no choice but to agree to an amendment containing the American version.[63]

Few of the Western participants in the Moscow conference could have been confident of the democratic consequences of the agreements.

Kennan recalls that he "deplored any and every effort to convey to the American public the impression that our own government had any residue of influence in the Soviet-dominated area, or that the countries in question faced anything less than the full rigor of Stalinist totalitarianism." While the conference was still in progress, he recorded in his diary that Byrnes's "weakness in dealing with the Russians is that his main purpose is to achieve some sort of an agreement, he doesn't much care what. The realities behind this agreement, since they concern only such people as Koreans, Rumanians, and Iranians, about whom he knows nothing, do not concern him."[64] The secretary of state could not be accused of being entirely in the dark about conditions in East-Central Europe, particularly after the return of the Ethridge mission, but evidently he had neither the inclination nor, at least in his own view, the mandate to take a firmer stand in defense of the Yalta principles and thereby accentuate even further the growing cleavage between East and West. Neither could he reasonably expect, however, that the longed-for peace treaties would mitigate the Soviets' and the local communists' predominance, when he himself had implicitly sanctioned this in Moscow. To jeopardize a potentially meaningless peace settlement with the ex-satellites by insisting on the implementation of wartime promises, and, as Kennan suggests, by refusing in the final instance to be a passive participant in their oppression, might well have been a small price to pay for principle and consistency.

Although, in his first major speech on foreign affairs, delivered on October 27, President Truman had stressed the goal of establishing peaceful democratic governments in the former enemy states, American involvement in the affairs of Bulgaria and Rumania became even more of an exercise in futility after the Moscow conference. The president was incensed at his secretary of state for failing to report back during the Moscow discussions. Having belatedly read the Ethridge report, the president told Byrnes on January 5 that he did "not think we should play compromise any longer. We should refuse to recognize Rumania and Bulgaria until they comply with our requirements. . . . I'm tired of babying the Soviets."[65] By his own account, Byrnes had "approved many adjustments" and "resolved many serious doubts" in favor of the Soviet Union, all in the hope that the two Great Powers would retain a "common purpose."[66] Despite Truman's harsh words, Byrnes remained in office for another year, until the conclusion of the peace settlements with the satellites. As for the president's apparently firm stand on recognition, it was reduced in practice to the application of criteria that were already a travesty of earlier promises.

The Moscow formula having been implemented in Bucharest, American recognition followed on January 5, but the persecution of noncommunists went on unabated. Through the summer of 1946 the two governments exchanged numerous notes, the Americans protesting at undemocratic practices, the Rumanians regularly denying the allegations (with one such note explaining that the noncommunist cabinet members preferred to act as observers rather than as participants). The elections, held on November 19, were well orchestrated and returned the expected procommunist majority; one week later, the first mass political trial opened in Bucharest.[67] On July 23, 1947, the first postwar U.S. minister to Rumania was officially named; included in the announcement was the rather forlorn comment that the appointment did not indicate U.S. approval of earlier malpractices.[68]

In regard to Bulgaria, Kennan had reported from Moscow on January 15, 1946, that the Soviet Union is "unrelenting in its insistence that Bulgaria be 'security sphere' of Russia. In Russian terms this means that power in Bulgaria must be exercised by elements which recognize themselves to be in relationship of disciplinary subordination to Moscow." Ambassador Harriman concurrently recommended that the United States withhold recognition from the Bulgarian regime, noting that the Moscow decisions remained unfulfilled.[69] Confident of Moscow's support, the Bulgarian communists proved totally unresponsive to Washington's blandishments, and their insistence that the cabinet could be broadened only on the basis of "conditions mutually agreeable to both the Bulgarian Government and the opposition" was clearly meant to discourage the participation of the latter. On February 15 Byrnes sent an official note to the Soviet Union protesting that the Russians and the Bulgarians were making it impossible for the U.S. delegation on the ACC to fulfill its functions, but to no effect;[70] when in October the American member proposed that the commission meet to discuss the modalities of the upcoming elections, the Soviet chairman replied that such a discussion would constitute unwarranted interference in Bulgaria's internal affairs and that the matter was therefore outside the ACC's jurisdiction.[71] The elections followed the Rumanian pattern, and the U.S. envoy, Maynard Barnes, reported that, with the formation of a new government, communist domination of all aspects of state control over the country's life had been completed.[72] In June 1947 G. M. Dimitrov's hapless successor to the secretaryship of the Agrarian party, Nikolai Petkov, was arrested on conspiracy charges and subsequently executed. The diplomatic protests that punctuated America's relations with Bulgaria and Rumania in this period served as a conscientious reiteration of Washington's dissatisfaction, but carried no expectation of preventing those countries' definitive incorporation into the Soviet orbit.

However lamentable in terms of Bulgaria's and Rumania's political future, the Moscow agreements did open the way for the drafting of the various peace treaties, a task that was pursued into 1946 in an unpropitious atmosphere of mistrust and mounting confrontation. This atmosphere was most pronounced in the discussions of Germany. In April the secretary of state had tentatively proposed a twenty-five-year treaty for the demilitarization of that country, only to have it rejected by Stalin, who momentarily seemed more interested in extracting the maximum amount of reparations. The centralized occupation control of Germany was rapidly breaking down as a consequence of Soviet unilateralism. In May, deliveries of reparations on an interzonal level were halted, and the Soviets' lack of interest in the problem of reconstruction finally led to the Anglo-American "bizonia" agreement of December 2, which established a separate economic unit and laid the foundation for what proved to be an enduring division of Germany. Disputes proliferated over Iran, which the Russians were persuaded to evacuate in May; over Greece, whose government charged that Albania, Yugoslavia, and Bulgaria were aiding the communist guerrillas (eliciting Soviet countercharges of British interference); and over the Trieste area, to which both Italy and Yugoslavia laid claim. Concurrently, the growing militancy of the communist parties of Western Europe, particularly in Italy and France, alarmed those who saw in them the vanguard of Soviet influence. Indeed, as the exigencies of war disappeared, the revolutionary messianism inherent in Marxism-Leninism reappeared as a tangible, if incalculable, element of Soviet foreign policy, a resurgence that owed far more to the Manichean world view of that ideology than to any novel and ill-founded hostility on the part of the West. In their election speeches in February 1946, Stalin and Molotov once again emphasized that the fundamental incompatibility between the communist and capitalist systems predetermined the Soviet Union's policies at home and abroad. On February 22, 1946, George Kennan dispatched to Washington a lengthy essay on Soviet intentions which foreshadowed his policy of containment.[73] The Russians, he wrote, were persuaded that, in view of the "capitalist encirclement," there could be no permanent *modus vivendi* with the United States, and would officially seek to extend their power and influence on their periphery while unofficially attempting by subversion to undermine the general political and strategic potential of the major Western powers; he urged the West to respond with careful study and by building up its self-confidence and strength so as to withstand these pressures. Similarly, the new U.S. ambassador to Moscow, Walter Bedell Smith, would report that the Russians were prepared to go to "almost any lengths" to maintain their control over the satellites (a term which thus enjoyed uninterrupted currency in its application to East-Central Europe), despite popular opposition, and that they had not set a definite limit to their objectives in Europe.[74] To the extent that these perceptions were shared in Washington, the operative question was to what lengths the United States would or could go in order to counter the new threat from the East. The precipitous withdrawal of American forces from the Continent that coincided with this growing awareness of Soviet strategic and ideological expansionism led to an asymmetry between political objectives and power which in turn left Washington almost no alternative but to pursue an essentially temporizing and defensive policy. Underlying that policy was an implicit, grudging acknowledgment that, in the circumstances, self-determination for the East Europeans was a chimera and that the latter would have to content themselves with a brand of liberation far removed from the rash precepts of the Atlantic Charter.

By mid-1946, Bulgaria and Rumania had been written off for all practical purposes, and in Poland the façade of democracy was eroding steadily, despite the occasional American protest. On the other hand, the normalization of political conditions in Czechoslovakia was viewed in the capitals of the West with a high and partially warranted degree of optimism. Pursuing his wartime strategy of accommodation with Stalin, Beneš traveled to Moscow in March 1945 to construct a coalition government that in the end had communists heading seven out of the twenty-five ministries; a notable inclusion was the former ambassador to Moscow, Zdenek Fierlinger, a nominal Social Democrat whom George Kennan described as a Soviet agent. This new regime first gathered in the Slovakian city of Košice and then, after the liberation of Prague, formally took office in the capital. One of its first actions was to negotiate a simultaneous withdrawal of all Allied forces, proceeding in phases to December 1, 1945; another decision, far less popular but unavoidable in view of Beneš' earlier commitments, was taken in June to cede Ruthenia, a region populated by a mixture of Ukrainians and Hungarians, to the Soviet Union. Initially the Americans encountered some difficulty in having representatives admitted to Prague because of Soviet resistance (efforts that Kennan, at least, deplored, on the grounds that U.S. envoys would be used to "lend respectability to a stooge government"), but, by January, Ambassador Laurence Steinhardt was reporting on the subtleties of Beneš' balancing act.[75] He observed a widening chasm between Masaryk and other moderates, on the one hand, and radicals such as Fierlinger and Gottwald, on the other, and noted apprehensively that communist control over the media, the police, and the courts had induced a "fear complex" in the moderates which made them ineffectual; he recommended that, before the United States negotiated an Export-Import Bank reconstruction loan, the Czechoslovak government should be required to make a full disclosure of its commitments to the Soviet Union in the areas of trade, industry, and finance.[76] In fact, the Czechs were at that moment engaged in discussions with the Russians on a wide range of economic matters, but President Beneš told Steinhardt a few days later that he did not expect the Soviets to insist on disrupting Czechoslovakia's trade relations with the West.[77]

The May 26 general elections were received with mixed feelings in the West, for, while their conduct had been by and large unexceptionable, the communists managed to poll a plurality of the votes, which testified to a popular feeling of gratitude and friendship toward the Soviet Union that was unique in East-Central Europe. The resulting cabinet was evenly balanced between leftists and moderates, and, although certain key posts went to communists, Steinhardt reported optimistically that Premier Gottwald was "a thorough Czech patriot . . . unlikely to embark on further extremist ventures."[78] Meanwhile, the concurrent negotiations with the United States on loans and credits were running into trouble. The Czechs had applied for a $300 million loan in September 1945, then had dropped their request, presumably as a result of Soviet pressure; in February, talks were resumed, but Washington set a $50 million limit at the outset and became increasingly diffident as difficulties arose over the settlement of American claims, the disclosure of Prague's economic policies and trade agreements with Moscow, and the violently anti-American attitudes of certain members of the Gottwald regime. The latter, cabled Ambassador Steinhardt on August 16, was "making use of individual Czechoslovaks who are moderates as a front for the purpose of extracting from the United States maximum benefits for Czechoslovakia [while] the leftist elements simultaneously belittle the assistance already assured, play down our aid and at the same time threaten the United States with a further orientation to the East if additional aid is not forthcoming."[79] Byrnes's impulsive action at the Paris peace conference blocked further contracts for surplus purchases by Czechoslovakia (see p. 68) and led to the suspension of loan and credit negotiations, apparently much to the satisfaction of the pro-West members of the Gottwald cabinet. Even President Beneš would confess to Steinhardt that the American move had strengthened his hand in reducing public attacks on the United States and in dealing with U.S. claims, but he defended his country's voting support for the Soviet Union at Paris by arguing that it had not harmed the West and had provided insurance against Soviet intervention in Czechoslovak affairs.[80] By 1947, Czechoslovakia was unique among the East European states (excepting Yugoslavia) in having preserved a large degree of national sovereignty; it remained to be seen how the United States and its friends in Prague could consolidate this independence against the mounting pressures of the Czech communists and their Soviet mentors.

American displeasure was far more pronounced with regard to developments in Yugoslavia, particularly after Tito threatened to make good his claim to Trieste and the surrounding province of Venezia Giulia by effecting a partial military occupation. The area, with mixed Italian, Croat, and Slovene population, was considered by Churchill, among others, to be of prime commercial importance to Italy, whose economic and political revival was becoming a matter of concern to the Western Allies. When, at the beginning of May 1945, British forces moved into Trieste and found themselves face to face with Tito's soldiers, the situation became explosive. Truman was convinced (although probably in error) that Yugoslavia's claim was Soviet-inspired; Allied consultations and veiled threats of force finally resulted in a temporary compromise, reached on June 9, which compelled Tito to withdraw and leave Trieste and its environs under Western control.[81] In the matter of Yugoslavia's domestic politics, the Western Allies were equally displeased. Although the Tito-Šubašić agreement had resulted in a joint provisional government that received Washington's blessing, it soon became evident that the partisan leader was not prepared to share power with the royalists, a fact which led Churchill to protest to Stalin in April that Tito's exclusively pro-Soviet orientation was hardly compatible with their 50-50 percentage agreement (but then, on other occasions, the prime minister would assert that that agreement had been superseded by Yalta).[82] The November general elections for a Constituent Assembly (which proceeded to abolish the monarchy and declare Yugoslavia a Federative People's Republic) served only to confirm Tito's monopoly of power; the American ambassador was instructed to advise the new government upon his arrival in Belgrade in December that the United States did not consider the elections to have been free and representative and that diplomatic relations were not to be construed as approval of the regime.[83] This setback to Western, and particularly Churchill's, hopes for a Yugoslavia friendly to both East and West owed less to the Kremlin's machinations than to Tito's tactics in his single-minded quest for power and independence. Washington, however, bore a large part of the blame for this estrangement, for it failed to perceive the fundamental differences between Tito and Moscow's satraps in the neighboring Balkan states. The Yugoslav leader sent a conciliatory letter to President Truman in January 1946, and intimated that he would like to visit the United States, but the reply he received was that such a visit would be untimely; Washington also refused Yugoslavia's request for an Export-Import Bank loan and did not extend any credits for the purchase of surplus matériel.[84] In the wake of these rebuffs (and the stalemate over Trieste), Tito veered to a more anti-American line; Yugoslav-American relations in 1946 were punctuated by protests over the harassment of U.S. planes and by the expulsion of the U.S. Information Service mission from Belgrade.[85]

The case of Hungary in the period of the drafting of the peace treaties is worthy of special note, for it was the only East European country that at once enjoyed a relatively representative government and was subject to joint supervision through the Allied Control Commission. One can only speculate why the Soviet Union did not immediately impose on Hungary a communist "front" regime like those foisted on Rumania and Bulgaria. Conceivably, the initial numerical weakness of the indigenous communists necessitated a period of recruitment and consolidation. The sweeping land reform effected in March 1945 by the provisional government had been supervised by the communist minister of agriculture, Imre Nagy, but, despite their collaboration in this and other popular reforms, the communists suffered unequivocal defeat in the November elections of that year. For the mass of the people, the relatively unfettered elections seemed to lend some credibility to the Yalta Declaration and to hold out hope that the depredations of the occupying armies and the purges of the more extreme anticommunists were only transitory phenomena. The Smallholder premier, Ferenc Nagy, and his noncommunist associates shared this hope, but at the same time had to contend with Soviet and communist pressures that steadily undermined their power.

From the start, the operations of the Allied Control Commission in Budapest were characterized by a Soviet unilateralism that, in the words of a Hungarian diplomat, "reduced Hungarian sovereignty to a minimum."[86] The reorientation of Hungary's commercial links toward the East, the tenure by communists of such key posts as the ministry of interior, and the isolation of Hungary from the West all were goals that the Russians pursued assiduously and with little interference from the West, which, recalls Ferenc Nagy, "was undivided in urging us to cultivate, at all costs, the friendship of Russia."[87] At the same time, the Americans warned Nagy that, unless he abandoned his coalition with the communists, he would lose control, but to such advice the premier replied that an exclusively Smallholder government would be destroyed even sooner through communist-fomented anarchy.[88] It was already evident from the experience of Bulgaria and Rumania that the "friendship" of Moscow would, in the absence of a countervailing influence from the West, make a travesty of democratic institutions. The American Minister to Budapest, H. F. A. Schoenfeld, reported on May 2, 1946, that, thanks to the Russian military presence, Hungary was virtually a Soviet economic colony in the hands of a communist minority; yet the following December he would respond to a plea for help from Cardinal Mindszenty with a reminder that the U.S. policy of noninterference in the internal affairs of other nations "has proven over a long period of time and through many trying situations the best guarantee of spontaneous, vigorous and genuine democratic development."[89] In the circumstances, such an attitude amounted to an abdication of responsibility by the leading Western signatory of the Yalta Declaration, which unquestionably required some measure of "interference." The legalistic argument stressing joint action and claiming exemption from any action in the event of a signatory's unilateral interference seemed rather low in principle to those Hungarians who tried to make democracy work. In the event, Western participation in the ACC proved to be an exercise in frustration. Communications between the British and American delegates and the Hungarian authorities were, on chairman Voroshilov's orders, to be channeled through his office; furthermore, the head of the Soviet High Command and the chairman of the ACC were one and the same man, and directives frequently failed to specify the precise status of the issuing authority. The chairman's veto power was most liberally interpreted by the Russians, notably, in the case of an American proposal in 1945 for an agreement to include Budapest in a network of air routes to the Far East.[90]

The Americans and the Russians were, in the period leading to the peace settlement, involved in two main issues of importance to Hungary. One was economic; the other, ethnic and territorial. The Potsdam agreement regarding the transfer of German assets to the Soviet Union had been so widely applied, observed Schoenfeld, as to "extend Soviet control to every sector of Hungarian industry and finance."[91] These assets were judged by the Russians to include all property seized by the Germans in the last months of the war. Moreover, reparations were exacted in such a way as to multiply the amount agreed upon. These measures, together with a Soviet-Hungarian trade agreement signed in October 1945, turned over to Soviet control one half of Hungary's industry. Because the ACC had not been consulted, the U.S. State Department charged that the trade agreement violated the spirit of the Yalta Declaration, but to no avail.[92] In December 1945 the American member of the ACC recommended the establishment of a subcommittee to deal with Hungary's economic crisis; a subsequent note dated March 26, 1946, again deplored "over-burdening the country with reparations, requisitions, and the cost of maintaining large occupation forces" and called for a jointly drafted program of rehabilitation. The Soviet reply claimed that such a plan fell within the competence of the Hungarian government and denied Soviet responsibility for the economic situation, which it attributed to America's failure to return Hungarian property from the American zones of occupation in Germany and Austria. On July 23, in yet another note, the State Department produced detailed statistics to prove its case, recalled that the Hungarian finance minister had asked in a report for an Allied commission to examine his country's economic and financial plight, and reiterated the request for concerted action. (Shortly after this note was sent, the Americans returned Hungary's $35 million gold reserve, which had been removed by the retreating Nazis.) Finally, on September 23, the Americans admitted to stalemate—"It is a matter of regret to the United States Government that the Soviet Government not only has refused to implement the undertaking assumed by it at the Crimea Conference, but moreover has failed to indicate its reasons for so refusing"—but expressed readiness "at any time" to engage in consultations in order to implement the Yalta obligations.[93]

American attitudes were even more passive regarding the ethnic problem in Hungary, a problem the armistice agreement had created by provisionally reinstating the Trianon boundaries without settling the fate of the sizable Hungarian minorities. Between April 1945 and July 1946 some 184 notes were sent by the Hungarian government to the ACC, protesting in particular the systematic persecution of Hungarians in Czechoslovakia, but they did not elicit a definite reply beyond a general condemnation of the collective punishment of ethnic minorities; a Hungarian proposal for an international commission to investigate the plight of these minorities also was rejected.[94] The problem of Transylvania, with its one and a half million Hungarians, was critical in the sense that upon its resolution rested much of the prestige of the Smallholder government. When a delegation headed by Ferenc Nagy journeyed to Moscow in April to present Hungary's case, Stalin and Molotov simply replayed the old Habsburg *divide et impera* game by promising to support the rights of the Slovakian Magyars and by urging Nagy to negotiate directly with Groza over the Transylvanian question.[95] The decision of the Council of Foreign Ministers (which met in Paris in May) to recommend awarding all of Transylvania to Rumania was received in Hungary with astonishment. Schoenfeld informed Premier Nagy that the United States had been willing to reexamine the issue, and that the secretary of state had even proposed some adjustments in Hungary's favor, but that Molotov had been adamantly opposed to Hungary's claims.[96] Later that month Nagy made an official visit to the United States to seek support for Hungary's interests at the upcoming peace conference. The return of the gold bullion was arranged and a previously granted $10 million credit for surplus U.S. war goods was increased by half, but, with regard to Transylvania, Byrnes merely told the premier that the United States might support Hungary's claims if the

Russians chose to reintroduce the matter; passing through Paris on his way home, Nagy learned from Molotov that this was out of the question.[97]

While, in the case of Rumania and Bulgaria, the Americans had tacitly come to terms with the *fait accompli* of communist domination, the existence in Hungary of a democratically elected and inalienably pro-Western government ought perhaps to have prompted a more tenacious effort to bolster it. All three nations were technically enemy states, and there was certainly no intrinsic reason to favor Groza's puppet regime in the Transylvanian dispute over that of Nagy, which publicly endorsed such American objectives as the international control of the Danube; in March of 1946 Schoenfeld had advised Washington that some rectification of the Transylvanian frontier would correct past injustices and had noted that it is "more important for us to consider the effect of a frontier revision on Hungarian internal politics than on Rumanian internal politics inasmuch as Hungary is still a twilight zone in respect to Soviet expansion whereas the shadows falling on Rumania are already of a deeper hue."[98] By its, at best, half-hearted defense of Hungarian interests that were essentially consistent with the principles propounded at Yalta, the United States succeeded only in demoralizing the anticommunists and in creating the impression that it had somewhat prematurely—in mid-1946—conceded to the Russians the right to determine the fate of even the remaining democratic rump of East-Central Europe. Washington's alternative was by now reduced to diplomatic pressure, but the prospect of ending the long months of uncertainty animated a spirit of compromise that invariably worked to the benefit of Soviet interests.

Although it was obvious at the time that peace treaties with the satellites could scarcely ameliorate political conditions in East-Central Europe unless the Soviet Union withdrew its armies of occupation, the Western powers persevered in their negotiations, even after the Russians had ruled out such a withdrawal by blocking progress on the key German and Austrian settlements. In the absence of such settlements, the maintenance of occupation zones in those countries necessitated a Soviet military presence in the East European hinterland to protect lines of communication, a phrase which Byrnes later admitted had a "very broad meaning" when translated into political interference.[99] When the Council of Foreign Ministers convened in Paris, however, Molotov simply declined to discuss either Byrnes's proposed treaty for the demilitarization of Germany or the Austrian peace settlement. Negotiations on draft treaties for the satellites (those for Bulgaria, Hungary, and Rumania having been submitted by the Soviet Union) dragged on through the summer of 1946, the principal concession extracted by the West being tentative approval for a "Free Territory of Trieste" under UN supervision. Reported Byrnes in a radio address on July 15: "The drafts of treaties agreed upon are not the best which human wit could devise. But they are the best which human wit could get the four principal Allies to agree upon."[100] Two days before the twenty-one-nation peace conference opened in Paris on July 29, he expressed the wish that "the compromises we have reached and those I hope we will reach will be compromises intended to reconcile honest conflicts of opinion and not to secure selfish advantages for ourselves or others."[101] In practice, however, the dictates of expediency tended to blur the distinction.

The peacemaking procedure agreed upon by the Allies had been for the Council of Foreign Ministers to draw up preliminary terms that would then be submitted to a conference of all the states that had fought the Axis, at which time a hearing would be given to representatives of ex-enemy states. These hearings proved to be of little consequence, however, for with one exception the satellites dutifully fell into line behind their respective patrons: the Western powers championed Italy and a relatively uncontroversial Finland (as well as Greek interests), and the Soviet Union led a chorus that included Czechoslovakia and Poland, as well as Rumania and Bulgaria—a "Slav bloc" which, in the words of an American delegate, "showed good teamwork and careful timing."[102] In fact, Byrnes became so incensed when he observed the Czech delegates applauding a Vyshinsky diatribe about American domination through economic aid that, having learned of Czechoslovakia's plan to let Rumania benefit from its $50 million U.S. credit for surplus war goods, he cabled Washington to stop the credit.[103] The Hungarian delegation, representing the last East European regime that, despite communist influence, diverged from Soviet policy in defense of its own national interest (the Czechs having maintained their tactical alignment with the Russians), arrived at the conference with well-documented briefs regarding territorial and economic issues, including a proposal for Danubian economic cooperation; ironically enough, its efforts were nullified by a conjunction of Soviet-led opposition and the fatalistic aloofness of the West.[104] The Russians consistently gave the impression, recalls a British observer, that they "interpreted the many polite assurances given to them during the course of the war as definite recognitions on the part of the Western powers of a wide Russian zone of influence in central and South Eastern Europe."[105] The West's reluctant acquiescence was much in evidence at the Paris peace conference.

In the matter of reparations, as stipulated in the armistice agreements the sum of $300 million payable by Finland, Hungary, and Rumania was reaffirmed, although the United States attempted to have Hungary's burden reduced by one-third, in view of that country's economic weakness (reparations accounted for 35 percent of its national income) and the Allies' inability to implement the Yalta promise to aid economic reconstruction in any other manner.[106] Bulgaria, already a dutiful client-state, saw its reparations to Greece and Yugoslavia reduced, upon Soviet insistence, to $70 million.[107] The restoration of, or compensation for, allied property also proved controversial, this time because of Anglo-American disagreement. The United States, again seeking to ease the ex-satellites' economic burden, proposed compensation at the rate of 25 percent, a figure which suited the Soviet Union, since it owned little property and was already benefiting from reparations; Britain, on the other hand, demanded full compensation. The matter was not resolved until a subsequent meeting of the Council of Foreign Ministers, at which the final figure was set at 66⅔ percent; this proved to be of little consequence to the East Europeans, however, for their communist regimes all defaulted on their payments.[108] Agreement on reciprocal, nondiscriminatory trade relations between the ex-enemy states and the United Nations was reached after Soviet accusations of capitalistic enslavement were aired, but this also proved to be of short-lived relevance to East-Central Europe. With regard to the administration of the Danubian waterways, Molotov denounced all previous international agreements as being imperialistic, and the question was postponed for consideration at a later conference.

Territorial disputes, which have perennially plagued international relations in the heart of Europe, were resolved to the Americans' satisfaction only in the case of Bulgaria; despite mutual claims by Bulgaria and Greece, supported respectively by the Soviet Union and Britain, the *status quo* was reaffirmed. With regard to Transylvania, Hungary had protested that the Council of Foreign Ministers had recommended the transfer of the entire region to Rumania without hearing its case; in reply, it had been told that the peace conference would provide an opportunity for this. In its briefs to the joint meeting of the Hungarian and Rumanian Political and Territorial commissions, Hungary's delegation asked first for 22,000 sq. km., then for 4,000 sq. km. (with a population that was more than two-thirds Magyar) and autonomy for the remaining 600,000 Hungarians in eastern Transylvania, but, after some expressions of sympathy by the Australian and American negotiators, the original award was unanimously upheld.[109] Having thus benefited from the support of the Russians and their friends, the Rumanians did not cavil at the transfer of northern Bukovina to the Soviet Union.

Yet another problem considered by the conference was the status of the Hungarians who became a Slovakian minority once again when the Trianon boundaries were re-established. The Czechoslovak delegation introduced two relevant amendments: one would authorize the transfer of

200,000 Hungarians as the final solution to a "disturbing minority problem"; the other involved the cession to Czechoslovakia of five Hungarian
villages that lay across the Danube from Bratislava and were said to be
essential to that city's economic expansion. The Hungarians proposed
instead that, since the Czechs were aiming to build a homogeneous state
devoid of Hungarians, the land upon which the latter lived also ought to
be transferred, and that an international commission be dispatched to
make an on-the-spot investigation; regarding the so-called Bratislava
bridgehead, they pointed out that the majority of the local population
was Hungarian and they were joined by the Americans in noting the
strange juxtaposition of proposals for transferring Hungarians both to and
from Czechoslovakia. Speaking for the Soviet "bloc," Vyshinsky supported the amendments and expressed surprise that Hungary was reluctant
to admit the Hungarians in question, since the expulsion of Germans had
left room for this transfer. The American representative on the Hungarian
Political and Territorial Commission, Walter Bedell Smith, retorted that
the United States could not agree to the incorporation in a peace treaty of
the principle of forced population transfers, but in reality neither he nor
the Western delegates on the subcommission studying Czechoslovakia's
claims felt it was appropriate to defend too strenuously the interests of an
ex-enemy state. In the end, the conference approved both an American
compromise proposal committing Hungary and Czechoslovakia to bilateral
negotiations within six months regarding the transfer, and a New Zealand
amendment proposing the cession of a smaller "bridgehead" of three villages.[110] In his report on October 18, Secretary of State Byrnes expressed
the rather forlorn hope that Hungary and Czechoslovakia and Rumania
would somehow cooperate and resolve their minority problems, but, in
spite of the strictly one-sided influence exerted by the Soviet Union, he
seemed only too happy to wash his hands of these admittedly complex
disputes; the secretary of the American delegation subsequently affirmed
that the United States had sought fair terms for Hungary but did not want
to place itself in the position of Hungary's champion against Allied nations.[111]

Each satellite treaty also embodied military and political clauses. The
former set a limit on the size of the domestic armed forces and specified
that occupation troops—except for those required to protect lines of communication—were to be withdrawn within ninety days of ratification.[112]
The political clauses enjoined the various governments to respect human
rights and fundamental freedoms and specified that any relevant disagreement be referred to the diplomatic representatives of the three Great
Powers, who ("acting in concert") were also charged with supervising the
general execution and interpretation of the treaties.[113] Given the con-

tinued presence of Soviet troops in Bulgaria, Hungary, and Rumania, there was, of course, little prospect that such supervision would be any more effective than the attempts by Western representatives on the ACCs to ensure respect for identical political and other freedoms stipulated in the armistice documents.

Meeting in New York through November and December, the Council of Foreign Ministers debated and finally approved, with only minor modifications, the recommendations of the peace conference. The ceremonial signing of the treaties took place on February 10, 1947, in the Salon de l'Horloge of the Quai d'Orsay; there was, observed the correspondent of the *New York Times*, "strangely little joy either in the room or in Paris itself which greeted the event with supreme indifference."[114] Relieved at having done with the problems of East-Central Europe, Secretary of State Byrnes attempted to rationalize and minimize the extent of his failure, commenting in his last major speech while in office:

> I admit that during the past year there were times when I was deeply discouraged. Our repeated efforts to achieve cooperation in a peaceful world seemed to be meeting only with constant rebuff. But we persisted in our efforts with patience and firmness.
>
> The treaties with Italy and the ex-satellite states . . . are not perfect. But they are as good as we can hope to get by general agreement now or within a reasonable length of time. . . .
>
> During the year or more that these treaties were under discussion it was inevitable that the differences between the Allies should be emphasized, and at times exaggerated. On the other hand, during the war some of these differences were minimized and overlooked.[115]

Byrnes's retrospective complaint that his critics wanted him to speak loudly and carry a twig was not, however, all that inaccurate.[116] He had tried to preserve the political bipartisanship that had bolstered America's wartime foreign policy by taking along Senators Connally and Vandenberg on his peacemaking journeys, and, indeed, congressional and public awareness of the extent of Soviet domination in the satellites grew only slowly— without any encouragement from the administration—and did not at the time give rise to any meaningful proposals for alternative courses of action. Despite a mounting hostility toward the Soviet Union, the American political climate was marked by a strong undercurrent of political disengagement from wide-ranging commitments which, with respect to East-Central Europe, had been evident in the compromises over Poland. In the 1946 elections the Republicans did make selective use in Polish districts of the charge that Roosevelt had capitulated to Stalin's hegemonic demands at Yalta, and in the process won the support of Charles Rozmarek, president of the Polish-American Congress, but bipartisanship in foreign policy matters continued to dominate the national political scene.

The combination of Soviet power and American demobilization unquestionably weakened the bargaining power of the United States and made disengagement and reliance on the United Nations an expeditious, if rather myopic, policy. Moreover, as noted earlier, a more forceful Western stand, dependent to a large extent on active military strength, would not have been easy, given the psychological climate of the period. Yet regretful reappraisals were not long in coming. Undersecretary of State Robert A. Lovett admitted to Forrestal in 1947 that "the great political error in the post-war period was the failure to insist upon the writing of the peace treaties while our troops and military power were still evident in Europe. Nothing . . . could have stopped the American forces which were at that time deployed in Germany."[117] Even in the absence of such a position of power, however, little benefit was to be derived from pressing on with the satellite and Italian treaties while progress was held up on the German and Austrian settlements, which alone could remove the legal justification for, if not the physical presence of, Soviet occupation forces stationed in East-Central Europe. A hypothetical American insistence on priority for the Austrian and German treaties might have resulted merely in the postponement of *all* settlements, but this eventuality could scarcely have worsened the existing political situation in the satellites or jeopardized the Western orientation of Italy (as was to be demonstrated in the case of Japan); on the other hand, such a postponement would have at least avoided the pretense that the East European satellites were sovereign states whose independence and domestic political self-determination could be guaranteed by peace treaties.

It appears, then, that American foreign policy in this period did not exhibit the combination of tactical flexibility and consistency of purpose which might have best served Washington's long-range interests in East-Central Europe. These interests, while recognizing the need to prevent a renascence of German expansionism and to assuage the historically warranted fears of the Soviet Union in this respect, required an independent and democratic status for the ex-satellites as well as for Poland and Czechoslovakia, not only for the sake of fulfilling the wartime commitments, but also in order to safeguard the security of Western Europe and restore some semblance of a balance of power on the Continent. Regrettably, as Hans Morgenthau later reflected, the United States was "slow to recognize that its victory in the Second World War, eliminating one threat to its security, opened the door for a new threat more dangerous than the one against which the Second World War had been fought."[118] Whether in 1946 the Soviet Union represented a greater threat than had Germany in the late thirties is debatable, but the fact remains that it did emerge as a powerful opponent possessed of an irreconcilable ideology and certainly more desirous of extending its influence than of collaborating with its erstwhile allies in defense of the principles of the UN Charter. The Russians did not waver in their quest for an impregnable buffer zone in East-Central Europe; in the words of Ambassador Bedell Smith, "there never was the slightest intention on the part of Stalin and the Politburo to allow any other pattern to develop in the satellite area or to honor—at any point or in any way—the many agreements they had made with the British and ourselves to allow the people of Eastern Europe freely to choose their own form of government and to decide on their own futures."[119] In the face of this determination, the military and diplomatic policies pursued by the United States in 1945 and 1946 amounted to little better than futile appeasement.

CONTAINMENT AND COLD WAR

Hardly had the ink dried on the satellite treaties than American foreign policy began to move into a new phase of undisguised hostility and confrontation with the Soviet Union, although, in the interests of ratification by an increasingly uneasy Congress, official statements retained a guarded optimism in the first days of 1947. Commented the president in his State of the Union message: "This Government does not regard the treaties as completely satisfactory. Whatever their defects, however, I am convinced that they are as good as we can hope to obtain by agreement among the principal wartime Allies. Further dispute and delay would gravely jeopardize political stability in the countries concerned for many years."[120] Testifying before the Committee on Foreign Relations, General Marshall, who had replaced Byrnes as secretary of state in January, offered a rather more speculative argument: "If these treaties are suspended or rejected, I think it would be exceedingly harmful to the prospect for completing a satisfactory treaty with Austria, and the development of one with Germany."[121] In the case of the East European satellites, political stability turned out to be far more precarious than Truman had implied; in his remarks on the occasion of formal ratification, on June 14, he expressed regret that the Bulgarian, Hungarian, and Rumanian governments "not only have disregarded the will of the majority of the people but have resorted to measures of oppression against them."[122]

While in Bulgaria and Rumania those measures served merely to consolidate existing procommunist regimes, in Hungary the process of attrition whereby a democratically elected and predominantly anticommunist government was liquidated gathered momentum in the months following the Paris peace conference. As early as July 1946, Premier Nagy had been confronted by a Soviet request (issued by the acting head of the ACC, General Sviridov, but under the authority of the Soviet High Command) to restrict the freedom of the churches, dissolve the Boy Scouts and religious youth organizations, and purge the "fascists" from his party.[123] The premier had become even more despondent after his territorial proposals were dismissed, and he had made a quick trip to Paris in September to complain to Byrnes that Hungary's free elections and relative independence had not been rewarded by any Western support; Byrnes failed to offer reassurance beyond expressing confidence about Hungary's economic revival, and a profoundly pessimistic Nagy returned to his capital.[124] More or less covert appeals for help continued to reach Washington, and in March 1947 Undersecretary of State Dean Acheson wrote to Nagy assuring him that "we here are giving close attention to the important problems affecting Hungary and, as you know, we are currently exploring . . . various possible means of extending further material assistance to your country. . . . It is unfortunately true that, in some instances, the solutions which have been adopted in connection with the peace settlements as the only ones possible of agreement are not entirely satisfactory."[125] Discernible in Acheson's note was an admission of impotence, since material assistance in the guise of credits for surplus goods was hardly adequate to contain the communists. The gap between Hungary's needs and America's ability to help was faithfully represented by Schoenfeld's account of a meeting with the beleaguered premier, who appeared "less interested at that moment in American economic aid than in knowing what political action the United States would take to prevent the collapse of the Hungarian Government, which he considered imminent."[126] Meanwhile, the "salami tactics" pursued by the Hungarian communists under the leadership of Mátyás Rákosi and by their Russian friends whittled away at the democratic parties, in the first instance at the Smallholders. Early in the year Béla Kovács, that party's secretary-general and a member of Parliament, was arrested by Soviet occupation forces; after repeated requests by the communists, Parliament had waived his immunity, and he was faced with charges of espionage. On March 5, Secretary of State Marshall sent off a stiff note of protest against "foreign interference in the domestic affairs of Hungary in support of repeated aggressive attempts by Hungarian minority elements to coerce the popularly elected majority." He deplored that the Western representatives on the ACC had not been consulted, qualified the charges against Kovács as "unwarranted," and demanded that no further measures be taken without the prescribed consultation. General Sviridov, the Soviet vice-chairman of the ACC, replied that a joint investigation of the "conspiracy" would constitute a direct intervention in the internal affairs of Hungary and he dismissed Marshall's protest as "an attempt to encroach upon the lawful rights of the Soviet occupation authorities to defend their armed forces in the territory of Hungary." Marshall's protest could not affect the situation (indeed, Sviridov did not even allow its publication until he had replied), and Nagy felt it necessary to advise his Smallholder colleagues "not to feel triumphant over this note, because it would aggravate the situation."[127] A further American note pointed out that "investigation of the plot against the state has to date been conducted only by Communist-dominated police organs," reiterated the charge that the communists were attempting to seize power through extraconstitutional tactics, and renewed the earlier request for a joint investigation. With chilling finality, the Russians replied that Kovács had "fully acknowledged his guilt in crimes against the Soviet Army."[128]

Premier Nagy recalls counting the days until ratification and the official termination of Hungary's status as an occupied country ninety days thereafter, but the race would have been an uneven one even if the pretext of guarding lines of communication had not ensured the continued presence of Soviet troops.[129] At the end of May, a communist-engineered coup ousted Nagy (who was on holiday in Switzerland) and replaced him with the more compliant Social Democrat Lajos Dinnyés. Although the takeover had been expected for some weeks, Washington's reaction was swift and vocal; President Truman called the coup an outrage and dispatched a note of protest to the Soviet military commander in Budapest, blaming him for actions that violated the Yalta agreement and warning that the United States might submit the case to the United Nations.[130] But normal diplomatic relations were already breaking down; on June 4 the Hungarian ambassador to Washington resigned and issued a statement refusing to recognize the legality of the new government, an act followed by his colleagues in several other capitals.[131] Predictably, the request of the American representative on the ACC, General Weems, to examine the incriminating information that had allegedly led to Nagy's resignation was refused. In order to give credence to the premier's treason, the communists charged that Nagy had sent his son to Acheson with a letter "asking for help so that the Truman Doctrine should be applied in Hungary also," and asserted that Acheson had replied promising support; the State Department felt it necessary to make public an exchange of letters between Acheson and Nagy to refute these charges.[132] The Hungarian government now supplanted the Russians in rejecting Western requests for a joint investigation, and in July it published a White Book charging that the United States had indeed conspired with the Smallholders.[133]

At the time of the coup, the possibilities of American intervention were severely limited. Military pressure was ruled out by the tactical weakness of the Americans in Europe, even if it had been contemplated by the administration. Safely out of office, James Byrnes argued that the Hungarian crisis came within the spirit of the Truman Doctrine and that the United States ought not to set a precedent for inaction, but even he proposed only a Security Council investigation.[134] Three possible avenues for retaliation remained: nonrecognition of the regime, rejection of the peace treaty in the Senate, and the cancellation of economic aid. Of these, the first was considered harmful, on balance, since it would eliminate the potentially useful listening-post of a diplomatic mission. Regarding the second alternative, it was argued that ratification would at least signify American support in principle for the basic rights embodied in the treaty. Only the third measure was implemented, with all credits being suspended on the morrow of Nagy's resignation and subsequently canceled; the secretary of state offered the rather disingenuous explanation that the new communist-dominated regime had exiled those Hungarian negotiators who had the confidence of the United States.[135] Perfunctory protests continued to issue from Washington (one note dated August 17 objected to new electoral laws for the upcoming elections which disenfranchised innumerable anticommunists), but by now Rákosi and his associates were totally impervious to the blandishments of the West. The resident of the Central Intelligence Group, whose cover identity was that of civilian adviser to the U.S. military mission, mounted a final Scarlet Pimpernel–like operation to arrange the escape of seventy-four leading anticommunists (including certain scientists requested by the U.S. Navy) before leaving the country himself.[136]

Moscow's ring of satellites already included Poland, where democratic forces had been routed even before the coup in Hungary. In the sphere of economic relations, American-Polish negotiations on a loan were broken off in May 1946 when Warsaw showed itself unwilling to provide information on its economic and commercial policies and agreements.[137] Some surplus deliveries were made in the course of the year, but the resumption of negotiations in December came too late to affect the process of communist subversion. Despite some interference by the communist-dominated government, the pre-election referendum held on June 30, 1946, resulted in an impressive show of strength by Mikolajczyk's Peasant party.[138] Thereafter the communists redoubled their efforts to harass the party and its supporters, and, when Mikolajczyk officially complained about this persecution to the three Great Powers, the Soviet Union branded his colleagues "criminal elements" and warned the West not to interfere in Polish affairs. There was, in fact, little likelihood of such interference. Mikolajczyk had proposed that the Yalta powers supervise the forthcoming election, but, in transmitting this suggestion, even the sympathetic American ambassador, Arthur Bliss Lane, had noted that the Polish and Soviet governments were bound to reject Allied observation as constituting unwarranted interference in the internal affairs of Poland and that in any case the difficulties of mounting such a large-scale supervisory effort were insuperable.[139] Moreover, the cause of the pro-Western elements in Poland was not advanced in a speech Byrnes delivered in Stuttgart on September 6, in the course of which he reiterated that the Potsdam decision on the Oder-Neisse line represented an interim settlement pending the final peace treaty with Germany; emphasis on this qualification could only arouse the ire of Poles, who to a man viewed the Oder-Neisse frontier as irrevocable.[140] Regardless of such irritations, what the State Department termed "wide-spread measures of coercion and intimidation against democratic elements" ensured that the general elections, held on January 19, 1947, would result in a communist majority.[141] After recommending that his government refuse to acquiesce in the outcome of the election, Ambassador Lane resigned in disgust at the "grievous errors which our government had made in following a policy of appeasement in its dealings with Stalin";[142] Mikolajczyk fled into exile. As in the case of Hungary, the United States found itself unable to compensate for earlier concessions and for the influence that derived from the presence of Soviet forces. When he accepted the credentials of Poland's new envoy on February 4, President Truman had to content himself with voicing a reproachful reminder of the long-dead Yalta agreements.[143]

While Stalin thus consolidated his East European buffer zone, a fundamental reappraisal of America's international commitments and objectives was proceeding in Washington. At the Conference of Foreign Ministers that opened in Moscow on March 10, 1947, the United States tried unsuccessfully to advance the prospects of Germany's reunification and demilitarization and Austria's evacuation; the Soviet negotiators turned all the more intractable when on March 12 the world learned that President Truman, acting upon an urgent appeal from London, had committed the United States to providing military and economic assistance to the embattled anticommunist regimes in Greece and Turkey. In what became known as the Truman Doctrine, the president declared that "totalitarian régimes imposed on free peoples, by direct or indirect aggression, undermine the foundations of international peace and hence the security of the United States."[144] News of the doctrine aroused some hopes in East-Central Europe, and, in the course of hearings on the proposed Greek-Turkish bill in the Foreign Relations Committee, Senator Vandenberg queried Acheson regarding its applicability in other areas of Soviet-American confrontation; the administration made it clear, however, that the Soviet presence in East-Central Europe ruled out any extension of the doctrine to that area.[145] The extent to which the Truman Doctrine's neat distinction between two hostile camps served as a self-fulfilling prophecy has been a matter of some debate;[146] in the final analysis, the palpable communist threat to the pro-Western regime in Greece necessitated an at least logistical rescue operation which the virtually bankrupt British could no longer provide, whereas the Russians were already so well entrenched in East-Central Europe that the doctrine could contribute only marginally to their resolve to maintain that strategic buffer zone.

Although the Truman Doctrine represented a scarcely debated response to an emergency, it proved to be the first step in the elaboration of a new American strategy of containment. Secretary of State Marshall returned from the Moscow conference (in the course of which he had had a private meeting with Stalin) convinced that the Russians were willfully obstructing progress on the resolution of Europe's political and economic problems and proceeded to establish within the State Department a Policy Planning Staff headed by George Kennan and charged with the task of elaborating new initiatives in foreign policy.[147] A study group which included the economist Charles Kindleberger had already produced a memorandum for the department's Committee on Foreign Aid which stressed the need for a program to strengthen Western Europe and recommended its extension to East-Central Europe and the Soviet Union, since the economies of the two areas were largely complementary.[148] Then, on May 23, Kennan's team reported with a proposal for a general European recovery program, to be introduced through the Economic Commission for Europe (a recent creation of the United Nations) in such a way that the Soviet satellites would "either exclude themselves by unwillingness to accept the proposed conditions or agree to abandon the exclusive orientation of their economies."[149] When Marshall wondered about the consequences of Soviet participation, Kennan explained that the United States would have to put the matter to the Russians in the following terms: "You, like ourselves, produce raw materials which western Europe needs, and we shall be glad to examine together what contributions you as well as we could make. This would mean that Russia would either have to decline or else agree to make a real contribution, herself, to the revival of the Western European economy." In this way, argued Kennan, "we would not ourselves draw a line of division through Europe"; clearly, however, the unstated expectation was that the Russians would draw appropriately negative conclusions.[150] At the first meeting of the Economic Commission for Europe, held in Geneva, the Soviets had already proven troublesome, and, in view of their own dire economic circumstances, they were not likely to devote their efforts to the reconstruction of a capitalistic, and at least latently antagonistic, Western Europe. Moreover, the Policy Planning

Staff's report stressed that the United States could not wait for Russian agreement to restore Germany's economy.

In a speech at Harvard on June 5, the same day that President Truman denounced the coup in Hungary, Secretary of State Marshall formally extended an invitation to the Europeans to join with the United States in a cooperative venture to facilitate their economic recovery, but he warned: "Any government which maneuvers to block the recovery of other countries cannot expect help from us."[151] The British and French foreign ministers met in Paris to take up Marshall's challenge and they invited Molotov to a preliminary conference that opened in Paris on June 27. When Bevin and Bidault proposed, however, that a steering committee be established to survey economic needs and draft a plan, Molotov retorted that this would constitute interference in the states' internal affairs, and he suggested instead that the United States be asked to specify the amount of aid it was offering, and that each individual country prepare estimates of its own requirements. Faced with the West's insistence on cooperation rather than unilateral planning, the Russians withdrew from the conference on July 2, to the obvious relief of all concerned.[152] The following day Bevin and Bidault issued an invitation to twenty-two other nations to meet on July 12 for further consultations. There was still some expectation that, in view of their pressing need for aid, the East Europeans would participate and thereby retain their traditional economic links with the West, but such hopes proved to be short-lived. In Hungary, Premier Dinnyés asked for the ACC's permission to send a delegate, then backtracked a few days later, allegedly because of disagreements among the great powers; evidently his initiative had been vetoed by the Russians, who also instructed the Polish, Rumanian, and the Yugoslav regimes to opt out.[153] Only Czechoslovakia, free of foreign occupation and still possessed of an ostensibly democratic government, officially accepted the invitation. However, when a delegation led by Premier Klement Gottwald and including Foreign Minister Jan Masaryk arrived in Moscow to discuss some other matters, they were told by Stalin that the so-called Marshall Plan was anti-Soviet and that therefore they must withdraw. On July 10 the government ignominiously revoked its earlier acceptance, leading Masaryk to comment privately: "It is a new Munich. I left for Moscow as Minister of Foreign Affairs of a sovereign state. I am returning as Stalin's stooge."[154] The Kremlin would not permit a degree of independence that invited a dangerous reassertion of Western influence, and thus it offered superfluous but incontrovertible proof that the East Europeans were no longer masters in their own houses.

Apart from the rather ominous surrender of the Czechs, the East Europeans' failure to profit from the first practical manifestations of the containment policy did not occasion much surprise in Washington, for that policy was directed not at the satellites but at more salvageable areas such as Greece; the Policy Planning Staff's report had pointedly warned against any misinterpretation of the Truman Doctrine as being applicable to all areas where the communists were reaching for power.[155] What George Kennan later regretfully termed the "indestructible myth" of a containment doctrine originated in a paper which he wrote and published in the July 1947 issue of *Foreign Affairs*.[156] His purpose, recalls the author, was not "to perpetuate the status quo to which the military operations and political arrangements of World War II had led," but rather "to cease at that point making fatuous unilateral concessions to the Kremlin, to do what we could to inspire and support resistance elsewhere to its efforts to expand the area of its dominant political influence, and to wait for the internal weaknesses of Soviet power, combined with frustration in the external field, to moderate Soviet ambitions and behavior." East-Central Europe received no mention in his thesis, and, although he saw it as having a potentially weakening effect on Soviet power, he clearly relegated it for the foreseeable future to a Soviet sphere of domination. Kennan viewed the Soviet threat as essentially political rather than military, a fact his article failed to make clear, and he therefore meant to advocate political initiatives such as the Marshall Plan rather than the network of military alliances foreshadowed by the Truman Doctrine.[157] The ambiguity of his thesis prompted a variety of criticisms that will be examined in Chapter III; for the present, however, it can simply be noted that containment offered no promise of early self-determination for East-Central Europe or of American initiatives to that end.

In the defensive atmosphere engendered by Soviet intransigence, the acceptance of the East European *status quo* implicit in containment aroused relatively little opposition in Western Europe or, at first, in the United States. Faced with communist-led strikes and the threatening prox-imity of Soviet power, most West Europeans regarded the fate of their Eastern neighbors with some indifference and concentrated on shoring up their faltering economies. Winston Churchill, now leader of the Opposi-tion, stressed the advantages of negotiating from strength to a Conserva-tive conference in October 1948: "The Western Nations will be far more likely to reach a lasting settlement, without bloodshed, if they formulate their just demands while they have the atomic power and before the Russian Communists have got it too." In private conversations with Amer-ican visitors, he would be even more unequivocal in urging that the United States wield its atomic potential in support of an ultimatum to the Rus-sians to withdraw from East-Central Europe.[158] His earlier warnings about the ebbing forces of democracy had fallen largely on deaf ears, and few now shared his fear that the bargaining position of the West to compel a satisfactory settlement could only suffer from postponement. Both the realistic and idealistic elements in American foreign policy militated against Churchill's forceful alternative. The democratic precepts and processes which had historically characterized that policy (allowing for occasional transgressions) could not accommodate the use of atomic blackmail in the absence of a direct threat to American security; that solution was also ruled out by more pragmatic considerations regarding Stalin's likely response to an ultimatum—there was at least a possibility that he might call the West's bluff and set his unopposed armies marching toward the Atlantic—as well as the long-range effects of such atomic diplomacy on the international system. Similarly, the wartime declarations of principle and the emerging status of the Soviet Union as a fundamentally insatiable adversary precluded official sanction of Soviet hegemony over East-Central Europe. Instead of open acquiescence or aggressive hostility, the mood that came to prevail in the West was one of consolidation and containment.

A process of consolidation also marked the Soviet sphere, where the rejection of Marshall's admittedly provocative overture was followed in quick succession by the announcement of the formation of the Cominform, whose task it would be to coordinate the operations of all communist parties, and of a series of trade agreements with the satellites (a rival "Molotov Plan") which drew the latter into even greater economic subjection to the Soviet Union. Meanwhile, official statements—notably, those made by Andrei Zhdanov at the Cominform's founding convention—grew in militancy in their denunciations of the Marshall Plan as an instrument of American imperialism and reiterated the division of the world into two irreconcilable camps. In terms of this world view, the position of Czechoslovakia was clearly anomalous, for, despite a strong representation of the communists in the ruling coalition, democratic processes and contacts with the West were preserved in apparent justification of the Beneš-Masaryk strategy of cultivating Soviet friendship. Czechoslovakia's reluctant refusal to participate in the Marshall Plan gave an early inkling of the subordination of that nation's sovereignty to Russian interests, and, as domestic communist agitation, particularly in the trade unions, escalated in the autumn of 1947, Kennan warned the secretary of state that the already foreseeable success of the European Recovery Program would in all likelihood prompt a Soviet-inspired coup in that country.[159] Apart from an American-Czech trade agreement, Beneš did not invite Western involvement or support, perceiving with some accuracy that no one would guarantee Czechoslovakia's independence if his long-standing policy of accommodation with Stalin should prove to have failed. On

February 19, U.S. Ambassador Laurence Steinhardt returned from Washington with the offer of a $25 million credit that was intended to strengthen the democratic elements in the government, but his arrival in Prague coincided with that of Soviet Deputy Foreign Minister Valerian Zorin, who presumably came armed with more persuasive arguments.[160] The following day saw the resignation of twelve noncommunist cabinet members, a move made ostensibly in protest against the outrageously partisan activities of the police, but in reality to impel the president to use his constitutional power to call for new elections. In the event, Beneš refrained from dismissing the government, but the calculated neutrality of Defense Minister Svoboda and communist influence in the armed forces prevented him from resorting to more forceful measures; faced with the unambiguous threat of Soviet intervention, he fatalistically approved on February 25 Gottwald's revamped communist cabinet. After this thinly disguised communist *coup d'état*, the single-list elections held at the end of May and the succession of Gottwald to the presidency merely confirmed the death of Czech democracy.[161] Whether or not Stalin subscribed to Bismarck's anticipatory dictum that the master of Bohemia was the master of Europe, his East European *Gleichschaltung* was now complete.

The Prague coup only heightened the atmosphere of crisis in Washington, where the concurrently hardening Soviet position regarding Berlin and the growing power of communist parties in Italy and France were regarded with grave apprehension. Although it is more likely that the Russians were momentarily intent upon strengthening their own perimeter, the West—the American military and intelligence establishments in particular—over-reacted.[162] The ensuing war scare led first to the signing on March 17 of the Brussels Treaty, which was the West Europeans' first collective defense agreement, and then on June 11 to the Senate's endorsement of the Vandenberg Resolution, a four-point program for the expansion of America's military strength, the extension of military and economic assistance to Western Europe and elsewhere as needed, and increased diplomatic and propagandistic activity to contain the Soviet Union, all of which provided the inspiration for the North Atlantic Treaty of April 1949. (The atmosphere of urgency engendered by the Prague coup also contributed to Congress' swift approval on April 8 of the Foreign Assistance Act, which would implement the Marshall Plan.) George Kennan once again found himself in a dissenting minority, arguing that, since the Soviet threat to Western Europe was political rather than military, there was no need for a joint American-European effort in the military sphere, while the Truman administration became more and more deeply committed to shoring up the defenses of the West, even at the expense of postponing indefinitely new initiatives in the diplomatic arena. As emphasis shifted in Washington to the questions of rearmament and Western collective security, the prospect of West German participation gradually acquired precedence over that of an all-German settlement; as long as the East and West failed to resolve the German problem, however, there could be no hope of moderating the extent of Soviet domination in East-Central Europe. Thus, in practice, containment manifested itself in a defensive, inward-looking posture that projected the failure of past negotiations into a fatalistic commitment to the preservation of the *status quo.*

After the breakdown of the Council of Foreign Ministers' meeting in December 1947, the Western powers reacted in sheer frustration by embarking on the "London Program," which envisaged the creation of an independent West Germany. The Soviet Union retaliated by initiating the blockade of Berlin in July 1948, but that measure (apart from arousing some unwarranted hopes among the East Europeans when the airlift successfully called the Russians' bluff) only strengthened the West's resolve to implement the program and ensured that in the concurrent American election campaign foreign policy would remain a relatively nonpartisan issue.[163] As an alternative to the London Program, the Policy Planning Staff had prepared a plan for all-German elections and a phased withdrawal of occupation forces leading to a reunited and demilitarized Germany, but Secretary of State Dean Acheson, who took over that office in January 1949, prudently, if somewhat unimaginatively, opted for the former course and reassured his French and British colleagues that the United States did not envisage any military withdrawal from Germany. Instead, recalls Kennan, the London Program was "being rushed frantically to completion with the scarcely concealed intention that it should stand as a *fait accompli* before the Big Four foreign ministers," who were scheduled to meet on May 23 in Paris; notes Acheson in his memoirs, "we soon came to believe that our chief concern should be the future of Europe, and that the reunification of Germany should not be regarded as the chief end in itself."[164] This Western strategy made it a foregone conclusion that the ensuing "Palais Rose" meetings would prove fruitless. The new Soviet foreign minister, Andrei Vyshinsky, urged the reactivation of the four-power Allied Control Council, the quadripartite control of the Ruhr, and the union of the two German economic councils, but the West responded with the even more disingenuous proposal that the Länder in the Soviet zone join in the London Program.

The Paris conference served only to reaffirm the division of Germany. That same month, the constitution of the new Federal Republic of Germany was promulgated; in October, following another unpublicized proposal for reunification, the Russians transferred the administration of their zone to a provisional East German government dominated by the communist Socialist Unity party (SED), which had all along been an impatient proponent of an independent German Democratic Republic (GDR).[165] Over the next three years, Washington steadfastly pursued its policy of integrating West Germany into its alliance system, a policy that had the enthusiastic support of the Adenauer government (though it was opposed by Kurt Schumacher's Social Democratic party (SDP), which still advocated a reunited, neutral Germany).[166] The Russians were above all concerned with preventing West Germany's remilitarization, but, rightly or wrongly, few in the West believed that they were prepared to trade off the GDR for a genuinely neutral, united Germany. With the outbreak of hostilities in Korea, the Truman administration became even more committed to rearmament and the consolidation of Western Europe. In September 1950 the three Western powers revised the Occupation Statute in preparation for West Germany's rearmament, thereby prompting a Soviet bloc conference in Prague which proposed a four-power pledge against the remilitarization of Germany and the creation of an all-German Constituent Council to prepare a new constitution and a peace treaty; Western disinterest and the Soviets' awareness that there was no immediate prospect of West German rearmament conspired to preserve the stalemate. A year later, in response to renewed Soviet calls for reunification, the Bonn government extended a fourteen-point proposal for all-German elections. When, to their astonishment, the East Germans accepted the overture in principle and suggested all-German consultations, the Western powers quickly buried the matter in the United Nations.[167] The official rationalization for this Western strategy was that the communists were, as in the past, insincere in their hints of compromise and aimed merely to hinder the entrenchment of NATO. Yet the most puzzling Soviet overture was yet to come. Confronted with evidence from the NATO talks in Lisbon in February 1952 of strong American pressure for a massive increase in NATO's military capacity, the Soviet Union on March 10 dispatched a note calling for quadripartite discussions on a draft peace treaty that envisaged a reunited, neutral, but not necessarily demilitarized Germany.[168] Subsequent evidence suggests that the Russians were indeed prepared to sacrifice the East German regime, but, at the time, the United States and its allies were clearly unwilling to exchange the certainty and security of a pro-Western, rearmed West Germany for yet another round of dilatory negotiations with the Russians; in his memoirs, Acheson dismisses the note as a "spoiling operation intended to check and dissipate the momentum toward solutions in the West brought about by three years of colossal effort."[169] Having rebuffed Moscow's overture (ostensibly because of the neutrality clause), the Western powers proceeded to sign on

May 26 a set of "Contractual Agreements" with Bonn which allowed for the creation of a West German army and its eventual participation in the alliance;[170] although disagreements over the proposed European Defense Community delayed this participation for more than two years, West Germany had become a linchpin in the ring containing the communists. East of the Elbe, a more confident Pieck-Ulbricht regime launched a program of administrative reorganization and centralization to assimilate the GDR even more closely into the Soviet sphere.

In the absence of adequate documentation, only speculation is possible in assessing the authenticity of Soviet proposals for German reunification. The delay in allowing Ulbricht to implant the orthodox "people's democracy" in East Germany and the signing in June 1950 of an East German–Polish agreement formalizing the Oder-Neisse frontier (which could scarcely have been calculated to enhance the domestic popularity of the Pankow regime) suggest a certain hesitancy on the part of Stalin regarding the desirability and viability of a communist East Germany; Ulbricht himself later admitted that a positive Western response to the March note would have "greatly endangered" the party's position in the GDR.[171] It is therefore conceivable that the Russians, faced with the alternative of a rearmed and revisionist West Germany in NATO, genuinely preferred the buffer of a reunited but neutralized Germany. However, an equally compelling logic lay behind the West's reluctance to respond. Endless rebuffs of American initiatives in the early postwar period—notably, the outright rejection of Byrnes's proposed demilitarization treaty—had engendered in Washington a profound conviction of Soviet intractability and duplicity. From 1948 onward, this skepticism regarding Soviet intentions and the emerging strategy of military containment only reinforced each other, while the Berlin blockade, the communists' victory in China, and the Korean invasion contributed to a warlike atmosphere that left few advocates of negotiation and compromise. Meanwhile, the West Europeans, Adenauer foremost among them, were clamoring for protection, protested at the slightest hint of American withdrawal, and, particularly in the case of France, viewed with some indifference the prospect of Germany's reunification. Yet another deterrent to negotiation was the consistent opposition of the American military establishment to even marginal disengagement on the Continent; the chairman of the Joint Chiefs of Staff, General Bradley, dismissed as strategically perilous the Policy Planning Staff's 1948 proposal for mutual troop withdrawals to enclaves on the eastern and western borders of Germany (as a preliminary step toward supervised elections and reunification), and, as long as the cold war atmosphere of confrontation endured, such arguments appeared eminently convincing to succeeding administrations.[172] The prevailing political climate in the United States also militated against relaxed negotiations, with the most violent criticism of Truman and Acheson coming from those who saw in them the agents of compromise and defeat. The Truman-Acheson strategy was, as noted earlier, one of consolidating the *status quo* rather than of changing it by force or by diplomacy, and it certainly proved successful in terms of the security and economic revival of Western Europe. The single-minded pursuit of this goal carried a heavy price, however, in the rejection of all opportunities for attenuating the division of the Continent. As long as Germany remained the divided prey of two armed camps, there was no chance of progress toward lightening the burden of Soviet domination in the satellites, no possibility of disengagement and neutrality in the heart of Europe. This is not to say that a successfully negotiated reunification and neutralization of Germany would necessarily have been followed by Soviet withdrawal from the satellites and the restoration of the latter's sovereignty. It would, however, have reduced the Russians' chronic fear of German aggression, made less tenable their excuse for maintaining a military presence in East-Central Europe, and represented a step toward a resolution of the European schism which might have liberated the satellite nations, if not from Soviet influence, at least from Soviet domination.

By the summer of 1948, with Czechoslovakia and Hungary firmly in Moscow's embrace, East-Central Europe (excluding Yugoslavia) had acquired a monolithic appearance that neither invited nor deserved a particularly differentiated involvement on the part of the West, and American policy makers concentrated instead on Western Europe, and later on the Far East, in their efforts to contain the communist world. Having acknowledged that the satellites were totally impervious to American influence, the administration did not formulate a specific new policy aimed in their direction; instead, it rationalized its impotence with containment's teleological reassurance that the Soviet system carried within itself the seed of its own decay and proceeded to conduct relations with East-Central Europe in largely haphazard, reactive, and propagandistic fashion. Since the unfulfilled promises to the East Europeans represented a significant defeat for a nation whose traditional external policy contained a strong moralistic impulse, American insistence on the legal obligations incurred by the Soviet and East European regimes was maintained long after it ceased to have anything but an exhortative function.

The peace treaties with Bulgaria, Hungary, and Rumania had stipulated that for a period of eighteen months following ratification (that is, from September 15, 1947) the heads of the Soviet, British, and American diplomatic missions in those countries should supervise in concert the implementation of the treaties. Many of the human rights clauses continued to be flouted, however, by satellite regimes intent on eliminating all political opposition, and neither the Western heads of mission nor their governments could alter the course of totalitarian rule, despite innumerable *démarches* and diplomatic notes; the latter were invariably dismissed by the Soviet Union and its satraps as illegitimate interference in their internal affairs.[173] On March 16, 1949, the United States and Britain issued a statement noting the flagrant violations of the human rights and demilitarization clauses and warning that, although the initial eighteen-month period had expired, they reserved the right to pursue enforcement through other channels.[174] Formal notes enjoining the satellites to "adopt prompt remedial measures" elicited only the now customary litany of "domestic jurisdiction," an excuse whose legality was emphatically denied by the U.S. State Department: "Persecution of all political leaders and parties not amenable to the dictates of the minority ruling group and denial of freedom of expression cannot properly be justified under any Article of the Treaty."[175] The United States thereupon transferred the debate to the forum of the United Nations, where on April 30 the General Assembly passed a resolution expressing "deep concern at the grave accusations" made against Hungary and Bulgaria and drawing the latter's attention "most urgently" to their treaty obligations.[176] When the two satellites declined to appoint representatives to the commissions provided for in the treaties in the event of disputes, the United States reintroduced the issue at the September meeting of the General Assembly. In the course of the debate, Australia suggested the creation of a special investigatory committee, but since there was no hope of gaining the admittance of such a committee to Hungary and Bulgaria the proposal was shelved. Instead, the Assembly adopted a resolution requesting the International Court of Justice to give an advisory opinion on the legal aspects of the dispute.[177] Reporting on March 30, 1950, the court advised that disputes did exist within the meaning of the peace treaties and that the accused governments were under obligation to carry out the enforcement provisions by naming representatives to the three-power commissions; clearly, however, the United Nations lacked the power to compel compliance with this ruling. In the Fifth General Assembly, on November 3, a further resolution reiterated the charges made earlier and deplored the satellites' disregard for the court's opinions.[178] (Another East-West deadlock, regarding the admission of certain satellites and of a number of other countries sponsored by the United States, was not resolved until 1955, in a package deal.)

Contemporary historians differed in their assessments of American tactics. One commented that the United States, "by its forthright challenge of the practices of 'people's democracy', might have given Eastern Europe's peoples some needed moral encouragement"; another expressed the fear that "repeated ineffectual protests may weaken the position of the United States."[179] As a principal party to the treaties, however, the United States felt obligated to go through the motions of seeking their implementation and, through the intermediation of the United Nations, to brand the recalcitrant regimes as pariahs in the international system. Without in any way altering the fate of the East European peoples, this policy at least prompted a wider awareness of their plight.

Soviet determination to isolate the satellites from the West was instrumental in the failure of negotiations on various issues, notably, those of Danubian navigation and an Austrian peace settlement. Following postponement at the Paris peace conference, the riparian states (including the Soviet Union since its annexation of Bessarabia) and the three Western powers met at Belgrade in July 1948.[180] In arguing for the maintenance of a system of international control which, since 1856, had included France and Britain as well as the riparian states, the latter sought not only commercial advantage but also to preserve what was left of the satellites' Western orientation. Coming on the heels of the Truman Doctrine and the Marshall Plan, the conference was not expected by the Western participants to achieve a consensus, and, in the event, they were outvoted by the Russians and their dutiful satellites.[181] The resulting convention, which restricted membership on the governing commission to riparian states (and in effect ensured Soviet control of Danubian navigation), was not signed by the three Western powers. In the matter of the Austrian peace settlement, negotiations were suspended in London on May 26, 1948, ostensibly because the United States would not countenance Yugoslavia's Soviet-supported claims to parts of southern Carinthia and Styria and to $150 million in reparations, but in reality because the Soviet Union was reluctant to lose its pretext for maintaining troops in Hungary and Rumania and the additional isolation of Hungary and Czechoslovakia from the West provided by its zone of occupation.[182] Talks were subsequently reopened and continued in desultory fashion until their collapse in late 1949; they were not resumed for four years.

Washington's bilateral relations with the several satellites presented an equally dismal picture in these early cold war years. In consolidating their positions the satellite regimes perpetrated outrages on foreign nationals as well as their own, while enjoying immunity from any effective Western retaliation. The carefully staged trial and the imprisonment of Hungary's Cardinal Mindszenty in early 1949 aroused world-wide indignation and prompted the U.S. Congress to pass a resolution charging religious persecution and violation of the UN Charter and urging the administration to raise the matter in the United Nations; the Rákosi regime then proceeded to declare the American minister to Budapest, Selden Chapin, *persona non grata* for his alleged involvement in the Cardinal's anticommunist activities. A year later, in another spectacular trial, two Western businessmen—the American Robert Vogeler and the Briton Edgar Sanders—were convicted of espionage and sentenced to long prison terms. After denying the charges, the U.S. State Department retaliated symbolically by closing the Hungarian consulates in New York and Cleveland.[183] American attempts to normalize relations led in April 1951 to Vogeler's release and the reopening of the consulates (although Washington balked at returning the ancient crown of Saint Stephen, which had been in safekeeping in the American zone of Austria since the end of the war), but this easing of tensions proved ephemeral. In June, Archbishop József Grösz was convicted of plotting to overthrow the government with the help of the United States, three American diplomats were expelled, and the U.S. Information Agency's office in Budapest was ordered to close down. Charging that the trial "established nothing except the fact that the Hungarian authorities are continuing by ruthless and unconstitutional measures to terrorize the Hungarian people into mute submission to the existing regime," the United States formally abrogated the 1925 Treaty of Friendship, Commerce, and Consular Rights.[184] Later in July, President Truman denounced the deportations of Hungarian citizens and accused the Rákosi regime of "infamous conduct."[185] The next crisis occurred in November, with the downing of an American military aircraft by Soviet fighters over Hungary. The crew was convicted of espionage, and Washington found no way out of the dilemma but to pay ransom in the amount of $120,000; a travel ban for American citizens was reinstated and the two consulates were closed once again.[186] Relations with the other satellites followed a similar course. The implication of the U.S. minister to Sofia, Donald R. Heath, in a Titoist purge trial led the State Department to suspend diplomatic relations with Bulgaria in February 1950.[187] Amid allegations of espionage, the Czechs imprisoned an American correspondent, William Oatis, in April 1951 and expelled some U.S. diplomats.

The causes of this spy hysteria remain obscure. It is possible that the ruling communists were still sufficiently insecure to be seriously concerned over real or suspected American subversion and were consequently searching for plots even where plots did not exist; in their terminology, espionage encompassed the mundane as well as the subversive. A more fundamental motive was the desire of their masters in the Kremlin to effect a total break between Washington and the satellites so as to allow communization to proceed with the minimum of observation and interference. Acheson noted in February 1950 that "the principal purpose of what these Governments have been doing is plainly to make the so-called Iron Curtain impenetrable," but in the interests of preserving at least diplomatic listening-posts he added that the Americans "still wish to maintain normal relations with [the satellites] regardless of differences in political philosophies and institutions."[188] If an ancillary purpose behind the spy hysteria of the early 1950s was to convince the satellite peoples that the United States was powerless to help them, the propaganda advantage lay with the communists, for, taking the events at face value, small dictatorships were with impunity irritating a Great Power.

In the face of such provocations and the more serious flouting of the peace treaties (Bulgaria, Hungary, and Rumania were already rearming well in excess of treaty limitations), the Truman administration had to concede momentary impotence. After the final Council of Foreign Ministers meeting ended in deadlock in late 1949, Secretary of State Acheson became convinced that it would be pointless for the United States to initiate further discussions regarding the satellites: "It is clear that the Russians do not want to settle those issues as long as they feel there is any possibility they can exploit them for their own objectives of world domination. It is only when they come to the conclusion that they cannot so exploit them that they will make agreements, and they will let it be known when they have reached that decision."[189] Equally consistent with the wait-and-see logic of containment was Acheson's only major reference to East-Central Europe. In a speech delivered at Berkeley in March 1950, he speculated that, should the Russians wish to give evidence of their peaceful intentions, they could "withdraw their military and police force and refrain from using the shadow of that force to keep in power persons or régimes which do not command the confidence of the respective peoples, freely expressed through orderly representative processes. In other words, they could elect to observe, in practice, the declaration to which they set their signature at Yalta concerning liberated Europe. . . . Nothing could so alter the international climate as the holding of elections in the satellite states in which the will of the people could be expressed."[190] Having, with somewhat hopeless pragmatism, placed the onus for altering the East European *status quo* on the Soviet Union, the administration fell back upon a number of secondary tactics, including the encouragement of Titoism, discriminatory trade policies, propaganda, and even subversion. These tactics were not expected, either singly or in the aggregate, to occasion any immediate change in East-Central Europe, but they found their place within the evolutionary strategy of attrition known as containment.

The first defection from the Soviet (as distinguished from the communist) camp occurred in the summer of 1948, when the long-festering feud between Stalin and Tito reached its climax. By purging his party of its most pro-Soviet members and by putting into practice economic policies that diverged from the Muscovite orthodoxy, Tito was persisting in his effort to turn the wartime partisan movement into an effective government unchallenged from within or without; his claim to Trieste and his plans for a Balkan federation elicited Moscow's lukewarm support and determined opposition, respectively. Stalin would not countenance such a show of independence, and on June 28 the Cominform formally expelled the "Tito clique." Why did Stalin not immediately intervene by force to replace Tito with a more pliant viceroy? The least likely explanation is that he still felt bound by the old percentage agreement, which hitherto had not prevented him from treating Yugoslavia as part of the Soviet sphere of influence. The difficult terrain and Tito's experienced army, Yugoslavia's marginal strategic importance for Russian security, the expectation that Tito could easily be toppled by subversion and, perhaps, the fear that President Truman would extend his doctrine to protect Yugoslavia were more relevant factors in deterring the Russians. In the event, Tito successfully overcame internal treachery and set a tentative course for independence from both East and West.

In Washington, news of the schism was received with puzzlement and mistrust, all the more so because Tito did not immediately modify his ideological hostility toward the West. At the Belgrade conference in July, the Yugoslav and Soviet bloc positions were identical; the ongoing harassment of Westerners, the downing of an American aircraft in 1947, and the Trieste dispute had embittered America's relations with Tito. The matter of Trieste had been temporarily resolved at the Paris peace conference, which awarded territorial fragments to both Italy and Yugoslavia and placed Trieste and its immediate hinterland under UN administration, but the latter decision was never implemented, owing to East-West disagreements, and Trieste remained under Anglo-American occupation.[191] In the face of this experience, it was nevertheless decided in Washington that it would be to the West's advantage to prolong the Stalin-Tito schism, initially by measures calculated to bolster the Yugoslav economy and compensate for its earlier reliance on Soviet trade.[192] The political implications of the $20 million Export-Import Bank loan, announced in September 1949, were inescapable: despite the earlier concerted rejection of the Marshall Plan, a communist state was accepting Western aid. When, at the meeting of the UN General Assembly later that autumn, the Yugoslav delegate openly attacked the Soviet Union for its hegemonic designs, the Western powers retained even fewer inhibitions about embracing Tito. Washington's courtship proceeded with the relaxation of credit and export controls, the granting of outright economic aid, support for Yugoslavia's short-run membership in the Security Council, and a military aid program that began in 1951. However, it did not go so far as to explicitly extend the Truman Doctrine to Yugoslavia; the closest approximation to such a commitment was made in December 1949 by the newly appointed American ambassador, George V. Allen, who, after meeting with the president, told the press that the United States was "just as opposed to aggression against that country as against any other, and just as favorable to the retention of Yugoslavia's sovereignty."[193] In practice, the American policy became to "keep Tito afloat" economically and to assist in the strengthening of his northern defenses. Strategically, Yugoslavia's defection represented a significant improvement in the West's position in the Mediterranean area, but its political benefits proved to be rather limited. Expectations that the Titoist virus would spread to the satellites and inspire other secessionist movements were soon shaken by a spate of purges that liquidated or imprisoned such alleged "Titoists" as Rajk in Hungary, Slansky in Czechoslovakia, Kostov in Bulgaria, Gomulka in Poland, and Xoxe in Albania; thus, the immediate effect of Tito's apostasy and the West's enthusiastic reaction was a reaffirmation of the satellite parties' allegiance to Moscow. Subsequently, the survivors of these purges made a comeback in certain satellites, but they never succeeded in duplicating Tito's version of national communism; as will be seen, such experiments in voluntarism and decompression invariably ended in a reassertion of Soviet suzerainty. Nevertheless, in the late forties and early fifties, American support for Tito, implying as it did that his system would be an acceptable intermediate stage in the weaning of the satellites, appeared eminently suited to the strategy of containment.

In restricting American trade with East-Central Europe the Truman administration resorted to its last remaining punitive tool, all the while maintaining that it was acting out of strategic necessity. Despite the agreements reached in 1947 by the Great Powers, the United States failed in its efforts to get compensation for nationalized or destroyed American property in the satellites. This and many hostile acts of the communist regimes prompted the administration to impose stringent trade controls; beginning on March 1, 1948, applications for export licenses were subjected to screening by an interdepartmental committee and by the secretary of commerce, with a view to eliminating all goods necessary to the development of the key satellite industries—in particular, of those with a military orientation. Exports of similar items to countries participating in the European Recovery Program were also banned if they were to be re-exported to East-Central Europe. The restrictions had an immediate effect: U.S. exports to the satellites fell from an annual rate of $400 million in the second quarter of 1947 to an annual rate of $125 million in the third quarter of 1948.[194] Ensuing bilateral trade agreements between the Soviet Union and the satellites and the creation of COMECON in 1949 were only incidentally encouraged by this policy, while the West Europeans, notably the British, stepped into the gap and actually increased their trade with the East. America's allies (Belgium, Britain, France, Italy, Luxemburg, and the Netherlands, later followed by nine others) did join in a Consultative Group which in turn set up a Coordinating Committee; from January 1950 the Coordinating Committee met periodically to revise the strategic embargo against the Soviet bloc. With the outbreak of the Korean War, congressional and public hostility to the communist world reached a peak and led to the "Battle Act" of 1951, which aimed to "impede the ability of nations threatening the security of the United States to conduct military operations," as well as to assist America's allies and reduced even further the West's trade with the satellites; it made the granting of aid contingent upon the recipient's agreement to abide by Washington's increasingly inclusive embargo. The multilateral controls eventually comprised three lists of goods that were either prohibited, under quantitative restrictions, or under "surveillance."[195] (The U.S. Senate would attempt to impose even more stringent controls the following year with the so-called Kem Amendment.) By 1952, American exports to East-Central Europe—excluding Yugoslavia—had dwindled to a yearly total of less than $6 million. While understandable as a political reaction to communist militancy, this restrictive trade policy made little economic sense, particularly in light of the constraints it imposed upon the West Europeans; indeed, it only accommodated Moscow's determination to isolate the satellites from the West and make them economically dependent upon—and exploitable by—the Soviet Union.

Another weapon of the cold war, propaganda, had been seized upon with enthusiasm in Washington as the ideal answer to a number of needs and pressures. Propaganda could serve as a symbolic outlet for the moral fervor of the anticommunist masses and, in particular, of the East European émigrés; it could also, in keeping with the scenario of containment, hasten the decay and disintegration of the Soviet empire. The flagging spirits of the satellite peoples would meanwhile be revived by assurances of American good will and commitment to their ultimate liberation. As Secretary of State Acheson observed on February 24, 1950: "We do not regard the people of Eastern Europe as responsible for the deterioration in our relations with their governments. . . . This country will maintain undiminished its concern for their rights and their welfare."[196] Normal means of reaching the East Europeans were progressively eliminated by the Stalinist regimes in their drive to isolate their subjects from the West. The borders were closed to all but a few official travelers in either direction, contact with the remaining diplomats and other foreigners was actively discouraged, the operation of Western information services was curtailed, and the inflow of printed matter was reduced to a trickle; however, these measures only heightened the East Europeans' thirst for untainted information, as well as for indications that the West was actively concerned with their liberation. The United States therefore resorted to the airwaves as the last remaining channel for communicating with the overwhelmingly anticommunist masses in the satellites.

Having originated in World War II, the Voice of America (VOA) carried on its operations in the context of the cold war. Initially, the VOA's programming was fairly objective in nature, emphasizing official speeches and communiqués, and as such it performed less a propagandistic than a straight informative function (which was even more the case with the BBC's East European services). In 1948, with the Iron Curtain firmly down, appropriations for the VOA were increased and the agency was reorganized to give "harder-hitting but still factual propaganda" on the theme of democracy versus totalitarianism.[197] It soon became apparent, however, that a purely official information organ was insufficient. Moreover, the relationship between the U.S. government's information agencies and émigré politicians was a source of embarrassment to the State Department. Thus, it was to provide a new propaganda outlet free of the drawbacks of direct identification with the U.S. government that in June 1949 a number of public and private notables, including ex-ambassador Joseph C. Grew, gathered to form the Committee for a Free Europe (FEC). The committee, wrote John Foster Dulles at the time, had as one purpose to "give aid and asylum to leading political exiles from Central Europe."[198] The State Department had been instrumental in the committee's establishment, with George Kennan in particular advocating a nonofficial solution to the dilemma of recognizing the communist regimes while maintaining the morale of émigré politicians, and Secretary of State Acheson proved amenable to this solution.[199]

The FEC's principal undertaking became the establishment of facilities for broadcasting to the East European area. The chairman of the Crusade for Freedom (the FEC's financing arm), General Clay, announced in May 1951 that the aim of the projected Radio Free Europe (RFE) was to "help those trapped behind the curtain to prepare for the day of liberation." "What we wanted to do," observed FEC president C. D. Jackson later that year, "was to create conditions of turmoil in the countries our broadcasts reached."[200] Meanwhile, in October, Radio Free Europe went on the air. The creation of RFE was simple enough, compared with the question of how its programming should differ from the VOA line. A contemporary analyst, observing correctly that the East Europeans needed not lectures on the value of freedom but assurances of Western determination to restore their right to national self-determination, concluded with the perhaps inevitably equivocal warning that it was as dangerous to hold out the promise of early liberation as to set the prospect of liberation beyond the listener's life span.[201] Faced with the problem of reconciling containment's evolutionary perspective with the aspirations of an audience only too ready to grasp at a promising statement, the FEC's crusaders opted for a potentially perilous optimism; a chronicler of Radio Free Europe concedes that in its early years RFE tended to function as a "prophet of early liberation."[202] In fact, the very existence of Radio Free Europe raised the question of whether a democratic government could afford to have an official and an unofficial foreign policy. The FEC was a brainchild of the U.S. government, and there is no doubt that it was the recipient, by covert channels, of public funds; consequently, RFE could well be called an "officially unofficial" instrument of statecraft.[203] Yet the intention to create conditions of turmoil went beyond the logic of containment, unless it was expected that such conditions would by themselves cause the Soviet monolith to crumble—or unless the Truman administration was willing to sacrifice the lives of East Europeans in order to impede Stalin's consolidation of his East European dependencies into a base for westward aggression (there is no evidence of such a Machiavellian motivation). Since official policy in the Truman era entertained no notion of imminent liberation by Western intervention, it can be argued that the administration should not have permitted even an ostensibly unofficial propaganda organ to prompt such dangerous illusions.

Although Radio Free Europe was welcomed by satellite peoples and by leading émigrés, to whom it offered employment, a chance to fight communism, and an implicit promise of eventual liberation and a return to their homelands, it represented a mere palliative to those exiled politicians who had hoped that the West would allow them to form governments-in-exile. For instance, in November 1947 the former president of the Hungarian National Assembly, Msgr. Béla Varga, announced the creation, with other refugee politicians, of a Hungarian National Council in New York; he argued that the council was a legal continuation of the Hungarian Parliament and that its Executive Committee filled the role of a government-in-exile.[204] This and similar initiatives concerned chiefly the United States, which would become the mecca for shadow governments, much as London had been during the war. But unhappy memories of wartime émigré politics and, at least in the late 1940s, a lingering hope that some settlement might be reached with the Russians regarding East-Central Europe deterred the Truman administration from recognizing any extraterritorial governments. The presence of the exiled and broadly representative politicians could not be ignored, however, particularly in view of the sizable East European ethnic groups and the growing anticommunist sentiment of the American public. (On May 1, 1949, more than 100,000 participated in a Manhattan Loyalty Day parade, mainly in protest against the Soviet Union's domination over the satellites.) Accordingly, the Committee for a Free Europe was set up as a diplomatic buffer to nurture and channel into productive endeavors the aspirations and energies of the émigré leaders without directly involving the U.S. government. For all that, the exiles did not curtail their lobbying, however, and busied themselves preparing analyses of prevailing conditions in their homelands and drafting plans for the future of East-Central Europe. In June 1952, at a meeting sponsored by the FEC, émigrés representing ten now-communist states (Albania, Bulgaria, Czechoslovakia, Estonia, Hungary, Latvia, Lithuania, Poland, Rumania, and Yugoslavia) issued the "Williamsburg Declaration," which, like the Philadelphia Declaration of the previous year, pledged a wide range of fundamental rights and economic and political reforms in their countries following the liberation of the latter; in an address to the meeting, former Undersecretary of State Adolf A. Berle, Jr., called for a united Central Europe within a United States of Europe. However remote the prospect of achieving any of these aims was, the *New York Times* was justified in claiming in its editorial columns that "these men at Williamsburg can be certain that opinion in this country and throughout the free world stands behind them."[205]

Beyond the tactics discussed above, none of which—apart from the occasional propagandistic flight of fancy—anticipated an early change in the status of the satellites, there lay the shadowy sphere of revolutionary subversion. Despite the Russian test of an atomic device in September 1949, America's strategic superiority remained unchallenged for several years thereafter, and it is therefore conceivable that, with Western coordination and assistance, popular revolts in East-Central Europe might have met with success. The risks were great, however, for most of the territory was densely populated and unsuitable for guerrilla warfare, and in order to deter repression the United States would have had to aim a credible atomic threat at the Soviet Union itself rather than at the satellites. In the event, tactical weakness on the Continent and a reluctance even to consider utilizing atomic weapons dissuaded the Truman administration from adopting such an aggressive policy, and its intelligence services limited their activities to maintaining contact with émigrés and the scattered oppositional elements in East-Central Europe. The one exception to this essentially passive posture was the Albanian farrago, a protracted and catastrophic undercover operation which the United States has not officially acknowledged to this day; revelations in the wake of the Philby affair leave little doubt as to its authenticity, however.[206]

Albania's annexation by Italy in April 1939 had not been recognized by the United States, and, when in early 1945 the communist partisans of Enver Hoxha set up the National Liberation Front as a provisional government, Washington dispatched an informal mission to investigate the political situation. The United States made recognition conditional upon the holding of free elections, but the Albanians declined to reply and held the customary communist single-list election on December 2, 1945; the informal U.S. mission was subsequently withdrawn and the matter of recognition was postponed indefinitely.[207] The following year the British, partly in the hope of relieving communist pressure on the Greek government, decided to mount a subversive operation in Albania under the aegis of their Secret Intelligence Service (SIS). The original plan was to airdrop reinforcements to the royalists in the Mati region of central Albania and to launch a guerrilla campaign and civil war that might spark similar revolts throughout the Balkans. By 1949, however, all that had been achieved were some isolated acts of sabotage, while the Balkan situation had altered owing to Tito's defection, the decline of communist resistance in Greece, and the large influx of Soviet advisers to Albania. With the concurrence of the U.S. State Department and the grudging agreement of British Foreign Secretary Bevin, plans were then drawn up for a new, Anglo-American operation to be executed by the SIS and the Central Intelligence Agency (CIA). Isolated from the Soviet Union, bordering on Greece and a neutral Yugoslavia, and accessible by sea, Albania was, geographically at least, a likely candidate for liberation, although in political terms the championing of the ineffectual "royalists" against the communists made ludicrous the State Department's private rationalization that it was furthering the cause of national self-determination. Nevertheless, an Albanian National Committee was created in New York, while in Cairo exiled King Zog was prevailed upon to send his more trusted followers to training camps on Cyprus and Malta and in Germany. For two years, beginning in the spring of 1950, small groups of guerrillas infiltrated by air and sea and across the Greek border; instead of being welcomed by enthusiastic royalists, however, they were almost invariably met by the guns of the Russians and the local militia. The total failure of the operation was not surprising, in view of the identity of the SIS coordinator, Kim Philby, who turned out to have been a double agent and who ultimately escaped to the Soviet Union.

That neither the Western powers nor the Soviet Union chose to publicize this experiment in positive intervention is understandable, for the former bore heavy responsibility for a disastrous operation that cost the lives of several hundred agents, while the latter did not want the other

East Europeans to be encouraged by such Western initiatives. It is even less surprising that, when in the fall of 1951 some Czech dissidents sent word that they were prepared to revolt, the Americans firmly advised against such action and said there was no chance of gaining U.S. assistance.[208] Despite the secret Albanian venture and mounting domestic pressures—manifested notably in the Kersten Amendment, which will be discussed in the next chapter—the Truman administration remained faithful to an interpretation of the strategy of containment that envisaged no drastic or early alteration of the *status quo* in East-Central Europe.

III

VARIATIONS ON LIBERATION

A foreign policy, to be successful,
must be commensurate with the power
available to carry it out.
                    HANS J. MORGENTHAU

Never befriend the oppressed unless
you are prepared to take on the
oppressor.
                    OGDEN NASH

Although the policy of containment dominated American foreign policy in the years 1947–1952, a wide range of adverse views found spokesmen at its very inception. According to the director of the State Department's Office of Public Affairs, the basic strategy for victory could be summed up as maintaining strength until the inherent weaknesses of the Soviet system caused it to disintegrate.[1] Opposition to this approach arose from three main sources. First, from the Left came voices such as that of Henry Wallace deploring the hard, uncompromising attitude toward Soviet communism; since Stalinism was at its zenith in East-Central Europe throughout this period, such criticism failed to strike a responsive chord either in the administration or with the general public, while Mao Tse-tung's victory in China and the subsequent invasion of South Korea made the already fragmented American Left only more impotent. Second, opposition arose on the grounds that containment was purely defensive and therefore, in the face of a revolutionary ideology, self-defeating. Finally, a variation of this second argument came from isolationists who, while sternly anticommunist, disliked the idea of a protracted struggle that would require great expenditures and a constant American involvement in world affairs. As the years went by, these last two schools of thought gathered adherents until in 1952 they approached the status of a new orthodoxy and gave rise to a new myth of liberation.

ATTACKS ON CONTAINMENT

Containment thus came under attack both for its aggressive stance and for its timidity. The first salvo was fired by Walter Lippmann, who misread some of Kennan's recommendations but nevertheless reflected widely held apprehensions. Lippmann's basic complaint was that the optimistic assumption of the eventual decay of Soviet power did not offer a sound premise upon which to build a foreign policy; he charged that "on [Kennan's] own showing, the policy cannot be made to work unless there are miracles and we get all the breaks."[2] Another prominent critic, the scholar-publicist James Burnham, echoed this view: "The strange truth is that the policy of containment has no goal. . . . Its inner law is: let history do it."[3] This apparent lack of initiative became the focus of the oppositional mainstream. To Lippmann, containment meant that "for ten or fifteen years Moscow, not Washington, would define the issues, would make the challenges, would select the ground where the conflict was to be waged, and would choose the weapon";[4] the subsequent crises over Berlin and in Korea only lent credence to his allegation. In deploring that the policy "excludes initiation of any action within the Soviet sphere," Burnham voiced another variation on the same theme.[5]

One historian later claimed that containment had been "psychologically and emotionally in contradiction with American values and experience in foreign affairs"—in other words, that a clear-cut choice between non-involvement and total commitment leading to an early solution would have been more appropriate.[6] Even Burnham believed that in the early stages there was no alternative to containment: "As a temporary expedient, there was something to be said for containment. In 1946–7 the United States and its friends were not politically, morally or intellectually prepared to undertake a positive strategy against Soviet power."[7] The long-run aspect of containment was less acceptable to its critics; Lippmann, among others, claimed that American military power was suited not to a "policy of shifts and manoeuvres" but rather to a "policy which has as its objective a decision and a settlement."[8]

From the very beginning, the status of East-Central Europe had drawn the attention of the critics of containment. On this question, Lippmann stood closer to Kennan in deploring that the United States had "guaranteed" Stalin's pledges regarding the area even though it lacked the power to compel their implementation, but most of the others saw the policy's shortcomings in a different light. Burnham typified this more aggressive approach: "By renouncing offensive action, containment abandons the satellite nations to Moscow. This implication of containment, which does not escape the Kremlin or the peoples of the satellite nations, helps create a political climate favorable to the consolidation of Moscow's control over the satellites and their integration into the Soviet system."[9] The communization of East-Central Europe came as an unpleasant surprise to the United States, where official opinion during the war had maintained that, at worst, that part of Europe would evolve into an ideological compromise between East and West. By 1948, however, there could be no question regarding the exclusiveness of Soviet hegemony in the area, and in the public mind the violations of wartime agreements became the symbols, as one observer put it, both of Russian perfidy and of American gullibility. A gradualist policy, no matter how wellfounded and realistic, was bound to suffer in such a political atmosphere.

Containment was attacked not only by independent observers. The "Great Debate" of the early 1950s also involved politicians and military men, and all the more so after the Russian A-bomb test, detected in September 1949, and the communist takeover in China shattered public confidence in America's invincibility and strategic posture. After a spell of isolationism on the part of some Republicans in the war years, the early postwar period had seen an excellent display of bipartisanship in foreign policy. Led by Senator Vandenberg, the Republican majority in both houses of Congress from 1946 to 1948 supported the Truman administration's stiffening stand against Moscow, a stand which received public approval in the 1948 elections, and Vandenberg proved to be instrumental in the success of the Marshall Plan and of the Greek-Turkish aid program. This bipartisan consensus did not, however, survive Vandenberg's death and the subsequent reverses suffered by the West.

What has been called a "nationalist-isolationist" sentiment gathered strength in 1950, and both Acheson and the State Department were subjected to a mounting barrage of criticism. Senator Joseph McCarthy, encouraged by many of his fellow Republicans and assisted by a team of investigators that included the notorious Cohn-Schine duo, launched virulent attacks upon that institution. McCarthy's conspiratorial theory regarding American setbacks perhaps found some minor justification in the Hiss trial, but was carried to extremes in his denunciations and allegations of treason in high places. At the time, popular support for McCarthyism was far from negligible, and the traumatic effect of China's loss was partially responsible for this. Although containment had never been explicitly defined to include China, Acheson and his department were blamed for that loss. In Congress, Republican caucuses pressed for the dismissal of the secretary of state, and an attempt was made to oust him by eliminating his salary from the State Department's budget.

In time the entire concept of containment—or, rather, misconceptions of that policy—came under attack. Public opinion had concurrently acquired an ambivalence that assisted the opponents of containment. On the one hand, there existed an impatience with anything but a dynamic and positive American strategy that would quickly nullify all external threats and the encroachments of communism along the periphery of the Soviet Union; on the other hand, there was a growing desire for relief from constant foreign involvement and for a reduction in American commitments and expenditures. The Republican party, its conservative-isolationist wing in particular, took advantage of both of these reactions. Its leaders, like Hoover and Taft, achieved the remarkable feat of appearing at once more aggressive and more isolationist than the Democratic administration.[10] One prominent proponent of this line was the much-respected senator from Wisconsin, Alexander Wiley, who took up the familiar charge regarding containment's alleged passivity: "The time is overdue for us to stop following a mere 'pantywaist' diplomacy—a mere wordy Voice of America program." Urging that the United States sponsor revolutions behind the Iron Curtain, Wiley suggested a "commando-type program of psychological and revolutionary penetration, including the use of 'silver bullets'—money." He argued that the rule of terror in the satellites had created "fertile ground for our liberal distribution of arms for vengeance," and that to foment unrest inside the bloc would detract from the Soviet Union's ability to wage war elsewhere; to implement this policy, Wiley proposed the appointment of a "commando-type leader with audacity and imagination" and a "board of revolutionary strategy consisting of the ablest experts in military science, experts in ethnic groups," all of whom would then work in close collaboration with the State Department, the Joint Chiefs of Staff, and the Central Intelligence Agency.[11] The senator failed to make clear whether the sole goal of his proposed revolts would be to divert Soviet attention from other objectives, or whether eventual liberation of the satellites was to follow. His statement was significant in that, for all its cloak-and-dagger extremism, it stopped short of engaging the United States in the provision of direct assistance in the event of a revolution; one must also surmise that the senator was unaware of the subversive operations against Albania then in progress.

What appeared to be a partial implementation of Senator Wiley's proposals came about through the efforts of another Wisconsin Republican, Congressman Charles J. Kersten. The occasion was the drafting in 1951 of a Mutual Security Program aimed at providing military and other assistance to countries friendly to the United States. Kersten testified at the preliminary hearings on July 25. Asserting that "unless the Soviet regime is undermined, subverted and overthrown it will bring us war," he advocated a number of concrete steps that would lead to the liberation of East-Central Europe. His first proposal—that the United States withdraw recognition from the Soviet Union and the satellite regimes and force (he did not specify how) the expulsion of the former from the United Nations—aroused little support at the hearings, but his further suggestion—that the United States grant asylum to all refugees from the satellites and incorporate escapees into a European Army—was well received. Confident that "Polish legions" or "Hungarian legions" would have tremendous propaganda value, Kersten went on to recommend that the United States "let the people behind the iron curtain know that we will do everything we can to work for their eventual liberation," and that "when the time is opportune we should actually assist the people behind the iron curtain to liberate themselves."[12] These suggestions went far beyond the bounds of containment and Secretary Acheson's general remarks at Berkeley the previous year, but they were nonetheless symptomatic of congressional, and more particularly Republican, disenchantment with official policy. It is interesting to note that Kersten also echoed another common Republican complaint when he deplored the great cost of the Mutual Security Program. Thus both the short-range and long-term aspects of containment received their share of criticism.

Congressional sympathy for Kersten's views—if not for each of his specific proposals—became evident when on October 10 the so-called Kersten Amendment was approved as an integral part of the Mutual Security Act. The amendment allocated $100 million in European military assistance funds "for any selected persons who are residing in or escapees from [the Soviet Union and the satellites] either to form such persons into elements of the military forces supporting the North Atlantic Treaty Organization or for other purposes."[13] Speaking in Congress after the approval of the Act, Kersten reasserted the aggressive intent behind his initiative:

> In this cold war against communism, we must do more than merely try to contain it. In [the Kersten Amendment] . . . we have the opportunity of taking the offensive in the cold war. Let us make some trouble for Joe Stalin in his own back yard.[14]

"Joe Stalin" did not tarry long in protesting at this provocative piece of legislation. The first note came on November 21, two days after an American aircraft was forced down in Hungary; it charged that the $100 million "are destined to finance subversive activities of persons and armed groups which [are] directed against the Soviet Union and other governments mentioned in the law."[15]

Washington's reply of December 19 maintained that "assistance of this nature is in keeping with the traditional United States policy of helping victims of oppression, in this instance those of Eastern Europe who have escaped or may escape to the free world," and stressed the defensive nature of NATO and of the Mutual Security Act.[16] Meanwhile, on November 22, the Soviet Union took the matter to the United Nations, asking the General Assembly's Political and Security Committee to consider the "aggressive acts of the United States of America and its interference in domestic affairs of other countries, as instanced by the appropriation of $100 million to pay for the recruitment of persons and the organization of armed groups in the Soviet Union, Poland, Czechoslovakia, Hungary, Rumania, Bulgaria, Albania, and a number of other democratic countries, as well as outside the territory of those countries."[17] American delegates repudiated the Soviet charges before the committee, stating that the real purpose of the amendment was "to assist refugees from political persecution to take part in the defense of the North Atlantic community," and that, in any event, no action had been taken by the administration up to that date, December 19.[18] One of the delegates, Representative Mike Mansfield, noting that the Soviet argument "rests on the assumption that the two words 'residing in' constitute a *prima facie* case of aggression and domestic interference," claimed that in reality the amendment applied only to those people who had already fled from the satellites.[19] The prevailing distribution of membership in the United Nations ensured that the Soviet charges would be defeated both in the Committee and in the General Assembly, as was the case on December 21, 1951, and January 11, 1952. The Soviet Union then sent a further note to Washington asserting that the Mutual Security Act defied the Soviet-American agreement of 1933 on noninterference in each other's internal affairs; Hungary and Poland followed suit in requesting abrogation of the Kersten Amendment.[20] All these protests were to no avail; a month earlier, Mansfield had emphatically denied any American violation of the Roosevelt-Litvinov agreement.[21]

The significance of the entire episode lay less in its diplomatic repercussions than in the cleavage it revealed between the Truman administration and Congress. Even before the passage of the appropriation bill, the former was busily burying the "liberation" aspects of Kersten's amendment. Subsequently, since the Mutual Security Act specified that the funds could be used at the president's discretion, the implementation of the amendment remained clouded in mystery. The 1953 report on the Mutual Security Act simply noted that "the President authorized the use of Kersten Amendment funds to help provide better facilities for the flood of escapees" and made mention of training and permanent resettlement.[22] According to unofficial reports, the administration also allocated some of these resources to aid in the escape of East European scientists and of other dissidents who wished to join NATO combat units with the aim of ultimately liberating their homelands. In fact, 1952 did see the creation of a small Special Forces unit (a precursor of the "Green Berets"); stationed in West Germany, it was composed mainly of East European refugees who would be trained in guerrilla warfare.[23]

There is little doubt that news of the Kersten Amendment aroused new hopes in the satellites, much as the Truman Doctrine had raised a flurry of false expectations four years earlier. The wording of the amendment renewed misapprehensions behind the Iron Curtain regarding American intentions. There and elsewhere in the world the amendment proved to be a source of embarrassment to Truman and Acheson, whose idea of containment stood in contradistinction to the crusading spirit of Kersten and his supporters. The administration tended to interpret the amendment moderately—notably, in its statements at the United Nations concerning the use of the funds—but the immediate impact could hardly be minimized; as one observer noted at the time, "the news of the hundred million dollars has travelled around the world and has assumed the proportions and weight of an army."[24] That the Kersten Amendment and the strong congressional reaction it represented ran contrary to the theory and practice of containment is obvious. This reaction found its logical outcome in the Republican "liberation" policy of 1952.

The question whether American foreign policy makers had any alternatives regarding East-Central Europe in the period 1948–1952 was touched on in Chapter II. To recapitulate, a twofold premise underlay the West's strategy: the Soviet Union was seen as inherently aggressive and therefore a threat to the *status quo*, but it was understood that under no circumstances would the United States act as the aggressor. From this double premise flowed the essentially defensive policy of containment and the various measures to rebuild the economic and military strength of the West. In theory there were three not necessarily exclusive policy options: containment, negotiation, or liberation. A decisive confrontation between the Soviet Union and the United States with a view to rolling back Russian hegemony carried grave risks. On the military plane, America's atomic quasi monopoly was balanced by the vastly superior conventional military power of the Soviet Union in continental Europe. The attempts to remedy this conventional gap resulted in NATO, an essentially defensive structure, while the war that broke out in Korea on June 25, 1950, spread limited American military power even more thinly. As one analyst argued convincingly: "there probably never was a time when preventive war would have been technically—not to say politically—feasible. When we had the atomic monopoly we did not have enough power; and when we developed the necessary power we no longer had the monopoly."[25] On occasion voices were raised, mainly outside the United States, in favor of brandishing America's atomic arsenal to compel a Soviet withdrawal; Winston Churchill and even the philosopher Bertrand Russell, in a rare retreat from pacifism, were among those who made this drastic proposal. As a realistic option, atomic blackmail was little short of fanciful. The inherent reluctance of a democracy to launch an offensive war would have been one key obstacle. Moreover, no American politician or pundit was prepared to take up the cry for atomic war; even the costly Korean conflict was waged solely with conventional arms, despite MacArthur's call for atomic retaliation. A major revolution in American attitudes would have been required for such risks to have been taken over East-Central Europe, where Soviet hegemony presented only a marginal threat to American security.

The prospects for altering the status of the satellites through negotiation were almost as dim as the chances for a war of liberation. From Washington's perspective, the relative political and military weakness of the West necessitated a period of consolidation undisturbed by potentially divisive and futile negotiations with the Kremlin, and this, together with what one scholar termed the "normal inertia of a democracy in foreign policy," led to the pursuit of the defensive strategy of containment.[26] Particularly after the formation of NATO, American policy with regard to East-Central Europe became in essence a *status quo* policy, and care was taken not to give the Russians the opposite impression. In its doctrinal rejection of negotiations, the Truman administration was not hampered by the critics of containment, most of whom—in Congress and outside— were equally convinced of the futility of talking to the Soviets.[27] Indeed, negotiation about the old promises of self-determination could scarcely have resulted in any relaxation of Soviet hegemony. Only on the question of German reunification was the West's fear of negotiation perhaps misplaced. Acting on their own premises, however, the decision makers in Washington concluded that between the Scylla of futile negotiations and the Charybdis of perilous war lay the path of containment.

THE DYNAMIC ALTERNATIVE

Attacks on containment were almost at their peak when President Truman delivered his last major message on the State of the Union. He referred to East-Central Europe in the following words:

> During the coming year, we must not forget the suffering of the people behind the Iron Curtain. In those areas, minorities are being oppressed,

human rights violated, religions persecuted. We should continue and expand the activities of the Voice of America, which brings our message of hope and truth to those peoples.[28]

This pious expression of concern no longer seemed to suffice at a time when containment was being subjected to criticism on grounds ranging from immorality to profligacy. Politically, Truman's policy was particularly vulnerable, for it envisaged victory over the Soviet Union only in the very distant future and appeared to be a policy less of action than of reaction to Soviet initiatives. For its critics, the temptation was great, in the election year of 1952, to offer easier and more popular solutions to the East-West deadlock.

Developments since the inception of containment were cited as evidence of its inadequacy and growing irrelevance. Wrote the editors of *Time*:

> The containing policy sickened as the free world realized that there was more wrong with Communism than its etiquette, and that it was probably strong enough to survive Stalin. Containment was doomed the day Americans realized that the Kremlin could make and deliver atomic bombs.[29]

In addition, critics of the Truman policy argued that, since Soviet power had grown to the extent that the Russians could start local wars almost anywhere in the noncommunist orbit, it was imperative that the United States take the initiative and "roll back" communism. The implementation of such proposals received less-careful attention, however. For instance, a military commentator called for a "strategic progression" whereby the example of a free and prosperous Germany and Austria would effect a "moral influence" sufficient to make Czechoslovakia break away from the Soviet bloc and be followed inevitably by Hungary and the other satellites.[30] Such wishful thinking was much in evidence throughout the long debate on foreign policy.

Most of the detractors of containment aimed, in the words of the French philosopher-sociologist Raymond Aron, at a caricature of the policy rather than at its reality.[31] Thus, in the course of the 1952 presidential campaign, Congressman Kersten demanded that containment should not endure, because it was "immoral and unchristian to negotiate a permanent agreement with forces which by every religious creed and moral precept are evil." He went on to charge that the policy was "un-American, because it violates the principle of the American Declaration of Independence"; that it would lead to World War III; and, last but not least, that it was an uneconomical strategy.[32] Such perceptions permeated the political grass roots. As the director of the State Department's Policy Planning Staff later wrote, "by the summer of 1952 the evolution of our policy had outrun public understanding and support."[33] It was the good fortune of the Republican party to be able to take advantage of the unpopularity of stalemate and of Acheson and his department, and in the heat of campaigning the Republicans did not shrink from laying the blame for the loss of East-Central Europe and of China on the Roosevelt and Truman administrations.

As was noted earlier, one of the chief ideological forebears of liberation was James Burnham, whose book *Containment or Liberation* advanced an alternative to the policies of Truman and Acheson. His views were even accepted abroad as being influential with the Republican policy makers; the respected Paris daily *Le Monde* called his book "without doubt the reference text of the new Administration," while *L'Humanité* attacked him as the "theoretician of American imperialism."[34] Burnham urged the concentration of America's efforts on the European heartland:

> So far as offensive action is concerned, action designed to weaken and defeat the opponent, an Eastern European concentration is the only strategy that can accomplish anything at all. . . . What the policy of liberation first and essentially means is a particular focus or perspective. . . . it means *the view that the key to the situation* is what happens and what can be made to happen in Eastern Europe.[35]

In his view the range of choice was restricted to appeasement, containment, and liberation. Containment, he argued, was a temporary expedient that had to lead to either of the other two alternatives, and, within the context of containment, American propaganda to East-Central Europe was ineffective, for it offered no ready solution. Since appeasement was an unthinkable alternative, future policy would have to involve a threefold commitment to liberation—"all-sided political warfare; auxiliary military and para-military actions where called for; adequate preparation for whatever military action may be required in the future."[36]

According to Burnham's blueprint, the captive nations were to be considered as allies, and, therefore, recognition was to be withdrawn from the ruling regimes in favor of governments-in-exile. Burnham also took up Kersten's call for the formation of military units under the flags of the nations of East-Central Europe and recommended that America express support for the principle of a Central European federation. While admitting that liberation presupposed the possibility of auxiliary military operations, Burnham denied that such intervention would precipitate a world conflict: "From Moscow's point of view, a mass revolt in part of her Empire, capable of spreading like fire in the dry season, is hardly a happy moment for starting a general war."[37] In Burnham's opinion, the mere fact of putting the Kremlin on the defensive would be a positive achievement for the West; he emphasized that the "essential element of the policy of liberation is *the commitment to a goal.*"[38]

This ambivalence concerning the extent of America's operational commitment was shared by most of the proponents of liberation. When faced with the logical possibility of outright hostilities, they tended to retreat to a more modest brand of liberation couched in terms of national interest. Thus another critic of containment, William H. Chamberlin, asserted that the "important thing, from the standpoint of American interest, is to do everything in our power to hinder the consolidation of the communist empire."[39] Unless it was to be backed up by the military commitment that Burnham had suggested, however, this relatively pragmatic goal would have endangered the peoples of East-Central Europe.

The name that became most closely identified with liberation in the public's mind was, of course, John Foster Dulles. A Republican with many years of experience in foreign affairs, and one who was frequently consulted by the Truman administration, Dulles became the prime candidate for secretary of state even before his party held its presidential convention. Although he came to personify the widespread reaction to containment, he was not, as one historian suggests, forced into a proliberation posture by the national mood.[40] As early as 1949, he had urged the Truman administration to take the offensive and to assure the peoples of East-Central Europe that their liberation was a goal of American foreign policy.[41] This idea had been elaborated upon to some extent in a book published the following year, in which he had argued that it was "time to think in terms of taking the offensive in the world struggle for freedom and of rolling back the engulfing tide of despotism."[42] While conceding that during the war it would have been difficult for the United States to insist more forcefully on freedoms that were denied within the Soviet Union itself, he saw no reason for further restraint. "The Communist structure is overextended, over-rigid, and ill founded. It could be shaken if the difficulties that are latent were activated." But, he went on:

> "Activation" does not mean open revolt. The people have no arms, and violent revolt would be futile. It would be worse than futile, for it would precipitate massacre. . . . We have no desire to weaken the Soviet Union at the cost of the lives of those who are our primary concern.[43]

This warning presaged the dilemma that would face him in two separate crises.

Clearly, then, it was not a new or uncharacteristic position that Dulles adopted in his election-year article, "A Policy of Boldness."[44] In this, his most authoritative and comprehensive statement on liberation, he reiterated the charge that prevailing policies were negative and fruitless, "merely reactions to some of the many Soviet threats."[45] It is interesting to note that, at a time when the arch isolationist, Senator Taft, was still in the running for the Republican nomination, Dulles criticized the isolationist stand for assuming that the United States was lacking in strength rather than misusing it; by then Dulles had committed himself to support the candidacy of General Eisenhower.

The alternative advanced by Dulles required, first, a military establishment capable of instant retaliation, and then, with this in hand, a political offensive by the United States. His profound concern with moral precepts was very much in evidence in the assumptions that underlay the proposed offensive; thus he asserted that "the dynamic prevails over the static," that "non-material forces are more powerful than those that are merely material," and that "there is a moral or natural law not made by man which determines right and wrong and in the long run only those who conform to that law will escape disaster." He added: "We should let these truths work in and through us. We should be *dynamic*, we should use *ideas* as weapons; and these ideas should conform to *moral* principles."[46]

Claiming that secret work then in progress to promote liberation was inadequate, Dulles insisted that such a goal could not be attained "*unless the United States makes it publicly known that it wants and expects liberation to occur.* The mere statement of that wish and expectation would change, in an electrifying way, the mood of the captive peoples. It would put heavy new burdens on the jailers and create new opportunities for liberation."[47] As means to this end, he suggested that a number of steps be taken by the United States. These included the declaration of liberation as a peaceful goal of American policy; the creation in the free world of political "task forces" of reliable émigrés who would develop a freedom program for each satellite; assistance in the escape of such men; the coordination of Radio Free Europe and the Voice of America with this freedom program; the coordination of America's cultural, economic, and commercial relations with the program; the cutting of diplomatic relations with the satellites if and when such action would promote the freedom programs; and the gaining of free world support for a "great new Declaration of Independence"[48] regarding the satellites. Dulles was careful to repeat his earlier denial that this strategy might set off revolts:

> We do not want a series of bloody uprisings and reprisals. There can be peaceful separation from Moscow, as Tito showed, and enslavement can be made so unprofitable that the master will let go his grip. . . . we can be confident that within two, five or 10 years substantial parts of the present captive world can peacefully regain national independence.[49]

This passage, in view of subsequent developments, is a critical one, for it brings to light Dulles' view that Titoism in the satellites might represent a satisfactory evolution as far as the liberation policy was concerned; it also illustrates his emphasis on *peaceful* means. Concluding his manifesto, Dulles justified the need for a new approach by asserting that "our policy makers have not found policies which would put us in command of the situation."[50] In sum, Dulles' views on foreign policy and East-Central Europe were formed well before 1952 and changed but little when he threw his energies into the campaign of that year.

THE POLITICS OF LIBERATION

A long commitment to bipartisanship in foreign policy was ended by John Foster Dulles when in March 1952 he resigned as adviser to President Truman and immersed himself in election-year politics. He had inherited Vandenberg's mantle as the voice of responsible Republicanism in foreign affairs, and consequently his services and support were sought both by the Taft isolationists and by the more diffuse "internationalist" wing of the party, whose putative leader was General Eisenhower. Feeling more in sympathy with the latter faction, he sent Eisenhower a memorandum (which formed the basis of his subsequent *Life* article) outlining his two-fold alternative: the creation of a military deterrent capable of instant and massive retaliation, and liberation. Judging from his reply, Eisenhower was favorably impressed by Dulles' advocacy of a credible American deterrent; significantly, he did not reflect on the proposed program for liberation.[51]

Early in May, Dulles journeyed to Paris for a decisive meeting with Eisenhower. The two men conferred at Allied Headquarters in the company of General Lucius Clay, a prime mover behind Eisenhower's candidacy, and Dulles decided then to support the latter, despite his lack of interest in liberation. The future secretary of state was most impressed to learn from Clay that in the fall of 1951 word had been received through the intermediation of Radio Free Europe that the United States could stage a revolution in Czechoslovakia any day it wanted to, and that Washington had replied advising the potential rebels to desist since it did not have the means to assist them. Reflecting on this overture, Dulles said to *New York Times* correspondent C. L. Sulzberger: "What on earth could we do with it under the present circumstances?"[52] The incident only strengthened his conviction that the United States must acquire the power and strategy to deal with such eventualities.

In the 1948 election campaign, bipartisanship on foreign policy issues had continued to prevail, notwithstanding the occasional Republican allegation of unholy compacts at Yalta in congressional districts with substantial Polish-American voting blocs. After Dewey's defeat, however, his foreign policy adviser, Allen Dulles, had voiced regret that the party had eschewed national debate on Yalta, and the following three years had witnessed the rapid erosion of bipartisanship and the growing influence of the Republican party's conservative-isolationist wing, which came to play a prominent role in the propagation of the myths of a Democratic sellout at wartime conferences with the Russians, of communist subversion in the State Department, and of the Truman administration's mishandling of China and of the Korean campaign.[53] Foreign policy was clearly destined to play a key role in the 1952 primary and national presidential races.

In September 1951 Senator Taft led off with scathing denunciations of the Democratic record. With the support of both the Taft and Eisenhower factions, John Foster Dulles set about drafting his party's foreign policy planks, producing after eight weeks' work a program which differed little from his earlier writings and pronouncements. The night before the convention was to open in Chicago, General Clay expressed some concern that Dulles' stress on retaliatory striking power might be inconsistent with the requirements for a flexible response to future revolts in the satellites; he observed that the United States could not keep calling off possible uprisings unless it wished to see its East European friends lose faith or be imprisoned.[54] Otherwise, little comment was made on the apparent contradictions in Dulles' proposed strategy, for the latter accurately reflected the dominant, belligerent mood of the party. Indeed, the more moderate, "internationalist" faction and its candidate, General Eisenhower, prevailed at the convention only by trimming their sails to the crusading and grossly partisan line of the party's substantial Taft wing and by adding one of its proponents, Richard Nixon, to the presidential ticket. Senator McCarthy spoke in the spirit of the convention when he declared that the "Yalta-Teheran-Potsdam crowd must go."[55]

The foreign policy plank stood first and foremost in the Republican platform adopted on July 10.[56] It excoriated the Truman administration for having "abandoned friendly nations such as Latvia, Lithuania, Esthonia, Poland and Czechoslovakia to fend for themselves against the Communist aggression which soon swallowed them," and charged that the Democrats "profess to be following a defensive policy of 'containment' of Russian communism which has not contained it." The Republicans would therefore end this "negative, futile and immoral" policy and give the Voice of America a real function, that of carrying the message of liberation to the captive nations: "The policies we espouse will revive the contagious, liberating influences which are inherent in freedom. They will inevitably set up strains and stresses within the captive world which will make the rulers impotent to continue in their monstrous ways and mark the beginning of the end." The ringing tones of Dullesian rhetoric were unmistakeable. The platform also incorporated the popular chimera of a Democratic betrayal by promising that a Republican administration would "repudiate all commitments contained in secret understandings such as those of Yalta which aid Communist enslavements. . . . It will be made clear, on the highest authority of the President and the Congress, that United States policy, as one of its peaceful purposes, looks happily forward to the genuine independence of those captive peoples." The tactical nature of such concessions to the party's right wing would become evident less than a year later, when Eisenhower and Dulles were successfully to oppose formal repudiation.

If the Republican platform was aimed at attracting the masses of voters frustrated by the gradualism of containment and weary of the Korean bloodshed, its liberation plank had a more specific function. This was to gain the votes of the large number of Americans who had fled from communism or were simply of East European stock and concerned about the fate of their ancestral lands; considerable concentrations of this ethnic vote existed in the major conurbations of the Northeast and the Midwest, as well as in California. In order to regain ethnic support from the Democrats, the Republican National Committee in 1951 created an Ethnic Origins Division and chose the former ambassador to Poland, Arthur Bliss Lane, to head its Foreign Language Group Activities. A man of strong anti-communist convictions, Lane later recorded that he "had numerous talks with Foster Dulles in Chicago, urging him, not only because of the international importance but for political purposes also, to make [the liberation] plank as strong as possible."[57] During the campaign Lane was charged with mobilizing ethnic support; campaign pamphlets—notably, two entitled *Betrayal! Over 100,000,000 Eastern Europeans by the Democratic Administration*, and *Republican Policy of Liberation or Democratic Policy of Containment* (the latter being the reprint of an earlier Taft interview)—propagated the theme of the Democrats' callous disregard for the fate of the East European nations. Candidates in districts with heavy concentrations of Poles and other concerned ethnic groups exploited these issues, emphasizing that the Republicans had had no part in the alleged secret wartime agreements and promising their repudiation. The Republican presidential candidate proved noticeably reluctant to resort to such sensational charges, and he had to be pressured by the National Committee to stress liberation in his speeches;[58] but on occasion, such as in a Pulaski Day address in Denver on October 11, he would repeat the platform promise to repudiate the Yalta agreements.

Consensus on the theme of liberation and its utilization in the campaign turned out to be elusive. Being particularly conscious of the political usefulness of liberation, Dulles arranged for a meeting between one of its principal proponents, Congressman Kersten, and Eisenhower on August 13 in order to seal the bond between the party's two wings. The encounter proved to be only moderately successful, for at the ensuing press conference the presidential candidate's press secretary, James Hagerty, denied that Eisenhower fully subscribed to Kersten's more activist version of the policy.[59] But, however tenuous the consensus might have been on the operational aspects of liberation and repudiation, as general Republican objectives they acquired widespread currency in the campaign. The first major statement was made by Eisenhower in his address to the American Legion Convention in New York on August 25. He vowed that "the American conscience can never know peace until the millions in Soviet satellites are restored again to be masters of their own fate," but he emphasized that liberation would be implemented by "peaceful instruments."[60] Throughout the campaign Eisenhower was careful to refer to "peaceful liberation," a caution which was encouraged by at least one of his speech writers, Emmet Hughes, who recalls that he consciously avoided presumptuous and offensive words such as crusade and liberation.[61] It is less certain whether listeners at home and abroad caught these nuances, which revealed that the incoming administration was making no practical commitment to free the satellites.

The ambiguity was only enhanced by Dulles, who in the heat of the campaign proved to be less concerned with keeping the liberation policy well qualified. His messianic fervor was evident in some notes he drew up for a foreign policy discussion that summer:

> Our so called "containment" policy has not, in fact, contained Soviet Communism, which has been proceeding at least as rapidly as it ever expected in its programme of encirclement. Containment has, in fact, "contained" the dynamic spirit of America and the contagious love of freedom which has, up to now, made our nation the hope of the oppressed and the despair of the despots.[62]

At a meeting of the American Political Science Association in Buffalo on August 27, he outlined once again his blueprint for liberation.[63] After a presidential declaration that the United States would not concede East-Central Europe to Soviet hegemony, said Dulles, the Voice of America and other agencies would begin to stir up the satellite peoples and assure them of America's moral support. Resistance movements would then spring up and be assisted by air drops and other communications from private organizations such as the Committee for a Free Europe. As a result the communist regimes would disintegrate and the Soviet Union, faced with similar problems at home, would relinquish its newly acquired empire. Mutual Security director Averell Harriman also addressed the association, asserting that "liberation" had spread the fear of war in Europe, whereas the Truman administration's policies were aimed not only at containment but also at "helping our friends." Dulles attacked Harriman's statement in a press conference:

> It is nonsense for Mr. Harriman to say that General Eisenhower's liberation policy is a trap and would lead to premature uprisings and more Warsaw massacres. There was nothing premature about the Warsaw uprising. What was wrong was that the Russians double-crossed the Poles. To suggest any analogy between this treachery and the General's idea is unthinkable. The only trap I see, is that in the Democratic platform which says, they look forward to liberation of all these peoples but they aren't willing to do anything about it. That's a trap to get votes, but I don't think it will work.[64]

Various conclusions and inferences could be drawn from Dulles' pronouncements at Buffalo. One was that he seriously envisaged the formation and activation of underground movements, which in the moment of need would be assisted at least by so-called private agencies. Another was that a full-scale uprising would elicit American support sufficient to prevent repression—any other reaction being tantamount to "treachery."

These polemics went beyond Eisenhower's bland statements about peaceful liberation, and the General immediately checked with Dulles, since the latter's exaggerated version was potentially harmful to the election; Dulles conceded that on this occasion he had erred in the direction of oversimplification.[65] In Philadelphia, on September 4, Eisenhower reiterated his stand on the peaceful intent of liberation: "There is also need to bring hope and every peaceful aid to the world's enslaved peoples. We shall never be truculent—but we shall never appease." Dulles also felt compelled to issue a clarification on the same day:

> It is, of course, absurd to suggest that General Eisenhower anticipates invoking wholesale insurrection by unarmed slaves. Premature revolt would expose the patriotic peoples to liquidation. There are countless peaceful ways by which the task of the Russian despots can be made so unbearably difficult that they will renounce their rule. That was shown in Yugoslavia.[66]

Once again he had used the example of Titoism as an acceptable precedent, but without explaining how Yugoslavia's apostasy, the success of which was due to a unique set of factors, could be repeated in the satellites. The vagueness of the policy of liberation did not fail to strike many observers, and much of the campaign was taken up with mutual recrimination about the respective merits and shortcomings of liberation and containment. Dulles himself told a journalist that as an individual he could not subscribe to some of the statements in the platform, but that as a platform writer he was merely advancing the Republican case against the Democrats' failure to implement the principles of the Atlantic Charter.[67] Nevertheless, the record shows that, if Dulles overstated the case, he did not do so under any compulsion from his party.

The Democratic party was sensitive to the popular appeal of liberation, and its election platform asserted, although with less emphasis than its Republican counterpart, that the Democrats looked forward to the day when the peoples of East-Central Europe would be free once again. They were also aware of the importance of the ethnic vote. Said Truman to a group of Rumanian émigrés in May, "if I can continue our program which I have inaugurated, you are going to be a free country again, before you pass on to the next world." A few weeks later, he assured exiled premier Ferenc Nagy of Hungary that it was "a vital responsibility of free peoples throughout the world" to encourage and support the aspirations of the Hungarian people.[68] Nevertheless, the main thrust of the Democratic campaign was to discredit liberation. In speech after speech Adlai Stevenson warned against propaganda and secret agents and any idea of a war of liberation; he denied that either party could pledge to free the captive peoples in the foreseeable future and said that, instead, the United States must be prepared to "negotiate and initiate negotiations . . . by give and take."[69] The basic Democratic position, that nothing more could be done for the East Europeans by any means short of force, which in turn carried impossible risks, was spelled out by Truman as the campaign gathered steam:

> All Europeans know quite well that insurrection in the Soviet borderland these days could only be successful with armed support from the outside world. . . . To try to liberate these enslaved people at this time might well mean turning these lands into atomic battlefields.[70]

He concluded, predictably enough, that the Republicans wanted neither war nor insurrections but only votes.

As the popularity of liberation became more apparent, its opponents changed tack and tried to minimize the differences between it and containment. Speaking in September, Stevenson pleaded that the fate of the satellites "should never be an issue among Americans, for we are all united in our desire for their liberation from oppression and in confidence that freedom will once again be theirs."[71] Secretary of State Acheson, who had a proprietary interest in containment, although he later acknowledged that the word provided an inadequate description of his policies and actions, argued that the United States was doing "more" by building up the strength of the free nations and warned that the Republican alternative was a "positive prescription for disaster." He spoke contemptuously of being urged to be dynamic by those who had hitherto had their hands on the horn and their feet on the brakes, and he derided Dulles' "glittering adjectives."[72] The latter counterattacked the following day by claiming that the Republicans had never advocated liberation by force but intended rather to "dislocate, by peaceful measures, the internal structure of the Soviet empire."[73]

Yet the Republicans persisted in stressing the "dynamic" nature of their program. Eisenhower talked in October of his commitment to a "more dynamic foreign policy which, by peaceful means, will endeavour to bring about the liberation of the enslaved peoples."[74] A week later, the campaign hit a low point when Dulles charged that the Democrats were "careful to keep in a position where they could use the captive peoples as chips in some future poker game which they may play with Stalin."[75] He voiced faith in the abilities of the East Europeans to exploit the possibilities of a peaceful divorce from Moscow once they had become convinced of the determination of the United States not to barter them away. Eisenhower echoed this optimistic view by promising more intense psychological warfare; the United States must, he said, "give to those already enslaved hope that will enable them to continue resisting the oppressor until his hold can be gradually weakened, and loosened from within."[76]

Such was the confused and confusing debate on liberation in the election year of 1952. Equivocal promises and a few unguarded statements led many observers to attribute a warlike connotation to the policy; thus *New York Times* correspondent C. L. Sulzberger concluded that "what the Eisenhower Republicans would like to make very plain is that any such revolt of free peoples in the future would be supported by this country and Soviet intervention would be warned off with a clear threat that it would be met with American reprisals."[77] Although the Voice of America, faithful to administration policy, made a point of emphasizing that Eisenhower's foreign policy pronouncements contained no new practical ideas, the reaction from Europe was anguished and uncomprehending.[78] Commented the usually judicious London *Economist*, "Unhappily 'liberation' applied to Eastern Europe . . . means either the risk of war or it means nothing." Two weeks before the election, the same source noted that the liberation policy "sent shivers down every European spine and seemed to confirm the insidious propaganda that paints the clumsy Americans as the chief threat to peace."[79] The American press was aware of the unpopularity of liberation in Western Europe; the *New York Times* reported that Eisenhower and Dulles were "offering a new American policy that no European statesman could follow."[80]

European suspicions of Dulles' real intentions regarding liberation lingered for several years, but the people's fears waned as they came to realize the essentially hortatory function of his dynamism. Europe, observed the admittedly partisan *Washington Post*, "will discover that Mr. Eisenhower cannot change the grim facts of international life and therefore cannot appreciably change the foreign policy of the United States."[81] It is certainly plausible that most West Europeans, profiting from the economic assistance and the peaceful stalemate brought about by containment, were reluctant to take new risks. Some of the American "liberators," such as James Burnham, concluded that the Europeans were only waiting for an initiative from Washington and would willingly espouse a militant policy. There is evidence that this assessment of the mood of Western Europe was ill founded. The West Germans were to react with more apprehension than enthusiasm to the revolt of their compatriots in the eastern zone; and one-time French Foreign Minister Georges Bidault would say subsequently, probably with relief, that Dulles "surely never believed in rollback from the start."[82] In fact, America's European allies relaxed only when they realized to what extent liberation had been exaggerated in the heat of the campaign.

Was liberation merely a campaign issue? The answer depends largely on the definition of the term, and unfortunately it was never clearly defined during the campaign. One function that it did serve was to present the American voters with the alternative of a foreign policy apparently different from that of the Democrats. How different it was in reality can only be ascertained by examining its implementation. As a potentially operational policy, it was attacked by most ranking pundits and scholars. When George Kennan, back from his abortive stint as ambassador to Moscow, observed that one group adopted the approach of the gardener and the other that of the mechanic, he clearly favored the former.[83] Walter Lippmann maintained that containment had failed, but he branded the Republican proposals as dangerously misleading, contrasting prophetically the implied incitement to revolt with the actual reliance on propaganda and subversion—the latter being "measures short of war and not carrying . . . a commitment to go to war if the revolutionists we incited and financed were to rebel, were about to be crushed by the Red Army, and were appealing to their American liberators to come in and help liberate them."[84] But then he went on to recommend the encouragement of Titoism, a tactic that Dulles himself had advocated. The potential incompatibility of the Republicans' avowed goals of liberation and of budgetary stringency also aroused much adverse comment. Indeed, it was difficult to see how Dulles' policy of boldness could be implemented along with budgetary and tax cuts, but the party's campaigners blithely ignored such inconsistencies.

Upon close examination the GOP's commitment to liberation yielded little beyond the old policy of psychological warfare stiffened by a vaguely new "dynamic approach," and editorial support for the policy also wallowed in generalities:

> If there is one practical lesson our diplomats have learned these last six years, it is that primeval toughness and a willingness to meet force with force are the only diplomatic stance that influences the Soviets at all.[85]

However misplaced, the primary role played by foreign policy in the 1952 campaign ensured that liberation would be taken seriously by many Americans as well as by the people who lived in East-Central Europe. The policy's most vociferous protractors were conservative politicians like Knowland, Jenner, and McCarthy, and the majority of émigré leaders also were seduced by its crusading optimism. The actual electoral benefits of the policy have never been conclusively ascertained. Among the East European ethnic groups it unquestionably struck a responsive chord, and subsequent voting studies showed a marked swing in the allegiance of Polish-American and other ethnic voters to the Republican party;[86] within the electorate at large, the personal appeal of the Republican candidate and his eventual promise to go to Korea and bring the armistice negotiations to a successful conclusion had a much greater impact. In retrospect, to the extent that liberation was calculated to win votes, it fulfilled this domestic political function only marginally.

Even if, for most Republicans, liberation was a handy campaign issue, arising logically out of the prevailing frustration with containment, to dismiss the policy as sheer political opportunism would be unfair to Dulles. What one historian termed his Wilsonian missionary passion, his moralistic approach to international politics, suffused Dulles' advocacy of liberation, and in this respect, at least, his sincerity was unquestionable.[87] He upheld an old and worthy anti-imperialist morality that had been codified in the wartime declarations, then neglected by the *Realpolitik* of the division of Europe into spheres of influence. His moralism appeared, however, to be tainted with an underestimation of Soviet power in East-Central Europe and with a legalistic view of Soviet obligations in that area; Hans Morgenthau pinpointed this bias bordering on self-delusion when he described it as the idea that with "the legalistic insistence upon the violations of the Yalta agreement we could build a bridge between our utopian ideals and the bitter realities of power politics."[88] The question of whether Dulles ever seriously contemplated the direct use of American power to affect the fate of the satellites has no conclusive answer. In his writings he carefully circumscribed the extent to which the United States would involve itself in the actual act of liberation, and, while some of his public statements carried the implication of American commitment, he himself expressed alarm at the resultant reactions and subsequently complained that Eisenhower's views on foreign policy had been "grossly distorted" during the campaign.[89] But oversimplification was the natural outcome of a situation offering few concrete possibilities. In advocating an active policy of liberation, Dulles did not really dismiss the expectation that the Soviet empire would disintegrate from within, an expectation which was also the key feature of containment. His policy merely emphasized certain pressures that might accelerate this disintegration. In fact, Dulles' commitment to liberation as an abstract goal did not carry with it too much concern with the immediacy of such a development or with the means of its implementation.[90]

The language of liberation aroused hopes among East Europeans, frightened America's allies, and nurtured false assumptions about U.S. foreign policy in the halls of Congress and among the grass roots. Unfortunately, without negotiation or the application of preponderant power, moral indignation and legalistic arguments were unlikely to budge Soviet hegemony over the satellites. The inherent limitations of the Republican alternative were already apparent in the contradictions of the party's platform, with its concurrent stress on economy and massive retaliation, and became even more striking when toward the end of the campaign Eisenhower made his famous promise to go to Korea. Was not the credibility of liberation tainted by his determination to secure peace in the Far East, and this by an armistice that, far from rolling back communism, would reaffirm the line separating the two blocs? The paradox of the Republican response to popular frustration with stalemate lay in the ease with which the newborn policy of moral dynamism was discarded in favor of a more expedient pragmatism.

FIRST REASSESSMENTS

Returning from his well-publicized trip to Korea a month after the election, the incoming president met on the cruiser U.S.S. *Helena* with his principal advisers, including Dulles, in order to review his administration's strategy.[91] There it was agreed that the Korean war would be liquidated by accepting stalemate; the meeting also dealt with what was called the Great Equation—"how to equate needed military strength with maximum economic strength." This became the over-riding concern of Eisenhower and his entourage of businessmen: to re-establish economic conservatism by means of a balanced budget. Dulles' views on deterrence, generally referred to as the policy of "massive retaliation," were in harmony with this goal, and a close adviser of the president, Robert Cutler, recalls that "the considerations that controlled the president's judgment were, first, the working up of a strategy for the 'long haul' that would be within the nation's capacity to pay and, second, a defensive and retaliatory power of such overawing strength as to deter the possibility of attack upon this country."[92] In terms of military spending, this meant, of course, a concentration on air power. As for the policy of liberation, there is no evidence that it figured in these discussions.

Nevertheless, liberation in its many facets remained an enduring legacy of the 1952 campaign. As a general policy orientation and expression of concern for the fate of the satellites, it was referred to by the new leadership on numerous occasions. In his 1953 New Year's message, Eisenhower addressed himself to the youth behind the Iron Curtain:

> I want to assure them that they are not forgotten. I know that many of them fought bravely in the underground against Nazi tyranny and that they tried to build up representative governments after the war. So long as the spirit of freedom lives in the youth, the future is one of promise.[93]

The one concrete commitment, repudiation, was also reiterated by the new president, notably in his first State of the Union message:

> We shall never acquiesce in the enslavement of any people in order to purchase fancied gain for ourselves. I shall ask Congress at a later date to join in an appropriate resolution making clear that this Government recognizes no kind of commitment contained in secret understandings of the past with foreign governments which permits this kind of enslavement.[94]

At least on the surface it appeared that the Republicans' obsession with a supposed betrayal of the nations of East-Central Europe by Roosevelt lingered on in the White House.

American foreign policy was to acquire a new character and style by virtue of the personality of the new secretary of state. Dulles, not Eisenhower, became the prime initiator in this field, and the president gave his secretary of state a relatively free hand in its management. The campaign had already demonstrated that Dulles was the more inflexible of the two; Sherman Adams recalls that Eisenhower was "well aware that his own approach to foreign problems was far more conciliatory than Dulles'."[95] Dulles viewed the satellite problem in moral terms, and this prevented him from relaxing his stand on the necessity and inevitability of liberation. The president, on the other hand, would say that he had "always thought Foster was a bit too optimistic about changes or up-heavals" in the Soviet bloc.[96] This shade of disagreement did not affect Eisenhower's faith in Dulles, however, or cause any modification of Dulles' crusading attitude. The latter constructed his policies without help from the State Department, and in the beginning, at least, created the impression of a drastically changed and aggressive American stand. Thus Sherman Adams' recollection—that "the hard and uncompromising line that the United States government took towards Soviet Russia and Red China between 1953 and the early months of 1959 was more a Dulles line than an Eisenhower one"—is essentially accurate.[97]

Because of his predominance in foreign affairs, it is particularly important to note the continuity in Dulles' views regarding East-Central Europe, both before and after the 1952 elections. Hardly had he taken office when he declared in an informal radio-television talk that, if the captive peoples nurtured their love of freedom, the Soviet Union's "in-digestion will become so acute that it might be fatal."[98] His testimony before the Committee on Foreign Relations, in connection with his nomination, was equally consistent. He stated that it is "only by keeping alive the hope of liberation, by taking advantage of that wherever opportunity arises, that we will end this terrible peril which dominates the world."[99] Lest this be taken as a commitment to direct assistance, he added with characteristic confidence, "It must be and can be a peaceful process, but those who do not believe that results can be accomplished by moral pressures, by the weight of propaganda, just do not know what they are talking about." Again he cited Yugoslavia as a case in point, noting that while the "rule of Tito is not one which we admire . . . it illustrates that it is possible to disintegrate this present monolithic structure."[100]

Apparently no comment was made by the committee on Dulles' reluctance to differentiate between the processes by which communist rule was established in Yugoslavia and those utilized in the satellites, between a relatively popular and home-grown regime and satrapies created by the overt or threatened pressure of Soviet military power. Furthermore, the geographical position of the other satellites, which were contiguous with the Soviet Union and in some cases formed a buffer zone between it and the still-feared Germans, contrasted with the marginal situation of Yugoslavia. The latter had never been part of a "monolithic structure" except in a purely ideological sense, whereas the satellites were very much a part of the Soviet bloc in a geopolitical sense. The earlier purges of real and alleged Titoists in the other East European satellites made it even more unlikely that those states would assert themselves in the image of Tito's Yugoslavia.

Meanwhile, conservative Republicans in the U.S. Congress were pressing on with what they considered to be the first step on the road to liberation; by the end of January 1953, five separate resolutions had been introduced by congressmen clamoring for "repudiation."[101] Much to their dismay, however, the Eisenhower administration's version omitted any spectacular denunciation of the "deals" made at Teheran, Yalta, and Potsdam. As drafted by Dulles and Eisenhower, the Captive Peoples Resolution deplored Soviet hegemony in East-Central Europe, expressed hope that the satellites would achieve self-determination, and rejected "any interpretations or applications of any international agreements or understandings, made during the course of World War II, which have been perverted to bring about the subjugation of free peoples."[102] Introduced in both houses on February 20, the proposed joint declaration by Congress and the president had, according to Dulles, two primary purposes: to "register dramatically" the breaches by the Soviet Union of wartime agreements; and to "register equally dramatically the desire and hope of the American people that the captive peoples shall be liberated." Dulles insisted that the resolution was not intended as a domestic political pronouncement.[103]

Early texts of the draft had referred to repudiation more forcefully, but they would have been unacceptable to most Democrats and were therefore altered to place the blame on the Russians for flouting the terms of such agreements as the Declaration on Liberated Europe.[104] Legal arguments were also advanced in favor of this watering down of Republican campaign promises. Repudiation of the agreements, wrote Dulles, "would be repudiation of the basis of those very rights which we are struggling to achieve for our own and other peoples."[105] Eisenhower recalled in his memoirs that he "refused to do what extremists asked: repudiate in their entirety the Yalta agreements and thus endanger United States rights in Vienna and Berlin, affirmed at Yalta."[106] The extremists in question were prominent members of his own party, and both he and Dulles had promised repudiation during the campaign. His change of heart may have resulted from one of two causes. The first of these, that new information making the charge of betrayal seem unfounded came into their hands once the new administration had taken office, is improbable. Dulles, for one, must have had access to the State Department's files in the course of his functions as adviser to President Truman, and the Yalta papers, rushed into publication on his orders, brought no spectacular revelations. It is more likely that the issue of repudiation had been a willful political ploy which outlived its usefulness.

Conservative Republicans in Congress were less willing to bury the matter, but they were warned by Dulles that a more partisan motion would be worse than no resolution at all. The secretary of state wrote to Senator Wiley on March 2 that, while the status of the wartime agreements was doubtful, the joint resolution could ignore this and look to the future;[107] in his statement before the House Committee on Foreign Affairs on February 26, he had pointed out that the proposed draft avoided the "realm of controversy" concerning the wisdom of past administrations. In defense of the resolution, Dulles argued:

> The captive peoples are oppressed by a great fear that at some future time the United States may agree to a partition of the world whereby we would accept and support Soviet dictatorship of alien peoples in the hope of gaining greater security for ourselves.

Urging that the United States "do what we peacefully can do, in order to revive the hopes of those now enslaved," he went on:

> This resolution is no call to bloody and senseless revolution. . . . it will, over the coming years, revive the inherent longing for freedom which persists within the captive peoples so that the longing becomes a mounting spiritual power which will eventually overcome the material power of Soviet dictatorship.[108]

This controversy regarding the Captive Peoples Resolution had repercussions throughout the world and no doubt raised new hopes behind the Iron Curtain. The debate, one of the first major ones involving the new administration, had its stranger aspects, for it placed conservative Republicans—the most outspoken proponents of liberation—in opposition to the milder stand taken by Eisenhower and Dulles. The House Foreign Affairs Committee had unanimously endorsed the joint resolution, but the more conservative Republican senators on the Foreign Relations Committee could not bring themselves to support a motion that amounted to a repudiation less of Yalta and Potsdam than of their own campaign commitments. Senator Taft accordingly proposed a compromise amendment to the effect that the resolution did not "constitute any determination" of the validity or invalidity of the wartime agreements. The amendment was carried in the committee over Democratic opposition on March 3, and the prospect loomed of a bitter, and for the Republicans a politically embarrassing, fight for congressional approval.[109]

The cleavage between Republican leaders in Congress intent upon a vindictive denunciation of the Democrats' record and an administration already more concerned with gaining bipartisan support was still unresolved when on March 5 news of Stalin's death reached the West. Sherman Adams records that this development ended the debate on the controversial resolution, to the "immense relief" of Eisenhower and Dulles, and, in the event, the latter told a meeting of congressional leaders four days later that the resolution was no longer necessary or appropriate; on March 10 Senator Taft bowed to the inevitable and had the resolution killed in committee.[110] Clearly, policy makers in Washington felt that the time was inopportune to antagonize the Soviet Union with a public condemnation of its rule over East-Central Europe. In a telephone conversation later that month with Congressman Walter Judd, who was interested in reviving the resolution, Dulles agreed that the United States had "missed the boat before the peace feelers began," but he objected that "it would be difficult now because it would look as though we were rejecting the peace bids."[111] There is no public evidence as to the nature of these Soviet "peace feelers," but Eisenhower as well as British and French leaders obviously came to favor a Western initiative to test the intentions of the new men in the Kremlin.

Although the fate of the Captive Peoples Resolution did not presage much action on the impassioned promises of the campaign, the debate did exhibit two characteristics that were to remain in evidence for many years. The first was Dulles' steadfast advocacy of liberation by "peaceful means" and his faith in "spiritual power." The second was the inclination of some conservative legislators—Republicans in the main—to interpret liberation more literally and to insist on forceful statements of American intentions regarding the freedom of East-Central Europe. The latter group was even more responsible than Dulles for the impression on both sides of the Iron Curtain that liberation was a concrete goal of American foreign policy instead of a pious hope for the distant future. Thus liberation, a principle never really translated into operational policy, survived and endured as a dangerous myth.

IV

IMPOTENCE
AND COEXISTENCE

*As long as these powers flattered themselves
that the menace of force would produce
the effect of force, they acted on those
declarations; but when their menaces
failed of success, their efforts took a
new direction.*

EDMUND BURKE

*The evils which are endured with patience
so long as they are inevitable seem
intolerable as soon as hope can be
entertained of escaping them.*

ALEXIS DE TOCQUEVILLE

The Eisenhower administration's tentative undertaking to turn the ongoing process of consolidation into a dynamic crusade against communism was still far from being translated into operational policy when the reins of power in the Kremlin passed into the hands of Malenkov, Molotov, and Beria, and this change raised hopes in the West that at long last a thaw in the cold war might be at hand. Stalin himself had made tentative overtures in the course of 1952—notably, in his March 10 note on German reunification and later in his suggestion of a meeting with Eisenhower. Foreshadowing the peaceful coexistence line of the later 1950s, Stalin in his directive for the Nineteenth Congress of the CPSU stressed a new "movement for peace." Whatever the reasons for his tactical shift—and one could cite in this context the domestic tensions arising from the rigors of reconstruction, apprehensions about America's flirtation with "rollback," consciousness of Russia's inferior strategic capability—Stalin appears, at least in retrospect, to have been the last Soviet leader sufficiently omnipotent to compromise on questions such as the division of Germany, but the West's preoccupation with shoring up its defenses dictated a tactical refusal to reopen negotiations. Having failed to take up Stalin's cues, the Western powers felt that the ostensibly conciliatory attitude of his successors, taken in conjunction with their more fragmented domestic base, warranted an at least *pro forma* response.

In the wake of Stalin's death in March 1953, President Eisenhower decided, with the concurrence of his psychological warfare advisers, that the time was ripe for a major pronouncement on the theme of peaceful coexistence. His secretary of state, however, remained convinced that offense was the best policy at a time when the enemy appeared to be wavering: "I grow less keen about this speech because I think that there's some real danger of our just seeming to fall in with these Soviet overtures. It's obvious that what they are doing is because of outside pressures, and I don't know anything better we can do than to keep up these pressures right now."[1] If Dulles was cool to the idea, the president's speech writers must have been diametrically opposed to him; one of them recalls that high on the list of omissions from the draft was "any allusion to 'liberation' of Eastern Europe."[2] Eisenhower's speech, entitled "The Chance for Peace" and delivered in Washington on April 16 before the American Society of Newspaper Editors, challenged the Russians to halt the arms race and coexist peacefully, but the president posited some stiff prerequisites in asking rhetorically whether the Soviet Union was "prepared to allow other nations, including those of Eastern Europe, the free choice of their own forms of government."[3] Over-all, the speech stressed peace and evolutionary change, but two days later, aware of the attention American pronouncements were getting behind the Iron Curtain, Dulles moved to dispel any fears of appeasement, noting that "it was of the utmost importance to make clear to the captive peoples that we do not accept their captivity as a permanent fact of history. If they thought otherwise and became hopeless, we would unwittingly have become partners in the forging of a hostile power so vast that it would encompass our destruction."[4] *Pravda* replied to the American challenge in a predictably offended vein: "Facts show that only by a stubborn struggle for their rights did the peoples of Eastern Europe come to the present popular-democratic form of government. ... It would be strange to expect the Soviet Union to interfere in favor of installing the reactionary regimes overthrown by these peoples."[5] Unimpeded though he was by the kind of doctrinal opposition to negotiating with the enemy that characterized Dulles' approach, even the president could not in all conscience refrain from raising the question of the satellites, and when the Soviet Union made it abundantly clear that the status of the latter was no more negotiable than it had been in the past "The Chance for Peace" became indistinguishable from the earlier ventures into propagandistic rhetoric.

In addition to this professed concern for the fate of the satellites, a more immediate and pragmatic consideration inhibited American policy makers from taking up the matter of a European settlement with the Russians once again—a consideration which had restrained the previous administration from engaging in such negotiations: the commitment to fully integrate West Germany into its alliance system, to rearm the Germans, and to ensure the rehabilitation of their economy. While the Western Allies had signed the European Defense Community Treaty on May 27, 1952, the hammering out of its modalities turned out to be a painfully slow process, and its ultimate ratification, particularly by the French, who were less ready than their partners to divest themselves of a historical fear of Germany, became increasingly doubtful as the months went by. The most enthusiastic proponents of this German policy were Dulles and Chancellor Adenauer, whose community of views led to a genuine friendship that only reinforced the immutability of the policy; and, if West Germany's status was nonnegotiable, Eisenhower's challenge to the Russians to demonstrate their peaceful intentions (he gave as an example the conclusion of a peace treaty with Austria) represented little more than an invitation to make unilateral concessions and therefore carried no promise of easing the division of Europe through disengagement. Visiting Washington early in April 1953, Adenauer found himself in agreement with Dulles (and, apparently, also with the president) that the Soviet peace feelers were merely an indication that Stalin's successors needed a lull in which to settle their internal affairs.[6] The joint communiqué issued on April 9 regarding Germany and European security called for free elections in East Germany and reunification (and the release of the German prisoners of war still in the Soviet Union), as well as ratification of the European Defense Community Treaty, but undoubtedly the latter goal received operational priority.[7] Eisenhower's trial balloon the following week and the relatively moderate Soviet reply prompted Prime Minister Churchill to deliver in the House of Commons on May 11 a major address advocating an East-West summit conference and anticipating a détente in the cold war.[8] Since the president and Dulles were basically in agreement that such a conference would have to await West Germany's rearmament and the further strengthening of NATO, Churchill's proposal was simply placed on the agenda for further discussion, and the opportunity for negotiating with a momentarily weakened and vacillating Soviet leadership was lost.

While Washington thus pursued its single-minded and perhaps unnecessarily cautious policy of consolidating the Western alliance, the Soviet Union for the first time faced serious unrest in its newly acquired sphere of dominance. The merciless imposition of the Stalinist system in Eastern Europe had thoroughly cowed even the most determined anticommunist elements in the satellites, but the indiscriminate application of the Soviet economic model engendered such structural disharmonies and individual hardships that discontent among the working classes acquired threatening proportions. The first outburst occurred in Czechoslovakia in the wake of a series of new economic decrees that in effect lowered the standard of living by devaluing the currency and instituting longer working hours. On June 1, 1953, the day after the reforms were announced, workers from the Skoda works in Pilsen sparked a riot that led to momentary seizure of the City Hall and to attacks on the symbols of communist authority. The protestations of the rioters soon surpassed the original economic grievances, but the unrest was quelled before it could spread to other centers, and thousands were placed under arrest. In setting a precedent for the forceful challenge of a satellite regime, the workers of Pilsen set the stage for a confrontation of far greater proportions that was to erupt in East Berlin later that month. The Pilsen riots had been too localized and short-lived to invite reactions from the American or other foreign governments, although the event no doubt added urgency to the subsequent introduction of the Soviet-sanctioned "New Course" in East-Central Europe. On the other hand, the magnitude of the East German uprising did necessitate the involvement of other powers; in the case of the United States, it served as the first, if somewhat premature, test of the new policy of liberation.

UPRISING IN EAST GERMANY

At the second conference of East Germany's ruling party, SED, convened in July 1952 after the failure of the latest round of negotiations on reunification, resolutions were passed which in effect quickened the pace of socialization. Following the Soviet model, emphasis was placed on the development of heavy industry and on a program of "voluntary collectivization" in the agricultural sector. At the same time, cultural russification and the campaign against "class enemies" and the churches were intensified. The harsh economic measures soon aroused widespread opposition, but those dissatisfied with the system had an option that was unique in East-Central Europe: to seek a new life via the escape valve of West Berlin. Nationalization certainly accelerated the ongoing exodus of the middle classes, but the concurrent raising of norms in the factories and the lowering of welfare benefits, all without any improvement in wages, prompted a growing dissatisfaction among the working classes which had potentially greater disintegrative consequences. The westward flight of skilled workers and of farmers unwilling to join collectives aggravated an already critical labor shortage and led not only to inefficiencies in industry but also to an embarrassing drop in food supplies; administrative reforms had replaced the old provinces with a new structure, but this in turn contributed to a breakdown of the distributive process. While the regime struggled with this economic dilemma, the number of refugees crossing into West Berlin swelled to an unprecedented total of more than 58,000 in March 1953. Then, on May 14, in an ill-advised and desperate measure to maintain a viable level of productivity, the Central Committee adopted a resolution recommending an average increase of 10 percent in working norms beginning June 1; but, even before the government moved to implement this recommendation, labor unrest and work stoppages provided tangible evidence of its unpopularity.

The Kremlin's vacillations in the wake of Stalin's death was reflected in Soviet policies concerning East Germany, which at the time was still under the administrative aegis of the Soviet High Command. The local political adviser, Vladimir Semeonov, engaged in tentative discussions with the SED leadership regarding the advantages of economic liberalization, then was recalled to Moscow in April. Following yet another reversal in Soviet policy, the military was relieved of its political functions and Semeonov returned to Berlin on May 28 as high commissioner. On his instructions the East German regime now attempted to effect a belated reconciliation with its alienated constituency. A Politburo resolution, adopted on June 9 and published two days later, admitted to "a series of errors" on the part of party and government and executed a major about-face; it recommended a shift of emphasis from heavy industry to consumer goods, a relaxation in travel restrictions, a normalization of relations with the Evangelical church, an amnesty for "economic criminals," the restoration of ration cards to large sections of the middle classes which had been deprived of them in April, the return of confiscated farms to those owners who chose to come back, and in general a more lenient treatment for returning refugees. In the aggregate these promised reforms amounted to a "New Course" in economic and social policy which was to be followed shortly by other satellites and which represented a radical alteration of the earlier Stalinist model. Concurrently, the Russians admitted that the defunct Soviet Control Commission had been "to a certain extent responsible for recent errors." Although the East German regime's concessions foreshadowed an improvement in the standard of living and in the status of farmers and the middle classes, they fell short of the mark in one important respect, that of the recently increased industrial work norms. The government announced on June 14 that the new norms and wage rates would remain in effect; by then a pay cut for East Berlin construction workers had already given tangible proof of the regime's obduracy. Despite the very real economic crisis, the government's failure to respond to the workers' demands was clearly ill advised, for the measures to appease other sections of the population only heightened the workers' dissatisfaction.

The catalytic force that transformed the long-simmering unrest into open revolt turned out to be the elite brigade working on the prestigious Stalinallee project in East Berlin. Having decided to confront the government en masse, the brigade set out on the morning of June 16 for the House of Ministries, carrying signs reading "We demand a reduction in the norms." By the time one of the ministers appeared to address the workers, voices from the crowd were calling not only for a reduction in norms but also for free elections by secret ballot and were threatening a general strike. The gathering size and momentum of the demonstration all but obscured the announcement by a shaken government that the Politburo had already recommended a revision of the norm decree. As had been the case in Pilsen a few weeks earlier, the initial economic demands soon became laced with slogans condemning Ulbricht, Grotewohl, and the rest of the communist leadership and with claims of wide popular support. Declared one of the workers: "We represent not only Stalinallee but the people of Berlin. This is a people's rising."[9]

Overnight, mobile units of the *Volkspolizei* and Soviet armored divisions moved into East Berlin, and when, on the morning of the seventeenth, tens of thousands of workers from the capital and its environs gathered once again in front of the government buildings, they clashed with the police and were repulsed, the area then being cordoned off by the Russians. Unorganized and uncertain whether to appeal for Western assistance or to avoid any provocation of the Russians and aim only to discredit the Ulbricht regime, the marchers moved their mass meeting to Marx-Engels Platz, but once again they were dispersed by Soviet tanks, and the first casualties testified to the growing belligerency of both sides. In what was becoming an unambiguously anticommunist and anti-Soviet revolt, 50,000 East Berliners gathered at the Brandenburg Gate and tore down the red flag as the spirit of rebellion spread through Ulbricht's domain. From Rostock on the Baltic to Karl Marx Stadt (formerly Chemnitz) in the south, from Magdeburg in the west to Frankfurt on the Oder, more than 370,000 workers in 274 localities participated in the strike;[10] farmers joined the chorus by attacking the collective system. In almost every instance the workers initially presented their demands in a disciplined, peaceful manner, although there were isolated cases of violence against party functionaries and of liberation of political prisoners by more impulsive elements. While numerous clashes occurred (the Soviet military authorities having declared a state of emergency and martial law in East Berlin and other cities), the restraint exercised by the *Vopos* and the Red Army and by the demonstrators resulted in only twenty-two fatalities. By nightfall, the strike that became an uprising had been effectively quelled.

Despite subsequent indications that a power struggle had been going on in the Kremlin concurrently with the uprising, the nature of its influence on events in East Germany remains clouded in mystery. The revolt occasioned protracted soul-searching within a divided SED leadership, but, following Beria's failure to overcome the united opposition of the Soviet party and military establishments and the arrest of the secret police chief in July, Ulbricht moved to consolidate his own position and to purge those elements which had allegedly followed Beria's star. His two principal victims, Wilhelm Zaisser, minister of state security and a Politburo member, and Rudolf Herrnstadt, editor of the SED newspaper *Neues Deutschland*, were accused of antiparty "defeatism," of having plotted to take power within the SED, to revive other left-wing parties, and to reverse the process of socialization in order to facilitate the reunification and neutralization of the two Germanies; Zaisser, Ulbricht charged, had negotiated with Beria's special envoys with a view to effecting such a coup.[11] Some years later both Ulbricht and Khrushchev would allude to Beria's inclination at the time of the uprising to liquidate the East German regime and resolve by some compromise the issue of reunification.[12] Whatever Beria's ulterior motives might have been, his apparent disposition to relinquish direct Soviet control over East Germany must have contributed to the determination of a security-conscious Soviet military establishment to block his road to power, and the outcome of the power struggles in both East Berlin and Moscow only reaffirmed the immutability of the *status quo*. A Soviet–East German communiqué, released on August 22, announced the upgrading of diplomatic missions, the cancellation of further reparations, and the granting of credits to East Germany, and testified to the Soviet Union's commitment to maintain the GDR.[13]

The West's response to the uprising must have reassured Ulbricht and his masters that they had little to fear from that direction, although they would protest against the alleged involvement of Western agents and agitators. Agents of every ilk did proliferate in Berlin, that microcosm of cold war confrontation, and some may well have played a supporting role once the uprising got under way, but there is no evidence that the initiative of the Stalinallee workers was anything but spontaneous. This is not to say that the Western powers were unaware of the growing economic dilemma facing their opponents in East Germany. U.S. High Commissioner James B. Conant records that when he visited West Berlin one week after taking up his post in February 1953, "Almost the first question I heard at the staff meeting was: When will the Soviets seal off their sector completely? The second was: What will we do?"[14] There was apparently no contingency plan to deal with such an eventuality, let alone with a mass uprising. The West's propaganda organs—the U.S.-sponsored "Radio in the American Sector" (RIAS) foremost among them—were rather less inhibited by the ambivalence and uncertainty that characterized Western policies regarding the Soviet sphere; in fact, RIAS was recognized as "the epitome of dynamic 'psych warfare.' "[15] For several years RIAS had been broadcasting special labor programs to East Germany, where its audience amounted to a majority of the population, and by focusing on the system's weaknesses it undoubtedly contributed both to the climate of unrest and to the mounting exodus westward. When, on the afternoon of June 16, a delegation from the Stalinallee workers appeared at RIAS headquarters and asked to be put on the air, its request was politely rejected, but RIAS did broadcast the workers' demands, which included payment according to the old norms, immediate measures to lower the cost of living, and free and secret elections.[16] The political director of RIAS, Gordon Ewing, recalls that he was well aware he would be "pouring gasoline on the flames" when at 6 A.M. the next day he allowed the station to broadcast a message from the West Berlin union leader, Ernst Scharnowski, calling for a general strike in the eastern zone; meanwhile, RIAS commentators spread word of the successful mass action of the Berlin workers and the weakness of the *Volkspolizei.* Ewing was confident the Russians would not invade West Berlin or fire into the East Berlin crowds "if they could possibly help it," so, despite the absence of instructions from Washington and the realization that the uprising would eventually be put down, he felt warranted in having RIAS spread the seeds of revolt.[17] That the broadcasts were instrumental in turning the Stalinallee strike into a nationwide uprising is beyond doubt; more difficult to estimate is the expectation of Western assistance that might also have been engendered. RIAS cautioned its listeners that "the ultimate decisions would lie with the Russian occupiers," but the eastern zone was rife with rumors that U.S. assistance was on its way, and RIAS as well as West German, American, and British agencies and authorities were besieged with requests for direction and material assistance.[18] Response to such pleas was of course beyond the competence of a propaganda outlet, for, while RIAS may have been an operational symbol of the rhetoric of liberation, it was in no position to go beyond that rhetoric in defining the nature of the West's commitments and objectives.

As the country most intimately concerned with the fate of the rebels, West Germany was the first logical source of encouragement and guidance. Having only recently overcome their fear that the Korean war was part of a general Soviet offensive that would also engulf Europe, and being preoccupied with rebuilding their economy, the West German people and their government reacted to the uprising with less enthusiasm than apprehension. Apart from the message of the West Berlin trade-union leader noted above, the uprising elicited only a few declarations of cautious sympathy; Jakob Kaiser, the federal minister for all-German affairs (a euphemistically named department concerned with the eastern zone), cautioned the East Germans against provoking their leaders and the Russians into bloody retaliation. Feelings of insecurity, the rapid course of events in the eastern zone, a reluctance to gratuitously provide the Russians with any evidence of a Western plot, and its dependence on American policy all contributed to Bonn's hands-off attitude, although the last factor gave rise to some rueful comments, notably, by West Berlin's mayor, Ernst Reuter, who broadcast on June 18: "The workers of Berlin have not asked for higher wages but for a change of the entire system. Can the world be silent to this call?"[19] During the few dramatic hours of the uprising the West Germans may have been looking to Washington for some initiative, but few among them dared to urge a forceful reaction which would turn their scarcely rebuilt homes into a potential battleground.

On the day the rebellion broke out in East Germany, U.S. High Commissioner Conant was in Washington defending his budget (which included the American information program) against the attacks of Senator McCarthy at hearings of the Senate's Appropriations Committee. At the same time, leading figures in the administration were reported to be involved in a "hot debate" regarding the meaning of liberation in the light of the new crisis. Eisenhower's psychological warfare advisers were apparently joined by Dulles in urging some form of positive response on the grounds that "the satellite resistance movements must take their chance, and that forcing the Red Army to move, into Czechoslovakia for instance, will amount to a major victory in the cold war," but with characteristic caution the president chose not to imperil the *status quo*.[20] Recalls Conant:

> By the time I got to Berlin three days later, nothing had been done and nothing said by the Allied powers. As a concession to American opinion, I wrote a public letter to General Chuikov protesting the complete closing of all crossing points between the United States and Soviet sectors. Reaffirmation of the right of free circulation through all of

Berlin was at best a mild gesture. And it came from only one of the three representatives of the Allies. Washington would have vetoed anything more drastic. A three-power statement was out of the question. London and Paris had little sympathy with the uprising. The British High Commissioner returned in a worried state from an interrupted vacation. He suggested that if the East Berliners were encouraged to insult the Soviet occupation forces, some of the West Germans might start making riotous protests against the American or the British or the French. Equating the legality of all occupying forces in Berlin may have been formally correct, but it in no way corresponded with the mood of the Berliners or the Americans in Berlin.[21]

Notwithstanding Conant's assertion that "smoldering disagreement" among the Western Allies precluded a more vigorous response, there is no evidence that French or British pressures played a dominant role in dissuading Washington either from mounting a propaganda offensive aimed at spreading the spirit of rebellion to other satellites or from seizing the opportunity to initiate wide-ranging negotiations with the Russians. The logic of containment continued to prevail over both the urgings of the "liberators" and arguments favoring détente and negotiation.

The temporizing attitude that materialized out of this debate within the administration was accurately reflected in the diplomatic exchanges that followed the short-lived uprising. On June 17, after repairing to the boundary of the Soviet sector for a quick visual appraisal of the battle, the Allied commandants and the West Berlin authorities issued a communiqué expressing full agreement "on the need of maintaining public order in the Western Sectors and on the advisability of adopting a completely calm attitude," and disclaiming any responsibility for the demonstrations. It was only on the following day that they dispatched a joint message to the Soviet military command condemning the "irresponsible recourse to military force." In his reply of June 20, the Soviet commandant dismissed the protests as devoid of any basis and charged that the disturbances had been caused by "groups of provocateurs and fascist agents from the Western sectors of Berlin who were sent here." On the twenty-first, four days after the uprising, Chancellor Adenauer appealed to the three Western powers to reinstate the violated human rights and reunify Germany, but his messages were as much in a propagandistic vein as was President Eisenhower's reply, which praised the courage of the East Germans and the unextinguished spirit of liberty behind the Iron Curtain. Three weeks later, in response to a more pragmatic suggestion from Adenauer, the U.S. government instructed its chargé d'affaires in Moscow to offer $15 million worth of foodstuffs to alleviate the critical shortages in East Germany; noting that the offer should have been addressed to the GDR government, Molotov dismissed it as a propaganda maneuver and asserted that the

Soviet Union was quite capable of supplying the needs of the East Germans. Nevertheless, several million food parcels were distributed to East Berliners in the western sectors, and, while many of these were confiscated upon their return to the eastern zone, the United States could at least be credited with a humanitarian gesture.[22]

Amid lingering public criticism of their passive stance during the uprising, the foreign ministers of Britain, France, and the United States gathered in Washington on July 10 to effect their own post-mortem on the event and to assess the opportunities for détente in the post-Stalin era. That the East Germans had inadvertently called Dulles' bluff could not, of course, be acknowledged officially. The secretary of state told the ministers that the revolt testified to the inherent weaknesses of the Soviet system and would eventually compel the Kremlin to "recognize the futility of trying to hold captive so many peoples who, by their faith and their patriotism, can never really be consolidated into a Soviet Communist world."[23] One result of the Washington meeting was a communiqué inviting the Soviet Union to join in fresh attempts to solve the German and Austrian problems through a four-power meeting and expressing a desire "to see true liberty restored" to the nations of East-Central Europe. The European participants had apparently been as reluctant as ever to join in the rhetoric of rollback, but had made a tactical concession to the crusading spirit of their hosts; in a cabinet meeting on July 17, Dulles reported that the joint declaration of concern over the satellites marked "the first time to my knowledge that London and Paris have been willing to embrace this principle."[24]

Preoccupied with the problems of collective defense, the West European leaders must have derived some secret comfort from the Soviet Union's swift repression of the East German rebellion. Adenauer himself had endorsed Dulles' liberation policy, but he understood perhaps better than most that it presented no short-range threat to the *status quo*, and neither he nor Dulles had expected the East Germans or any other satellite people to take to arms. The chancellor waited until the uprising was well and truly crushed before appealing to his allies for some initiative to resolve the German problem. Eisenhower's response, dispatched on July 23 and intended to amplify the foreign ministers' communiqué, was appropriately vague and optimistic. The president averred that "certain definite patterns are emerging from the situation in East Germany and the Eastern Europe satellite countries—patterns which will unquestionably have a profound effect upon the future." Noting the spontaneity of the uprising and the workers' (as distinct from "bourgeois reactionaries' ") demands for free elections, he pledged that the United States would "lend the full force of its political, diplomatic, and moral support" to the achievement of their goals: "This increasing contrast between Western and Eastern Germany, the latter with its bankrupt regime and impoverished economy, will in the long run produce conditions which should make possible the liquidation of the present Communist dictatorship and of the Soviet occupation."[25] Such professions of faith in the ultimate triumph of good over evil did not add up to a firm operational commitment or reconcile the impassioned promises of the election campaign with American inaction in the face of the uprising, but they served to reaffirm the moral superiority of the West without endangering Erhard's "economic miracle" or the consolidation of the Western alliance. Paeans to the East Europeans' indomitable spirit provided an outlet for the more frustrated proponents of rollback; on August 3 the U.S. Senate adopted a concurrent resolution praising "heroic resistance throughout Eastern Europe" and asserting that "this sacrifice for freedom will aid the cause of freedom in all Communist enslaved nations."[26] Concluded an official of RIAS, "The East Germans proved to themselves that men can be men, even under a totalitarian dictatorship."[27] Such patronizing compliments could scarcely compensate for the shattered hopes of the imprisoned rebels.

Yet, in the final analysis, the West had few realistic options in responding to the East German revolt. A local military intervention in Berlin aimed at maintaining free passage between the zones might have been legally warranted, but it would have necessarily entailed confrontation with the Russians, and the small Western garrisons were no match for the 275,000-strong Soviet army deployed in and around East Berlin. A threat to activate U.S. contingents in West Germany would have been equally injudicious in view of the overwhelming superiority of Soviet land forces in East-Central Europe and would certainly have been unlikely to deter the Russians from carrying through their police action. As for the suggestion of Eisenhower's psychological warfare advisers that the other satellite peoples be urged to follow the example of the East Germans, this might well have stimulated risings in other parts of the Soviet empire, but the Soviet Union had both the military capability and, judging by its behavior in East Germany, the will to maintain the *status quo*; furthermore, in the absence of direct U.S. involvement such incitement would have saddled the administration with a heavy moral responsibility for the potentially disastrous consequences. Conceivably, a combination of military intervention and mass uprisings might have shifted the balance against the Russians, but this would have amounted to total war, a price that no American policy maker was willing to pay for the liberation of the satellites. Only the option of negotiation appears—if only in retrospect—to have had the remotest chance of success. The coincidence of the leadership struggle in the Kremlin with the East German revolt might have provided a unique opportunity for a Western diplomatic initiative to resolve the German and Austrian questions. If such an initiative had strengthened the hand of Beria, an unholy bargain might have been struck to neutralize a reunited Germany, as well as Austria, and to legitimize Soviet hegemony over the rest of East-Central Europe, but a multiplicity of factors and interests militated against a settlement of this magnitude—notably, the opposition of the Soviet military establishment to any strategic withdrawal (and to Beria's gamble for power); the incompatibility of any partial bargain with a host of explicit and implicit American commitments stretching from the Atlantic Charter to the policy of liberation; the refusal of the West Europeans, Adenauer foremost among them, to countenance an even marginal reduction in the protective American umbrella; and Washington's vested interest in West Germany's economic revival and integration into the Western camp. In the event, the brevity of the revolt mercifully obviated the need for lengthy debate in the West's chancelleries on the advisability of negotiation. As for the men in the Kremlin, the extent of popular opposition to the communist regimes in East Germany and the other satellites must have made them realize that without the presence of Soviet power their protective glacis would evaporate overnight and that, therefore, partial or area-wide neutralization of East-Central Europe was in terms of Soviet security a dangerous illusion. Even if they had seriously contemplated a negotiated détente in the early months of 1953, their disposition to compromise did not survive the East German experience.[28]

Thus, none of the participants, with the exception of the unfortunate East German dissidents, was altogether unhappy with the outcome of the uprising. Ulbricht emerged confident of Soviet support and of immunity from Western intervention and set about restoring the authority of his regime on a somewhat more popular basis. Adenauer and the more intransigent Americans, such as Dulles, viewed with ill-concealed satisfaction the inevitable adjournment of any major East-West negotiations over Europe, for they had convinced themselves that time was on the side of the West and that by creating an atmosphere of uncertainty and by delaying military integration such negotiations would only serve the interests of the Soviet Union.[29] Despite the lip service they paid to détente, the French and the British were less than sanguine about the prospects of a reunited Germany and a westward retrenchment of their lines of defense. In terms of the American policy of liberation, Washington's passive stance somewhat tarnished Dulles' image as a champion of the oppressed, but the uprising nevertheless vindicated his claim of the East European masses' profound anticommunism and hostility to the Soviet Union, and to this extent it provided a modest propaganda victory for the West. In light of the East German revolt, American policy makers might have been expected to redouble their efforts to revise and translate the electoral rhetoric of liberation into a comprehensive operational policy; in particular, the ability of propaganda organs such as RIAS to inflame popular passions invited careful study and correlation with the broader orientations of American foreign policy. Since no one could exclude the possibility of similar outbursts in one of the other satellites, prudence dictated that the lessons of the East German episode be applied in planning for future contingencies.

THE NEW COURSE

The death of Stalin, economic stagnation and popular unrest in the satellites, and the Dulles-inspired propaganda offensive all contributed to an atmosphere of reappraisal and cautious compromise in the Kremlin throughout the spring and summer of 1953. The earlier procrustean efforts to apply the Stalinist economic model were now relaxed in several of the satellites by a process of decompression that became known as the New Course. The first evidence of a new tack had come in East Germany even before the uprising. Despite the rash of arrests and the party purge that took place in the wake of that event, the Ulbricht regime remained faithful to the reforms it had enacted in early June and moved to pacify the workers by moderating the production norms that had been the initial cause of unrest. The next satellite to benefit from the New Course was Hungary, where the repressive measures and economic mismanagement of the Rákosi regime had been responsible not only for the massive political alienation of the population but also for food shortages and an 18 percent drop between 1949 and 1952 in the real incomes of the workers. Summoned to Moscow in June 1953, Rákosi was warned by the Soviet leaders that his tactics were no longer appropriate and was ordered to relinquish the premiership in favor of Imre Nagy, a veteran communist who had been in disgrace for some years after directing the ministries of Agriculture and Interior in the immediate postwar period. Nagy thereupon attempted to forestall the spread of popular unrest by restoring some civil rights, by shifting the emphasis from heavy industry to consumer goods, and by relaxing the pressures on the peasantry to join collective farms; in the political arena he revived the Patriotic People's Front, partly to encourage wider political participation, and also to provide himself with an alternative power base to the Communist party, which remained under Rákosi's guidance. The favorable popular response to Nagy's program and the increasingly liberal and critical stance of the intelligentsia only strengthened Rákosi's fears that decompression would lead to disintegration of the party's monopolistic position, and he continued to intrigue against Nagy and to obstruct reforms until the New Course was reversed at the time of

Malenkov's demise in early 1955 and Nagy was forced once again to retire in disgrace. The New Course also materialized tentatively in Czechoslovakia, where in September 1953 the Novotny-Siroky regime announced economic reforms similar to those instituted in East Germany and Hungary.

While the selective launching of a New Course in East-Central Europe inspired a momentary, guarded optimism among the peoples most directly affected, the profound cleavage between the masses and their communist leaders endured well into the 1950s and produced among the former a highly idiosyncratic view of international politics. One significant finding of a study based on information provided by escapees in the years 1951 and 1952 was that a very real hope for a war of liberation existed in the satellites. As one young Hungarian refugee observed: "Everyone wants war. . . . It doesn't pay to live like this anyway, being afraid all the time of what would happen the next night."[30] The East Europeans apparently reasoned that by virtue of the irreconcilability of the two camps—and Leninist dogma as well as their own domestic propaganda stressed this— war was inevitable, and they therefore searched for evidence that such a war and the consequent liberation from the Kremlin's yoke was imminent. Because of this premise, listeners tended to give Western broadcasts their selective attention in order to have their hopes for liberation reinforced; one refugee noted that news of possible liberation was his only motive for listening to the Voice of America. Corroborating evidence was advanced by a 1953 report prepared for the State Department on Hungarian reactions to propaganda broadcasts. The report concluded that Hungarians listened to and judged the VOA in terms of its contribution to "hope for liberation from the Communist yoke"; the United States was their "only source of hope," and they craved assurance of America's strength and determination to free them.[31]

That despair at their collective and individual impotence led the East Europeans to anticipate a war of liberation is perhaps understandable, but public opinion in the West clearly did not countenance such a forceful resolution of the cold war. Preoccupied with their own security and economic problems, West Europeans were not in a crusading mood, and their cautious sympathy for the satellite peoples manifested itself only in vague support for diplomatic initiatives. In the United States, on the other hand, public opinion reflected a greater sense of responsibility for the fate of the East Europeans; this arose partly from a feeling that the United States had somehow failed to stand by its wartime commitments, and partly from the deeply rooted assumption that as the bastion of democracy the United States had a duty to liberate those oppressed by godless communism. An elite opinion survey, conducted for the Council on Foreign Relations in late 1953, found overwhelming opposition to any East-West bargain that would trade a Soviet guarantee of nonaggression in Western Europe for American recognition of the legitimacy of Soviet hegemony in East-Central Europe; observed the council's analyst, "no other question in this inquiry aroused such fervor and indignant rejection."[32] Yet the survey found no clear indication of preferred means, for, having rejected compromise, the majority of the respondents nevertheless supported continued U.S. diplomatic efforts to end the cold war and opposed congressional prohibition of trade with the satellites. While the American public strongly favored the ultimate liberation of the East Europeans, it certainly did not envisage liberation by force, particularly after the costly Korean experience, and it therefore offered little guidance to Washington's policy makers beyond supporting their refusal to legitimize the *status quo*.

This ambivalence was not entirely absent from the views of that more directly involved, if still heterogeneous, interest group within the American body politic, the émigrés and the descendants of earlier immigrants from East-Central Europe and from the Soviet Union. Like their predecessors in history, the refugee politicians proved to be a fractious lot, and, as noted earlier, one of the functions of the Committee for a Free Europe was to channel their energies in politically useful directions. Official advocacy of liberation only encouraged those among them who wanted to ride back to their homelands on the crest of a great American crusade; typical of this group was the president of the Ukrainian Congress Committee, Professor Dobriansky, who recommended to the Committee on Foreign Relations that a billion dollars be set aside for the task of fomenting revolution behind the Iron Curtain.[33] While many émigrés perceived the dangers inherent in a policy of incitement, the political climate of the early 1950s favored their more aggressive compatriots; official acts such as the establishment of propaganda outlets and the recruitment of refugees into a Special Forces unit based in West Germany led the latter to believe that liberation was indeed an operational policy.[34]

The next step in the consolidation of the various émigré groups occurred in September 1954, when, under the aegis of the FEC, representatives from the various satellites, including the Baltic states, met at the Carnegie International Center in New York, across the street from the United Nations, where the ninth session of the General Assembly was about to be convened. The delegates, for the most part prominent democratic politicians, proceeded to found the Assembly of Captive European Nations (ACEN), whose "paramount purpose" they declared to be "to serve the cause of the liberation of the Central and Eastern European nations from the Soviet-Communist yoke." ACEN was to be not only a source of information about conditions in the satellites but also, rather ambiguously, a forum for promoting "courses of action which would enable the free world to help the enslaved peoples to help themselves." Later that same year, in a Christmas "Appeal to the Nations of the Free World," ACEN urged those nations to declare the satellite regimes illegitimate, to have the United Nations recognize this and supervise free elections, and to demand that any government obstructing these measures be declared an aggressor by the United Nations. On a slightly more realistic level, ACEN also recommended a trade embargo ("Western efforts to expand East-West trade relations would have the most detrimental effect on the morale of the captive peoples") and warned the West against succumbing to Soviet enticements to peaceful coexistence ("which can only lead to the condonement of past and present Soviet aggression and thus to the consolidation of the Soviet grip on a region ideally suited to serve as a basis for the final assault against Western Europe"). In its advocacy of "a consistent policy of liberation" by nonviolent means, ACEN was ostensibly attuned to the prevailing official attitudes in Washington; but, by nevertheless taking a hard line on such issues as trade, recognition, and UN membership, it spoke for the anticommunist crusaders who were in the majority among the émigrés and who represented a substantial proportion of the population at large. Although Washington had long ago dismissed the option of setting up governments-in-exile, the various émigré organizations collaborating within ACEN represented with some accuracy the values and aspirations of the anticommunist majorities in their homelands, so that at this stage in the cold war (in contrast to the late fifties and the sixties) ACEN could with only a modest degree of exaggeration claim to be the "authentic voice of the subjugated nations of Central and Eastern Europe."[35]

On the other hand, the effectiveness of ACEN, and of the émigrés in general, as a pressure group within the American political system must not be overrated. The East European ethnic groups were not well represented in positions of political or economic power, and, while their electoral support was sought by both parties, their influence on the formulation of U.S. foreign policy arose from a momentary coincidence of interests rather than from their limited political leverage. Particularly in the first term of the Eisenhower administration, ACEN received substantial vocal support from official circles (and it must be noted that its activities were largely, if indirectly, financed by the government); in replying to ACEN's first Christmas appeal, Secretary of State Dulles observed that its deliberations were "illustrative of the Free World's just concern with the problems of the captive countries." But the signifiance of the émigré organizations lay less in their influence on U.S. foreign policy than in the impact their activities had on the satellites. By giving them a propagandistic function and by providing them with facilities to broadcast their message behind the Iron Curtain, the U.S. government endowed the exile groups with a quasi-official status that was open to serious misrepresentation by the satellite peoples. News of ACEN's activities and of official and public American support was regularly relayed by Radio Free Europe to listeners who, as was noted earlier, were only too ready to receive indications of imminent liberation by the West.

The question of liberation also continued to draw the attention of at least the more conservative members of the Republican-dominated U.S. Congress. The chairman of the Foreign Relations Committee, Senator Wiley, declared in July 1953 that Beria's fall provided "one of the greatest opportunities for the West for exploiting the boiling tensions behind the Iron Curtain."[36] After the Berlin riots, Congressman Kersten introduced a number of House concurrent resolutions urging the withdrawal of recognition from the satellite regimes and asking the Eisenhower administration to reaffirm its commitment to liberation. In the event, official congressional reaction to the uprising was limited to the previously noted resolution in the Senate, and those politicians who had in the heat of the campaign espoused the cause of liberation grew increasingly disillusioned with the administration's apparent inaction; the ranks of the disenchanted included Arthur Bliss Lane, who charged that the government had no intention of implementing the campaign pledge of liberation and who in late 1953 resigned from the Republican National Committee.[37] The administration's growing interest in the stabilization of East-West relations and in peaceful coexistence only further alienated conservatives such as Senator Knowland, who repeatedly expressed concern that the new trend in foreign policy would lead to "peace at any price."[38]

In an interim report, the Kersten Committee on Communist Aggression condemned peaceful coexistence as a "Communist myth" and recommended the curtailment of diplomatic relations and a ban on trade with the Soviet bloc.[39] The committee also noted that, although Congress had authorized the formation of national military units of escapees within the framework of the Mutual Security Act, nothing had in fact issued from this proposal. (Nonetheless, the Mutual Security Act of 1954 included the original Kersten Amendment providing $100 million for the assistance of "selected residents and escapees from Iron Curtain countries.") On January 2, 1955, the committee published a report which asserted that the "time was never more opportune, or the world situation more demanding for a bold, positive offensive by the United States and the entire free world; this is the only course which gives reasonable hope for avoiding all-out war." The committee urged that the U.S. "immediately launch a positive, bipartisan, political offensive against the international Communist conspiracy and in behalf of the enslaved nations." Again deriding the concept of peaceful coexistence, it proposed, *inter alia*, that greater government and private support be given to international information programs, such as the Voice of America and that of the Committee for a Free Europe, because they were relaying the truth to those who wanted to revolt against communism.[40] Almost simultaneously, the Committee on Foreign Relations released a series of studies on "Tensions within the Soviet Captive Countries." In its report on Hungary, the committee noted that "there exists widespread popular antagonism to the Communist regime in Hungary, and this regime has reached a low ebb both economically and politically," but it warned that it would be a mistake to conclude that the whole communist structure is on the verge of collapse: "The Red Army and the secret police present formidable barriers to revolt."[41] While these congressional opinions largely coincided with the stand taken by ACEN and the majority of émigrés, they, too, fell short of prescribing a comprehensive course of action for the administration, for diplomatic and economic isolation of the Soviet bloc and the concurrent encouragement of the East Europeans' feelings of frustration could hardly be expected to achieve the goal of liberation without some further, explicit American commitment to intervene.

This, then, was the domestic and foreign context within which the Eisenhower administration had to elaborate its policies in the wake of the East German uprising. In his first State of the Union message the president had deplored the West's "paralyzed tension" and had manifested some of the dynamism promised in the election campaign by countermanding Truman's order to the Seventh Fleet and unleashing Chiang Kai-shek, by recommending increased aid for South Korea's rearmament program, and by promising some action in the matter of "repudiation." The first two measures, together with the deployment of nuclear-armed Strategic Air Command units, served to persuade the Chinese and North Koreans that the Republic of Korea would be maintained at all costs; repudiation, as has been seen, was quietly shelved after Stalin's death. In fact, long-term policy remained under review for much of the administration's first year. At a meeting in the White House on May 8, 1953, it was decided to set up task forces to study three alternative strategies, which according to a reliable source were "to continue on with the Truman containment doctrine," "to draw a line around certain threatened areas—Formosa, Southeast Asia, the Middle East—and serve notice on the U.S.S.R. that a violation of these lines would invite general war," and "to pass over to the initiative and subject Russia to intense political and economic pressure."[42] By November the outlines of the strategy adopted had become apparent: containment was to be extended to certain extra-European sections of the perimeter by means of new alliances, while in the military sphere a "New

Look" indicated that emphasis would be placed on strategic retaliatory power and drastic cuts in conventional forces. Thus massive retaliation, Dulles' original recommendation to Eisenhower when the latter was still one of several Republican candidates, became official policy. As a defensive strategy which reduced American flexibility at least in military terms, the New Look carried little promise of new initiatives aimed at the liberation of East-Central Europe; yet the administration, and principally the secretary of state, was loath to abandon its vocal advocacy of rollback.

After the turmoil in East Germany, Dulles appeared a shade more careful in circumscribing the practical aspects of liberation. In a major address before the United Nations General Assembly on September 17, 1953, he maintained as before that "it is not in the interest of peace, or the other goals of our charter, that the once independent peoples of [East-Central Europe] should feel that they can no longer live by their traditions and their faith," but he made an unusually strong declaration as to the means of liberation: "[Our] creed does not call for exporting revolution or inciting others to violence. Let me make that emphatic. We believe that violent change destroys what it would gain. We put our hopes in the vast possibilities of peaceful change."[43] The official communiqué that issued from the Bermuda conference of Eisenhower, Churchill, and Laniel later that year reiterated this revisionist but essentially passive line: "We cannot accept as justified or permanent the present division of Europe. Our hope is that in due course peaceful means will be found to enable the countries of Eastern Europe to play their part as free nations in a free Europe."[44] The stress on peaceful change would lead French Foreign Minister Georges Bidault to conclude after the Berlin conference in January 1954 that Dulles "surely didn't believe in [rollback] at that conference as far as I could see. That was buried with the electoral campaign in the United States."[45] Yet the secretary of state continued to make hopeful and even inflammatory remarks about the satellites. In a speech in Chicago on November 29, 1954, he contrasted the increasingly deferential treatment accorded to the Yugoslavs by the new Soviet leadership and noted that this "may embolden the satellites to demand for themselves a measure of independence." His attitude toward negotiation remained unchanged: "The scope of conferences with the Soviet Government is necessarily limited by our attitude towards the captive peoples, for the Soviets know that we will not make any deal which would condone and perpetuate the captivity of men and nations."[46] Thus American policy regarding the satellites continued to wallow in ambiguous generalities while ruling out diplomatic initiatives. The speed with which America's strategic superiority was being reduced by the Soviets, who had successfully tested a nuclear device in August 1953, and the concurrent formulation of a policy of deterrence by the threat of massive retaliation contributed to the official view that a drawn-out but relatively stable struggle with the Soviet Union was inevitable. The stress on stability and peaceful coexistence was of course diametrically opposed to any really dynamic concept of liberation, but Dulles, at least, refused to acknowledge the inconsistency; instead, he continued to profess his confidence (scarcely distinguishable from that of the originators of containment) that the example of a strong and prosperous free world, uncompromising and unwavering in its principles, would induce the decay and ultimate collapse of the Soviet imperial order.

Two policies relative to East-Central Europe were inherited by the Eisenhower administration: that of containment, which assumed that the satellites were to remain members of the Soviet bloc until the internal disintegration of the communist system was set in motion; and that of assistance to Tito, which was based on the hope that the success of his system of national communism would accelerate the process of disintegration. The subsequent policy of liberation does not seem to have arisen in response to some significant change in the international environment; rather, it represented a new messianism, the principal function of which was to rally around the Republican party the masses of voters frustrated by the prevailing stalemate. But, while containment, derided as passive and unproductive, had been implemented by practical initiatives such as the Truman Doctrine, the Marshall Plan, and NATO, the policy of liberation never acquired a similarly tangible form. From the outset it manifested itself in a deluge of moralistic and legalistic rhetoric that may have been intrinsically unimpeachable but that proved ineffective in easing the satellites' subjection; it is likely that the vocal liberation campaign only reaffirmed the Soviet leaders' resolve to bind the satellites even closer to their ideological fountainhead.

Ironically, the Eisenhower administration demonstrated a greater inflexibility than its predecessor in responding to changes within the Soviet bloc, for the New Course phase, most notably in Hungary, passed without any tangible reaction from Washington. While American propaganda organs rapidly adjusted to the New Course, the State Department gave no official indication that Imre Nagy represented a more liberal, quasi-Titoist brand of communism and therefore deserved treatment different from that accorded to Rákosi; Hungary and the other satellites continued to be viewed as undifferentiated appendages of the Soviet Union. Popular unrest and the launching of the New Course in certain satellites should perhaps have provided the incentive for a selective relaxation of American economic and diplomatic sanctions. Instead, these developments were perceived by Dulles to justify continuation of his hard line, and he allowed no compromise on the admission of the satellites to the United Nations or with respect to the restrictions on trade. Even cultural exchanges were discouraged, although, in the face of popular opposition to the visit of eleven Czechoslovak and Hungarian clergymen in July 1954, even the State Department would remark that "the spiritual foundation on which this country rests is too strong to be adversely affected" by such a small group. In retrospect, it is doubtful whether even a positive American response to the tentative liberalization in Hungary would have saved Nagy from his eventual demotion in 1955, but the logic of liberation and the official encouragement of Titoism should nevertheless have prompted a more flexible approach to such developments.

In the event, American relations with the satellites in the early years of the Eisenhower administration were marked by the same pattern of petty aggravations that had prevailed in the Stalinist era. In January 1953, the Bierut regime charged that U.S. aircraft had violated Polish territory the previous November and alleged that the Americans were sponsoring subversive activities in Poland; the continuing harassment of American diplomats induced the State Department to order the closure of the Polish consulates in New York, Chicago, and Detroit. Rumanian employees of the formerly U.S.-owned oil companies at Ploesti were brought to trial in February on charges of espionage and sabotage, while a Czech note dated January 30 protested against American-financed espionage and subversion. At the United Nations, Ambassador Lodge dismissed the Czech allegations, stating that 95.7 percent of the Mutual Security Act funds was spent on regular military and economic aid, the remaining $4,300,000 being used to provide transit facilities for escapees.[47] These various protests may have been largely the result of the paranoia that characterizes all totalitarian regimes, but CIA director Allen Dulles admitted in an interview in March 1954 that, since the communists were pursuing subversive activities in the West, the Americans would be stupid not to assist anticommunists in the satellites.[48]

The satellites' support for the communists in the Korean war had only strengthened American opposition to any commercial intercourse with them, and the volume of trade continued to decline,[49] although a momentary jump in American exports occurred in 1954 owing to food shipments under the president's emergency program for flood relief in East Germany, Hungary, Czechoslovakia, and Yugoslavia. The last-named country remained the one notable exception to the dismal pattern of mutual recriminations and distrust. Bolstered in his independent stance by U.S. economic and military aid, Tito took the bold step of signing a treaty of friendship and cooperation with Greece and Turkey in February 1953; the treaty was expanded into a mutual defense pact in August 1954, and the following October Yugoslavia at last settled its long-standing feud with Italy over Trieste. Although the Balkan Pact declined in significance with the Soviet-Yugoslav rapprochement and the Turkish-Greek dispute over Cyprus, it did for a time serve to symbolize the latitude in foreign policy enjoyed by a Western-supported national communist regime. By 1955 the total cost to the United States of ensuring Tito's friendly neutrality stood at close to $1.5 billion, of which only $55 million consisted of repayable loans, but this was arguably money well spent in terms of the Kremlin's irritation, improved Western security in the Mediterranean, and the benefits of propaganda among the satellite peoples.

The greatest impact of the policy of liberation lay in the realm of psychological warfare, which Dulles had designated at the outset as the principal instrument of rollback. In the course of the Senate Foreign Relations Committee's hearings on his nomination, he had reiterated the view that the United States ought to intensify its psychological warfare efforts with a view to liberating the satellites, and shortly afterward President Eisenhower appointed a special committee to study the question, headed by William H. Jackson and including the principal White House adviser on psychological warfare, C. D. Jackson; since the latter had been among the founders of the Committee for a Free Europe, it was foreseeable that the study group's recommendations would entail an intensification of the U.S. propaganda effort. Such a course was an eminently suitable compromise for the administration, for it was at once consistent with Dulles' doctrine, satisfying for the émigrés and other interested groups, and comforting for the disaffected East Europeans; furthermore, to the extent that it was implemented by ostensibly private and independent outlets such as RFE and Radio Liberty (which beamed its broadcasts to the Soviet Union), the United States could conveniently disclaim any direct responsibility for the content or the consequences.

The teleological quality of "liberation" created no small dilemma for the propaganda organs, and an RFE policy directive during the 1952 election campaign explicitly warned against any interpretation of political statements which might "encourage militant anti-communists to go over from passive to active resistance in the expectation that such resistance will be supported by Western elements."[50] Even unadorned reporting on the campaign was likely to arouse the East Europeans' optimism, however, as had been the case with news of the Kersten Amendment and its recommendation that escapees be organized into military units. Now, after years of improvising in an official policy vacuum, Radio Free Europe found itself the unofficial spokesman for an administration elected on a platform that declared the liberation of the satellites to be a key goal of U.S. foreign policy. The messianic tone was eminently suitable for propaganda, but, when it became clear that no specific guidance or elaboration on the theme of liberation was about to issue from Washingon, RFE proceeded to improvise as before. However, even though liberation was ill defined, it provided a policy context inherently different from that of the Truman administration; in declaratory if not operational policy, liberation had replaced containment as the fundamental goal regarding the Soviet sphere. Reliance on a nongovernmental agent for the elaboration of a declaratory policy incurred grave risks, but, in spite of this, Radio Free Europe did not suffer from a lack of official encouragement. Dulles himself commended it on many occasions, citing as a proof of its effectiveness communist efforts to jam its broadcasts; in the same context he noted that the programs kept alive the hope of eventual *self-liberation.*[51]

From the events in Czechoslovakia and East Germany in the first half of 1953, the policy makers at RFE drew lessons that were to form the basis for the next phase in their propaganda effort. They noted the existence of a large, unorganized, inarticulate opposition that included the young and even some communists; observed that, partly as a result of the state of flux in the Kremlin, local leaders were hesitant to crush this opposition; and concluded that if the workers stood firm they might extract concessions from a leadership obsessed with the achievement of production goals. RFE's response, outlined in its June 30 policy guidance for Czechoslovakia, was to make the workers aware of their potential power, to undermine the loyalty of the police and the armed forces to the party, to encourage party officials to save their skins by sabotage or by defection, and to urge young people to prepare for the building of a postcommunist society.[52] This policy was first implemented in mid-July in Operation Prospero, when an intensive four-day radio barrage supported the dropping of some twelve million balloon-carried leaflets over Czech cities. When toward the end of the year the Siroky-Novotny regime announced that ongoing economic reforms would be followed by elections at various levels, RFE concluded that its offensive was bearing fruit and in April 1954 launched a longer-range action program called Operation VETO. Claiming to speak as the voice of the People's Opposition, RFE set about propagating this opposition's "Ten Demands," which involved such pragmatic goals as smaller quotas, less bureaucratic oppression, and less official interference in the workers' free time. The radio campaign was complemented by the expedition of more sophisticated, controllable hydrogen-filled balloons carrying leaflets that at first bore only the mysterious number "10," then outlined the ten demands. Concurrently, RFE attempted to explain the rationale underlying the operation—that, since Western liberation by war was as unlikely as a voluntary Soviet withdrawal, liberation could come about only as a result of a "favorable confluence of events within and outside" Czechoslovakia. "Given . . . a favorable relationship of internal and external components, and given the right moment when in the course of international events the Soviet Union finds it less painful not to intervene than to intervene, then coordinated mass opposition becomes coordinated mass action actively supported by the 'Opposition Center' outside." While this was clearly a long-range expectation, RFE nevertheless felt that a limited but realistic action program had to be initiated and advised its listeners to support the least inimical candidates in the upcoming elections (which, in the event, were postponed by the regime). The dangers inherent in this strategy were inescapable. First, internal resistance would have to be managed masterfully to keep it growing constantly and at the same time to prevent it from erupting prematurely; second, a conclusive assessment of the exact moment when the "confluence of forces" reached the critical stage was well-nigh impossible. There is evidence that RFE's incitement of the workers did worry the communist leadership, and some officials were demoralized when RFE publicized their misdeeds and warned of eventual retribution; the ten demands furthermore reflected with accuracy the most immediate grievances of the population. RFE even made subtle appeals to Slovakian nationalism by dismissing the Slovak National Council as an instrument of communist centralism.[53] But, if Operation VETO did succeed in focusing the latent opposition within Czechoslovakia, its promise of ultimate liberation remained shrouded in ambiguity.

On October 1, 1954, Radio Free Europe launched its second major campaign, Operation FOCUS, which was directed at Hungary in an attempt to take advantage of Imre Nagy's New Course.[54] It followed the general pattern of Operation VETO: millions of leaflets carrying the letters NEM (for Nemzeti Ellenállási Mozgalom, or National Opposition Movement) or the number "12" (indicating its twelve demands) as well as "Liberty Bell" medals with the inscription "Hungarians for Freedom—All the Free World for the Hungarians," were dropped; and the broadcasting schedule was expanded to elaborate on the same themes. When the Czechoslovakian and Hungarian regimes issued official protests against these campaigns (complaining incidentally that the balloons represented a hazard for aircraft), the State Department replied ingenuously that the leaflets, originating with what was in any case a private organization, only recommended remedies for well-known shortcomings.[55] Operation FOCUS was canceled early in 1955 following Nagy's demise, but Radio Free Europe continued its area-wide propaganda offensive both on the airwaves (by means of twenty-nine powerful transmitters located in West Germany and in Portugal) and, in the case of Poland, Hungary, and Czechoslovakia, by means of balloons.

The operations carried out under the aegis of the Committee for a Free Europe were not, however, purely propagandistic; the committee's Munich headquarters also had a research-and-analysis section which drew upon private as well as public sources in the satellites, and the accumulated data were no doubt relayed to interested agencies in Washington. In West Berlin, meanwhile, RIAS was pursuing what one analyst has called its "strategy of constructive subversion" in the direction of East Germany.[56] Such a strategy did not form an integral part of any comprehensive American program that envisaged specific outcomes and involved appropriate contingency planning, however, and thus it imposed on the propagandists an immense and unfair responsibility for the consequences of their actions.

The problems of misperception and misinterpretation became particularly acute in these early years of the Eisenhower administration, when political warfare was viewed as an inexpensive and suitably nonviolent means of winning the cold war. For the people in the satellites, it seemed inconceivable that the United States would sponsor massive propaganda campaigns without further committing itself to the achievement of their liberation. Even before the term "rollback" acquired official currency, there was a tendency among the East European anticommunists to overestimate the West's concern and determination to free them; as one refugee observed, "Everyone knows that Hungary will never be able to shake off the yoke of the USSR by herself and that she can do so only with outside help."[57] Since the propaganda organs, and particularly the émigrés on their staffs, had a vested interest in liberation, it is not surprising that, having taken their cue from the occasional Dullesian flight of rhetoric, they would indulge in a certain amount of exaggeration. A collaborator of the Voice of America observed that "no one at the State Department or the Voice was in a position to know at any given time precisely what was being broadcast. . . . It was not always easy to persuade the desk heads to temper the promises they made to the captive peoples so as not to exceed the realities of American policy." On the one side, the "comforting generalities" of the liberation policy were open to misinterpretation by the broadcasters; on the other, the listeners were only too ready to "transmute vague implications of eventual liberation into *explicit promises* of *imminent* liberation."[58] Thus a critical asymmetry developed between the views of liberation held in Washington and those held in East-Central Europe. Even at the time this did not escape the notice of some analysts: "To aid and abet [the East Europeans] in opposing or conspiring against their dictators without recognizing that we ourselves may thereby be committed at the appropriate time to more thoroughgoing action . . . is naiveté or cowardice. Who wills the end wills the means—and all the necessary steps en route."[59] But most contemporary critics, while advocating prudence and an emphasis on straight news and cultural programs, conceded that freedom had to be the essence of the message of the West. For its part, the administration found it difficult to acknowledge publicly the purely exhortative nature of the liberation policy. Noted the *Manchester Guardian* on July 2, 1954: "Mr. Dulles has retreated from the concept of 'liberating' the countries behind the Iron Curtain. But he still believes that the hope of freedom must be extended to all these captive peoples." Indeed, official statements, such as that of Dulles on the occasion of the one hundred seventh anniversary of Hungary's Independence Day, when he broadcast that "we can view the future with quiet resolution and confidence," or the Dulles message assuring the Poles that the United States "joins them in their desire for independence from the unhappy bondage of Communism," were superficially unexceptionable and innocuous.[60] Perhaps neither the propagandists nor their targets could be expected to discriminate consistently between fine shades of encouragement. Yet the administration and the general public manifested a dangerously naïve faith in the effectiveness of political warfare; unless the secret, underlying motive was to weaken the Soviet Union's strategic position in East-Central Europe at any price, including the sacrifice of East European lives (and there is no evidence that the profoundly religious and moralistic Dulles was quite so Machiavellian), propaganda tactics should have been carefully integrated into a comprehensive American strategy. Subsequently, many observers—notably, the late Charles Lerche—deplored that this was not done:

> The deepest-rooted cause of the ineffectiveness of American propaganda would seem to be found in the rather common lack of understanding, both in government and among the general public, of the nature, limitations, and effectiveness of the propaganda instrument.
>
> To the extent to which American propaganda is not consonant with or implemented by policy, the propaganda itself becomes almost valueless and may on occasion prove harmful.[61]

The liberation propaganda fell on fertile ground, but the harvest, particularly in Hungary, would be bitter and bloody.

THE SPIRIT OF GENEVA

Brought to power on a platform of strident revisionism, the Eisenhower administration rapidly demonstrated a fundamental and cautious commitment to the preservation of the *status quo*, which precluded any adventurous experiments in rollback. In 1953, the United States resigned itself to the permanent partition of Korea; the following year the president over-ruled a rather more adventurous Dulles on U.S. military intervention in Indochina, where the French were fighting a losing battle against the nationalist-communist forces of Ho Chi Minh. By 1954 it was evident that revisionism, manifested in psychological warfare as well as in the intransigent stand taken at the conference tables, was only a secondary aspirational element in a strategy that defined the vital interests of the United States in terms of the avoidance of nuclear war and the strengthening of the free world's perimeter defenses. This strategic posture was reinforced by the fact that, as James Reston observed, the Republicans had "a military policy for the extremes of war and no really effective halfway policy for dealing with the halfway war now in progress."[62] Although Washington's inclination to accept the *status quo* in Europe was not reflected in American propaganda, it necessarily outweighed in practice the more abstract and expendable desire to liberate the peoples of East-Central Europe. The midterm elections in 1954 aroused little of the polemical debate on liberation which had characterized American politics two years before, and in its official statements the administration took pains to tone down the language of rollback. Said Assistant Secretary of State Livingston Merchant in an address on May 14: "In our diplomatic moves on behalf of the peoples behind the Iron Curtain, we do not attempt to prescribe what shall be the way of life of these people once they regain their freedom and independence. . . . For the future of this region, all we can legitimately expect is that the form of government and economic system to be established will correspond to the freely expressed will of the people."[63] For at least another year, however, the administration would prove unwilling to abandon completely the theme of liberation.

The problem of a divided Germany continued to take precedence over the satellite issue, and pressure came from some Western Allies—in particular, from Prime Minister Churchill at the Bermuda conference—to resume high-level negotiations with the Russians. There was no indication, however, that either side was prepared to take the first step in dismantling its alliance network, and rumors of disengagement and a nonaggression pact prior to the Berlin conference of January 1954 proved to be, at best, trial balloons. That conference, the first meeting of the four foreign ministers since the Palais Rose affair in 1949, served only to confirm the stalemate. Since the conference was, in James Conant's words, "conceived by the Americans and the British as an instrument to convince France that the rearming of the Germans was a necessity and therefore the treaties establishing a European Army must be ratified," its failure to produce a compromise on the question of reunification could scarcely be attributed to Soviet obduracy.[64] Molotov nevertheless played his part by opposing free elections (arguing that Hitler had come to power by such means); he proposed instead the creation of a coalition government drawn equally from East and West Germany and the neutralization of the country. For their part, the Western foreign ministers refused to recognize the government of the GDR as a valid interlocutor and insisted that supervised free elections precede the formation of a unified government.[65] Since Molotov would not countenance any discussion of Austria until after the German problem had been resolved, the impasse was complete, but it was not altogether unsatisfactory to the West, as witnessed by Harold Macmillan's illuminating comment at the time that "the truculence of Molotov is much less dangerous than a show of moderation. The neutralist forces in France and Italy have been correspondingly weakened."[66] The Western leaders attached a far more urgent priority to the rearmament of the Federal Republic of Germany than to the goal of reunification, and the two objectives were at least in the short run mutually exclusive.

Moscow's fear of a remilitarized Germany declined marginally with the growth in Soviet strategic military capability, and when on August 30 the French National Assembly defeated the proposal for a European Defense Community with an integrated army the Russians felt vindicated in their policy of procrastination. Two months later, however, a set of agreements signed in Paris overcame the West's divisions; under a formula devised by Foreign Secretary Anthony Eden, Germany and Italy joined an organization called the Western European Union, which in turn placed its armed forces under NATO command. This unexpected success impelled the Soviet Union to launch a penultimate series of diplomatic initiatives aimed at postponing or decelerating West Germany's rearmament program. When the West rejected its proposals for a general conference on Germany and European security, Moscow called a meeting of its satellite leaders in late November to consider possible countermeasures. Largely as a result of this new activism, 1955 turned out to be a vintage year in the annals of diplomacy. The first sign of a change of heart over Austria came with Molotov's address to the Supreme Soviet on February 8, 1955, in the course of which he asserted that an Austrian peace treaty was necessary in order to "preclude the possibility of Germany carrying out a new Anschluss."[67] The reasons for this *volte-face* are obscure, but in all likelihood the principal ones were, first, a rather forlorn hope that the example of a neutralized Austria would prove attractive to the West Germans and induce the latter to reconsider their commitment to the Western alliance, and, second, the expectation that the gesture would mollify the Americans' resistance to a summit meeting. On March 24, the day after Bonn ratified the Paris Pacts, Molotov invited Austrian Chancellor Julius Raab to bilateral talks in Moscow and the two parties quickly reached a tentative agreement. Four-power negotiations ensued in Vienna (while the West Germans reassured their allies that they remained immune to the bait of neutralism), and on May 15 the four foreign ministers signed the Austrian State Treaty in the Belvedere Palace amid wild public rejoicing.[68] The rejoicing was rather less marked in the satellites, where the negotiations had momentarily fanned hopes that the Austrian model would find wider application; the day before the ceremonies in Vienna it had been announced that the Soviet Union and its satellites had concluded in Warsaw a treaty of "friendship, collaboration, and mutual assistance," which confirmed Moscow's determination to consolidate its sphere of dominance and provided a new pretext for maintaining Soviet troops in Hungary and Rumania now that the old excuse of protecting communication lines to the zone of occupation in Austria was no longer valid.[69]

By abandoning its long-standing opposition to an Austrian peace treaty and by negotiating the compromise bilaterally, with ostentatious disdain for the other occupying powers, the Soviet Union won a minor, if undeserved, propaganda victory. It also achieved a more tangible goal, for on May 14 the assembled foreign ministers agreed to the holding of a summit conference that summer. Dulles believed that the Austrian State Treaty had been the price paid by the Russians for such a conference and could not resist the temptation to put it in the context of liberation; in a television interview on May 18 the secretary of state observed that the treaty represented the first major Soviet retreat since the war and that Austria's satellite neighbors, Czechoslovakia and Hungary, "may find freedom contagious."[70] In fact, the neutralization of Austria represented at best a symbolic retreat on the part of the Russians; in strategic terms, its most immediate consequence was to cut the Western Allies' most direct line of communication between Italy and West Germany.

Apart from the settlement of the Austrian question, the Khrushchevian New Look manifested itself in a number of other spheres. Within the bloc, and particularly in Hungary, the process of decompression threatened to acquire a momentum of its own and was accordingly slowed down, while new emphasis was placed on military and economic integration. Internal consolidation was necessary to provide a secure basis for the new Soviet regime's attempts to create a thaw in its relations outside the bloc. Khrushchev's most striking success was the reconciliation he engineered with Tito. Swallowing their pride, Soviet leaders traveled to Belgrade in May and, after apologizing for Moscow's ostracism of Tito (the safely dead Beria being used as a scapegoat), promised to coexist peacefully. The resulting "Belgrade Declaration" marked the first public appearance of the "several roads to socialism" thesis and symbolized the normalization of relations between the Soviet Union and heretical Yugoslavia.[71]

Apart from their courtship of Tito, the Soviet leaders must have concluded that there was little room left in which to maneuver in Europe, and consequently they redirected the main thrust of their activities toward the Third World. Without expecting to disturb the *status quo*, they now sought to secure their European sphere by lulling the West into a relaxed mood of peaceful coexistence and thereby retarding the military build-up of NATO and, more particularly, of West Germany. This new conciliatory image had an effect, for, throughout the West, public pressure mounted in the early months of 1955 for a summit conference that would somehow enshrine the incipient détente. The British had been urging such a meeting for two years, and now Eden came forward with a plan for a demilitarized strip in Central Europe and for a general limitation of armaments; Chancellor Adenauer made similar proposals for limited military disengagement, but remained firm in his commitment to NATO.[72] Eisenhower proved predictably susceptible to the popular clamor for détente, but even his secretary of state, whose aversion to summit meetings dated back to the Paris peace conference of 1919, became increasingly optimistic in his perception of Soviet weakness. Dulles still clung to the idea that the right mixture of firmness and promises of peaceful relations might convince the Soviet Union to grant more independence to its satellites, and he found encouragement in the progress of the New Course in Hungary and Czechoslovakia.[73] For their part, the satellite regimes viewed the upcoming conference with some trepidation (apparently the Rumanians even made some tentative overtures to imprisoned noncommunist politicians), despite Soviet assurances that their future was secure.

In view of its earlier advocacy of liberation, the administration could not afford to ignore the thorny question of the satellites, and both Dulles and Eisenhower issued statements to the effect that the status of East-Central Europe ought to be discussed at Geneva; the latter noted in his memoirs that this was one of the priority subjects considered before the conference.[74] Although the Soviets' acceptance of the tripartite invitation included objections to the placing of the satellite question on the agenda—and an additional warning in the notes sent to Britain and France, as if to lessen their already lukewarm concern for the problem—Dulles persevered in advocating greater sovereignty for East-Central Europe.[75] Testifying before the House Appropriations Committee on June 10, he stressed again that the neutralization of Austria had created a "new frontier of freedom" for Hungary and Czechoslovakia and new pressures on Moscow to relax its grip.[76] The Soviet reaction was adamant:

> It should be clear that no "problem of the countries of Eastern Europe" exists. The people of these countries, having overthrown the

rule of the exploiters, have established in their countries a people's democratic government and will not allow anyone to interfere with their domestic affairs.[77]

The preconference preparations of the administration were further complicated by the urgings of some conservative politicians that the policy of liberation be re-activated. Senator Joseph McCarthy, though past the peak of his power, submitted a resolution in which he argued that failure to discuss the satellites at Geneva would imply recognition of their status and would demoralize internal opposition; warning against another Yalta, he recommended that "the only possible way of getting the subject discussed is securing the Communists' prior agreement to that effect." But by now even such hard-line Republicans as Senators Mundt and Knowland were tiring of the Yalta myth and saw no reason to challenge the testimony of Undersecretary of State Herbert Hoover, Jr., that, while the president and Dulles sympathized with the humanitarian objectives of the resolution, their hands ought not to be tied by such an engagement.[78] Following the overwhelming rejection of McCarthy's initiative, a sense-of-Congress resolution was adopted urging that the United States help countries under foreign rule to achieve their independence.

As the date of the conference approached, it became increasingly evident that Washington would not allow the satellite issue to jeopardize the prospects of détente with the Soviet Union. Wrote Dulles in a memorandum to the president, "Probably, in private conversation, you can do more along this line than can be done in formal conference."[79] The secretary of state warned Molotov in the course of an informal meeting at the end of June that the status of East-Central Europe required discussion, but the American position was marked by a sense of futility and impotence. At a press conference prior to the summit, the president asked rhetorically: "If you believe [that liberation is desirable], how far are you going to go? You are certainly not going to declare war, are you? So there, instantly, you fix yourself limitations on how far we, as a people, will go in accomplishing this thing."[80] America's allies exhibited a notable lack of enthusiasm for the issue; French Foreign Minister Antoine Pinay tactfully informed Dulles that his advisers disagreed with his (Pinay's) stand in favor of frank discussion of the satellites.[81] When on July 12 Eisenhower and Dulles met with leading legislators to discuss the impending conference, the president remarked disparagingly that America's European allies tended to see the East-West struggle in terms of power politics rather than as a moral issue. But clearly the Soviet terms—broad discussion on the subject of relaxation of tensions, and no agenda reference to East-Central Europe—were not to be rejected at this late date.[82]

The drastic attenuation of the policy of liberation is well illustrated in a set of status papers, drafted by Dulles, which outlined the respective goals of the Americans and the Russians at the conference.[83] The paper on U.S. objectives relegated to fourth place the satellite question, and Dulles expressed profound pessimism regarding its outcome: "It will be difficult to get any formal undertaking from the Soviet Union with reference to the topic or even their acceptance of it as a proper topic for discussion." He did note the remote possibility that strong American pressure might have some effect, adding rather ambiguously that "what we ask for is less than what the Soviets gave Tito." The primary goal set down by Dulles was progress toward German reunification without neutralization or demilitarization; he anticipated that the Soviet Union would temporize and that the question would be referred to a subsequent foreign ministers' meeting. His second goal was an agreement on "European security" which would involve some reduction of forces by both sides, and with which the European allies were counted on to concur. Dulles felt that the Soviets might agree to negotiate on this second goal, but he himself was skeptical: "Care must be taken lest this arrangement operate in effect to accept and consolidate the Soviet control over the satellites." Other postulated American goals concerned arms control, curtailment of Cominform activities, cultural exchanges, and an "atoms for peace" plan.

Significantly, Dulles expected that the first and foremost Soviet goal would be to create "an appearance that the West concede the Soviet rulers a moral and social equality which will help the Soviets maintain their satellite rule by disheartening potential resistance." American policymakers evidently anticipated that their Soviet counterparts were unlikely to concede on major issues and were primarily interested in exploiting the propaganda advantages of a summit meeting. Dulles estimated the real predisposition of the British and the French to this goal to be one of indifference, and he acknowledged that the Soviets would "probably make considerable gains in this respect," adding that "the extent of Soviet gain could be limited by public knowledge that the occasion was being used by the United States to push for satellite liberation and liquidation of International Communism." The second Soviet goal, according to Dulles, was a relaxation of military activities by the West (to which the U.S. and Britain were opposed, but which France favored), and he considered that the Soviet Union might gain here in terms of the level of NATO forces and German rearmament. The third Soviet goal was thought to be nuclear disarmament without extensive safeguards, which ran counter to the modalities of the third American goal. The Russians were also expected to press for freer trade, agreement on a "statement of principles" that would give the impression of Soviet moral leadership, a

European security system devoid of all U.S. bases, and a legitimization of the status of Communist China.

In light of the foregoing, it is scarcely surprising that no progress was made at the summit in solving the fundamental issues that divided East and West. Just as predictably, the status of East-Central Europe received little attention. Harold Macmillan recalls that, when on July 17, the day before the conference opened in Paris, the Western participants met at Eisenhower's villa to discuss the summary of his address, "No one seemed to have any particular view about it, except to ask that the passage about the 'satellites' and 'tyranny' might be modified. This was done."[84] Conscious of the lingering popularity of liberation with certain politicians and interest groups back home, the president was determined to make at least passing reference to the satellites "so as to leave no doubt of their importance," and he declared in his opening speech that the American people "feel strongly that certain peoples of Eastern Europe . . . have not yet been given the benefit of this pledge [of self-determination] of our United Nations wartime declaration, reinforced by other wartime agreements." Premier Bulganin's rebuttal was blunt:

> It is common knowledge that the regime of people's democracies has been established in those countries by the people themselves of their own free will. Besides, nobody has authorized us to consider the state of affairs in those countries. Thus, there are no grounds for discussing this question at our Conference.

On the question of Germany, the Soviet Union proposed the disbandment of NATO and the Warsaw Pact and the withdrawal of foreign troops from Europe as a prerequisite to any discussion of reunification; the matter was conveniently tabled for consideration at a subsequent meeting of foreign ministers. As for the president's "Open Skies" proposal, a propaganda gambit devised by his psychological warfare advisers, it attracted much public attention but represented no practical advance toward an East-West agreement on disarmament.[85]

The summit conference's most immediate result was a short-lived euphoria, labeled by the press "Spirit of Geneva," which symbolized, however, a more fundamental alteration in Soviet-American relations—a mutual concession that the immense risks of war in the nuclear age ruled out forceful attempts by the superpowers to alter the *status quo*, at least in those areas where their vital interests were at stake. As Dulles had forecast, the Soviets made the most of this spirit's propaganda value; the photograph of a smiling Ike and Bulganin was widely circulated in East-Central Europe, intimating to the satellite peoples that a "deal" had been made at their expense. (Having been informed of this, Dulles pointedly avoided cameras at the October meeting of foreign ministers.[86]) Indeed, from the point of view of the Russians the spirit marked the success of their policies, for it enhanced their image as the agents of détente, particularly in the eyes of the Third World. With respect to East-Central Europe, the summit's impact was twofold. On the one hand, the apparently cordial spirit of the protagonists carried at least a suggestion that the West had abandoned its advocacy of liberation and tacitly acquiesced to Soviet hegemony; on the other hand, the relaxation of tensions offered some encouragement to those satellite leaders whose inclination to liberalize had hitherto been inhibited by the virulent antagonism of the two camps and it arguably paved the way for the particularistic developments of the following decade.

In the aftermath of the summit the administration manifested some concern about the American public's reaction to the relative neglect of the satellite question. At a post-mortem meeting with congressional leaders, the secretary of state claimed that American concern for the satellites had been voiced at the conference table and in informal talks, but noted that he had "never expected that the Soviet Union would agree to establish international procedures to deal with these matters."[87] (Dulles, observed an anonymous French diplomat at Geneva, "no longer really believed in rollback, but he had not yet quite drawn the conclusion that he would have to accept the status quo."[88]) The secretary subsequently sent to the president a memorandum intended to serve as a guideline for the reassertion of their theoretically revisionist attitude regarding the satellites:

> As the risk of war has diminished, so have become downgraded the security reasons which are the pretext for the Russians holding on to East Germany and maintaining a tight rule over the satellite countries. Both the President and the Secretary of State at Geneva told Bulganin and Khrushchev that the satellite states would be watched as a barometer of Soviet real intentions.[89]

In a television address on July 25, Eisenhower had already assured the public that at unofficial meetings he and Dulles had "specifically brought up, more than once, American convictions and American beliefs and American concern about such questions as the satellites of Eastern Europe."[90] One month later, speaking at a convention of the American Bar Association in Philadelphia, he reiterated that the "domination of the captive countries cannot longer be justified by a claim that this is needed for purposes of security."[91] Radio Free Europe made wide use of this and similar statements in order to dispel the East Europeans' apprehensions, but such propaganda only obscured the reality of a new world order consensually based on the European *status quo*.

In the interval between the summit and the foreign ministers' conference that began on October 27, there were few indications that the "Spirit of Geneva" would produce any substantive changes in East-West relations. Bulganin made much of this spirit in his report to the Supreme Soviet on August 4,[92] and a week later Moscow announced a reduction in the strength of its armed forces (with the satellites following suit in quick succession), but the popular pressures for liberalization in East-Central Europe made the Russians wary of concessions, particularly with regard to East Germany, that could be interpreted as a sign of weakness. As if to underline the permanence of the division of Europe, Adenauer appeared in Moscow on September 8 to negotiate the release of some 10,000 German "prisoners of war" and agreed to establish diplomatic relations with the Soviet Union; when the Russians thereupon signed a treaty with the GDR to indicate its sovereign equality with West Germany, the Western powers acceded to Adenauer's request and retaliated by declaring that the Federal Republic was the sole legal representative of Germany and that, pending a peace conference, the eastern frontiers had to be considered provisional. (The first in a long series of tactical probes occurred on November 27, when, to demonstrate that East Berlin was no longer occupied but was sovereign East German territory, the *Volkspolizei* detained two visiting American congressmen.)

At the actual meeting of foreign ministers in Geneva, the West endorsed Eden's plan for free elections in the two Germanies followed by reunification and a mutual security arrangement whereby the four Great Powers and Germany, Poland, and Czechoslovakia would renounce the use of force, guarantee each other's sovereignty, and undertake to limit armaments in a zone 100–150 miles wide along Germany's eastern frontier; as before, the Russians proposed an all-European collective security treaty that would exclude all "foreign" troops from the Continent and supersede NATO. The deadlock was complete, and the conference ended amid mutual recriminations that owed little to the "Spirit of Geneva." The fact that Dulles' talks with Molotov had by his own account been "futile" could scarcely have disheartened the secretary of state, in view of his immutable distrust of Soviet intentions;[93] the failure of Geneva II and the postponement of any tampering with the European *status quo* probably occasioned some relief, at least on the part of the two principal protagonists.

The foreign ministers' stormy meeting passed apparently without major reference to the problem of East-Central Europe. Dulles had promised to raise the question with Molotov, and he drafted identical letters to the latter and to Macmillan and Pinay requesting its inclusion in the agenda, but for some reason the letters were not sent.[94] In his closing address, the secretary contented himself with noting the Soviet Union's reluctance to permit free elections in the satellites. Taking advantage of a three-day recess in the conference, Dulles traveled to Brioni to confer with Marshal Tito and ascertain the extent of the latter's recent rapprochement with the Soviet Union. There had been earlier indications that the Yugoslavs expected the satellites to draw appropriate conclusions from this rapprochement. On the eve of the Belgrade conference, the Yugoslav ambassador to Washington had speculated that the meeting might stimulate the East Europeans to strive for greater independence and freedom of action; two months later Tito publicly attacked the most unregenerate Stalinist among his neighbors, Rákosi, saying that "there are still people who do not like the normalization of relations. They will not recognize what the Soviet leaders have said. . . . They say that what has happened is only a manoeuvre."[95] The Brioni meeting reinforced Dulles in his conviction that Titoist evolution was the answer to the satellites' dilemma, and the two men issued a joint communiqué:

> The final subject of our talk was the problem of the States of Eastern Europe. We reached common accord on recognizing the importance of independence for these States, noninterference from the outside in their internal affairs, and their right to develop their own social and economic order in ways of their own choice.[96]

Although the declaration understandably skirted the issue of free elections, and subsequent Yugoslav comment negated any impression that Tito and Dulles were of one mind on the desirable political, social, and economic goals for the satellites, the secretary of state observed optimistically after the meeting:

> I don't mean to suggest that there will be an early breakaway of the satellites from Moscow. But I think there will soon be visible signs of evolution toward governments which command more popular support than those which now exist, and which are markedly less the paid hirelings of Moscow.[97]

The Brioni visit undoubtedly contributed to this sanguine expectation, and, while in Hungary, at least, the New Course had been checked by Rákosi's return to power, Dulles appeared more confident than ever that the disintegration of the Soviet bloc was well under way. His emphasis on Titoism was a far cry from the earlier, confident promises of full self-determination, but Dulles, as one of his senior assistants observed, had "undoubtedly revised his notion of how long rollback would take—in other words, he saw that it would take a very long time. He could not find a formula to promote it with greater speed. But he never deviated from the notion that Eastern Europe would some day emerge in freedom."[98]

At the mid-December gathering of the NATO foreign ministers in Paris, Dulles reviewed the achievements of the two Geneva conferences. Geneva II, he said, had unveiled the Soviet leaders' two-faced attitude at Geneva I—"our security proposals forced this into open"—and had furthermore revealed their rigidity on the satellite question and their fear of the "contagious effect" of Tito; he concluded that the only positive outcome of the summit had been "the repudiation of war as a present means of extending [Soviet] influence" and observed that the cold war was entering a new phase, in which the East-West confrontation would shift to the Middle East and South Asia.[99] Concurrently, the Western powers decided to end the deadlock over new admissions to the United Nations (by December 1955 twenty-one states awaited admittance) by means of a package deal; the United States abstained on the question of membership for Albania, Bulgaria, Hungary, and Rumania and thus allowed them to join the world body,[100] much to the dismay of the Assembly of Captive European Nations, which had been campaigning strenuously against their admission. But clearly this compromise in no way signified American approval of the regimes concerned. When at the end of the year Eisenhower and Dulles drafted routine sympathetic Christmas messages to the satellites, their action was attacked by the Russians as "not in accord with the spirit of Geneva"; the official note replying to this charge, as well as the president's State of the Union address, maintained that the American policy of liberation remained a valid and enduring answer to the "bondage of millions."[101] Commented the *New York Times*: "On the eve of 1956, in which a President and a new Congress will be elected, the Republican Administration welcomed the opportunity to reaffirm its support of eventual freedom for the peoples of Eastern Europe."[102] Few anticipated the convulsions that would shake the Soviet empire and the dilemmas that would face the West in the course of that year.

DECOMPRESSION IN POLAND

If, as one historian suggested, the Geneva summit amounted to a tacit nonaggression pact between the superpowers, this was largely a result of their common awareness that the military balance had undergone both a qualitative and a quantitative transformation.[103] Early in the year, Secretary of the Air Force Donald A. Quarles proclaimed the advent of a new era:

> If we are to credit recent Communist statements as to their capabilities and intent, we must conclude that we are now passing, or will before long pass, from a phase of unilateral deterrence to a phase of mutual deterrence. That is, from a phase in which the Soviets have been de-

terred from an attack by our air-atomic retaliatory power to a phase in which each side would be deterred by the retaliatory power of the other.[104]

This change was significant, for America's capacity to wage limited war had already been curtailed by the Eisenhower administration's policy of reducing military expenditures, particularly for ground power (U.S. Army strength on June 30, 1956, was 700,000 men weaker than it had been in 1953), and of concentrating upon strategic retaliatory capability. As long as the United States possessed a quasi monopoly of nuclear weapons, the latter could serve not only the prevailing defensive strategy but also a hypothetical offensive one. Although American superiority in these weapons remained overwhelming for some years, Eisenhower reported that at the summit all had agreed "a nuclear war would be an intolerable disaster which must not be permitted to occur."[105] The perceived state of mutual deterrence meant that reliance on nuclear weapons at the expense of conventional forces would lead to an even greater inflexibility in military strategy and tactics than before, but the administration remained steadfast in its commitment to a strategy of nuclear defense.

Against the background of this altered power balance, it was becoming evident that, as the president put it, the conflict between international communism and freedom had taken on a new complexion. Yet the makers of American foreign policy still sought to reconcile the reality of this state of mutual deterrence with their moral, and perhaps utopian, yearnings. On the one hand, it was acknowledged that nuclear stalemate and developments in the Soviet bloc called for a reappraisal of American attitudes. Referring to the Austrian State Treaty and the Kremlin's reconciliation with Tito and normalized relations with Bonn, the secretary of state concluded on February 26 that the Soviet leaders "pursue their foreign policy goals with less manifestation of intolerance and less emphasis on violence."[106] On the other hand, as Dulles had declared earlier in the year, the United States would accept no compromise with the Russians in its pledge to work for the liberation of the East Europeans. In defense of this pledge, a prominent conservative columnist wrote that "there had never been any deviation from the original position, which is that the United States intends to use moral force only—not military force—to help attain the objective of liberation of the captive peoples"; he understood the means to be "encouragement and stimulus to the people there, so that some day they will rise up against their tyrannical masters and achieve their freedom."[107] Although this policy seemed to aim at the impossible, it retained wide public support. On April 16 the House of Representatives unanimously approved a resolution calling for the peaceful liberation of the peoples "now under Soviet and Chinese Communist bondage."[108]

The Soviet leaders meanwhile manifested a growing confidence in their intrabloc and external policies. The difficulties of determining a successor to Stalin had been overcome with the emergence of Khrushchev as *primus inter pares* in the Politburo, the rapprochement with Tito had momentarily ended internecine bickering, the offensive in the Third World was reaping its first rewards (notably in the case of Egypt's Nasser), and much was expected of the new five-year economic plan. In this atmosphere the relaxation within the Soviet sphere took the form of de-Stalinization. Dulles held a press conference on April 3 to comment on the rumors of an anti-Stalin campaign:

> [The] fact that the Soviet rulers now denounce much of the past gives cause for hope, because it demonstrates that liberalizing influences from within and without can bring about peaceful change. . . . [The] yearnings of the subject peoples are not to be satisfied merely by a rewriting of past history. Thus we can hope for ultimate changes more fundamental than any that have so far been revealed.[109]

Three weeks later, having asserted that the apparent doctrinal shift had "put a certain premium now upon Titoism," Dulles elaborated: "If the Soviet Communists now say that it is all right to have communism on a national basis, that offers a great prospect to the Poles, the Czechs and so forth, who would much rather have their own national brand of communism than be run by Moscow."[110] Factors that contributed to the secretary's optimism included the dissolution of the Cominform on April 17, the Soviet announcement a month later of reductions in the armed forces, the demotion of Molotov on June 1, and Tito's visit to Moscow in June, which ended in a reassertion of the "different roads" line.

The bombshell of Khrushchev's anti-Stalin speech before the Twentieth Congress of the CPSU, made public by the State Department on June 4, did not eradicate all doubts about a basic change in Soviet aims. Dulles himself warned that Khrushchev's purpose "may be merely to persuade the subject peoples that the present dictatorship is good because it condemns the past dictatorship."[111] The policy of supporting Titoism suffered a setback, however, not so much as a result of second thoughts on the part of the administration as because of the apprehensions of the mass public and of a good proportion of Congress that Tito's visit to Moscow symbolized his reintegration into the Soviet sphere. Dulles tried to argue the contrary, testifying before the Senate Foreign Relations Committee that it would be "incredible that [Tito] would give up his ambition to exerting an independent influence in Eastern Europe and to promote the independence of the satellite states, as he publicly stated in his conference with me at Brioni," and he stressed that "at the present time Tito sets an example of independence which is important to maintain in view of our efforts to bring about the liberation of the satellite countries."[112] The more sophisticated pundits tended to support this stand. C. S. Sulzberger wrote in the *New York Times* on April 18 that "the greatest fault of our satellite policy, both as announced and as applied, is that it has not concentrated upon the attainable. . . . But there is a realizable goal. That is Titoism." George Kennan, no longer an active participant in policy-making, published an article advising the West to refrain from putting too much pressure on the satellites to break away from Moscow: "Whether we like it or not, the gradual evolution of these Communist regimes to a position of greater independence . . . is the best we can hope for as the next phase of development in that area."[113] But in the end the political exigencies of the election year prevailed, and the Eisenhower administration timidly suspended its program of military and economic aid to Yugoslavia, although the latter was reinstated in October on the scarcely novel excuse that Tito's independence rested in large measure on American economic sponsorship.[114] The possibility of a visit by Bulganin and Khrushchev to Washington (following their trip to England that summer) was similarly rejected on the grounds that neither the American nor the East European publics were ready for such a display of hospitality. That the administration wavered in this fashion was a reflection of the difficulty it faced in reconciling its doctrinal and popularly based opposition to communism with the concept of peaceful, if competitive, coexistence, which had been sanctioned at the summit; the clear-cut confrontation of the early cold war years had given way to a set of complex relationships that required more highly differentiated responses from an administration whose strategic and internal political options were severely limited.

Meanwhile, American propaganda continued to be the subject of a wide range of criticism. Acknowledging the existence of "internal people's opposition" in the satellites, Soviet authorities charged that it could be directly attributed to "lying propaganda aimed against the people's regime" by Western broadcasts and balloon-leaflet campaigns.[115] Clearly the Russians were apprehensive that their experiment in de-Stalinization might become uncontrollable as a result of Western incitement of the East Europeans. Indeed, Radio Free Europe lost no opportunity to exploit the Kremlin's tactical shifts. It saw that the "several roads to socialism" thesis could have a powerful centrifugal impact in the satellites and with renewed vigor proceeded to elaborate that theme in its broadcasts after Khrushchev's Twentieth Congress speech, arguing that "the logic of de-Stalinization demands revising the system in order to make it impossible for any new Stalin to arise."[116] At the same time, and somewhat paradoxically, RFE assured its listeners that the West remained skeptical about the real extent of the Kremlin's inclination to liberalize. This ambivalence was criticized by an unnamed American diplomat in Eastern Europe:

> The United States has always encouraged these peoples to overthrow the Government. Our propaganda still implies this purpose. We have done nothing or said nothing to give the impression that we will ever make our peace with this regime. Yet we *must* do business with it—and do so. This schizophrenic attitude puzzles the local population.[117]

The FEC's policy adviser denied in reply that either RFE or VOA had ever broadcast incitements to revolt,[118] but evidently the old problem of attuning official statements of encouragement to the hypersensitive receptiveness of the satellite peoples had not been successfully resolved. In fact, a reappraisal of American propaganda policy was concurrently in progress; it was reported that in the U.S. Information Agency a review of the entire program had been initiated—"a country by country study of information policy with relation to the satellites to insure that programme content takes into account the different situations in each country."[119] As will be seen, however, even after the 1956 upheavals in East-Central Europe no consensus was reached as to the role played by the propaganda organs before and during those events.

The ongoing process of cautious liberalization in the satellites received a new impetus from Khrushchev's anti-Stalin speech and Tito's triumphal visit to Moscow, but, concurrently, warning signs appeared that the East European masses might try to force the pace of decompression. The first outbreak occurred in the Polish industrial center of Poznań. Poland's Stalinist party boss, Bierut, had expired in Moscow in March after attending the Twentieth Congress, and was replaced by the marginally less dogmatic Edward Ochab after Khrushchev flew to Warsaw to personally supervise the succession. The local intelligentsia had been urging the regime to liberalize its policies for some time, and the peasantry was doggedly resisting collectivization, but, as in Pilsen and East Berlin three years earlier, the initial challenge came from the workers. On June 28, after false reports that a delegation sent to present their economic grievances had been arrested, the workers of Poznań took to the streets and stormed the party and secret police headquarters; troops and armored vehicles were sent in, and after three days of fighting and some fifty casualties the rioting ceased. Momentarily, at least, it seemed that the forces of reaction in the regime had prevailed.

On the day following the eruption in Poznań the State Department issued a bland statement noting that "all free peoples will be watching the situation closely to see whether or not the Polish people will be allowed a government which will remedy the grievances which have brought them to a breaking point."[120] Dulles exhibited an equally cautious optimism in his news conference of July 11: "It is not a matter for this year or next year, but I believe that this second post-war decade . . . will see these new forces take charge of the situation and that we can really hopefully look forward to a transformation of the international scene." He added that a genuinely new Soviet policy would have to include greater independence for the satellites.[121] Thus, America's response to the Poznań riots differed little from its reaction to the East German uprising, and once again material assistance in the form of surplus food was offered and rejected, but the administration was rather more confident than it had been in 1953 that an irreversible process of liberalization was at work in the satellites.

On the Soviet side, the disturbances in Poland and the West's reactions to them were ill received, for it was probably thought that the policy of de-Stalinization had been dangerously misinterpreted both in the satellites and in the West. As if to add fuel to the fire, on June 29 two amendments to the Mutual Security Act were introduced in the U.S. Senate which were intended to encourage private organizations "engaged in keeping alive the will for freedom" in Eastern Europe. Senator Dirksen's proposal was that $5 million be expended at the president's discretion; the Douglas Amendment provided for $20 million as well as an agency—a "Freedom Administration"—to distribute the largesse. Both senators made extensive reference to the old promises of liberation and to the ongoing events in Poland, but their initiatives—calculated at least in part to appeal to the ethnic vote—appeared to embarrass the administration and eventually died quiet deaths.[122] In the meantime, a resolution of the Soviet Central Committee testified to the Russians' alarm:

> At the height of the "cold war" . . . the U.S. Congress officially (in addition to unofficial allocations) appropriated $100,000,000 for subversive activities in the people's democracies and the Soviet Union. . . . [Evidence that the Americans are stepping up the cold war] is seen in the decision of the U.S. Senate to appropriate an additional $25,000,000 for subversive activities, which is cynically described as "encouraging freedom" behind the "iron curtain." . . . It is clear that the anti-popular demonstrations in Poznań were financed from this source.[123]

And on July 21, while visiting Warsaw, Premier Bulganin warned against Western efforts to upset the satellite regimes and against allowing "national particularism" and "opportunistic vacillations" to arise from a misperception of the liberalizing tendencies within the Soviet bloc.[124] As of mid-1956 the "spirit of Geneva," if not its underlying premise of mutual deterrence, had become a dead letter.

The concurrent election campaign in the United States saw much less emphasis placed on liberation than had been the case in 1952, but the fate of the satellites was still too powerful an issue to be ignored completely by either party. Early in the year the Democrats attacked the administration for failing at Geneva to implement its promises of liberation, and the party's election platform repeated these charges:

> We condemn the Republican Administration for its heartless record of broken promises to the unfortunate victims of Communism. Candidate Eisenhower's 1952 pledges to "liberate" the captive peoples have now been disavowed and dishonored. . . . We shall press before the United Nations the principle that Soviet Russia withdraw its troops from the captive countries.

The platform even denounced the Republican administration for "standing silent when the peoples rise in East Germany and Poland."[125] Meanwhile, Democratic presidential candidate Adlai Stevenson publicly and completely disagreed with an earlier assertion by George Kennan that the status of East-Central Europe was final.[126] The Republican platform, adopted on August 21, mentioned liberation in the context of NATO ("Instead of being merely a military alliance, NATO will provide a means for coordinating the policies of the member states on vital matters, such as the reunification of Germany, the liberation of the satellites, and general policies in relation to the Soviet Union"), but clearly the party of an incumbent president could not afford to indulge in the crusading cadences that had distinguished the GOP's 1952 campaign; the platform merely expressed confidence that "our peaceful methods, resolutely pursued, will finally restore freedom and independence to oppressed peoples and nations."[127] (It is worthy of note that one sentence that appeared in an early draft—"We rejoice that the hold of Soviet Communism [over the satellites] is today shaken"—was missing from the final version.[128]) The Republicans distributed a pamphlet entitled *Republican Policy of Liberation to Turn the Tide Against Communism*, and in his campaign speeches Vice-President Richard Nixon reiterated the hoary promise never to write off the captive millions,[129] but, by and large, Eisenhower and Stevenson avoided the issue of liberation until the last moment, when it was thrust into prominence by the Hungarian revolt.

Meanwhile, developments in Poland appeared to testify to the validity of the "peaceful liberation" thesis.[130] In August, Wladyslaw Gomulka, who had been deposed as first secretary in 1949 because of his alleged sympathies for Tito's version of national communism, was restored to full party membership. Even more surprising was the openness of the trials of the Poznań rioters, which began on September 27; breaking with the traditional pattern of East European political trials, the regime allowed the defendants to make candid statements regarding the deplorable social and economic conditions in Poland. But this permissiveness only accentuated the popular sentiment against collectivization, economic centralization, and the continued presence of seven Soviet divisions, sentiments which found their champion in the person of Gomulka. By early October the state of unrest was reaching a critical point; while workers and intellectuals stepped up their demands, students in Warsaw, Kraków, and other centers took to the streets to demonstrate. Responding to Moscow's alarm at the disorder, Defense Minister Rokossovsky (Polish-born, but a Soviet citizen and unquestioningly loyal to the Kremlin) placed the Soviet base at Legnica on alert, but the balance of power did not necessarily favor him, for the Polish army's performance at Poznań in June raised doubts as to its reliability, while the newly released General Waclaw Komar was busily reorganizing a 50,000-strong workers' militia that was even more immune to Russian influence.

Caught in the crossfire of domestic and Soviet demands, the Polish leadership demonstrated a remarkable unity of purpose in opting for greater independence. On October 15, just four days before the Central Committee was to convene, the Politburo secretly welcomed Gomulka back to its ranks and decided to recommend his appointment as first secretary; the move was urged most forcefully by the premier, former Social Democrat Joseph Cyrankiewicz, but even Ochab, incensed at the Kremlin's interference, agreed to his own demotion. The stage was set for an extraordinary test of wills when, on October 19, an imposing Soviet delegation (including Khrushchev, Mikoyan, Molotov, Kaganovich, and Warsaw Pact commander Marshal Koniev) arrived in Warsaw. Concurrently, Soviet units in Silesia and East Germany began to move ominously toward the capital, while in Warsaw the Gomulka forces mobilized workers' committees in the factories and the militia took up defensive positions around the city. In the course of a protracted and acrimonious debate, Khrushchev reportedly shouted, "We shed our blood for this country, and now you want to sell out to the Americans and the Zionists,"[131] but the Poles remained united and adamant. Ochab told the Russians that he would call off the negotiations unless the advance of Soviet troops on Warsaw was halted, and Gomulka threatened to broadcast to the nation the nature of the Soviet pressures and to arm the workers of Warsaw. The visitors thereupon turned conciliatory, having probably decided that in the final analysis Gomulka was a reliable communist and that Poland's strategic position ruled out outright secession à la Tito. They sanctioned Gomulka's appointment; agreed to curtail Soviet interference, particularly with regard to religious affairs, collectivization, and the secret police; and promised to revise their trade policies and to recall the hated Rokossovsky and other military advisers. In the immediate aftermath of this climactic confrontation Gomulka demonstrated consummate skill in pacifying both the Polish masses and the Russians. After making public promises to hold elections, carry out economic reforms, and safeguard Poland's sovereignty, he did not hesitate to call upon the support of the workers in quelling explicitly anticommunist demonstrations by students in Warsaw on October 22. Both the regime and the Polish people responded sympathetically to the revolution that broke out in Hungary that same week, but, when a fortnight after its repression a delegation headed by Gomulka traveled to Moscow to negotiate the cancellation of debts, the extension of new credits, and other contentious issues, the Poles had no choice but to endorse the Kremlin's foreign policy in general and in particular its application to Hungary. This was a small price to pay for the stabilization of what appeared to be a major advance in the internal liberalization of a satellite regime.

Poland's success in moving toward national communism without any supportive action on the part of the West was greeted in Washington as a vindication of the policy of peaceful liberation. In the course of a radio interview on October 21, the secretary of state was asked what the United States would do in the event of a Polish bloodbath: "Well, we don't think that there will be a 'blood bath.' . . . There could be some repression. But when you have a whole people rising up, it is likely that efforts will be made to put it down by mass military measures. That has never been attempted before. I don't think it would succeed. I think what we see going on is part of a process."[132] Noting that the Poles would not want any outside involvement which could precipitate a world war, Dulles went on to state categorically that the United States would not intervene militarily in the event of a repressive action by the Soviet Union. Since Dulles openly referred to the Kremlin's dilemma between the potentially centrifugal effects of liberalization and the drawbacks of a return to Stalinism, he must have calculated that an assurance of American nonintervention would strengthen the hand of the more conciliatory Soviet leaders; it is an open question whether, particularly in light of the events in Hungary, the converse calculation might have been tactically more appropriate. Even from the perspective of peaceful liberation the American response to the Polish October was notable mainly for its ponderous caution; bilateral talks on economic aid were initiated shortly after Gomulka's accession to power, but it took Washington some eight months to advance the first in a series of loans.

If the apparent victory of reform in Poland owed nothing to the West, and, if, judging from its passive reaction, Washington did not really anticipate another Yugoslavia, then the policy of liberation was left devoid of any operational significance. Yet Dulles continued to insist on the validity and effectiveness of that policy. Addressing a delegation of Polish-Americans on October 22, he said that "there had been a tendency in West European countries to be unsympathetic to the U.S. attitude on the satellites. These countries feared that any change in the status quo in Eastern Europe might threaten their own security. However, in the last year and a half, the European governments have come around largely to our way of thinking."[133] It seems likely that if the West Europeans now accepted the American point of view, it was because they perceived the absence of concrete planning behind the occasionally violent rhetoric. A statement by Undersecretary of State Robert Murphy before the House Foreign Affairs Committee on October 11 had testified to the fundamentally innocuous nature of Washington's satellite policy:

> We can facilitate the exposure of Soviet and satellite citizens to free societies. We can keep before the satellites their ancient national traditions. We can show them how the free world is able to accommodate diversity within it. It is our policy to do these things. We do not expect that they will bring the tyranny down tomorrow or the next day. But we must do what we can to promote an evolution in the U.S.S.R. toward a society devoted to the welfare and national interests of its people and not expansion and the domination of other nations.[134]

Regrettably, only another bloodbath would finally persuade the East Europeans of America's impotence.

V
HUNGARY'S CHALLENGE

*The insurrection in Hungary has of late
made so much progress that Russia cannot
possibly remain inactive.*
CZAR NICHOLAS I, April 27, 1849

*The present Congress will do nothing to
sustain the cause of Hungary, or to maintain
that great law of nations which is violated
when one power endeavors to interfere in the
domestic affairs of another.*
NEW YORK DAILY TIMES, January 5, 1852

Momentarily, the temporizing philosophy that underlay containment and
had been adopted even by the principal proponents of liberation appeared
to be bearing fruit. Washington's policy toward the Soviet bloc, an elusive
amalgam of rhetoric calling for the relaxation of tensions and for liberation, and of operational commitments stressing the defense of Western
Europe and demarcating the division of that continent, found vindication
both in the strategic consolidation and growing economic strength of the
Western alliance and in the ostensible success of national particularism in
Poland. The free world's common resolve stood in contradistinction to the
feverish efforts of the Soviet leadership to liberalize in the domestic
sphere and to maintain its alliance system by means of apparent compromises with the infection of Titoism. At least to the more optimistic observer, these developments within the communist system seemed irreversible

173

and full of promise. Yet, within the span of a few weeks in the autumn of 1956, the image of Western solidarity, as well as the illusion of peaceful and gradual liberation, suffered shattering setbacks. Crises that had been brewing for months in the Middle East and in Hungary culminated almost simultaneously, presenting Washington's policy makers with a double dilemma.

The impending confrontation over the Suez had profound historical roots. France and Britain were uneasy owing to the erosion of their traditional influence in the Mediterranean, the former being engaged in a bloody battle to maintain control in Algeria, the latter straining its diminished power to protect British interests in the Middle East. Their efforts were scarcely aided by the increasingly intense Soviet-American competition to displace these discredited remnants of European imperialism. Yet another complicating element in the Middle Eastern puzzle was the struggle of the young state of Israel for survival. In the course of 1956, this proliferation of forces and interests focused on the person and actions of Gamal Abdel Nasser. The Egyptian president's dreams of Arab solidarity threatened British and French interests; his threats of a new holy war caused acute concern in Tel Aviv; and his professed neutralism and contacts with the communist bloc offended the Manichean world view personified by Dulles. Earlier in the year, Nasser had recognized Red China, contracted for the delivery of Czech-made arms, and approached the Soviet Union for development loans. In July, to show its displeasure and call the Russians' bluff, Washington withdrew its support for a major loan to finance the Aswan project; one week later, Nasser announced the nationalization of the Suez Canal Company. This act prompted London and Paris to draw up plans for a military intervention that was expected to topple Nasser and assure the security of the canal, while, in Israel, pressure also mounted for a pre-emptive blow. Despite Dulles' belated attempts to effect a compromise, notably through a Suez Canal Users' Association, and over his pointed public references to European colonialism, the secret Anglo-French preparations for Operation Musketeer proceeded apace and were dovetailed into Israel's own designs. When on October 19 Ambassador Dillon reported to Dulles from Paris that a concerted attack on Egypt appeared to be imminent, the rift between the United States and its two principal allies was complete.

While the Middle Eastern cauldron was coming to a boil and the decompression in Poland was reaching a precarious but peaceful plateau, yet another confrontation approached its unexpected climax in Hungary. With the realignment of forces in the Kremlin following Malenkov's demise came the shelving of the New Course in Hungary and the replacement of its principal proponent, Imre Nagy, by the former Stalinist dictator Mátyás Rákosi. Through the latter half of 1955 and early 1956, Rákosi made desperate efforts to restore the *status quo ante*, efforts which were thwarted by a growing number of domestic and external factors. Internally, the New Course had fostered a spirit of criticism, or, in the jargon of communist ideology, of "revisionism," which found more and more vocal expression among the hitherto sycophantic but now restive intelligentsia and among the students. Following his expulsion from the party, Imre Nagy proceeded to compose a "dissertation" in explanation of his earlier activities; the document, a damning exposé of the costs of Stalinism, went so far as to criticize Soviet influence and to recommend a neutral stance for Hungary.[1]

Purges of the intelligentsia in the early fall of 1955 prompted fifty writers to issue a boldly phrased memorandum on October 18 attacking the "despotic, anti-democratic methods of leadership in the cultural field."[2] In putting renewed pressure on the intellectuals, Rákosi may well have miscalculated, for it was his harsh treatment of Nagy and the writers which caused the public to take note of their admittedly equivocal hostility to the party and to follow their debates with growing enthusiasm. The final blow to the unity of the party was dealt by Khrushchev's anti-Stalin speech at the Twentieth Party Congress in February 1956. As the most rabidly Stalinist of the satellite leaders, Rákosi felt directly threatened, but he continued to cling to power; he publicly supported a Central Committee resolution endorsing the recommendations of the Congress and placed the blame for earlier excesses on the already imprisoned secret police chief, Gábor Péter. The subsequent Soviet reconciliation with Tito, who denounced Rákosi for having his hands "soaked in blood," only further weakened the Hungarian leader's position.

Meanwhile, in March 1956 a new forum had been founded; named the Petőfi Circle after the nineteenth-century poet-patriot, it was not restricted to writers. The Petőfi Circle was originally approved by the party as a relatively harmless escape valve, but it became the intellectual birthplace of open revolt. By July, one of Rákosi's lieutenants referred to it as the "second leading centre" in the country—in other words, a rival to the party.[3] With more and more debates turning into mass protest meetings, Rákosi decided to strike back, and on July 16 he presented the Politburo with a plan to purge the dissenters.[4] No decision had yet been reached on his proposal when Soviet Presidium member Anastas Mikoyan appeared in Budapest to "suggest" the dismissal of Rákosi. The resolution relieving Rákosi of his post and appointing Ernő Gerő as first secretary was adopted by the Central Committee on July 18, with Rákosi admitting that his mistakes had been "much more serious than I had previously believed."[5] The change in leadership reflected Moscow's view that Rákosi was too unpopular both at home and with Tito to warrant further tenure, although the choice of the intrinsically doctrinaire Gerő offered little promise of a Polish-style revolution from above.

Nevertheless, some signs pointed to peaceful change rather than to revolution. Although an American correspondent had reported in May that the Hungarians "apparently have ceased to believe, as they believed a few years ago, that the United States was getting ready to free their country," the successful stand of the Polish revisionists led many Hungarians to expect that a similar orderly evolution could take place in their country.[6] Gerő attempted to still the voices of protest by ostensibly steering a middle course between "sectarianism" and "right-wing opportunism"; he promised to improve economic management and to institute "socialist legality," all under the now obligatory collective leadership. An early victim of the anti-Titoist purges, László Rajk, was reinterred with great pomp on October 6; one week later the Politburo reinstated Nagy to party membership, though with the caveat that he had indeed committed political errors. Meanwhile, the Foreign Ministry announced that an improvement in Hungarian-American relations was imminent, noting in support of this development the issuance of visas to American newsmen and the relaxation of travel restrictions for foreign diplomats; this spirit of accommodation came in the wake of mutual protests and diplomatic sanctions following the arrest in January of AP and UP correspondents, together with some employees of the American legation, on charges of espionage.[7]

Despite real and promised concessions, the groundswell of popular protest gathered momentum. Encouraged by developments in Poland, diverse groups, including the Writers' Union and the Central Council of Trade Unions, pressed for sweeping reforms. In mid-October, while Gerő was in Belgrade trying to reach an eleventh-hour accommodation with Tito, the reactivated Petőfi Circle adopted a resolution listing ten demands that ranged from the public trial of prominent Stalinists to the publication of foreign trade agreements, including those concerning the exploitation of Hungarian uranium. The idea of manifestos spread like wildfire, and student groups throughout the country voiced similar demands. It was at the Technical University in Budapest that, early on the morning of October 23, students adopted a program which was to represent the ideology of the revolution; they called for the immediate withdrawal of all Soviet troops, reconstitution of the government under Imre Nagy, general elections by secret ballot and the participation of several political parties therein, the right to strike, and a re-examination of the planned economy.[8]

Although Gerő and his associates had been sufficiently concerned about the growing unrest to make tentative plans to provoke a minor insurrection and purge the opposition, the rapid escalation of demands caught them out of the country and unprepared. Apprised of student plans for a demonstration of sympathy for the Poles upon his return on the twenty-third, Gerő lashed back with an inflammatory speech that characterized the potential demonstrators as "enemies of our people."[9] Later in the day the government rescinded its prohibition of the demonstration, but the gesture was a mark of its own impotence. The students' march quickly turned into a mass demonstration, and when that same evening shots were exchanged with the secret police guarding the broadcasting center, peaceful protest turned into open revolt. With the army either joining the rebels or remaining passive, Gerő saw his support reduced to the deeply implicated secret police; he thereupon named Imre Nagy prime minister (a delaying tactic, since the latter was advised only *post facto*) and announced that Soviet military assistance had been requested. Russian troops stationed in Hungary had been on alert for some time; units of two mechanized divisions reached Budapest by 2 A.M. on the twenty-fourth.

HOPES AND FEARS IN WASHINGTON

Although West German intelligence—the famous Gehlen organization, until April 1956 the CIA's European branch—apparently gave advance warning of an uprising in Hungary, it is not clear to what extent official Washington apprehended the imminence of the outburst. By an unfortunate coincidence the American minister to Hungary, Christian Ravndal, had recently left his post. He told reporters that the uprising "came sooner than we had thought. We had expected something of this sort around the end of the year."[10] According to a knowledgeable historian, the State Department had as early as October 20 "got wind" of serious unrest that was likely to lead to an uprising.[11] On the other hand, Undersecretary of State Robert D. Murphy subsequently asserted that Washington had "no advance information about this uprising, no plan of action. . . . The State Department had welcomed the stimulation which Tito seemed to be giving to a liberalizing trend, but nobody anticipated anything like this Hungarian insurrection."[12] Some years later President Eisenhower also recalled that "the thing started in such a way . . . that everyone was a little bit fooled."[13] Since there is no evidence that the revolution began according to a prearranged plan, it is understandable that its outbreak carried with it an element of surprise, but most critics found the official claim that the uprising was totally unexpected somewhat less convincing in light of the earlier disturbances in Poland and the steadily mounting popular unrest in Hungary.

When at 7 P.M. on October 23 Dulles was informed of the outbreak of fighting in Budapest, his elation knew no bounds:

> Did I not tell you that our financial aid to Yugoslavia . . . would come back tenfold? . . . the people of Poland and Hungary, their leaders, have seen that it is possible to be independent of Moscow! We kept alive the yearning for freedom. It worked in Yugoslavia; it will work in Poland and Hungary. The great monolith of Communism is crumbling![14]

For a moment, at least, Dulles could claim that his liberation policy—i.e., peaceful liberation by means of propaganda and encouragement of the captive peoples—had been successful. The Republicans did not tarry in taking some of the credit for the apparent disintegration of the Soviet bloc; a GOP "truth squad"—part of their campaign effort—claimed the next day that the revolts were tangible proof of the wisdom of the Eisenhower administration's foreign policy.[15]

As recorded in his memoirs, the president held twenty-three conferences in the course of that first day, almost all of which touched on the situation in Hungary.[16] Apart from the recent precedent of Poland, there was little to guide the decision makers in Washington, for the State Department had lost contact with the Budapest legation, and the world press wallowed in confusion and wild speculation. Thus, despite Dulles' elation and the premature boasting of some electioneering Republicans, the administration maintained, at least outwardly, an attitude of extreme caution. The view was expressed in official quarters that it would be best if the revolts in Poland and Hungary did not move so fast as to invite Soviet military intervention, and that for the moment the U.S. government would have to remain a passive observer; echoing this caution, Walter Lippmann wrote that, "in the interests of peace and of freedom—freedom both from despotism and from anarchy—we must hope that for a time, not forever but for a time, the uprising in the satellite orbit will be stabilized at Titoism."[17] Meanwhile, the Voice of America was broadcasting sixty additional news programs behind the Iron Curtain, where the unrest was spreading, particularly within the sizable Hungarian minority in Rumania.

While Soviet units engaged the insurgents (with some reluctance, since these troops, stationed for some time in Hungary, failed to see how workers and students could have turned into fascist enemies overnight), the Gerő regime broadcast on October 24 that "dastardly armed attacks of counter-revolutionary gangs" had caught it unprepared and had necessitated a request for help in accordance with the Warsaw Pact.[18] In fact, the fifth clause of the pact provided for such assistance only in the event of external aggression, and Article 8 specified noninterference in the internal affairs of the signatories, but respect for legalistic niceties clearly was not opportune. On the following day a bloody clash occurred in front of Parliament when demonstrators who were fraternizing with Russian troops while waiting for Nagy to appear were fired upon by the secret police. Thereupon a crowd assembled at the American legation to plead for some assurance of Western assistance; concerned primarily with the safety of American nationals in Hungary, Chargé d'Affaires Spencer Barnes told the gathering that this was up to the U.S. government and the United Nations. In the absence of any instruction or communication from Washington, Barnes and his subordinates withdrew into a stunned isolation that was to endure throughout the revolution.

The fighting in Budapest in this first phase of the revolution inflicted heavy losses on the Russians and on the secret police, and it left the regime in control of only a few public buildings. Some Stalinists had been dropped from the Central Committee, but Gerő remained in charge, though he was increasingly powerless to influence the situation. At this juncture Moscow dispatched Suslov and Mikoyan to Budapest, and at their recommendation Gerő was replaced by János Kádár, an early victim of Rákosi's purges, as first secretary. Kádár and Nagy then proceeded to broadcast conciliatory speeches that must have had the blessing of the Soviet envoys. Nagy announced that the government would begin negotiations on the withdrawal of Soviet forces, promised that an "all-embracing and well-founded" reform program would be presented by him to a reconvened National Assembly, and indicated that a major transformation of the government would be forthcoming.[19] On October 26, after Gerő and other leading Stalinists had disappeared from view, the party issued a declaration reiterating Nagy's promises and confirming that the country was now to be led by Nagy.

After conferring with Eisenhower on the morning of the twenty-fourth, Dulles announced merely that they had been "particularly interested today in Poland and Hungary."[20] Later in the day the secretary received a delegation of Hungarian-Americans in a prearranged meeting that was part of the election campaign. The visitors asked him to review the situation in light of the UN Charter and the Hungarian Peace Treaty and came away with the assurance that "our Government views the situation in Hungary with alert interest and attention and is wholly sympathetic to the efforts of the Hungarian people to move to regain freedom and independence."[21]

On October 25, while the press reported that Washington was considering various possible gestures to show support for the revolution—including a protest to Moscow against the use of force, and the extension of economic aid to regimes that demonstrated independence from the Soviet Union— and that it had begun consultations with Britain, France, and other friendly governments regarding the advisability of taking the Hungarian question to the United Nations, President Eisenhower issued the first official comment on the crisis: "The United States considers the development in Hungary as being a renewed expression of the intense desire for freedom long held by the Hungarian people." He went on to note that the demands of the rebels involved human rights affirmed in the UN Charter and specifically guaranteed by the peace treaty to which Hungary and the Allies, including the Soviet Union, were parties, and concluded, "the United States deplores the intervention of Soviet military forces which, under the treaty of peace, should have been withdrawn."[22] Although Robert Murphy subsequently criticized Eisenhower for having strengthened the impression that the United States was sponsoring the Hungarian revolt, the president had in fact carefully eschewed any hint of American intervention; later that night, after telling a Republican rally in Madison Square Garden that the United States would do all in its peaceful power to help the Poles and Hungarians, he would remark to *New York Times* correspondent C. L. Sulzberger: "Poor fellows, poor fellows, I think about them all the time. I wish there were some way of helping them."[23]

Amid conflicting reports of developments in Hungary, the president, Dulles, and UN Ambassador Henry Cabot Lodge engaged in discussions with British and French representatives as to possible action in the Security Council and the legitimacy of Soviet intervention; although the Warsaw Pact guaranteed the territorial integrity and sovereignty of its signatories, as far as Washington was aware the Soviet troops had been called in by the new premier, Imre Nagy, and it was reluctant to jeopardize the latter's chances of consolidating his regime.[24] The American press tended to praise the moderation of the administration's reaction while urging nonmilitary action. Observed one editorial: "Had there been any indication that American or other Western governments were encouraging revolt aimed at a return to capitalism, the Soviet-inspired countermeasures might easily have been more severe than they have been."[25] The *New York Times* claimed that there could be no clearer case of foreign interference in a country's internal affairs and, invoking "all the weapons of international law" and the "moral force of our outrage and horror," urged that there be no delay in bringing "these crimes" before the United Nations.[26] In much the same vein, Democratic candidate Adlai Stevenson pledged his support for responsible action involving the United Nations and for economic aid once Hungary was free.[27] For the time being, however, the revolution appeared successful, and no official action was taken within or without the United Nations. Hungarians in exile were less confident of the revolution's success in the absence of any Western action; writing on behalf of the New York-based Hungarian National Committee, Msgr. Béla Varga urged Dulles to immediately dispatch UN "truce commissions" to Hungary.[28]

At the National Security Council meeting on the morning of October 26, Hungary continued to be, in Eisenhower's words, the "compelling news." CIA Director Allen Dulles saw the situation in a favorable light:

> The Chinese Communists may not be unhappy over what's happening in Hungary. If so, we might at this moment be seeing the beginning of the first rift between China and the U.S.S.R. . . . Bohlen recently saw Bulganin and Khrushchev together at a reception in Moscow. Khrushchev, he said, had never looked so grim. His days may well be numbered.

As usual, the president was more concerned with the possible complications:

> I doubt that the Russian leaders genuinely fear an invasion by the West. But with the deterioration of the Soviet Union's hold over its satellites might not the Soviet Union be tempted to resort to extreme measures, even to start a world war? This possibility we must watch with the utmost care.

Eisenhower's primary concern was clearly to avoid provoking the Russians. Upon his request a position paper was drafted on Hungary and Poland; the document reaffirmed Washington's assurance that the United States had no intention of making Poland or Hungary its allies, and asserted that any Soviet attempt to remove Gomulka by force would be countered by American support for UN action, "including the use of force." Later that day the Defense Department and other security agencies were put on special alert (a move that arose from Eisenhower's perception of the threat of war and that certainly was not calculated to influence developments in Hungary) while the president checked over a speech that Dulles was to make the following day.[29]

The secretary of state traveled to Dallas on the afternoon of October 27 to deliver a major address in which he made it clear that direct U.S. assistance to the Hungarian rebels was out of the question. The captive peoples, he said,

> must know that they can draw upon our abundance to tide themselves over the period of economic adjustment which is inevitable as they

rededicate their productive efforts to the service of their own people, rather than of exploiting masters. . . . Nor do we condition economic ties between us upon the adoption by these countries of any particular form of society. And let me make this clear, beyond a possibility of doubt: The United States has no ulterior purpose in desiring the independence of the satellite countries. . . . We do not look upon these people as potential military allies. . . . We are confident that their independence, if promptly accorded, will contribute immensely to stabilize peace throughout all of Europe, West and East.[30]

Dulles' speech carried a number of important implications. First, it provided a perhaps gratuitous assurance that the United States would under no circumstances use force to alter the course of events in East-Central Europe; it is safe to assume that such a reassurance strengthened the hand of those Soviet leaders who favored total repression. Second, in its reference to "any particular form of society," the speech indicated that Washington anticipated nothing more than the spread of Titoism. The one practical proposal, that dealing with economic aid, seemed to reflect a remarkable confidence in the Hungarians' ability to achieve a large measure of independence without the help of Western pressure.

The cautious optimism underlying Dulles' address was further qualified by almost concurrent developments in East-Central Europe. At dawn on Sunday, October 28, teletype messages reaching the State Department reported that Soviet troops were crossing the Carpathian frontier into Hungary.[31] Evidently the original setback suffered by the Russians in the first three days of the revolution had prompted the Kremlin to bolster its forces in that country as insurance, in case the overthrow of the Nagy regime became necessary.

On October 27, as fighting receded in Budapest, the Hungarian government underwent a major reorganization which resulted in the inclusion of several noncommunist politicians of the postwar era. It is one of the imponderables of history whether, had the Hungarian people been more pragmatic and compromising, the revolution could have ended with the consolidation of this regime. In the event, the gulf separating Nagy and other moderate communists from the mass of the people was too great to allow this government any degree of permanence. The cleavage owed less to the still preponderantly communist character of the regime than to the continued presence of Russian troops. While a multiparty government was one of their avowed aims, the revolutionaries proved to be most adamant in their demands for Soviet withdrawal. Nagy lacked Moscow's mandate to promise this, although he repeatedly stressed that negotiations with the

Soviet Union were in progress. A man of limited charisma, Nagy labored under the stigma of his communist past—Radio Free Europe would comment on his pleas for a cease-fire that he wanted to "revise and modernize the Trojan horse episode"—and lacked the unquestioning support that had brought Gomulka to power. Faced with the prospect of national communism, the vast majority of Hungarians chose to follow a different drummer.

The new government's program was broadcast by Nagy on October 28, with the preamble that the "present formidable movement" manifested a national and democratic, rather than some counterrevolutionary, spirit.[32] In addition to the usual promises of economic reform, Nagy announced that the withdrawal of Soviet forces from the capital would occur simultaneously with the formation of a new Hungarian army. The government repeated its earlier cease-fire orders, while the Communist party announced its reorganization and approval of the Nagy program. The party, however, failed to represent the aims of the nation in revolt. Some of the strongest voices in favor of radical reform came from the provinces. On October 28, the Workers' Council and Student Parliament of the northeastern Borsod county issued a manifesto demanding the formation of a broadly based provisional government pending the holding of general and free elections within two months with the participation of several parties; the abolition of the secret police; and the withdrawal of Soviet troops, not only from Budapest, but from the entire territory of Hungary.[33]

The appeal coincided with a *Pravda* editorial ominously entitled "Collapse of the Antipopular Adventure in Hungary," which claimed that the "Hungarian working people" were determined to defend their people's regime against the schemes of imperialist reaction. In Poland and Yugoslavia, comment was more moderate. Warsaw's *Trybuna Ludu* expressed doubts that "alien agencies which should have been isolated and cut off from the nation might have succeeded in mobilizing vast masses for the struggle"; Belgrade's *Politika* concluded that "this has not been a counterrevolution."[34] The press in the other satellites followed the Moscow line. In Budapest, the October 29 edition of the party daily *Szabad Nép* took issue with the *Pravda* editorial, arguing that the events in Hungary had been neither antipopular nor an adventure, and that what had in fact collapsed was the "reign of the Rákosi-Gerő clique." Nevertheless, the official emanations from Moscow indicated little flexibility on the part of the Soviet leadership. Foreign Minister Shepilov observed that same day that "the sooner the activity of anti-national and anti-democratic elements stops, and if there is no danger, the sooner would Soviet troops withdraw"; the provisions of the Warsaw Treaty, affirmed Marshal Zhukov, applied also to internal aid.[35] The Kremlin's hard line was also evident in *Pravda*'s charges that the rebels acted according to a prearranged plan and in the instructions to Soviet forces that they were fighting a fascist revolution supported by the West.[36]

The confused situation in Hungary was further complicated in its impact on Washington when on the afternoon of Sunday, October 28, a cable arrived from the American ambassador in Tel Aviv reporting massive Israeli mobilization.[37] Upon his return from Dallas, the secretary of state warned the French and British chargés d'affaires that the use of force would damage the West's case against Soviet repression in Hungary.[38] In the course of the day, Dulles disclosed plans for Red Cross and government relief aid for Hungary. He also took time to dismiss as tommyrot Russian charges that American agents and American funds had fomented the uprising; more recent evidence does suggest, however, that the Gehlen organization had been active in Hungary and that, when the revolt broke out, it dispatched a team of Hungarian agents to the scene, where the latter were joined by a CIA unit.[39] On Monday morning Dulles was scheduled to give his final instructions to Edward T. Wailes, who was leaving to take up his post as the new minister to Hungary, but while in transit the diplomat would complain that he had not been briefed on his assignment.[40] Until Wailes' arrival on November 2, Budapest remained without an experienced and ranking American envoy.

For the next few days the Hungarian situation was relegated to a secondary role by the outbreak of military operations in the Sinai. Hungary had been discussed in the Security Council on October 28, but the Israeli offensive the following day focused world attention on the Middle East. Apprised of the Anglo-French ultimatum on the afternoon of October 30, a furious Dulles told French Ambassador Hervé Alphand that the action of France and Britain was just the same as the behavior of the Soviet Union in Budapest.[41] Meanwhile, the lull in the fighting in Hungary prompted the American press to talk of "victory" and "miracle" in editorials concerning the revolution.[42] A reputable political commentator wrote that Washington had concluded that the satellites should be trusted to break away from Soviet control eventually and that therefore the West should not push them toward a speedier break than had occurred in Poland lest the Russians be provoked into a repression which would retard the process; he also reported that a possible *quid pro quo* involving the neutralization of Germany in exchange for self-determination in East-Central Europe was being studied.[43] More forceful gestures were beyond consideration; when asked whether NATO would react to events in Hungary, Secretary-General Ismay noted that no member state had been attacked and that therefore, if "reaction means taking action, the answer is no."[44]

At this crucial juncture in the course of the Hungarian revolution Moscow still seemed to be hesitating. According to Khrushchev the Soviet Presidium had been divided on the question of intervention, with the Peking Chinese opposing and the other satellites, notably Rumania, advocating military measures.[45] Mikoyan and Suslov paid a second visit to Budapest on October 27 and yet another four days later. In the interval, on the thirtieth, the Kremlin issued a remarkable policy statement upholding peaceful coexistence between the Soviet Union and other socialist states "on the principles of complete equality, of respect for territorial integrity, state independence and sovereignty, and of non-interference in one another's internal affairs." Voicing willingness to negotiate—specifically with the Hungarian government—on the stationing of Soviet forces, the declaration noted that the Warsaw Treaty stipulated that the consent of the host country be obtained. It ended on the warning note that the Soviet Union "expresses confidence that the peoples of the socialist countries will not permit foreign and domestic reactionary forces to shake the foundations of the people's democratic system."[46]

Mikoyan appeared willing to negotiate on the basis of this declaration. On the thirty-first he met with Zoltán Tildy, a member of Nagy's cabinet, to discuss four specific points: the immediate recall of Soviet forces, Hungary's withdrawal from the Warsaw Pact, the re-establishment of a multiparty system, and preparations for free elections and the assertion of Hungarian sovereignty and self-determination. Reported Tildy after the meeting, "I raised all the problems and he agreed with everything."[47] Nevertheless, the mood in the Kremlin must have been anything but conciliatory once the Hungarian leaders' position had been conveyed back by Mikoyan. A sham withdrawal of Soviet troops earlier that day may well have been calculated to give Nagy a chance to consolidate a national communist regime, but a few hours later a new influx of forces began, while the units that had withdrawn from Budapest dug in to form a cordon around the capital. It remains unclear whether the Moscow declaration and Mikoyan's sympathetic attitude were temporizing measures that served to draw attention away from the military build-up, or whether they reflected a genuine inclination to compromise. In the event, the hardliners in the Kremlin must have gained the upper hand when they learned that Nagy was unable to limit his demands commensurately with the preservation of a communist Hungary under Soviet suzerainty.[48]

The new offensive's first stage, involving the securing of all airfields, was camouflaged as a security operation designed to facilitate the imminent evacuation of Soviet personnel. Alarmed by the reports of troop movements, Imre Nagy assumed the direction of the Ministry of Foreign Affairs on November 1 and dispatched a flurry of protests. In a telegram to Marshal Voroshilov, chairman of the Soviet Presidium, he requested immediate negotiations on withdrawal. Notifying Secretary-General Hammarskjold of his protests against the Russian troop movements and of Hungary's official withdrawal from the Warsaw Pact, Nagy asked the "four great powers" for recognition and protection of Hungary's neutrality. (It is worth noting that the Warsaw Treaty was repudiated by the Nagy government only when it became apparent that the Soviet Union was actively planning its overthrow and was violating the treaty by moving troops into Hungary without prior agreement.) Finally, in a radio address to the nation, Nagy affirmed Hungary's neutrality and noted that "today our people are as united in this decision as perhaps never before in their history."[49] Still, aware that open hostilities could have but one outcome, he tried to avoid clashes between freedom fighters and the Russians, and therefore rested his case with the UN in the hope that the Soviet Union would respect that body's endorsement of Hungary's neutrality.

Also on November 1, First Secretary János Kádár announced the formation of a new Communist party, in the name of which he fully supported the new government's decisions. His speech, however, was laced with references to the dangers of "menacing counter-revolution" and of "intervention from abroad."[50] Clearly, unlike Nagy, some communists could not stomach an overnight renunciation of their lifelong dogma. Later in the day Kádár and several of his associates surreptitiously departed from the capital.

The Hungarian revolution passed its point of no return with the renunciation of the Warsaw Pact, but even at this juncture the Nagy regime refrained from appealing directly to the West, although individual insurgents would repeatedly seek reassurance from Western diplomats and correspondents in Budapest. With his country in the grip of two deepening crises, President Eisenhower prepared to make a radio-television address on the evening of Wednesday, October 31. His usual caution was much in evidence. Upon hearing Allen Dulles hail Moscow's October 30 declaration as "one of the most significant to come out of the Soviet Union since the end of World War II," the president had retorted, "Yes, if it is honest."[51] He decided with one of his speech writers to alter the draft submitted by John Foster Dulles—to divide it equally between Hungary and the Suez, and to "tone down Dulles' references to 'irresistible' forces of 'liberation' unleashed in Eastern Europe."[52] The secretary of state then came to the White House to work on the final draft, changing the phrase "There seems to appear the dawn of hope" to "There *is* the dawning of hope." In his actual address, Eisenhower reverted to the original version. To have tried to fulfill the wartime pledges regarding East-Central Europe by force, he said, "would have been contrary both to the best interests of the Eastern European peoples and to the abiding principles of the United Nations. But we did help to keep alive the hope of these peoples for freedom." Referring to the Soviet declaration that indicated a disposition to review satellite policy, the president continued:

> The United States has made clear its readiness to assist economically the new and independent governments of these countries. We have also—with respect to the Soviet Union—sought clearly to remove any false fears that we would look upon new governments in these Eastern European countries as potential military allies.[53]

The remainder of his address dealt with the Middle Eastern situation. On the following day Eisenhower allocated $20 million from his emergency fund for relief in Hungary.

The official tone of modest optimism did not prevent much unofficial concern over the possibility of massive repressive action, and rumors of continued Soviet troop movements only added to this concern. To begin with, congressional and other criticism focused on the lack of preparedness of the State Department and American intelligence, although one high official argued later that it would have been impossible to draw up a blueprint for such an intangible situation.[54] During the crisis, some members of the administration pressed for American intervention, while congressmen, foreign envoys, émigrés, and others descended on the State Department with pleas for American aid to the Hungarians.[55] Subsequently, the deputy undersecretary of state commented:

> I would analyze for each complainant the possibilities of "action" adequate to liberate Hungary, and would point out that palliatives could not possibly settle the issue but would only provoke the powerful Soviet armies to further massacre.[56]

In the course of Un-American Activities Committee hearings on November 1, Béla Fabian, a prominent émigré, suggested that the United States organize a Berlin-type airlift to fly in supplies and provide moral encouragement to the rebels, but a key objection to this idea had been that Austria adamantly opposed the use of her airspace for such purposes.[57] In the days preceding the final repression, most officials clearly favored noninvolvement; there was little support in Washington or in other capitals for a military confrontation between the Soviet Union and the United States. The Yugoslav ambassador told Robert Murphy that his country was "trembling on the thin edge of war against the Soviet Union" and urged that everything be done to confine the conflict to Hungary.[58] The administration's primary goal, then, was to contain the crisis. It was reported that the State Department used Tito as an intermediary to assure the Kremlin that the United States would not exploit the Hungarian situation, while an American diplomat in Budapest reportedly advised Premier Nagy to refrain from too great a show of friendship for the West as long as Soviet troops remained in Hungary.[59]

There was no official reaction in Washington when on November 1 Nagy announced Hungary's withdrawal from the Warsaw Pact and asked for recognition and protection of the country's neutrality. Although little doubt remained regarding the regime's legitimacy, U.S. recognition was not forthcoming; nor was any statement issued concerning Hungary's neutrality. The reasons for this strange passivity remain obscure. It may have been the result of a multiplicity of crises which left little time for policy formulation. More than likely it was the product of a tacit hands-off policy that was rationalized by wishful thinking. This optimism was evident in an intelligence review given to the president by Allen Dulles on the day of Nagy's declaration of independence:

> The occurrences in Hungary are a miracle. They have disproved that a popular revolt can't occur in the face of modern weapons. Eighty per cent of the Hungarian Army has defected. Except in Budapest, even the Soviet troops have shown no stomach for shooting down Hungarians.[60]

Dulles went on to conclude that the problem in Hungary was a lack of strong leadership.

Meanwhile, the *New York Times* expressed the "gravest apprehension" at the increasingly ominous deployment of Soviet forces in Hungary and reported that some members of the administration had urged various threatening gestures—"demonstrative movements" by the Strategic Air Command and cancellation of military leaves—in the hope of deterring repression.[61] At a State Department conference, however, the secretary of state listed three arguments against military intervention. First, limited intervention by American forces stationed in southern Germany would not succeed; second, full-scale military intervention would entail the risk of nuclear war, which the United States would not take over Hungary; and, third, any intervention would destroy rather than save Hungary. The secretary considered these reasons to be valid irrespective of the Suez crisis, although at the NATO conference in December he would tell the

French foreign minister that one factor militating against American acqui-escence in the Suez operation was that "it would have encouraged minor-ity groups in the United States to urge military action to liberate the East European satellites."[62]

The case against the use of force was overwhelming. Intervention would necessarily have violated Austrian neutrality, since it was unthinkable that the Western powers should infringe upon Czech or Yugoslav sovereignty. Participation by Great Britain and France in any military operation was ruled out by the Suez crisis and would have been unlikely in any case, despite vocal support for the rebels; as early as October 26 the French foreign minister had warned against attempts to exploit the uprisings in Hungary and Poland.[63] Some years later Eisenhower would ruefully recall this lack of international support:

> [The] only way that the United States could have ever moved would have been one as of coalition, because you couldn't have jumped over Germany, Austria or France, or any other direction and gone in there, because it would not have been allowed. . . . There was no European country, and indeed, I don't believe ours, ready to say that we should have gone into this thing at once and tried to liberate Hungary from the Communist influence. I don't believe . . . that we had the support of the United Nations to go in and make this a full-out war. . . . [We] had no agreement by Hungary. We had no government that was asking us to come in.[64]

The president also wrote in his memoirs, "I still wonder what would have been my recommendation to Congress and the American people had Hungary been accessible by sea or through the territory of allies who might have agreed to react positively to the tragic fate of the Hungarian people."[65] In fact, all these *ex post facto* speculations clouded the key issue, America's unwillingness to test its relatively reduced strength over Hungary. The emphasis on massive retaliation—"maximize air power and minimize the foot soldier," in the words of Secretary of Defense Wilson—had weakened the country's conventional military power to the extent that even for defensive purposes its NATO contingent was barely ade-quate. Intervention in time and with sufficient strength simply was not feasible.

In the early hours of Saturday, November 3, John Foster Dulles was taken to Walter Reed Army Hospital for an emergency operation, and Herbert Hoover, Jr., took over as acting secretary of state; although the latter was subsequently criticized for not providing strong enough leader-ship in the final days of the Hungarian revolution, there is no evidence that he deviated from established policy. On the afternoon of the third the question of Hungary was briefly discussed in the Security Council, then was postponed for two days with Lodge's assent. The news that negotiations had begun between the Nagy government and the Russians had apparently lessened Washington's concern. However, an unnamed administration official was quoted as saying:

> We still have reasons to fear the Russians have decided to drown the Hungarian revolution in blood. If our fears materialize and the Hungarians manage to hold out for three or four days, the pressure on America to help militarily might become irresistible. The President, being constitutionally minded, will do no such thing without Congressional approval, and Congressmen will not vote for war, not at least until the election on Tuesday. If the Hungarians are still fighting on Wednesday, we will be closer to a world war than we have been since August 1939.[66]

The official was bitter at the British and the French, whose Middle East farrago had removed Russian fears of propaganda losses among the neutralist nations. It was also reported that the Pentagon strongly opposed any offer to pull out American troops from Germany in exchange for a Russian withdrawal from Hungary; Eisenhower and Dulles agreed that an offer along these lines would be a sign of weakness.

In Budapest, the pressure on Imre Nagy was building up from both sides. A multitude of revolutionary organizations clamored for a speedier Soviet withdrawal and a removal of the last vestiges of communist control over the state apparatus; even the recently released Cardinal Mindszenty refrained from bestowing an unequivocal endorsement upon the Nagy regime. Then, late on November 1, Soviet Ambassador Yuri Andropov delivered an ultimatum to Nagy to retract his renunciation of the Warsaw Pact. The latter protested and demanded negotiations on Hungary's political status and on the question of Soviet evacuation, naming two delegations for this purpose; he also sent a message to Hammarskjold reporting the massive movement of Soviet troops into Hungary and repeating the earlier request for recognition of Hungary's neutrality. The following day, the Russians somewhat unexpectedly agreed to negotiations on military withdrawal. Meanwhile, Western diplomats in Budapest continued to function as necessarily helpless observers of the drama unfolding around them. Representatives of the Great Powers had been summoned singly to the foreign office to be formally notified of Nagy's declaration of October 31, but this was to be their only official communication with the Hungarian government. Although Nagy was also the titular foreign minister, he and his cabinet were, particularly in the last days of the revolution, in almost continuous session; they had no time for consultations with the West's envoys. The American minister-designate, Edward Wailes, arrived in Budapest on November 2, but he did not have an opportunity to present his credentials to the Hungarian government before the ultimate collapse of the revolution. In reality, the passivity of the American and other Western diplomats in Hungary only reflected—and in no way did it contribute to —the impotence of their governments.

November 3 saw the final reorganization of the Hungarian government into a four-party coalition which, as the subsequent UN report observed, "commanded the support of all sections of the nation. The four parties now sharing power had received 4,632,972 of the 4,717,256 votes cast and had won 407 out of 409 seats in the free elections of 1945."[67] According to a Hungarian participant, the initial meeting with the Russians produced "full agreement . . . on the withdrawal of Soviet troops, and the last day the Soviet troops have to leave is January 15." Late that night the negotiators met again; in the words of one official, the Hungarian delegation "entered the Soviet headquarters with good faith, intending to sign the final text of [the] Soviet-Hungarian agreement which already was agreed upon in the Hungarian Parliament."[68] The discussions were interrupted by the appearance of Soviet Security Police Chief Ivan Serov, who, breaking every international law and convention regarding diplomatic immunity, summarily arrested the members of the Hungarian delegation, including Defense Minister Pál Maléter.

Throughout the night the final Soviet offensive mounted, with ten divisions moving into Budapest assisted by jet fighters and bombers. Facing the inevitable, Nagy broadcast a desperate appeal:

> Today at daybreak Soviet forces started an attack against our capital, obviously with the intention to overthrow the legal democratic Hungarian Government. Our troops are fighting. The Government is in its place. I notify the people of our country and the entire world of this fact.[69]

Concurrently, two broadcasts by Kádár and his associates originating from Soviet territory announced the formation of a new government and its request to the Soviet army to "help our nation in smashing the sinister forces of reaction and restoring order and calm in the country."[70]

First news of the Soviet attack reached the State Department before dawn on Sunday; it was announced that the matter remained momentarily in the hands of Henry Cabot Lodge, who called for a meeting of the Security Council. As reports of bitter fighting, interspersed with broadcast pleas for help, reached the West, the White House issued a statement by the president:

> I met today with the Secretary of State at Walter Reed Hospital and later with the Acting Secretary of State, some of his staff, the Director of the Central Intelligence Agency and some of my staff, to discuss the ways and means available to the United States which would result in . . . [the] withdrawal of Soviet troops from Hungary, and . . . achieve for Hungary its own right of self-determination in the choice of its own government. I have sent an urgent message to Premier Bulganin on these points.[71]

In his message to Bulganin, Eisenhower expressed shock and dismay and urged the Russians to desist "in the name of humanity and in the cause of peace." His letter crossed one from Bulganin which arrived on Monday and which suggested that the United States join the Soviet Union in military action to stop the fighting at Suez; concurrently, the Russians issued an ultimatum to the British and the French to stop their operations or face the possibility of nuclear retaliation.[72] The president and his aides were thunderstruck, and Eisenhower expressed the fear that the combination of internal pressure and Western disarray was making the Russians aggressive:

> Those boys are both furious and scared. Just as with Hitler, that makes for the most dangerous state of mind. . . . we may be dealing here with the opening gambit of an ultimatum. We have to be positive and clear in our every word, every step. And if those fellows start something, we may have to hit 'em—and, if necessary, with everything in the bucket.[73]

The official White House statement called Bulganin's letter an "obvious attempt to divert world attention from the Hungarian tragedy. While we are vitally concerned with the situation in Egypt, we are equally concerned with the situation in Hungary."[74] The Soviets' reply to Eisenhower's earlier message on Hungary arrived November 7:

> [The] problem of the withdrawal of Soviet troops from Hungary . . . comes completely and entirely under the competence of the Hungarian and Soviet governments. . . . there is absolutely no reason to doubt that the Soviet Government's policy has been guided and will be guided by the principles outlined in [the October 30 declaration].[75]

Although some policy planners urged American military intervention, the general feeling was that there was no possibility of using force to help the insurgents; Eisenhower recalls that Bulganin's note, "written of course in the knowledge that Hungary was, in the circumstances, as inaccessible to us as Tibet, was almost the last provocation that my temper could stand."[76] A high official gave what must have been the central argument in this most frustrating of crises:

> Whether we like it or not, the nuclear bomb stalemate does create two spheres of influence, the Russian and the Western. Much as we would have liked to help Hungary we had to decide that interference there might have precipitated a third world war involving hundreds of millions of people and the whole of civilization.[77]

He added that this decision was reached "against the emotional urges of some Cabinet members." Indeed, the dominant sentiment in Washington was one of fear that the Soviet Union might be provoked into lashing out beyond its sphere. Although the State Department had previously denied that the United States entered into secret contact or negotiations with Moscow regarding East-Central Europe, it was later reported that the administration had warned the Russians that West Berlin and Austria would be defended by force if necessary.[78] Such a warning could only serve to reinforce the division of Europe into two spheres. The United States branded as grossly false the Soviet charges that it had sent aid to the revolutionaries from neutral Austria; in fact, although some arms had reached the rebels—presumably through CIA sponsorship—the revolution had been an essentially self-generated and self-supporting phenomenon. Nevertheless, the Russians went on to charge that "it is perfectly obvious that the attempt to carry through a counterrevolutionary putsch in Hungary was an integral part of the extensive imperialist conspiracy against the countries of the socialist camp" and even made the ludicrous allegation that the U.S. had staged the revolt in order to restore the monarchy under Otto von Habsburg.[79]

The brutality of the repression aroused widespread revulsion in the United States. The *New York Times* editorial on November 5 was headlined "We Accuse the Soviet Government of Murder." AFL-CIO president George Meany cabled Eisenhower asking for a complete economic boycott of the Soviet Union, and massive opposition to any diplomatic recognition of the Kádár regime prevailed. Senator Knowland proposed that an international force of military volunteers launch a "crusade for freedom" if Soviet forces were not withdrawn; he also urged that the Soviet Union be expelled from the United Nations, that diplomatic recognition of Moscow be withdrawn, and that economic sanctions be applied against the communist bloc.[80] One congressman suggested that "the least we could do is to break off diplomatic relations with the butchers in the Kremlin who have ordered this terrible slaughter."[81]

The administration reacted with irritation to this internal pressure for more forceful action. A member of its UN delegation commented off the record: "We do think that the Hungarian situation is an important matter and we are studying it with great care, but we have to take up these problems one at a time. Right now our immediate objective is to see that a UN 'police force' is set up and actually in being in the Suez area."[82] Washington had realistically chosen to concentrate on the more manageable of the two crises. In anticipation of later discussion, it must be noted here the both during and after the event several voices were raised in favor of negotiation with the Soviet Union. Walter Lippmann charged that American policy had been sorely lacking in the field of diplomacy and said that the United States had the "moral responsibility of a full-dress attempt to bring about a negotiated settlement in which the Hungarian nation would achieve a position comparable with that of Poland or Yugoslavia"; another commentator complained that the Hungarians were "victims of the fact that there has been no productive negotiation toward a European settlement in 11 long years."[83] In the event, Washington concluded that the most suitable channel for its policies regarding Hungary was the United Nations.

RHETORIC AT THE UNITED NATIONS

Once the decision not to intervene militarily had been taken, the United Nations became the main forum for diplomatic action, and to a large extent the United States delegated to that organization any responsibility for the fate of Hungarian independence. It is therefore necessary to trace American behavior in that forum and to examine how the United Nations as an institution coped with the Hungarian problem.

In strictly legal terms, official UN involvement with the events in Hungary dated from October 24, when the Hungarian government requested the assistance of Soviet troops in accordance with Article 5 of the Warsaw Treaty, which provided for mutual aid in case of attack; when drafted, the treaty had been declared compatible with Article 51 of the Charter (regarding regional alliances for self-defense), and had stipulated that the Security Council be advised of any measures taken under its terms. This proviso was not complied with, and, as one UN staff member recalled of the early days of the revolution, "There was complete ignorance at this point as to what was going on in Hungary. Hardly anyone knew who Imre Nagy was."[84] Thus the United Nations had to wait for an initiative from the West before it could officially consider the Hungarian question.

The revolution had hardly begun when requests for action poured in to the United Nations. The New York–based Assembly of Captive European Nations sent a series of telegrams to UN officials and to heads of governments represented on the Security Council, urging them to condemn the

Soviet intervention on the grounds of Article 2, paragraph 4, of the Charter, which prohibited members from threatening or using force against the territorial integrity or political independence of any state.[85] Meanwhile, as was noted earlier, discussion continued among the three major Western powers regarding the feasibility of bringing the matter to the attention of the Security Council; one technical problem was the Hungarian legation's advice, given to Robert Murphy, that the Russian action was "quite legal."[86] Finally, on the morning of October 27, the chief representatives of the three powers—Lodge, Sir Pierson Dixon, and Bernard Cornut-Gentille (who was also president of the Council for the month of October)—met with Secretary-General Hammarskjold and then drafted an official letter referring to "foreign military forces . . . violently repressing the rights of the Hungarian people which are secured by the [Peace Treaty] " and requesting on the basis of Article 34 an urgent meeting of the Security Council to discuss the situation in Hungary.[87] At noon on the same day the Spanish chargé d'affaires called on Hammarskjold to lodge a protest against the "bloody intervention of Soviet troops in the internal affairs of Hungary."[88]

Early on the twenty-eighth the permanent Hungarian representative, Dr. Péter Kós, requested that a "Declaration of the Government of the Hungarian People's Republic" be distributed to Security Council members.[89] It is not clear whether this letter originated with the Nagy regime or with its predecessor, but in any event Kós was soon relieved of his functions. The declaration challenged the proposed consideration of the Hungarian situation, claiming that "the events which took place on 22 October 1956 and thereafter, and the measures taken in the course of these events are exclusively within the domestic jurisdiction of the Hungarian People's Republic." In spite of this protest, the Security Council convened at 4:00 P.M. that day.

The Soviet delegate, Arkady A. Sobolev, opened the proceedings by making procedural objections to the calling of the meeting and to the placing of the Hungarian question on the agenda. Referring to the letter from the three Western powers, he said: "In our view, the purpose of their action is to give further encouragement to the armed rebellion which is being conducted by a reactionary underground movement against the legal Government of Hungary." After mentioning the Kersten Amendment and America's "provocative 'Christmas' messages" and "open calls to revolt," he proceeded to present what was to be the stock Soviet argument throughout the crisis. Because Hungary was a sovereign state, he said, any UN action would be contrary to Article 2, paragraph 7, of the Charter, which prohibits member states from interfering in matters "essentially within the domestic jurisdiction of any state"; Article 34, claimed Sobolev, empowered the Security Council to investigate only situations of an international character and therefore was not applicable to the Hungarian situation. Sir Pierson Dixon pointed out that the presence of foreign troops in Hungary gave the matter an international character, and the Yugoslav delegate implicitly acknowledged this fact. The agenda was then adopted, with the Soviet Union voting against and Yugoslavia abstaining. The Hungarian representative, who had been given permission to sit in, tried to raise a point of order but was immediately overruled. Sobolev then introduced what was to be another regular delaying measure, asking for postponement of the debate in order to "obtain information on the substance of the issue." Once again his motion was defeated by nine votes, with Yugoslavia abstaining.[90]

In the formal debate the American delegate, quoting John Foster Dulles' Dallas address, expressed the hope that the Soviet Union would "cease its oppressive measures," and he urged the Security Council to consider what steps it could take to end the repression: "The Hungarian authorities say they are negotiating with the Soviet Union for the withdrawal of all Soviet troops, but at the same time it is reported that Soviet military reinforcements recently entered Hungary and that large-scale fighting ensued." Sir Pierson Dixon then related the events in Hungary since October 23 and quoted the human rights clause of the Hungarian Peace Treaty, as well as Article 8 of the Warsaw Treaty, which enjoined the contracting parties to respect each other's independence, in arguing for UN action: "The situation is urgent. The toll in human suffering is great. It does not brook delay." The French, Cuban, Peruvian, Chinese, and Australian delegates made similar statements, whereupon Sobolev returned to the attack. He repeated his earlier references to Washington's liberation pronouncements, charged that the "anti-popular elements" in Hungary were supported and directed from outside, and asserted that Hungary had officially requested Soviet assistance. After more debate and a statement by the Hungarian representative to the effect that he had no further instructions from Budapest, the Council adjourned; it would meet again at the discretion of its president. Throughout the proceedings, the secretary-general had remained silent; he had, as one analyst noted, adopted a hands-off attitude in order not to mar his usefulness as a neutral intermediary.[91]

Thus, after a somewhat perfunctory debate, consideration of the Hungarian question was postponed indefinitely, ostensibly on the grounds that the situation in Hungary was confused and that the Nagy regime was to all appearances consolidating itself. Despite renewed appeals from other member states, the secretary-general took no action.[92] It was not suggested that he fly to Budapest during that week of uncertainty, and no precedent existed for him to do so on his own initiative. Hammarskjold subsequently explained: "There was certainly not a single member of the Security Council who at that stage felt that the situation was clear enough to make such a proposal or felt that it was a good idea to send the Secretary-General away."[93] With the eruption of the Suez crisis, the Hungarian affair sank into the background at the United Nations, and Hammarskjold devoted himself almost exclusively to the cease-fire negotiations and the projected peace force. Washington's preoccupation with this new crisis elicited bitter and not altogether altruistic comments from Britain and France. Prime Minister Anthony Eden recalls in his memoirs:

> Five days passed without further Council meeting upon Hungary despite repeated attempts by ourselves and others to bring one about. The United States representative was reluctant, and voiced his suspicion that we were urging the Hungarian situation to divert attention from Suez. The United States Government appeared in no hurry to move.[94]

Indeed, if the Kremlin had ever been concerned about American action through the United Nations, it is doubtful whether this concern survived the first inconclusive debate.

At 10:26 A.M. on Thursday, November 1, a preliminary call came in on the UN teleprinter from DIPLOMAG, the code name of the Hungarian Foreign Ministry.[95] The message was not sent immediately, but there could have been little doubt that it was to be an important one, for the Hungarian government by-passed its UN delegation; however, the secretary-general's office was not notified. In Budapest, the Nagy cabinet had just reached its decision to renounce the Warsaw Pact, a decision that was announced over Budapest radio at 12:15 P.M. Six minutes later the formal message, signed by Imre Nagy in his capacity as president of the Council of Ministers and designated minister of Foreign Affairs, started to come over the UN teleprinter:

> Reliable reports have reached the Government of the Hungarian People's Republic that further Soviet units are entering into Hungary. The President of the Council of Ministers in his capacity as Minister of Foreign Affairs summoned Mr. Andropov, Ambassador Extraordinary and Plenipotentiary of the Soviet Union to Hungary, and expressed his strongest protest against the entry of further Soviet troops into Hungary. He demanded the instant and immediate withdrawal of these Soviet forces. He informed the Soviet Ambassador that the Hungarian Government immediately repudiates the Warsaw Treaty and at the same time declares Hungary's neutrality, turns to the United Nations and requests the help of the four great Powers in defending the country's neutrality. The Government of the Hungarian People's Republic made the declaration of neutrality on 1 November 1956. Therefore I request

Your Excellency promptly to put on the agenda of the forthcoming General Assembly of the United Nations the question of Hungary's neutrality and the defense of this neutrality by the four great Powers.[96]

After a formal acknowledgement was relayed to the Hungarian government, the communication was sent by special messenger to the secretary-general's office; Hammarskjold was out to lunch, and his office issued no statement regarding Nagy's appeal.[97]

European press reports of Nagy's declaration on Budapest radio prompted correspondents in New York to enquire at the United Nations, whereupon the UN press chief went to Hammarskjold's office, found the message in an "In" basket, and read out the contents at a press conference at 2:00 P.M. The appeal was then mimeographed and distributed to the delegates' pigeonholes without any indication that the matter was a special or urgent one; most delegates did not actually see it until late that evening. In the meantime, a second message had arrived from Budapest at 12:45 P.M. announcing that "Mr. János Szabó, First Secretary of the Permanent Mission, will represent the Hungarian People's Republic at the special session of the General Assembly to be convened November 1, 1956, in New York."[98] Apart from signifying the regime's lack of confidence in Kós (who in an earlier incarnation had been a Soviet national named Konduktorov), this message had other implications; while the earlier communication had merely mentioned the regular meeting of the General Assembly to be convened on November 12, this one made specific reference to the special session. The teleprinter circuit was still operative at this time, but no attempt was made by the Secretariat to contact Budapest and request further information.

There was not a total lack of concern among delegates that afternoon; a few of them, along with leading exiles and some Secretariat officials, actively urged early consideration of the Nagy appeals, acquiring in the process the informal name of the "Cassandra Club." The Cuban delegate, Dr. Emilio Nunez Portuondo, became the most assiduous advocate of UN action and recommended that the Hungarian situation be discussed at the special session of the General Assembly slated to open at 5:00 P.M. This session had been called to deal with the Suez crisis, but Nunez Portuondo pointed out that it was the first extraordinary session to be held under the "Uniting for Peace" procedure and argued that it could choose to discuss Hungary by a two-thirds vote: "We are going to make our own precedents today. Let us make good ones."[99] To the objection that the Security Council was still formally concerned with Hungary, the Cuban delegate would reply that the Council could meet and, following the predictable Soviet veto, refer the matter to the Assembly. Still another objection was the one noted above, that the original Nagy message had mentioned the "forthcoming" (i.e., regular) meeting of the Assembly and that he could not have known of the special session. Against this the "Cassandra Club" argued that Nagy was not likely to view complacently an eleven-day delay in the consideration of Hungary's neutrality, and that it was most improbable that at such a crucial moment the Hungarians were unaware of the special session. The Secretariat did not attach special significance to the second Nagy message. An enquiry to Budapest could have settled the issue, but by the time the secretary-general attempted to acknowledge Nagy's original message—at 1:05 A.M. the following morning—the link with Budapest was no longer operative.

At this juncture the attitude of the United States was bound to be critical, for without its support the "Cassandra Club" had little hope of gaining a hearing. Early that afternoon one member of the group approached an American delegate, who checked with Washington and then reported: "The Department says it has no confirmation of these reports from our people in Budapest. They think they're probably a bit exaggerated."[100] Members of the U.S. delegation then decided to communicate the latest dispatches relative to Hungary to the secretary of state, who received them on his way to New York, where he was to address the emergency session on Suez. There appeared to be little expectation that the United States would take any immediate action.

To place the problem in its proper perspective, the importance of the Suez affair was enhanced by the concern of the African and Asian delegations; even if Washington had considered the Hungarian question to be of prime urgency, it is uncertain whether at this point it could have mustered sufficient support in the Assembly to give the matter priority for debate. Said Hammarskjold in retrospect: "If you disregard all other aspects and look at the time sequence, I think it is perfectly clear to you that Suez had a time priority on the thinking and the policy-making of the main body in the UN. That was not their choice. It was history itself, so to say, which arranged it that way."[101] In the event, not even the United States seemed to consider Hungary that pressing a problem. During the first sitting of the emergency special session Hungary was mentioned only once, in passing, by the British delegate; Dulles, in his initial speech, made no reference to the revolution.[102] The diplomats who favored immediate consideration of Hungary realized that any attempt to bring it up during the Suez debate would only arouse the ire of the Afro-Asian members, and the American delegation also opposed such a move. Therefore, at 10:00 P.M. on November 1, shortly after the beginning of the second sitting, the decision was made (with American approval) to wait until a vote had been taken on the Suez question before raising the question of

Hungary.

During the night, while the debate was in progress, a member of the "Cassandra Club" read a dispatch on the Reuters teleprinter which gave notice of Russian troop movements and the surrounding of the Budapest airfields. He proceeded to send copies to the secretary-general's office and to some of the delegations; Dulles read the dispatch in the Assembly chamber. At about 3:30 A.M., following the adoption of an American resolution censuring Britain, France, and Israel, the Italian delegate rose on a point of order to draw attention to the Nagy appeal: "Hungary asks for the help of the United Nations. . . . I hope that the United Nations— and, if necessary, this special emergency session—will immediately take whatever action is possible with regard to the request of the Hungarian people." Following a similar statement by the Peruvian delegate, the debate reverted to the Suez issue. Finally, in his summation, Dulles made passing reference to Hungary. Having endorsed Italy's intervention and noted the news of further Soviet troop movements, he concluded: "I hope that this matter, which is on the agenda of the Security Council, will be kept urgently before it and that we shall not be preoccupied with the Middle East to the exclusion of assisting the State of Hungary to regain its independence."[103]

The Western powers were sufficiently aroused to call the following morning, November 2, for an urgent meeting of the Security Council, "in view of the critical situation in Hungary."[104] The Council met at 5:00 P.M. and spent the first hour debating the credentials of János Szabó, who had been invited to sit in as an observer. Standing in for Hammarskjold, Undersecretary-General Dragoslav Protitch at first denied that Szabó had been accredited, then, in the middle of his statement, was advised of the Nagy message relevant to Szabó which had been received the previous day. This preliminary discussion had its stranger aspects, with Lodge insisting that credentials had to be presented twenty-four hours before a meeting, and with the president, Nazrollah Entezam of Iran, noting that "as the Council was called on only three hours' notice, it was very difficult to ask the representative of a country to submit his credentials twenty-four hours before a meeting." Finally, the Soviet delegate himself spoke in favor of Szabó's right to participate in the debate. More argument ensued over whether Szabó, even if entitled to speak in the Assembly, could do so in the Security Council.[105]

In his principal statement, Lodge contrasted the Moscow declaration of October 30 with Nagy's subsequent protests, went on to call the situation in Hungary "confused," and suggested that Hammarskjold ask Budapest to send a representative to the United Nations to provide further information. Evidently the U.S. was not ready to introduce a resolution on the

Hungarian question, although in the face of a Soviet veto it would not have been difficult to find the minimum of seven votes needed to transfer the matter to the General Assembly; Britain, France, Australia, Belgium, Cuba, Peru, and Nationalist China all would have supported such an initiative. In fact, Cuba's delegate retorted that "none can allege that the Council has insufficient evidence at its disposal" and proceeded to outline a possible draft resolution:

> In the first place, it should contain an urgent appeal to the Government of the Soviet Union to withdraw its troops from Hungarian territory; this is in keeping with the provisions of the United Nations Charter. Secondly, it should expressly state, or rather reiterate, that the Hungarian people have the unquestionable right to determine, through free elections, the system of government under which they wish to live. Thirdly, it should provide for the establishment of a Security Council commission to supervise the position and to report on compliance with measures adopted by the Council to ensure the national independence and political freedom of the Hungarian people.[106]

Other noncommunist delegates made somewhat milder speeches, but all seemed to agree that the issue involved a *prima facie* case of foreign intervention. In his concluding remarks Lodge quoted Eisenhower's offer of $20 million in surplus foodstuffs and medical supplies, noting that "entirely apart from the political developments in Hungary, we in the United States want to do everything we can to ensure that the Hungarian people shall not have to suffer in the winter which lies ahead of us."[107]

While Sobolev delivered a speech charging that the West was trying to divert attention from Suez, denying Nagy's claims about the new influx of Soviet troops, and asserting that Soviet-Hungarian negotiations were in progress, a new communication from the Hungarian premier was circulated to the delegates assembled in the Council chamber.[108] The letter reiterated the earlier report of Soviet reinforcements crossing the border, advised that the Hungarian government had "forwarded concrete proposals on the withdrawal of Soviet troops stationed in Hungary as well as the place of negotiations concerning the execution of the termination of the Warsaw Pact," and requested the secretary-general to call upon the Great Powers to recognize Hungary's neutrality and to "instruct the Soviet and Hungarian Governments to start negotiations immediately." The meeting adjourned upon agreement to reconvene the following day at 3:00 P.M. Only that same afternoon did the secretary-general report that satisfactory credentials for Szabó had been received from Budapest.[109]

The third meeting of the Security Council on the situation in Hungary proved to be as inconclusive as the previous ones.[110] Henry Cabot Lodge again asked Szabó for more information and repeated his request that the secretary-general contact the Hungarian government "in order that this Council may know the facts." Then, without actually proposing it, he referred to an American draft resolution calling on the Soviet Union to stop its intervention and withdraw, affirming Hungary's right to a representative government, requesting Hammarskjold to study the question of relief, and urging all UN members to assist in relief work.[111] The Hungarian representative eventually replied that as far as he knew negotiations were in progress and that the two sides would meet again at 10:00 P.M. Budapest time. Walker of Australia, who had been one of the more energetic proponents of UN action, reluctantly agreed to wait and see, but he warned, "There is, of course, a considerable danger that, in those circumstances, negotiations between the Hungarian Government and the Soviet authorities may not be conducted on a basis of equality and respect for Hungarian rights." The Yugoslav delegate suggested that the Council adjourn, pending the outcome of the negotiations, and, although Dixon and de Guiringaud of France voiced reservations and urged the adoption of a resolution along the lines of the American draft as a fitting response to Nagy's appeal, Lodge was inclined to temporize: "We believe . . . that adjournment for a day or two would give a real opportunity to the Hungarian Government to carry out its announced desire to arrange for an orderly and immediate evacuation of Soviet troops."[112]

The remainder of this session was spent in debate over the time of the next meeting. Sobolev confirmed that negotiations were in progress, and, when Walker proposed that the Council reconvene the following day (November 4) at 5:00 P.M., the United States voted in the negative (supported by Iran, with the Soviet Union, Yugoslavia, and Peru abstaining) and the proposal was defeated. The Council president then suggested Monday, November 6, at 10:30 A.M., and this was adopted with only Australia abstaining; both Lodge and Sobolev thus approved of the postponement. After the vote had been taken, the Australian and French delegates reserved the right to call for an earlier meeting if necessary. The Council adjourned at 6:00 P.M. ; an hour later the General Assembly would convene once again to debate the Suez issue. Proposals during the foregoing debate to split delegations and carry on into the night had not received Lodge's support, and much of the subsequent criticism of American behavior would center on this postponement; some time after the crisis Lodge would issue an explanatory statement:

> The fact that a short time later it became clear to the Hungarian Government that the Soviet Union was lying does not alter the fact that on November 3 the Hungarian Government had some hope that the Soviets

were telling the truth. This was a decision which it was the Hungarian Government's to make. . . .

At that particular time, Washington could not be sure of all the facts of the situation. . . . Washington was confronting these things: the Suez crisis; a fog of uncertainty about events in Hungary; and the very real possibility of a clash with the Soviet Union—with the world shattering consequences which this could entail.[113]

These arguments failed of course to cover all important aspects of the situation as of November 3. Nagy's three-day-old appeal had failed to elicit any meaningful response; there was no "fog of uncertainty" concerning the massive influx of Soviet troops; the question of UN observers had been left in abeyance; and the ostensible American confidence in the outcome of negotiations held in such unpromising circumstances appeared, particularly in view of Washington's long-standing mistrust of Soviet negotiating tactics, somewhat disingenuous even at that time.

The General Assembly had been sitting for less than three hours when the Russians launched their massive offensive. At 11:19 P.M. (5:19 A.M. Budapest time) Premier Nagy made his radio announcement, and shortly afterward the Reuters report of these events reached the United Nations; then a group of Hungarian émigrés headed by Msgr. Varga arrived to meet with Lodge, but was refused entry. When approached by Walker, Lodge still seemed to favor delay and suggested a council meeting the following afternoon, but the Australian pressed for an immediate special session, and Lodge finally agreed. At about 1:00 A.M. Walker interrupted the proceedings on a point of order and requested that the Security Council be convened. Twenty minutes later Lodge also rose on a point of order, announced the receipt of dispatches reporting that Budapest was under heavy bombardment, and gave notice that he had called for a meeting of the council.[114] After further debate on Suez the General Assembly adjourned, and at 3:05 A.M. the special session of the Security Council got under way. Lodge opened with an impassioned piece of oratory: "If ever there was a time when the action of the United Nations could literally be a matter of life and death for a whole nation, this is the time. . . . A few minutes ago, we received word from the Prime Minister of Hungary for help from the whole world while his capital city is burning." Recalling Sobolev's earlier assurance regarding negotiations, he observed that it could "scarcely be equalled for its total lack of candor and its indifference to human suffering" and went on to address the beleaguered Hungarians: "By your heroic sacrifice you have given the United Nations a brief moment in which to mobilize the conscience of the world on your behalf. We are seizing that moment, and we will not fail you." The American delegate then introduced a slightly revised draft resolution which was immediately endorsed by Britain. In a lengthy and temporizing speech, Sobolev claimed lack of information and warned, "Any intervention by the United Nations and the Western Powers in the further course of events in Hungary can only lead to complications, and would in any event be illegal and incompatible with the Charter." Hungary's disoriented representative confessed that he was cut off from Budapest but said that "unofficially" he had been informed of the formation of a new government headed by Kádár. The American motion having been vetoed by the Soviet Union, Lodge invoked the Uniting for Peace resolution of November 3, 1950, and called for an emergency special session of the General Assembly "to make appropriate recommendations concerning the situation in Hungary." Even Yugoslavia concurred in this, and the motion passed, with Sobolev casting the only dissenting vote.[115]

The second emergency special session of the General Assembly was convened that same afternoon. Over Sobolev's objections—he called Nagy's appeals "unconstitutional"—the agenda was adopted and the American delegate took the floor:

> We have seen no passage of governmental authority from one Hungarian Government to another, but only the creation of a puppet clique and the overthrow of a liberal socialist government responsive to popular will in its desire to see [Soviet] troops go.

> Two hours after the attack began, the new puppet group appealed to the Soviet Union to come to its assistance. It cannot be maintained, therefore, that the Soviet action is undertaken in response to any request for assistance. The "assistance" ... arrived long before the call.[116]

Lodge then submitted a draft resolution calling for Soviet withdrawal and for an investigation by the secretary-general.[117] (Canada's L. B. Pearson also suggested the establishment of a UN mission or UN supervisory machinery, but without success.) A slightly amended American resolution was adopted by fifty votes, with eight states voting against and fifteen abstaining; although Lodge had made pointed reference to the Bandung principles of nonalignment, only eight among the signatories of that declaration chose to endorse the resolution.[118] The following morning, November 5, Hammarskjold received a telegram from Kádár's "Revolutionary Worker-Peasant Government" claiming that the Nagy appeals "have no legal force and cannot be considered as requests emanating from Hungary as a State."[119] (The subsequent UN report on Hungary concluded that the legality of the Nagy government under the Hungarian Constitution could not be contested.)[120] The outlines of a protracted stalemate appeared: the General Assembly had condemned Soviet action and had requested an investigation by the secretary-general, who in turn was faced by the *fait accompli* of a Soviet-supported regime.

While Washington waited for Hammarskjold to act, the situation lost some of its urgency, despite domestic pressures. Early on November 4 Adlai Stevenson cabled the president, urging him to "at once set in motion machinery to activate the Peace Observation Commission which was created in 1950 under the Uniting for Peace Resolution. This would make it possible for the United Nations to mobilize large teams of official observers and fly them into Hungary, or at least the still-free parts of Hungary."[121] The administration dismissed such alternatives, sharing with Hammarskjold the predilection for concentrating on Suez. As Hammarskjold subsequently recalled: "On the 4th I had in my hand a request for a report on UNEF within 48 hours. I do not think that the General Assembly or any member of the General Assembly would have asked me to do that and at the same time check what was going on in Budapest. They could not have done it."[122] Three days after the original resolution, the secretary-general apologized publicly for concentrating on the Middle East and promised that he would "shortly be in a position to report on further steps that we are taking for the implementation of the resolution."[123] Meanwhile, the meeting of the General Assembly scheduled for that afternoon to discuss Hungary had been postponed until the following morning in order to allow further debate on the Suez question.

On November 8 the General Assembly sat twice in its second emergency special session. The Soviet Union and its allies (now including the unfortunate Szabó) insisted that the debate constituted interference in the internal affairs of a member state. Finally, a five-power resolution sponsored by Cuba, Ireland, Italy, Pakistan, and Peru, requesting a Soviet withdrawal and free elections in Hungary under UN auspices, was introduced by the Italian delegate.[124] When the Assembly met again the following day, Lodge sounded fatalistic: "It is some measure of the deep sadness which is in our hearts that the speeches here have had some of the quality of funeral orations. We must not let the memory of this outrage die."[125] Noting that the five-power draft dealt with "longer-range objectives," he proposed a resolution which dealt with relief and refugees and which called on the Soviet Union to cease its activities in Hungary. The two motions, together with another humanitarian resolution introduced by Austria, were approved by the Assembly, which also heard a message from the secretary-general asking Hungary to admit observers. An air of futility permeated the proceedings, however. France's delegate observed that the Security Council had taken more than a week to decide that the Hungarian situation warranted immediate action and that five days had gone by without action on the Assembly's resolution: "It is as though we were waiting for a whole nation to be finally crushed before issuing a death certificate."[126] In the Assembly's last special session, on November 10, an American resolution transferring the question of Hungary to the provisional agenda of the upcoming eleventh regular session "as a matter of priority" was approved over Szabó's objections.[127] In his closing speech the president of the Assembly noted that "lack of time, resulting from the complexity of the grave problems created by the outbreak of hostilities in the Near East, has prevented the Secretary-General from submitting a report to the present session."[128]

The interval between the conclusion of the Assembly's special session and the opening of its regular session saw repeated attempts to have UN observers admitted into Hungary as well as a protracted controversy over the credentials of Hungary's representatives. On November 8 and 10 Hammarskjold sent two messages to Hungary, and one directly to the Soviet Union, regarding the admission of observers; the Russians disclaimed any responsibility in the matter, and the Kádár regime replied that, while it was willing to accept relief, it considered observers an unwarranted interference in Hungary's internal affairs.[129] A few days later, when Hammarskjold offered to go to Budapest, the Hungarians countered that, since he was in any event planning to visit the Middle East, he could meet with Kádár's representatives in Rome. "I turned thumbs down to that," observed Hammarskjold.[130]

The General Assembly had given Hammarskjold a broad mandate to investigate the Hungarian affair, without, however, specifying how he was to go about it. Originally the secretary-general had planned to set up two advisory bodies, one to investigate the situation brought about by the Soviet intervention, the other to observe conditions in Hungary firsthand, but opposition from the Soviet bloc ruled out the latter and he had to content himself with naming former OAS Secretary-General Dr. Alberto Lleras Camargo, India's permanent representative Arthur Lall, and the Norwegian judge Oscar Gundersen to fulfill the first function. Despite this initiative, a wide gulf prevailed between public expectations and the actual performance of the United Nations. Asked at a televised press conference why there was any question of sending observers to Hungary when a police force was being sent to Egypt, Lodge replied:

If you sent an expeditionary force into Hungary, you'd simply be making the whole situation worse and running the risk of a new war. . . .

The Soviets have made it clear they won't withdraw, whereas the British and French and Israelis have made it clear they will withdraw.

There's the difference. If they don't permit observers in Hungary then we'll have to have another meeting of the General Assembly and we'll have to exhaust every peaceful means. I don't know what the means will be.[131]

Meanwhile, Szabó held onto his UN accreditation and acted as the representative of the Kádár regime. Apparently Imre Nagy had planned to go to the United Nations on Monday, November 5, to present Hungary's case, but Mrs. Anna Kéthly, a prominent member of the old Social Democratic party, arrived in New York that day claiming to be Nagy's special UN representative.[132] Despite popular support, her claim to Hungary's seat was turned down on the grounds that she lacked the proper letters of accreditation.[133] When Kádár's foreign minister, Imre Horváth, appeared on November 13 to head Hungary's delegation, an informal committee of Latin-American members met to study ways of challenging his credentials, and a few days later an American spokesman was quoted as saying that Washington would support a move to give Mrs. Kéthly a hearing at the United Nations if some other country took the initiative. At a meeting of the General Assembly on November 27, Cuba's delegate declared that, if no progress was reported by the secretary-general, the Assembly should consider further action, beginning with the expulsion of the Hungarian delegation; his opinion was endorsed by the *New York Times*, which wondered why the administration continued to pretend that a legal government existed in Hungary.[134]

On December 6 Henry Cabot Lodge circulated a statement among delegates which proposed that the General Assembly consider action against the Hungarian delegation and which charged that Horváth had "deceived and deluded" the United Nations. At a seventeen-power meeting the United States put forward a resolution to suspend the delegation unless UN observers were promptly admitted; then, allegedly because the proposal was not assured of sufficient support, the Americans decided to defer consideration of the delegation's suspension. Nevertheless, the Hungarians walked out of the Assembly on December 11, having been "rudely and disgracefully offended" by the debate. The *New York Times* suggested that the Assembly should invite Mrs. Kéthly—"the only free member of the last legal Government of Hungary"—to step into the breach. In the continued absence of official American initiatives, Cuba's delegate announced that he would seek the cancellation of the delegation's credentials after the Christmas recess.[135] The rather anticlimactic outcome of the entire episode came on February 21, 1957, when the General Assembly accepted the Credentials Committee's recommendation to take no decision regarding the Kádár delegation. In practical terms this meant that the possibility of alternative representation had been ruled out, since clause 85 of the Assembly's rules of procedure states that *de facto* recognition of a delegation and toleration of its presence permits its full participation in the Assembly's activities. Although formal accreditation of the Kádár regime's delegation was delayed for some years, it was never prevented from representing Hungary.[136]

Some UN members—notably, the Latin-American bloc—persisted in their efforts in Hungary's behalf. On November 16 Cuba's delegate introduced a draft resolution which, noting the deportations that were taking place in Hungary, branded the Soviet measures as violations of the Convention on Genocide and demanded the curtailment of the deportations and the repatriation of those already affected.[137] The United States welcomed Cuba's initiative, but over the weekend before the Assembly convened Dr. Nunez Portuondo had to revise the text twice to water down the reference to genocide and thus gain wider support.[138] In the Assembly, Henry Cabot Lodge charged, over Soviet Foreign Minister Dmitri Shepilov's denials, that as of November 14 some 16,000 persons had been deported from Budapest alone. Finally, on November 21, three resolutions dealing with Hungary were adopted. The first was the Cuban draft condemning the deportations; the second, a three-power resolution sponsored by Ceylon, India, and Indonesia, urged Hungary to admit the secretary-general and UN observers "without prejudice to its sovereignty" and requested the secretary-general to report without delay; the third, introduced by Argentina, Belgium, Denmark, and the United States, concerned relief for refugees.[139]

Hammarskjold reported to the General Assembly on November 30 that Hungary had not reacted to his latest request for the admission of observers, although he had received a letter from the Soviet Union qualifying the talk of deportations as "slanderous rumors." (In fact, even Budapest radio had alluded to these measures.) The following day the United States asked the Assembly to give priority consideration to a resolution which again called on Kádár to admit observers and which urged as an alternative "first step" the dispatch of observers to the Hungarian border, across which more than 200,000 refugees were fleeing to the West. It was not clear what might follow this first step, but some U.S. legislators urged drastic measures; Senator Knowland suggested that the Soviet Union be barred from the United Nations pending its compliance with the various resolutions, and House Majority Leader John McCormack proposed that UN observers enter Hungary with or without permission. They were joined by union leaders George Meany and Walter Reuther in calling for the unseating of Kádár's delegation.[140]

Budapest replied on December 1 with a refusal to admit observers, adding, however, that the secretary-general would be welcome at a later date; the Soviet Union and India saw in this reply an approval, in principle, of UN observation.[141] Hammarskjold thereupon offered to visit Hungary for three days beginning December 16—noting that it was "impossible for me to be absent from headquarters for another week"—but his offer was rejected.[142] Meanwhile, another resolution, sponsored by the United States and thirteen other members, was adopted in the General Assembly.[143] Noting "with deep concern" the Soviet Union's failure to comply with earlier remonstrances, it called upon the Russians and the Hungarian authorities to advise the secretary-general by December 7 of their consent to receive UN observers and recommended that in the meantime Hammarskjold arrange for the eventual dispatch of such personnel to Hungary and other countries as would be appropriate. In the absence of any positive reaction from either Budapest or Moscow, the United States decided to launch yet another resolution, which would in no uncertain terms condemn the actions of the Russians. This eventually became a twenty-power resolution and was adopted on December 12. It declared that, "by using its armed force against the Hungarian people, the Government of the Union of Soviet Socialist Republics is violating the political independence of Hungary"; condemned this flouting of the Charter; demanded that the Soviet Union "make immediate arrangements for the withdrawal, under United Nations observation, of its armed forces from Hungary and to permit the reestablishment of the political independence of Hungary;" and requested that the secretary-general "take any initiative he deems helpful in relation to the Hungarian problem."[144]

With the passage of time each new resolution became more of an exercise in futility, although some interpreted these attempts as admittedly bitter propaganda victories for the West. In January, acting upon Hammarskjold's recommendation, the General Assembly established a Special Committee on the Problem of Hungary and named as members the representatives of Australia, Ceylon, Denmark, Tunisia, and Uruguay.[145] Unable to enter Hungary, or to visit Imre Nagy in Rumania, the committee carried out most of its investigations in Austria and submitted its report six months later. [146] A fitting epitaph for the revolution, the report denounced the Soviet Union's forcible repression of a "spontaneous national uprising." After lengthy debate the General Assembly endorsed the report and appointed a special representative to pursue the matter of compliance with its earlier resolutions.[147] Even this final phase in the United Nations' consideration of the Hungarian problem failed to pass without adverse publicity. Povl Bang-Jensen, a Danish diplomat of unimpeachable integrity who had served on the staff of the special committee, was forcibly expelled from the Secretariat after refusing to divulge the names of Hungarian witnesses who had testified before the committee on condition of anonymity; in another case, a Ceylonese UN employee was dismissed for having delivered verbatim testimony from the committee to the Soviet delegation.[148] These scandals cast doubt on the efficacy of an international and necessarily heterogeneous body of civil servants in handling a matter in which the interests of the superpowers were directly involved.

In evaluating the performance of the United Nations in the Hungarian crisis, it is difficult to divorce the institutional aspects of the question from the policies of the member states, since in the final analysis the latter had to provide the motive force for any collective action by that organization. Indeed, as one American scholar observed, the capacity of the United Nations for action was directly dependent upon U.S. policy.[149] Whether or not its reliance on the United Nations can be called an abdication by the United States of one of its major responsibilities, the fact remains that through various resolutions of the Security Council and the General Assembly a great load was placed on the shoulders of the secretary-general, who was allowed to exercise wide powers in investigating the Hungarian revolution even while that event was in progress. The record shows a remarkable lack of urgency in the Secretariat's response to the Nagy appeals, and Hammarskjold himself did not seem inclined toward swift action following various members' requests for investigation. These delays on his part have been explained by his preoccupation with the Suez crisis and by "a natural tendency to allow the situation to untangle itself."[150] That Hammarskjold chose to devote his energies to Suez at the expense of Hungary reflected at least in part a personal reluctance to involve his office and the prestige of the United Nations in a seemingly hopeless conflict.

POST-MORTEMS ON A MYTH

Although fighting in Hungary continued sporadically until mid-November, the overwhelming odds left no doubt as to the final outcome. In the face of the adamant enmity of the workers' councils, which had supplanted the Nagy regime as spokesmen for the revolution, and of the general population, the Kádár government abandoned its initial promises of reform and imposed harsh repressive measures. Imre Nagy, who had taken refuge in the Yugoslav embassy, was kidnapped by the Russians and spirited out of the country. The unlimited powers exercised by the Soviet Military Command and the total submissiveness of Kádár symbolized Hungary's reintegration into Moscow's sphere of dominance. The Hungarian fugue had come to a tragic end, leaving a *crise de conscience* in the West, felt most strongly in the United States, as its reproachful legacy.

Much criticism stemmed from the high expectations of UN assistance, as was recorded with commendable frankness by the Special Committee on the Problem of Hungary:

> It was thought that a visit by a delegation from the United Nations or by the Secretary-General might stave off the Soviet armed advance and its final overthrow of the Government. There was some hope among the public for United Nations moves similar to those which were then being undertaken with respect to the Middle East situation, a call for a cease-fire and possibly the sending of a United Nations Force. . . . Undoubtedly, there was disappointment that the United Nations was not acting with greater speed and determination.[151]

Not all of the retrospective judgments went beyond the bounds of reality. In the view of General Béla Király, commander of the revolutionary forces in the later stages of the uprising, "had the UN acted on Prime Minister Nagy's telegram of November first, the Russians would have accepted the revolution as a *fait accompli*. By the second, however, it became a matter of lulling us into the belief that we had won our point, while they prepared to crush us."[152] One possible reaction would have been for the secretary-general to fly to Budapest, Suez notwithstanding. Király mentioned a few others:

> The UN could have announced: "Hungary, an independent country negotiating with the USSR, announces its neutrality and places itself under the guarantee of the United Nations." We hoped for such a solemn announcement that the UN had taken notice of Nagy's statement that Hungary was asserting itself as independent and neutral.

> If they wished to go further, the UN could have sent 300 neutral soldiers to symbolize this international interest. They could have served as a symbolic picket line of Hungary's neutrality.[153]

The last suggestion, repeated by many critics, probably would not have passed the gamut of the General Assembly, even with American support. Direct and immediate international observation of the events in Hungary would have been more feasible and within the prerogative of the secretary-general. At least until November 3, a visit by Hammarskjold or even the appointment of diplomats already in Budapest as UN observers could have assumed symbolic significance. It is difficult to be sanguine, even in retrospect, regarding the preventive effectiveness of such observation, given the Nagy regime's open challenge to Soviet hegemony; nevertheless, a UN presence in Budapest would have been more in keeping with the lofty principles of the Charter, and it is a fair criticism that in Hungary the world organization "remained eyeless."[154]

This is not meant to deny that, as noted earlier, the issue was essentially one of Great Power politics. When the British ambassador said in New York that the United Nations "should not lay down one law for Asia and another for Europe, one law for the Soviet Union and another for the other powers," he was merely reflecting on the fact that, while Britain and France and Israel eventually gave in to the pressure of the two super-powers (and only incidentally to a nebulous "world opinion"), in the case of Hungary one of the superpowers was directly involved, and therefore any credible challenge had to come from its counterpart in the West.[155] Despite the initially disappointing performance of the United Nations in investigating the Hungarian problem, the decisive factor was the reluctance of the United States to risk a major confrontation. As Hammarskjold observed in his introduction to the secretary-general's annual report for 1957:

> The Assembly may recommend, it may investigate, it may pronounce judgment, but it does not have the power to compel compliance with its decisions. . . . in the case of Hungary, when compliance was refused, no delegation formally proposed a recommendation by the General Assembly to the Member States that they apply sanctions or use force to secure the withdrawal of foreign troops. The judgment of the majority of Member States as to the course to pursue . . . was, instead, reflected in the General Assembly's resolution of condemnation and decision to order an investigation.[156]

The only delegation that could have authoritatively recommended the use of force was that of the United States, but, as Eisenhower recalls in his memoirs, "if the United Nations, overriding a certain Soviet veto, decided that all the military and other resources of member nations should be used to drive the Soviets from Hungary, we would have a major conflict."[157] Thus, Washington's delay in pressing the case of Hungary at the United Nations until the revolution's failure was an accomplished fact stemmed from a consistent effort to avoid giving unwarranted encouragement to the rebels. Even at that clearly hopeless stage, expectations of assistance were easily kindled among Hungarians, as illustrated by the story of the freedom fighter who, upon hearing Western broadcasts of the UN proceedings and of the censure of the Soviet Union, recalled the Korean precedent and returned to battle with renewed optimism.[158]

Following the revolution, numerous critics focused on the real and imagined inconsistencies of American policies toward East-Central Europe. Typical of these was Walter Lippmann, who commented, "there can be few in this country who have not felt how sharp is the contrast between what we have been saying about Hungary and what we are doing.''[159] In a more partisan vein, Senator Kefauver denounced the Republican campaign pamphlets on liberation: "Taken individually, these statements might be dismissed as immoral but harmless political propaganda. But the cumulative effect, falling on hopeful ears abroad, could very well lead to the false hope that the United States was ready and willing to do what it was not prepared to do."[160] Amid the widespread disillusionment with Western propaganda, Radio Free Europe predictably emerged as a convenient scapegoat.

The Twentieth Congress of the CPSU had prompted the drafting of major policy guidelines at RFE which aimed to "stimulate a greater variety and intensity of legitimate and realistic demands" regarding de-Stalinization, political participation, and contacts with the West. Concurrently, however, RFE was committed to emphasize that no likelihood of Western intervention by force existed and that, in light of the Geneva conferences, the prospects of liberation through negotiation were almost equally remote. The fine balance between caution and encouragement proved difficult to maintain. On June 29, 1956, following the Poznań riots, RFE broadcast to Hungary: "The system of oppression is increasingly unstable everywhere, with the people's battle for freedom gaining hope. Success, however, depends on unity, patience, and discipline." With the onset of the revolution, RFE concentrated on disseminating the rebels' demands. Between October 25 and November 1 its commentators denounced Imre Nagy and his government. Although prompted by the assumption that the veteran communist had been responsible for the initial Russian intervention, this policy was not supported unanimously by RFE's policy makers; those in New York preferred to suspend judgment on Nagy. Otherwise, the station reported extensively on all relevant Western statements—notably Eisenhower's "dawning of a new day" speech—and on deliberations at the United Nations. On November 5, with the revolution virtually crushed, the daily guidelines read in part: "There can be no question but that none of our audiences will be too receptive to strong propaganda words and strident voices while the victims of Soviet imperialism lie unburied." By implication, a certain crusading spirit had been present in more propitious days.[161]

Indeed, an American correspondent who witnessed the revolution reported that the Hungarians had been thoroughly convinced the United States would help them against the Soviet Union, an illusion for which, according to the report of the Special Committee on the Problem of Hungary, Radio Free Europe was partly to blame.[162] From their exile in Vienna, three rebel leaders claimed that RFE broadcasts had intimated the imminent intervention of "volunteers"; the station issued a strong denial and later asserted that Hungarian-language broadcasts originating in East

Germany had reported the massing of Western forces preparing to come to the aid of the Hungarians.[163] In the wake of charges in the West German press of "opportunistic agitation," the Bonn government conducted a formal investigation of RFE's broadcasts during the uprising. The results were claimed to exonerate the organization. Specifically, the screening of the broadcasts showed that, of 308 programs, 4 were found to be "in clear violation of RFE's standing policies or daily guidances on the Hungarian revolt," and 16 more contained "distortions." Some Hungarian broadcasters had given military advice to the insurgents. The news report, quoted earlier, which suggested that if armed resistance lasted until after the U.S. elections Washington might feel compelled to intervene was rather inadvisedly relayed by RFE. The station had also placed great emphasis on the United Nations and its consideration of the conflict, and this apparently created the impression in Hungary that the world organization could offer tangible assistance.[164] Of course, even straight reporting had unforeseen effects. Reflecting on the verbatim broadcast by RFE of the original UN censure motion, two psychological warfare analysts observed: "To use the truth to enlighten involves a thorough analysis of how the listener, given his beliefs and attitudes and his situation, will interpret the truth and translate it into action."[165] A revolutionary situation like the one in Hungary made such an analysis at once more critical and less feasible.

An assessment of the real effect of U.S. propaganda must, however, go beyond RFE's occasional errors in judgment in the course of the Hungarian uprising. Even in the absence of unequivocal Western commitments, as one critic noted, the "gap between the actual promises and implied promises was easy to bridge for people under the maximum of mental stress."[166] Postrevolution surveys among refugees showed that, while few blamed RFE for inciting the Hungarians to revolt, a large proportion had the idea that the very existence of American propaganda stations signified America's willingness to fight for Hungary.[167] Perhaps the best illustration of how the East Europeans perceived the West's message came from the pen of István Bibó, a Hungarian scholar and minister in the last Nagy government. Writing of the satellites in an essay smuggled out after his arrest, Bibó said:

> The Western world did not promise to start an atomic war in their interest, nor did it call on them foolishly to take up arms. Their encouragements, however, did say that if ever the international political situation and the attitude of these peoples justify it, the Western world will use all its economic, political and moral weight to bring these issues up for consideration and satisfactory solution. The Hungarian Revolution brought about all the requisite conditions and legal claims.

The gravest consequences the Western world must face as a result of the defeat of the Hungarian Revolution are that a ten-year-long policy and propaganda referring to principles and morals can now be contested not only in terms of its effectiveness and true meaning, but in terms of its honesty as well.[168]

The revolution had aroused strong emotions, and not only behind the Iron Curtain. Popular revulsion at the Russians' brutality reached a high intensity particularly in Western Europe; on the evening of November 4 some 100,000 West Berliners rallied in protest and were barely restrained from storming the Brandenburg Gate. When, in the immediate aftermath of the revolution, this revulsion engendered a widespread mood of self-criticism, the Eisenhower administration re-emphasized that its policy had always been constant and consistent.

In his first news conference after re-election, the president attempted once again to clarify the meaning of liberation, defining it as a responsibility to keep alive the spirit of freedom and hope in the captive countries and to relieve suffering, without, however, encouraging actual revolution:

Nothing, of course, has so disturbed the American people as the events in Hungary. Our hearts have gone out to them and we have done everything it is possible to do in the way of alleviating suffering. But I must make one thing clear: the United States doesn't now, and never has, advocated open rebellion by an undefended populace against force over which they could not possibly prevail.[169]

Probably ruing his earlier optimism at Occidental College, where on October 29 he had boasted that the events in Poland and Hungary testified to the success of American policies, Vice-President Nixon also took pains to explain the administration's actions:

Because we stood firmly against the use of force in Egypt, we were in a moral position to condemn the ruthless and barbarous Soviet conquest of [Hungary]. The UN has no armies that it could send to rescue the heroic freedom fighters of Hungary. There were no treaties which would invoke the armed assistance of the free nations. Our only weapon here was moral condemnation, since the alternative was action on our part which might initiate the third and ultimate world war.[170]

Nixon concluded that the revolution was a major turning point leading to the peaceful defeat of communism. The legal argument that no treaties bound the United States to involve itself in a satellite rebellion could scarcely have been calculated to mitigate the feeling of disillusionment exemplified by István Bibó's manifesto to the West.

The chief crusader for rollback, Secretary of State Dulles, now faced the unhappy task of rationalizing disaster. Asked at a press conference on December 2 whether the United States bore any responsibility for the events in Hungary, he recalled that in 1952 Eisenhower and he had formulated a policy of evolutionary liberation: "I think it has been United States policy since this administration has been in office to adhere to that point of view; . . . the broadcasts and the like which have been made by the Voice of America have all adhered to that basic philosophy of an evolutionary process." Dulles then engaged in a long series of questions and answers regarding diplomatic recognition of the Kádár regime, in the course of which he admitted that he had forgotten the name of the American minister-designate; the gist of his answers was that the United States was maintaining its legation but that Wailes would postpone the presentation of his credentials. When a newsman wondered if it would be correct to label the policy regarding the ultimate liberation of the satellites as one of containment, Dulles stuck to his guns:

> I wouldn't so describe it, no. In fact, the contrary. Containment implies that you accept the Soviet rule over the satellites. We believe that that rule can and must be ended. But we believe that the processes must be evolutionary processes, and not violent revolution. . . . We did not encourage violent revolution because we did not see how violent revolution would prevail.[171]

As will be seen, many disagreed with Dulles' differentiation between containment and liberation.

On December 3, in a belated gesture of reprisal, the United States suspended its cultural exchange program with the Soviet Union. Three days later, a show of force by Soviet armored vehicles in front of the American legation in Budapest drew an official protest against the use of Russian troops to intimidate Hungarian civilians; the protest was rejected as an "unjustified attempt to interfere in the relations between the USSR and the Hungarian People's Republic."[172] In fact, the dominant sentiment within the Eisenhower administration was one of concern that the Soviet Union might start a war as a way of overcoming its weakened position in East-Central Europe; fears were expressed that, if the spirit of open rebellion spread to Poland and East Germany, the West Germans would feel compelled to intervene and thereby escalate the conflict to a critical level.[173] One month after the Hungarian revolution, to which the liberation policy had contributed to a certain extent, the main objective of American policy makers was to limit the turmoil to that country and prevent any further outbreaks behind the Iron Curtain.

The impact of the revolution gave rise in both official and unofficial quarters to what John Foster Dulles termed, in another context, an agonizing reappraisal of American aims and policies. Shortly after the repression, Hans J. Morgenthau wrote to the *New York Times*:

> The first week of November, 1956, is likely to be remembered as one of the most calamitous episodes in the history of United States diplomacy. Some of the basic assumptions of our policy have been put to the test of actual performance, and they have failed that test.

> One of these assumptions has been our commitment to the independence of the nations of Eastern Europe. It was over this issue that the Cold War started and was in good measure waged. Yet when the Russian empire started to disintegrate, the United States renounced from the outset the use of force and thus gave the Soviet Union, for all practical purposes, a free hand.[174]

This was a serious indictment of American policy, and one which found echo in many quarters. Capitol Hill was the scene of much soul-searching in the months following the revolution. A common criticism was voiced by John McCormack in the House: "How could our policymakers be removed so far from the world of reality as to believe that there was a finality to the Communist enslavement of people behind the Iron Curtain and that revolt against the tyranny of Moscow was impossible? . . . It seems incredible that we . . . did not even have contingency plans to fall back upon in this situation of unparalleled opportunity."[175] Subsequently, a special study mission of the House reported that the revolution had caught the free world totally unprepared: "The failure of the United States to have a plan or plans of action concerning the Hungarian events indicates either a serious weakness in our intelligence service or a serious misapplication by the administrators of our foreign policy of facts reported." The report noted that there were "4 fatal days during which the United States was paralyzed by inaction. This inaction in effect weakened the morale of the freedom fighters and emboldened the Soviets to take their ruthless action without fear of countermeasures from the free world."[176]

The criticisms spanned a wide range of alternative courses of action. On the question of the use of force, it was observed that the United States had from the outset declined to intervene. At the time of the revolution suggestions had been put forward—even by certain congressmen—that international volunteers or arms be sent to the insurgents. When Congressman Bentley subsequently inquired about this possibility, the State Department took a month to reply that military action, even by means of hypothetical volunteers, would have created a risk of war and would incidentally have violated Austrian neutrality. To a similar enquiry by McCormack, Assistant Secretary of State Robert C. Hill responded that the provision of arms would not have improved the situation and that in any case the avowed policy of the administration had been to deal with the problem through the United Nations.[177] The administration's key argument, that the Russians were in a belligerent mood and were prepared to precipitate a nuclear conflict at the slightest provocation, does not bear conclusive rebuttal; Eisenhower and at least some of his advisers had perceived Soviet intentions in this light and had acted with appropriate caution. Indeed, it is unlikely that at that time the majority of Americans favored an ultimatum similar to the one issued by Bulganin to Britain and France. A lingering doubt remained in the minds of some regarding the certainty of nuclear war in the event of a threat of American intervention, but no one could deny this grim possibility. In the course of hearings by the House Committee on Foreign Affairs a few weeks after the revolution, Paul Nitze speculated:

> Perhaps we should have taken that risk. Maybe the Russians would have backed down, if we had really been determined. . . . I do not believe that this administration was prepared to take any such risk. Frankly, I think the last administration was a much more courageous administration than this one.[178]

The official view, restated by Dulles at a news conference in Canberra in March 1957, necessarily prevailed: "There was no basis for our giving military aid to Hungary. We had no commitment to do so, and we did not think that to do so would either assist the people of Hungary or the people of Europe or the rest of the world."[179] In the final analysis, and despite the implicit or misperceived promises inherent in the policy of liberation, no responsible administration could risk nuclear annihilation for the sake of a small and faraway nation. Granting this, the question remained whether, in reassuring the Russians at the outset that the United States would remain a benevolent observer, Washington did not give away a potentially useful diplomatic counter; such a reaction, arising from the fear of war and from an overoptimistic assessment of Nagy's domestic influence, in effect gave *carte blanche* to the hard-liners in the Soviet Politburo at a time when that body was still divided on the wisdom of massive repression. The symbolic significance of Washington's pledge of nonintervention did not escape the eye of lay observers such as Hans Morgenthau, who noted that it was "tantamount to a unilateral recognition of a Russian sphere of influence wherein the United States concedes, without receiving any concessions in return, what she consistently refused to concede since Yalta."[180]

The main body of postrevolution criticism dealt with alternatives short of military intervention. Observed Senator Dodd, "We could have made it emphatically clear from the first minute that we recognized the government of Imre Nagy as the legitimate government of Hungary."[181] The administration's argument that the confusion reigning in Hungary precluded such a step might have carried a certain validity up to November 1, but the broadening of Nagy's government and its appeal to the United Nations should have removed any doubts as to its legitimacy.

American behavior in the United Nations also came under fire; the Eisenhower administration was attacked for not calling an emergency session of the General Assembly prior to the final repression, for failing to urge the creation of an observation commission, and for not supporting the accreditation of Anna Kéthly as Hungary's representative.[182] To these arguments Henry Cabot Lodge replied that the Suez issue took precedence at the United Nations, that Nagy had not invited observers (a questionable argument in view of the premier's plea for the recognition and protection of Hungary's neutrality), and that Mrs. Kéthly did not possess adequate credentials; he insisted that the United States had taken every step short of war. Washington's much-publicized reliance on the United Nations during the Hungarian episode was in fact a logical outcome of its policy of nonintervention. Secretary of State Dulles later claimed that by centering world opinion on the revolution the United Nations had made a recurrence of "such evil deeds as the suppression of the desire of the Hungarian people for independence" less likely, and privately he maintained that the organization "would have taken a stronger stand on Hungary had it not been for the Suez incident. I would dearly have loved to focus the eye of world public opinion uniquely on what was happening in Hungary."[183] The president, as usual more realistic than Dulles about the value of propaganda, recorded in his memoirs that even without Suez the reaction of the West would not have been more forceful.[184] Preservation of the United Nations must have been an additional restraining influence, for it is not idle speculation to suppose that any attempt to use it to force the Russians out of Hungary would have destroyed it, much as the League's impotence in the Manchurian and Abyssinian crises destroyed faith in that institution. Viewed in the long span of American policies toward the United Nations, the Hungarian revolution marked the early stage of a growing common interest in Washington and Moscow, born of an era of nuclear stalemate and booming UN membership, to settle differences over their respective spheres of interest outside the institutional framework of the world body.

Finally, the suggestion came from many sources that the United States should have seized the opportunity presented by Hungary to initiate negotiations aimed at an entirely new East-West agreement on European security; such negotiations were ardently hoped for in Hungary. Typical of this viewpoint, one European scholar argued that, at a time when the satellites were attacking Soviet hegemony, the West could risk proposing a simultaneous dissolution of NATO and the Warsaw Pact. American withdrawal from the heart of Europe, he postulated, would have made the Russians less reluctant to release their East European subjects.[185] Some British observers also urged the United States to explore the feasibility of disengagement to achieve the reunification of Germany and independence for the satellites.[186] It was argued that, faced with a mutinous empire, the Soviet Union might have been amenable to proposals that would provide effective guarantees of Russian security in exchange for an independent neutral belt in Europe and a reunited Germany. These suggestions were, of course, part of the protracted debate on disengagement, but it is significant that many proponents of such a solution to the division of Europe considered the Hungarian revolution a propitious occasion for a determined attempt by the West to initiate negotiations.

Although it would have required a revolution in Soviet policy for the Kremlin to relinquish control over East Germany and the other satellites—a move which would have amounted to ideological as well as strategic retrenchment—Washington concentrated on potential disadvantages for the West rather than on the possibility of failure. The Pentagon abhorred any initiative that could be interpreted as a sign of weakness. The Suez affair, by temporarily dividing the West and straining the time and energy of American policy makers to their limits, reduced even further the likelihood that any drastic revision would occur in the two alliance systems dividing Europe. Nevertheless, Moscow's hesitations and its momentary weakness in the satellites should have provided a consequential incentive for the policy makers to propose a major settlement.[187] In the event, on November 10 President Eisenhower rejected a Swiss proposal for a new summit conference and declared that the interests of all would be better served within the forum of the United Nations.[188] Once order was restored in Hungary, Premier Bulganin sent messages to the West's chancelleries and to the United Nations proposing a disarmament program which would involve a test ban and the reduction and eventual elimination of foreign armies in Europe, but his apparently conciliatory overture was coolly received in the West; in all likelihood the Kremlin foresaw this negative reaction and gambled that the offer might divide the West even further. At a press conference on December 18, the American secretary of state allowed that the United States was open to suggestions for changes in the status of the satellites through neutralization, but when asked about Bulganin's proposal he said that the "potential Soviet strength in Europe is so large that even after [the unreliability of the satellite armies is taken into account] the problem of military balance does not yet permit, in my opinion, and in the opinion of our military advisers, of any reduction in the strength of NATO forces in Europe." Maintaining that it was the Russians who rejected genuine negotiation, Dulles said that in any case he would not contemplate discussions which equated the Warsaw Pact with NATO and made it appear that the United States recognized the former. He countered the Russian overture by stipulating genuine independence for the satellites and a freely reunified Germany as conditions (rather than as consequences) of military disengagement.[189] Clearly, Dulles' moralistic distaste for negotiating with the Russians only strengthened the American preference for maintaining the prevailing strategic balance in Europe. Whatever opportunities had been present during Hungary's short-lived defection, the postrevolution mood in the West was scarcely one of compromise, and talk of disengagement remained an academic parlor game.

Was Washington's reaction to the Hungarian uprising consistent with the policy of liberation? Some years later President Eisenhower responded in the affirmative: "I was always very careful in the 1952 campaign; I always said, 'By every peaceful means.' I said, we will never accept the theory that these nations are to be forever enslaved. But we are not going to war to liberate them."[190] Indeed, as noted earlier, only rarely did the proponents of liberation venture beyond this cautious interpretation. Nevertheless, a certain ambiguity of purpose and means, inherent in the language of liberation, resulted in the widespread conviction that, in the words of an American analyst, "there was a serious and unjustified hiatus between pronouncement and policy, promise and performance. We spoke loudly and carried a small stick."[191] Liberation had been possessed of an essentially psychological orientation: to formulate a purpose which could stimulate American morale in the cold war, to create a long-range aim consistent with the moralistic element in Washington's world outlook, and perhaps only incidentally to win the hearts of the East Europeans and thereby weaken Soviet security. But hortatory policies that consist entirely of frequently repeated principles invite misinterpretation, and in the case of liberation the illusion of a definite goal carried with it the implied promise of assistance in case of revolt.

The Hungarian revolution illustrated dramatically the dangers of carrying on a multilevel foreign policy characterized by internal contradictions between principles and operational tactics. Granting that the primordial national interest of the United States lay in the prevention of nuclear war, it is still not certain that all alternatives short of war had been fully explored by American policy makers aspiring to dislodge the satellites from under direct Soviet rule. Despite the promises of de-Stalinization and of the spread of Titoism, common sense should have dictated planning for a contingency in which the East Europeans would demand full self-determination. Dulles, of course, denied that the revolution had in any way called the bluff of his liberation policy; on the contrary, he looked upon the uprisings in East Germany and Hungary and upon the evolution in Poland as evidence of its appropriateness. It is true that these events confirmed his predictions of internal collapse, but it is also true that they confirmed the futility of rebellions in the absence of Western support. In the event, he himself seemed to admit tacitly that the policy might have been misleading, for, as one of his subordinates in the State Department later observed, the words "roll back the aggressors" disappeared from his speeches.[192] Commented Dulles at a press briefing in Paris in mid-December, "I don't think that we should encourage violence unless we are in a position to help, but that doesn't mean that the day has passed when people of their own volition may not perhaps want to fight and die for freedom."[193] In prompting this clarification of American intentions, the people of Hungary had paid a heavy price and could draw only cold comfort from Jefferson's dictum that the tree of liberty must be refreshed from time to time with the blood of patriots and tyrants.

VI
NEW MYTHS
AND OLD REALITIES

Policy is only the glimmering of intention
through the manifold distractions of
reality.

C. R. FAY

The decade following the critical events of 1956 saw little alteration in the earlier pattern of East-West relations. Three different administrations grappled with the same core problems—the unity of the Western alliance; the maintenance of preponderant power; the control of endemic instability, particularly in the Middle East and in Southeast Asia; the containment of Soviet influence, whether over Berlin or in the Caribbean; and, above all, the limitation of the risk of nuclear conflict. Despite variations in the style and philosophy of presidents and secretaries of state, a common assessment of the prevailing balance of power and the continuity in Soviet aims allowed for no major modification in the foreign policy of the United States. In keeping with the enduring strategy of containment, the American sphere of influence was to be maintained by direct intervention—by Eisenhower in Lebanon, by Kennedy in Vietnam, by Johnson in the Dominican Republic—as well as by the more orthodox diplomatic and economic instruments. The rollback of communism, however, proved to be beyond the capacity of the three administrations, with the most notable net gain—Castro's Cuba—accruing instead to the Soviet Union. The policy of liberation, that albatross around the neck of the Eisenhower administration, had lost any semblance of actuality by the time of the Hungarian revolution, but succeeding administrations did not totally relinquish a moral and strategic interest in loosening the links that bound the satellites to Moscow. Encouraged by evidence of polycentric tendencies in the Soviet bloc, American policy makers persisted in advocating measures designed to encourage pluralism within the bloc, and, although various euphemisms supplanted the discredited terminology of liberation, that goal remained an integral, if increasingly long-range, part of U.S. foreign policy. The extent to which the new tactics inspired a modified myth of liberation, were actually implemented, and were consonant with secular trends within and without the Soviet sphere is the subject of the present chapter.

GRADUALISM

The year 1957 was one of active reappraisal in several spheres of American foreign policy. Having contributed, if only indirectly, to the decline of European influence in the Middle East, the Eisenhower administration now attempted to step into the breach by means of a program of military and economic aid for that area which was promptly dubbed the Eisenhower Doctrine; in application it would turn out to be a pale reflection, indeed, of the Truman Doctrine, at least partly because the communist influence it was designed to combat was peripheral to the fundamental national and ethnic conflicts in that area. In March, at a top-level conference in Bermuda, the British and the Americans attempted to restore some of the pre-Suez harmony and produced the predictable affirmations of NATO solidarity and of the desirability of German reunification, together with a sympathetic reference to the plight of Hungary. In the case of East-Central Europe, however, domestic and external constraints guaranteed that policy reappraisal would be an almost imperceptible process.

Among the satellite peoples themselves, America's popularity stood at its nadir in the months after the Hungarian tragedy, a fact which must have been particularly humiliating for an administration that prided itself on perceiving and encouraging their aspirations. Of more immediate consequence was the reaction of the American public and Congress, and in this sphere the administration could draw some comfort from the general understanding shown for its prudent response to the revolution. Popular revulsion at the brutality of Soviet repression in turn generated some self-criticism, but, with rare exceptions, this criticism was tempered by the grudging recognition that a more forceful response would have incurred the unacceptable risk of nuclear war. Having declared that the West's inaction constituted "the lost opportunity of our generation," the Foreign Affairs Committee's study group on satellite policy could do little more than deplore the lack of contingency planning: "While it was not expected of the United States to send troops or military weapons into Hungary for fear of provoking a third world war, the fact remains that we were without any means or devices at our disposal to meet the crisis." The study group recommended that the United States be better prepared for activating the United Nations in such contingencies and that the UN Charter be revised to ensure the enforcement of resolutions even against the Soviet Union; on a more realistic plane, it urged that the United Nations withhold recognition from the Kádár regime, that Hungary and the Soviet Union be subjected to economic sanctions, and that permanent mobile observer teams be created within the UN framework. Noting that seemingly innocuous speeches and broadcasts may have "an entirely different connotation to an audience under the stress of an intense struggle for freedom," the group further recommended a "reassessment of our present system of intelligence" and a reform of the VOA and of RFE which would result in the presentation of "our way of life on a strictly factual basis."[1] In its own report on foreign policy, the Foreign Affairs Committee favored the encouragement of nationalism in the satellites.[2] Such relatively modest recommendations were echoed by a number of prominent legislators. Observing that a single policy toward East-Central Europe was no longer adequate, Senator Mansfield advised the administration to implement a more differentiated policy of commercial, diplomatic, and cultural contacts with the several satellites; another Senator, after a visit to Hungary in the course of which he met Kádár and Cardinal Mindszenty, similarly concluded that the primary objective of the United States ought to be to increase contacts and exchanges with the Soviet bloc.[3] The prevailing attitudes in Congress, while inflexibly anticommunist, no longer imposed impossible demands for liberation on the administration.

In the aftermath of the revolution, President Eisenhower had charged the National Security Council with the tasks of analyzing that event and recommending guidelines for similar future contingencies. The resulting report testified to the impotence of the superpowers to affect each other's areas of vital interest; it concluded that, with respect to Hungary, the United States had possessed no alternative course of action, would be equally helpless if faced with another satellite revolt, and therefore should orient its policies toward preventing the recurrence of such a crisis.[4] The outcome of this policy review was an accelerated shift in emphasis from the hard-sell liberation line to more subdued support for evolutionary change. This new approach, unofficially designated "gradualism," was adopted without great difficulty even by Dulles, for, while in earlier days the secretary of state may have exhibited a predilection for messianic rhetoric, in guiding America's fortunes he never allowed the adventurism implicit in that rhetoric to obscure the constraints of the balance of power. Once the Hungarian affair had driven home the folly of liberation by political warfare, Dulles trimmed his language to the realities of the East-West stalemate in Europe. At a meeting of congressional leaders in the White House on New Year's Day, 1957, he outlined the essentials of the gradualist approach; it comprised a disavowal of American military designs in East-Central Europe, assistance to Hungarian refugees, economic aid for "semi-independent" Poland, sustained political pressure in the United Nations, and acceptance of national communism "as means to end."[5] Notably absent from the new policy was the prerevolution stress on psychological warfare. In his first major public address after the election, delivered on April 22, the secretary of state underscored that "we do not ourselves incite violent revolt. Rather we encourage an evolution to freedom."[6] The time scale of gradualism would necessarily be broader than that of liberation; as Dulles observed later that year, "American policy is conducted on the assumption . . . that free governments in the long run are going to prevail and despotic governments in the long run are going to go under."[7] Moscow, however, predictably seized upon the gradualist approach as evidence that the United States had lost interest in the satellites, and Washington was compelled to issue denials carefully phrased so as not to rekindle false hopes. Thus, on July 1, 1959, in the course of "Freedom Day" celebrations at the base of the Statue of Liberty, Assistant Secretary for Public Affairs Andrew H. Berding categorically denied Khrushchev's allegation that in the last period of his life Dulles had weakened in his opposition to the East European *status quo* and to recognition of the two Germanies; Berding reiterated America's refusal to accept the "permanent subjugation of the once-free captive peoples of Eastern Europe."[8] By now such phrases aroused scarcely any attention, either at home or abroad. While appreciably altered in tone since the violent propaganda warfare of the early liberation years, American policy as publicly expressed still reflected the basic and optimistic expectation which had been inherent in containment and liberation—that self-determination would come to the satellites in the course of time with little if any American involvement.

If war was more than ever ruled out as a means of altering the *status quo* in Europe, the future of negotiations also looked dim in the postrevolution period. Nevertheless, the very realization that change could not occur by other means made 1957 and 1958 vintage years in the history of disengagement proposals. On the communist side, the overtures were of course official and represented the latest phase in the Kremlin's campaign for a general agreement on European security that would sanctify the *status quo* and weaken the Western alliance. After meeting Khrushchev in February 1957, Chester Bowles, a prominent Democrat, reported that the Soviet leader considered the situation in Central Europe unnatural and favored a phased mutual withdrawal, by NATO forces from West Germany, France, and the Benelux, and by Soviet troops from East Germany and the satellites.[9] Then, in October of that year, Polish Foreign Minister Adam Rapacki proposed in an address before the UN General Assembly that a nuclear-free zone be created in Central Europe, covering the two Germanies as well as Poland and Czechoslovakia.[10] In the West the cause of disengagement was espoused by various unofficial advocates. George Kennan and Walter Lippmann advised the Eisenhower administration to consider mutual withdrawal as an acceptable price for German reunification and self-determination in the satellites; the ineffable Senator Knowland made the unquestionably original suggestion that Norway be neutralized in exchange for free elections in Hungary.[11] Among other Europeans, British Labour leader Hugh Gaitskell took up the theme of the Rapacki Plan and proposed that it be extended to include the evacuation of conventional forces from Eastern Europe and West Germany, the reunification of Germany through free elections, and a security pact guaranteeing the frontiers of the states concerned, but he himself observed that "the assumption underlying the plan is that the Soviet Union has decided it is worth while to achieve a permanent settlement and that so long as her own security is not impaired she is prepared to loosen the bonds on her satellites," acknowledged that the Russians had given no indication of this, and concluded that a more modest approach stressing a reduction of forces and partial disarmament might be more realistic.[12]

Disengagement received short shrift in official Washington, the administration being convinced that for strategic, political, and economic reasons the Soviet Union would not voluntarily effect a military withdrawal from the satellites. This was the consensus of a number of experts, quoted in a staff study of the Foreign Relations Committee, who argued that the Russians would never accept the disappearance of communism from East-Central Europe in exchange for some disarmament agreement.[13] On the other hand, partial disengagement without any alteration in the political status of the satellites and without German reunification would, in Washington's view, disproportionately weaken the defenses of Western Europe by excluding American troops and missile bases from

West Germany. Indeed, Germany remained the insoluble problem that overshadowed the broader question of the satellites. The hypothetical negotiating position of the West was made clear in the Berlin Declaration, signed on July 29, 1957, by the United States, Britain, France, and West Germany; it proposed the free reunification of the two Germanies and promised a "significant and far-reaching" security arrangement for the Soviet Union and the satellites in case a reunited Germany wished to join NATO.[14] Undoubtedly the signatories fully anticipated Moscow's rejection of this proposal, but the declaration was more noteworthy in another respect, for its references to the satellites carried the scarcely veiled implication of Western recognition of an inviolable Soviet sphere of influence in East-Central Europe.

Soviet attitudes in this period also contributed to the impression that the division of Europe was permanent and that disengagement—at least as understood by its Western proponents—was a mere chimera. In May 1957, shortly before Hungary and the Soviet Union concluded an agreement on the "temporary stationing" of Soviet troops on the former's territory, Khrushchev declared that, "if we are confronted with conditions such as Dulles likes to put forward such as the liberation of East European countries from 'slavery', it might take 200 years before we ever come together. For on these matters we are inflexible."[15] The Soviet leader's victory over the so-called antiparty group in June strengthened his position internally, and the successful testing of a long-range ballistic missile later that summer and the Sputnik flight in October served notice on the world that the Soviet Union was at least America's equal in military technology. Despite the embarrassment of the Hungarian affair, Khrushchev persisted in the strategy first developed two years earlier at the time of Geneva. Its basic premises were simple. Since mutual deterrence precluded violent change in the European *status quo*, it was in the Kremlin's interest to reduce the American presence on the Continent and to weaken the bonds of the Western alliance in order to enhance not only Soviet security but also Soviet influence in Western Europe. Moreover, détente in Europe would allow the Russians to concentrate their resources on modernization at home and on their proselytizing mission in the Third World.

Accordingly, the Kremlin approached the Western powers in December with a proposal for disengagement and disarmament which ignored the question of German reunification and specifically ruled out the possibility of change in the status of East-Central Europe, then followed this up early in 1958 with the suggestion of a summit meeting, possibly in Washington.[16] This new diplomatic offensive placed the administration in something of a dilemma, for an outright rejection of the overtures would only lend credence to Soviet charges of American warmongering, and a summit conference that avoided the questions of Germany and the satellites also would tend to serve Soviet interests. Official Washington was as reluctant as ever to publicly renounce its commitment to liberation and thereby antagonize not only the East Europeans but also the dogmatically anti-communist American public, and, accordingly, in his reply to Bulganin's proposal, President Eisenhower requested that the matter of the satellites be placed on the summit agenda.[17] Retorted Khrushchev in an address at Minsk on January 22: "If the status quo is not recognized, if the socialist states are ignored, their sovereign rights violated, and their domestic affairs interfered in, then it is, of course, absolutely impossible to come to terms."[18] As for German reunification, the Russians now declared that it was a matter for the two German governments to consider and therefore was not fit for discussion at the summit.[19] Secretary of State Dulles thereupon publicly denounced the "fiction that the cold war has come to an end" and insisted that preparatory consultations and some indication of progress on these key issues precede a meeting of heads of state.[20] Memories of Hungary were still too vivid to allow a revival of the spirit of Geneva.

As the prospects for a summit receded, Moscow decided to concentrate on one of its objectives, Western recognition of the German Democratic Republic, more forcefully. On November 10, 1958, in an address to the Soviet-Polish Friendship Society, Khrushchev threatened to hand over responsibility for Berlin to the Ulbricht government, and the ensuing official note gave the West six months to turn Berlin into an independent and demilitarized city.[21] In the event, the West's refusal to comply (reinforced by Chancellor Adenauer's adamant opposition to any legitimization of the GDR) called Khrushchev's bluff, but the continuing embarrassment to Ulbricht and Moscow of the escape valve of a free and prosperous West Berlin ensured that the crisis had merely been postponed. Meanwhile, the Dulles era was coming to an end. The former secretary of state had only a few days to live when on May 20, 1959, Vice-President Nixon visited him in Walter Reed Army Hospital to discuss Nixon's upcoming trip to Moscow for the opening of an American exhibition in Sokolniki Park. Dulles' characteristic skepticism showed up unaltered in his assessment of Khrushchev: "He says he is for peaceful coexistence. What he means, as he has shown in Hungary, is that while a revolution against a non-Communist government is proper and should be supported, a revolution against a Communist government is invariably wrong and must be suppressed. Thus, the peaceful coexistence which he advocates represents peace for the Communist world and constant strife for the non-Communist world."[22] Delayed by the Hungarian revolution and momentarily jeopardized by the Berlin crisis, the exhibition and Nixon's visit were nevertheless direct outcomes of the spirit of Geneva and the adminis-tration's reluctant flirtation with the concept of peaceful coexistence. This recognition of the necessity to normalize East-West relations was rather less evident in Congress, however, where the Democrats had sub-stantially increased their majority in 1958. In the sphere of domestic policy the new Congress proved to be more liberal than the administra-tion, but in foreign affairs it demonstrated an inflexibility that frequently embarrassed the executive branch.

On July 6, 1959, while Vice-President Nixon was preparing for his trip to Moscow, Congress unanimously endorsed a joint resolution which had been introduced in the Senate by Senator Paul Douglas and in the House by Congressman John McCormack. The Captive Nations Resolution charged that "the enslavement of a substantial part of the world's popula-tion by Communist imperialism makes a mockery of the idea of peaceful coexistence between nations" and called on the president to proclaim the third week in July "Captive Nations Week," during which free people were to pray for the liberation of the "enslaved peoples." While some Democrats may have had partisan motives, the unanimity in Congress reflected the widespread popular appeal of the sentiments expressed in the resolution, and on July 17 President Eisenhower complied by means of his Captive Nations Week Proclamation, which was to be repeated annually "until such time as freedom and independence shall have been achieved for all the captive nations of the world."[23] The resolution was extensively reported in the press, and emotional ceremonies and church services en-sued in numerous American localities. Vice-President Nixon subsequently described it as "simply the expression of a well-known opinion in the United States, and not a call to action," but the Soviets' reaction was predictably furious. Returning from a visit to Poland minutes before Nixon's arrival on July 23, Khrushchev proceeded to a rally in the Mos-cow sports arena to deliver a blistering attack on the American resolution. At a meeting in the Kremlin the following day, Khrushchev asked rhetori-cally, "Any action by an authoritative body like Congress must have a purpose, and I wonder what the purpose of this particular action can be?" He added that the changes implied by the resolution could only lead to war. Nixon recalls that when he "pointed out that the resolution did not call for our intervention, or even for our support of a revolution in the satellite nations, but only expressed moral support and asked for prayers for those who want freedom in those nations," an unimpressed Khrush-chev shouted, "This resolution stinks."[24] The episode reflected not only the Russians' apparent ignorance of the subtleties of the division of power in the American political system but also the asymmetry in the attitudes toward the Soviet bloc of the Administration and Congress, an asymmetry which would bedevil the attempts of Eisenhower's successors as well to acknowledge the *fait accompli* of Soviet hegemony in East-Central Europe. On his way home from Moscow the vice-president stopped over in Warsaw, where he was met by a huge crowd (word of his arrival having been spread by Radio Free Europe) whose enthusiasm stood in sharp contrast to the earlier, staged reception given Khrushchev. The popularity of America among the Poles evidently had not suffered permanent damage as a result of the Hungarian affair, and this despite the fact that Khrushchev had offered a unilateral guarantee of the Oder-Neisse frontier, which the United States consistently refused to endorse until a final peace treaty with Germany had been signed.[25]

Despite his anger at the Captive Nations Resolution, Khrushchev persisted in his campaign on the theme of peaceful coexistence, and once the Berlin crisis had faded away the Eisenhower administration proved increasingly responsive to the Kremlin's overtures. After protracted negotiations between foreign ministers it was announced on September 7 that agreement had been reached on the creation of a ten-nation committee to discuss the problems of disarmament in Geneva. One week later Khrushchev arrived for his famous shoe-banging appearance at the United Nations and subsequently conferred with Eisenhower at the latter's Camp David retreat. The visit had been viewed with acute apprehension in émigré circles, and the Hungarian Committee sent a letter to the president protesting that "the sojourn in the United States of the Soviet leader most responsible for the massacre of the Hungarian people again will subject this people's morale to a very severe test."[26] Although the president went through the motions of publicly reasserting America's hopes for the eventual liberation of the captive peoples, his meeting with Khrushchev resulted in a display of cordiality that the press promptly and unimaginatively labeled the spirit of Camp David.[27] The attempt to reinforce this spirit at a summit conference in Paris the following May collapsed, thanks to Eisenhower's clumsy handling of the U-2 incident, but it is unlikely that any substantive agreement would have emerged even if the conference had been allowed to proceed, for, without major concessions by one side or the other, the rhetoric of peaceful coexistence could not resolve the problem of Berlin. Meanwhile, the popularity of disarmament was waning rapidly in the wake of allegations that a "missile gap" had developed in favor of the Soviet Union.

It was within this broader policy context that the Eisenhower administration tried to implement its gradualist approach to East-Central Europe, although it could not eliminate the logical inconsistency between peaceful coexistence and an implicitly revisionist policy. The problem of reconciling the two perspectives was cogently expressed by Assistant Secretary of

State Andrew Berding in a public address shortly after Khrushchev's visit:

> There is reason to conclude that the Soviet Government as well as the Soviet people are now aware that they have a practical, vested interest in preservation of the peace. . . .
>
> Accepting peaceful coexistence means accepting the *status quo* whereby the Soviet Union dominates a Communist bloc of nations. We have given the Soviet Union solemn assurances that we have no desire to turn these nations against Moscow, that we do not seek military alliances with them, that we do not wish to impose the American way of life upon them, that we do not wish a return to their prewar processes of government. But we do desire for their peoples true freedom, genuine national independence, and ability to establish whatever form of government and economic and social institutions they wish. We cannot accept a *status quo* which makes this impossible.[28]

While the new policy subsumed a continuing interest in liberation, in its differentiated treatment of the individual satellites it represented a significant departure from the crusading spirit of the early Eisenhower years.

Washington's relations with the new "Revolutionary Worker-Peasant Government" of János Kádár were reminiscent of the darkest days of the cold war. The American minister-designate, Edward Wailes, lingered on in Budapest after the collapse of the uprising but was not permitted by the State Department to present his credentials, "because we thought the present Government did not represent the people."[29] For some months he remained incommunicado in an unofficial limbo, and, when the Hungarians finally insisted that he be accredited or leave the country, he was recalled to Washington. In the face of this snub, the Kádár regime demanded a reduction in the American legation's personnel and expelled two military attachés; in turn, the United States ousted a Hungarian air attaché and cut the size of its Budapest mission even further than had been requested. Meanwhile, various suggestions originated within and without the U.S. Congress—for withdrawal of recognition from all members of the Soviet bloc, for expulsion of the Soviet Union from the United Nations, for some "bold American diplomatic initiative" which would neutralize Hungary under international guarantees—but the administration, having long ago decided that the satellite problem was no *casus belli*, focused its disapproval on the Kádár regime and carried on its rather futile propaganda campaign at the United Nations while at the same time collaborating in the international effort to resettle some 200,000 Hungarian refugees.[30]

When, in June 1958, news reached the West of the execution of Nagy, Maléter, and two of their associates, the State Department denounced this as a shocking act of cruelty and endorsed the report of the UN General Assembly's special committee on the matter.[31] Hungary complained of Washington's unsympathetic attitude and proposed a normalization of relations, but the United States insisted that this depended upon Hungary's compliance with the Charter and the Paris peace treaty. On December 12 the General Assembly once again adopted a resolution condemning the actions of the Soviet and Hungarian governments and appointed Sir Leslie Munro of New Zealand as the United Nations' special representative for the Hungarian problem.[32] On Washington's insistence the "Question of Hungary" was inscribed on the agenda of the Fourteenth General Assembly, and on November 23, 1959, Ambassador Lodge bitterly attacked his Soviet counterpart, asking: "why don't you do something to show that you really believe in the true spirit of Camp David? Why don't you take down the barbed wire and the observation towers which now divide the poor Hungarians from Austria and the free world and which have turned Hungary into a vast human cage?"[33] When Sir Leslie Munro reported that he had not been admitted to Hungary and that, according to his investigations, political conditions in that country had not improved, the General Assembly performed the now annual ritual of censuring the regimes in question.[34] At the International Labor Conference in Geneva in June 1959, the U.S. delegate, Horace E. Henderson, argued that the Hungarian candidates represented a government which had been imposed by force by a foreign power and which defied the UN Charter. Protesting that the United States exerted "immense economic and political strength" to muster support against the seating of the Hungarian delegates and "stubbornly persists in attempting to use the Hungarian people for its cold war aims," the Budapest regime retaliated by imposing travel restrictions on American diplomats. The State Department then denied charges that the latter had engaged in spying and imposed similar restrictions on Hungarian diplomats.[35] The mutual prohibitions were lifted in April 1960, and, as a minor concession on the part of the West, Hungary was named to the twenty-four-member UN Committee on the Peaceful Uses of Outer Space in December 1959, but the fruitless cold war between Washington and Budapest continued virtually unabated. While there could have been little expectation on the American side that official hostility would lead the Kádár regime to moderate its policies, the lingering public horror at the Soviet invasion and the deportations and widespread repression that had followed the revolution left the administration little alternative.

If Hungary was viewed as a throwback to the Stalinist dark ages, Poland represented the principal hope of the gradualist strategy, which aimed to encourage the particularistic leanings of certain East European regimes. In the elections of January 1957 Gomulka had been endorsed even by the

Roman Catholic church, and the following month a Polish delegation arrived in Washington with a request for credits in the amount of $300 million. The administration moved with extreme caution on this politically sensitive issue (the minority leader in the Senate, William Knowland, was one prominent opponent of aid to the communists), and after protracted negotiations agreed in June to guarantee a $30 million Export-Import Bank loan and to sell $18.9 million worth of cotton, fats, and oils for Polish currency; two months later, after Congress extended the Agricultural Trade Development and Assistance Act, a further agreement was signed for the sale of $46.1 million worth of surplus cotton and wheat, again payable in zlotys.[36] Concurrently, a cultural agreement was signed which would bring some 300 Poles to the United States between 1957 and 1959 under the sponsorship of the Ford and Rockefeller foundations. In February 1958 the United States undertook to provide an additional $98 million in aid, but there already were signs that the evolutionary approach would yield few positive results.

From the point of view of the Polish regime, the rejection of the Rapacki Plan, the impending installation of nuclear weapons on West German territory, and the U.S. refusal to formally recognize the Oder-Neisse frontier all served to reinforce the threat of German revisionism and the consequent need for Soviet protection. Furthermore, the Soviet Union viewed Titoism with renewed alarm in the wake of the Hungarian uprising and sought to consolidate East-Central Europe politically and economically by reviving the Council for Mutual Economic Assistance (COMECON) and turning it into a tangible integrative institution. A Polish-Soviet trade protocol announced on April 11 indicated an expansion in commercial relations and in the economic integration of the communist economies. At a news conference on June 18 President Eisenhower observed with some dismay that, despite American aid and trade concessions, there was no evidence of increased independence on the part of Poland or Yugoslavia.[37] In November, when Gomulka traveled to Moscow and joined Khrushchev in violent attacks on the West, the State Department hinted that the aid program might be revised. The 1959 credits totaled only $50 million, but an economic crisis that developed in Poland in October led to new negotiations and an emergency credit for $11.8 million worth of surplus feed grains.[38] In 1960 the United States agreed to sell to Poland a further $60 million worth of agricultural surpluses on advantageous terms; as a *quid pro quo* the Poles had to undertake to pay compensation in the amount of $40 million over twenty years for American property confiscated at the end of the war.[39]

The administration was manifestly dissatisfied at the regressive policies of the Gomulka regime, which was in the process of tightening economic controls and cracking down on the restive intelligentsia. When Gomulka visited the United Nations in September he was the only communist leader received by Secretary of State Herter, but Eisenhower pointedly refused to see him; the only substantial concession Gomulka could extract was the restoration of Poland's most-favored-nation status.[40] The failure of the evolutionary strategy with respect to Poland was acknowledged with profound disappointment in Washington. It had never been expected that economic aid would literally liberate Poland from the Kremlin's grasp, but the administration had nevertheless anticipated a greater display of friendship and domestic permissiveness on the part of Gomulka. Lying between the Soviet Union and its East German satrapy and threatened (at least in the perception and propaganda of its leaders) by West German revanchism, Poland was geopolitically an unlikely candidate for gradual liberation, however, and these factors would have limited Gomulka's options even if he had not been a convinced and fundamentally inflexible communist. In its application to Poland, the gradualist policy might even have been counterproductive by reinforcing the Kremlin's campaign for economic integration, but there is no real evidence that the two developments were more than coincidental. On the other hand, by carrying on negotiations and by providing material assistance, the administration demonstrated in tangible fashion its concern for the welfare of the East Europeans and certainly enhanced America's popularity among the Polish masses.

With respect to Yugoslavia, Washington had been pursuing an evolutionary policy since 1949, but, once Tito became convinced that Stalin's heirs would not directly threaten his independence, he adopted a nonaligned posture that many in America interpreted as a regressive step. As Robert Murphy had argued in October 1956, aid to Yugoslavia did not signify endorsement of its form of government but was aimed rather at propping up its independence from Moscow.[41] Nevertheless, congressional opposition and Tito's new feeling of security conspired to reduce the significance of American assistance. In July 1956 the Mutual Security Act was amended to include a provision that aid to Yugoslavia be halted unless the president could assure Congress that Yugoslavia was "not participating in any policy or program for the communist conquest of the world" and that the national security of the United States required its continuance. Eisenhower subsequently reported in the affirmative and requested that the conduct of policy be left to the president's discretion.[42] Meanwhile, the Mutual Security Appropriation Act for 1957 had stipulated that no new military matériel be delivered to the Yugoslavs. Military aid was restored the following May after an on-the-spot investigation by an emissary of the State Department, but a resentful Tito abrogated the agreement as of December

1957.[43] By criticizing NATO and by allowing the Balkan Pact to die a quiet death, the Yugoslav leader only reinforced Congress's perception that his nonalignment was anti-American, and outright foreign aid grants were also curtailed at the end of 1957. American aid continued in the sale of agricultural surpluses for Yugoslav currency, in loans from the Development Loan Fund for specific projects, and in a program of technical assistance. In April 1958 Tito assured the Seventh Congress of the League of Communists that he had "not made any concessions to the United States, political or otherwise, nor did anyone at that time ask for any such conditions."[44] It is somewhat paradoxical that the U.S. Congress began to demand assurances of his friendship at the very time when he ceased to fear Soviet hostility.

The Eisenhower administration's gradualist approach achieved only marginal improvements in relations with the other satellites. Agreement was reached with Bulgaria in March 1959 to resume diplomatic relations and with Rumania the following year to initiate cultural exchanges and settle American claims.[45] With the strategic embargo still in force, the volume of U.S. trade with the communist bloc showed only a slight increase except in the case of Poland. As for American propaganda, the Hungarian experience brought about a certain moderation of tone which was in keeping with the readjustment of official policies. Shortly after the revolution the Hungarian section at Radio Free Europe was purged of most of its former staff, an act prompted not so much by their incompetence as by the need to symbolically mark the beginning of a new era. In sum, the significance of gradualism lay less in its questionable influence on developments in the satellites than in its rejection of the former optimistic expectations of early liberation. The task of elaborating on this evolutionary theme and reconciling it with the demands of domestic politics devolved upon Eisenhower's successors.

PEACEFUL ENGAGEMENT AND THE BERLIN WALL

If the myth of liberation in its various guises played a negligible role in the election campaign that pitted Vice-President Nixon against John F. Kennedy, it did so because both candidates shared the view that the freedom of East-Central Europe was a desirable but distant goal that was unlikely to be brought nearer by crusading rhetoric, and also because neither of them could offer a genuine alternative to the policies of the later Eisenhower years. Although President Eisenhower remained largely aloof from the campaign, he proclaimed Captive Nations Week once again, and in an address to the Polish-American Congress on September 30 expressed his continuing hope for liberation while admitting that the expectations voiced in 1952 remained unfulfilled; two days later, speaking before the Polish National Alliance in Chicago, Undersecretary of State C. Douglas Dillon declared that the United States accepted the East European *status quo* only as "a temporary nightmare before the inevitable dawn of freedom" and boasted of the ongoing aid program to Poland.[46] Meanwhile, both Kennedy and Nixon disclaimed any intention of arousing revolutionary movements in the satellites. The former advocated peaceful economic measures to bring about closer relations with the East Europeans and particularly with Poland, and, as the campaign drew to a close, the latter promised that if elected he would visit each satellite to remind the world that they would ultimately be delivered from their bondage.[47] Clearly, however, liberation was no burning issue in the 1960 election and did not contribute in any perceptible degree to Kennedy's narrow victory.

While still a senator, Kennedy had addressed his colleagues on August 21, 1957, on the subject of the captive nations. On that occasion he had attacked the incumbent administration for its attitude "of merely waiting and hoping—that caused us to be caught wholly unprepared for the events in Poland and Hungary" and had deplored its inadequate response to the Polish request for economic assistance; he had proposed, *inter alia*, that the president be given more discretion in granting aid to deserving satellites, that commercial and cultural relations be expanded, and that a permanent UN observation commission be set up "ready to fly at a moment's notice to any spot where an advance toward freedom is menaced by Soviet intervention."[48] Speaking at a Pulaski Day dinner two years later, Senator Kennedy urged that the United States "finally begin to recognize that there are varying shades and degrees within the Communist world."[49] This flexible and evolutionary strategy surfaced once again in Kennedy's first State of the Union message, in which he referred to historic ties of friendship with the East Europeans, repeated the by now ritualistic hope for their eventual freedom, and announced that he would ask Congress to give him special authority to develop economic relations with Poland and the other satellites.[50] In the context of his "Grand Design," however, Kennedy's East European policy was of only marginal significance. Anticipating a more pluralistic international system and scornful of Dulles' simplistic and Manichean world view, the new president and his advisers brought into office what they considered to be a radically revised foreign policy. This Grand Design laid first stress on the maintenance of peace by improving America's military preparedness, which together with the much-publicized but fictitious missile gap had been a key issue in the campaign; other priorities were the consensual reinforcement of the Western alliance and aid for economic development in the Third World. Détente would evolve from the state of mutual nuclear deterrence; as the *New York Times'* Max Frankel wrote three years later, "though no one ever quite said so, it was to be the product of an unmentionable division of the world into clear spheres of influence and an unadvertised cooperation in controlling the conflicts that were bound to arise in the vast no-man's land between those spheres."[51] The Kennedy administration tacitly recognized a Soviet sphere of influence in East-Central Europe, but in doing so it was only following the lead of its predecessor; its prime concern in regard to that part of the world became to encourage the growth of pluralistic tendencies.

As in the case of liberation the most comprehensive proposal for a new policy toward East-Central Europe came from outside the administration. In an article entitled "Peaceful Engagement in Eastern Europe," Professors Zbigniew Brzezinski and William E. Griffith outlined a dual policy which focused on both the regimes and the peoples and which was predicated on the East Europeans' awareness that change could come only through internal evolution.[52] Such a policy, they wrote, should

(1) aim at stimulating further diversity in the Communist bloc; (2) thus increasing the likelihood that the East European states can achieve a greater measure of political independence from Soviet domination; (3) thereby ultimately leading to the creation of a neutral belt of states which, like the Finnish, would enjoy genuine popular freedom of choice in internal policy while not being hostile to the Soviet Union and not belonging to Western military alliances. Finally, American policy must dissociate itself from any notion that it favors a restoration in Eastern Europe of an economic system patterned on that of the West.

In furthering this peaceful transition, the United States should foster closer economic and cultural relations; the first would do no harm and might even induce the Soviet Union to liberalize the terms of its trade with the satellites, while the second could only attenuate the isolation of the satellites, particularly if exchanges were extended to humanists and social scientists. The authors went on to suggest that West Germany reconsider its Hallstein Doctrine (which ruled out relations with states that recognized the Ulbricht regime) vis-à-vis the satellites, that the West Europeans develop economic links with the East, that Washington and Bonn take a more positive stand on the irrevocability of the Oder-Neisse frontier, and that the question of Hungary be kept on the UN agenda "as long as the Soviet Union makes capital out of posing as an anti-colonial power." For reasons of morality and East European morale, the United States should continue to insist on the principle of self-determination, but "a general attitude of disapproval does not preclude our attempting to improve our political, economic and cultural relations with the Eastern European states, provided these regimes refrain from hostile acts toward us." There is no doubt that the theory of peaceful engagement expounded by Brzezinski and Griffith was compatible with both Kennedy's emphasis on a world of diversity and the aspirations of the East European masses, and with minor alterations it came to form the basis of Kennedy's, as well as Johnson's, policies toward that area. Concurrently, pluralistic tendencies did materialize in East-Central Europe, but domestic constraints were to bedevil the policy's implementation, while the actions of the Soviet Union would raise serious doubts as to its effectiveness in promoting genuine self-determination.

The new president's most immediate concern in the realm of foreign relations was to take the measure of Khrushchev and of the prospects for détente, particularly in the perennial problem area of Berlin. For their part, the Russians appeared eager to test the posture of conciliatory flexibility that Kennedy had adopted in the election campaign. At the end of 1960 Foreign Minister Gromyko voiced the hope that "the relations between our countries would again follow the line along which they were developing in Franklin Roosevelt's time."[53] The façade of restrained good will tactically adopted by both leaders did not survive their encounter in Vienna in June 1961. Khrushchev presented Kennedy with an *aide-mémoire* calling for a peace conference to "formally recognize the situation which has developed in Europe after the war"—i.e., to recognize the two Germanies and to turn West Berlin into a demilitarized free city. In the absence of such a conference, threatened Khrushchev, he would unilaterally sign a peace treaty with the East Germans and thereby abrogate the West's rights in Berlin, and he intimated that he would implement this decision by force if necessary.[54] The American position proved to be equally inflexible. In a report commissioned by Kennedy earlier that year, former Secretary of State Dean Acheson had predicted that a crisis over Berlin was likely to materialize and had recommended the full use of American power to ensure the freedom of the West Berliners, to maintain the Western garrisons, and to guarantee unimpeded access to the city.[55] Kennedy was acutely conscious of the weaknesses of the prevailing Western strategy, which allowed no halfway measures between resistance by the hopelessly outnumbered garrison and nuclear retaliation, and he proceeded in the weeks following his confrontation with Khrushchev to improve the credibility of America's determination to stand fast in Berlin by ordering a build-up of U.S. ground and air forces in Europe and other emergency measures involving the reserves and the Strategic Air Command; the crisis only strengthened his determination to increase defense expenditures in order to improve the military's capacity for flexible response. In a somber television address on July 25, the president declared that West Berlin had become "the great testing place of Western courage and will" and that the communists would not be allowed to drive the West out of that city "either gradually or by force." "We recognize the Soviet Union's historical concern about their security in Central and Eastern Europe, after a series of ravaging invasions," continued Kennedy, "and we believe arrangements can be worked out which will help to meet these concerns, and make it possible for both security and freedom to exist in this troubled area." The essence of his message, however, was that the United States would not suffer an unfavorable revision of the Central European *status quo*.[56]

Meanwhile, the steadily mounting pressures on Berlin had only increased the flow of East German refugees, who feared that their last escape route might be closed, and by the summer of 1961 their total number had reached some 3.5 million. The resultant drain on the East German economy placed the Ulbricht regime in an untenable position. At the end of July it imposed new travel restrictions, and the U.S. embassy in Bonn reported the possibility of a popular uprising.[57] But another Budapest was just what Kennedy and his allies wanted to avoid; the president recognized that Ulbricht's dilemma would lead to the sanctioning of some preventive measure by Khrushchev, who was already infuriated by the July 25 address, and he observed to an adviser, "I can get the alliance to move if he tries to do anything about West Berlin but not if he just does something about East Berlin."[58] On August 13 it became clear what the communists would do as an astonished world watched the first embryonic stages in the construction of the Berlin Wall. As in 1953, the Western powers had no plans for such a contingency, being concerned exclusively with the security of West Berlin proper. Secretary of State Dean Rusk protested that a unilateral decision to sever communications between the two parts of Berlin violated the 1949 four-power agreement, but the United States and its allies tacitly accepted the *de facto* legitimacy of the East German action, and Rusk himself commented reassuringly that the "measures taken thus far are aimed at residents of East Berlin and East Germany and not at the allied position in West Berlin or access thereto."[59] The administration's chief concern was to minimize the chances of direct confrontation which in turn might incite the desperate East Germans to revolt. A biographer of Kennedy records that "not one responsible official—in this country, in West Berlin, West Germany or Western Europe—suggested that Allied forces should march into East German territory and tear the Wall down," and, indeed, a token foray by the Berlin garrison probably would not have deterred the communists; as Kennedy later told his critics, the use of force ran the risk of "a very violent reaction which might well have taken us down a rocky road."[60] Sitting in continuous session, the president's "Berlin Task Force" recommended only an acceleration of the American military build-up and took all of four days to draft an official protest.[61] When West Berlin's mayor Willy Brandt, alarmed by the possible psychological effect of this inaction, wrote to the president on August 16 asking for at least some symbolic retaliation, Kennedy dispatched Vice-President Johnson and General Lucius Clay (the latter being a legendary figure to West Berliners because of his role in beating the blockade) with his pledge that a free West Berlin would be maintained at all costs. At the same time, a 1,500-man battle group was sent down the East German autobahn to reinforce the Allied garrison. Chancellor Adenauer warned Kennedy that Western compromises over Berlin might stimulate neutralist tendencies in his country, but even he would caution the East German masses against resorting to force and was concerned more about the morale of the West Berliners and his own prospects in the upcoming election than about the Wall itself.[62]

In retrospect, East Germany's hemorrhage at Berlin had dictated the creation of some physical barrier, and the Wall, however infamous, served as a stabilizing factor that was not entirely unwelcome in the West. The dominant feeling in the Kennedy administration was that the border closure did not endanger West Berlin's survival and, by ending the refugee problem, might even facilitate future negotiations with the Soviet Union over the status of West Berlin and the recognition of East Germany (although such negotiations were opposed by Acheson and by the Joint Chiefs of Staff).[63] Persisting in his quest for an easing of tensions, President Kennedy told the UN General Assembly on September 26 that the United States was not committed to any rigid formulas regarding Berlin, and he subsequently initiated preliminary consultations with both the Russians and his allies. A possible settlement, outlined in an American note to Britain, France, and West Germany on April 12, 1962, entailed the normalization of relations between the two Germanies and an agreement between NATO and the Warsaw Pact to respect existing borders and demarcation lines in Europe.[64] This trial balloon (leaked to the press by Bonn) reflected the Kennedy administration's tentative willingness to stabilize the European *status quo* at the price of recognizing East Germany and giving up any hope of reunification. Negative reactions, particularly on the part of Adenauer, and East-West crises in other spheres led to the shelving of these proposals, while Soviet and East German attempts to erode the Western presence in Berlin would recur with monotonous regularity; but, if the German problem remained unresolved, the early actions of the Kennedy administration demonstrated unambiguously that the United States no longer challenged the legitimacy of the Soviet sphere of influence in East-Central Europe.

Although the Berlin Wall did not deter the administration from continuing its pursuit of an easing of tensions, its construction, added to evidence of communist pressures in Cuba, South Vietnam, and Laos, drove the American public and an otherwise relatively liberal Congress into an increasingly inflexible anticommunist posture. Thus, if the early Eisenhower years had been notable for an asymmetry between declaratory and operational policies regarding East-Central Europe, the Kennedy era was marked by a deepening cleavage between the administration and much of the body politic in that same policy area. Illustrative of the renewed congressional concern were the hearings on the captive nations conducted by the Foreign Affairs Committee's Subcommittee on Europe between March and September 1962. Among those testifying was Assistant Secretary of State for European Affairs William R. Tyler, who argued on behalf of the administration that Soviet policy toward the satellites had become more flexible and tolerant of diversity (alluding to Gomulka's defense of private farming and Kádár's new slogan that "he who is not against us is with us"), that pursuit of the Hungarian question at the United Nations retarded the development of "any effective program of contact with or through the Government," and that the United States could best respond to these changes by maintaining and developing more normal and active relations with the satellites and by increasing trade.[65] In its final report the subcommittee voiced lukewarm support for the broader aspects of the administration's policy, but urged the president to take "prompt, continuous, and energetic steps" to make it clear that the United States did not recognize the *status quo*, to persist with the Hungarian question at the United Nations, to expand VOA coverage of émigré activities, and to develop exchanges and contacts.[66]

It was over the issues of trade and aid that the administration ran into the most determined resistance in Congress. After a special study mission to Poland in 1961, one congressman had reported that although there was some popular appreciation of American efforts, the official Polish image of the United States was still distorted and the United States was given little credit for its aid.[67] Moreover, many legislators felt that both Poland and Yugoslavia had in recent years been moving closer to the Soviet Union, particularly in their foreign policies—as evidenced by Gomulka's anti-American stand on Germany and Cuba and by Tito's endorsement of most aspects of Soviet foreign policy at the Belgrade Conference of allegedly nonaligned nations in September 1961—and they questioned the benefits of existing aid and trade programs toward those two countries.[68] The debate came to a head when in June 1962 Congress moved to reconsider the Foreign Assistance Act of 1961. Senators Proxmire and Lausche introduced an amendment, passed by a wide margin, which denied the president discretionary power to allocate surplus commodities for aid. "Tito identifies his type of neutralism with the victory of communism over freedom. This is what he is working to achieve, not only in Yugoslavia, but also in Asia and Africa," charged Senator Proxmire.[69] The administration had been campaigning for many months to forestall just such a measure. Secretary of State Rusk had testified before a House Select Committee on Export Control in October 1961 that Yugoslavia's economic system was markedly dissimilar from that of the Soviet Union, and that Poland, while a member of the Soviet bloc, reflected nationalist sentiments and therefore deserved American support; in June 1962, apprehensive about the revolt in Congress, he had warned against giving the impression that the United States was "permanently writing off to Soviet domination" the satellite peoples.[70] These efforts were now intensified in order to overthrow the Proxmire-Lausche amendment, which, wrote presidential adviser McGeorge Bundy to Senator Mansfield, "would play into the hands of those who are most hostile to the United States. The intent of the amendment is obviously to oppose communism—but if it is adopted the hard line Communists will be delighted." Ambassadors Kennan and John M. Cabot were recalled from Belgrade and Warsaw to testify, the Polish-American Congress was mobilized, and the president called a major press conference, all in support of a compromise amendment, introduced by Senators Mansfield and Dirksen, which would allow the president to provide agricultural surplus aid after assuring Congress that the recipient was not engaged in aggressive efforts on behalf of communism. Thanks largely to the endorsement of the minority leader the amendment was passed in the Senate, but the House insisted on the further assurances for all aid that it was necessary for U.S. security, that the recipient was "not controlled by the international Communist conspiracy," and that the aid would promote the recipient's independence, and this version was finally adopted by both houses. The battle was renewed over the appropriation bill, for the chairman of the House Subcommittee on Appropriations, Otto Passman, reported the bill with a provision that none of the funds be expended in communist areas and the House approved it as such; it was only by a narrow margin that the Senate removed this new qualification.[71]

By withstanding this offensive on its already severely circumscribed powers to grant aid, the administration achieved a modest victory, but almost simultaneously it suffered a major setback when Congress included in the new Trade Expansion Act a provision denying the president the power to grant most-favored-nation treatment to communist states and thereby compelled the withdrawal of that privilege from Yugoslavia and

Poland. As one student of the entire controversy has noted, "the opposition to the Administration was national—i.e., bipartisan, inter-sectional, and devoid of any sharp cleavage along the domestic 'liberal' and 'conservative' lines" on the question of aid and trade with the satellites.[72] Moreover, the defeat stood in striking contrast to Kennedy's successful advocacy of sweeping tariff reductions within the context of the General Agreement on Tariffs and Trade (GATT). Throughout 1963 the president would insist that he needed the means "to exploit or to develop whatever differences in attitude or in tempo . . . may take place behind the iron curtain," but despite his remonstrances an obdurate Congress refused to delete the limiting paragraphs from the Foreign Assistance Act of 1963. He did manage to have the Trade Expansion Act amended, once again by a narrow margin, to allow the restoration of most-favored-nation treatment to Poland and Yugoslavia.[73] The legislative restrictions did not prevent Kennedy from giving the appropriate assurances in order to continue the sale of surpluses to Poland. In October he went even further by allowing American grain dealers to sell wheat to the Soviet Union and the rest of Eastern Europe (to be transported in U.S. ships). Kennedy argued that other Western powers were already making such sales and that by using their hard currency for food the communist regimes would have that much less to expend on military equipment.[74] However, the administration also wanted the freedom to sell the grain on credit and once again ran into stiff congressional opposition. First Senator Mundt, then other legislators, introduced restrictive amendments to the foreign aid appropriations bill being considered in the final months of 1963. The forceful intervention of the new president, Lyndon B. Johnson, was required to gain approval on December 24 for a bill free of credit restrictions.[75] Concurrently, the administration had been pursuing the relaxation of the West's strategic embargo through the gradual attrition of exclusively American listings as well as of those of the multinational Coordinating Committee.[76] Largely as a result of the wheat sales, American exports to East-Central Europe increased by one-third from 1962 to 1963, but this was scarcely indicative of any firm expansionist trend in East-West trade.

In the sphere of political relations, the administration decided after quiet negotiations that the Kádár regime had slowly turned a new leaf and could now be released from purgatory. From 1960 onward, meetings between State Department officials and Hungarian diplomats had brought about painfully slow progress toward a face-saving formula satisfactory to both parties. The Kádár regime, smarting from international ostracism, insisted on the normalization of relations and the dropping of the Hungarian question from the UN's agenda as preconditions to any consideration of a full amnesty in Hungary. The sequence of events preferred by the State Department was exactly the reverse. Finally, the deadlock was broken by an "unofficial" memorandum given by Assistant Undersecretary of State Richard Davis to the Hungarian chargé d'affaires on October 20, 1962. The note expressed the hope that the Hungarian government would visibly demonstrate that the revolution's consequences would be erased, and indicated that the United States would end its anti-Kádár activities at the United Nations.[77] A month later, at the Hungarian Socialist Workers' party's Eighth Congress, Kádár announced that 95 percent of people sentenced for "counterrevolutionary crimes" had already been amnestied and (with the blessing of Khrushchev, who was keen to ease tensions in the aftermath of the Cuban missile crisis) he called for good will in settling American-Hungarian differences.

As a result, U.S. delegate Carl T. Rowan advised the December 18 meeting of the UN Special Political Committee that his government wished to take a "fresh approach" to the Hungarian problem and proposed that the post of UN special representative be terminated and that the secretary-general be requested "to take any initiative that he deems helpful."[78] Two days later, the General Assembly approved the American resolution, which repeated one last time the annual demand for the withdrawal of Soviet troops and the re-establishment of basic human rights in Hungary. (The number of abstentions, principally by Third World members, had been growing year by year and contributed to Washington's decision to drop the issue.) The Budapest regime took the cue and announced a general amnesty for political prisoners, István Bibó being among those released in March 1963. The State Department thereupon reported to Congress that a genuine amelioration had occurred in Hungary's domestic political climate, and on June 5 the UN Credentials Committee was told that the United States "takes note of the recent announcement in Hungary of a general amnesty for prisoners arrested in connection with the events of 1956. We have reports of a number of steps taken in that country that appear to have improved the lot of the Hungarian people. We hope that the actions of the United Nations have had a helpful influence in this regard. In this connection, we note with satisfaction that the Secretary-General will be visiting Hungary in July." The United States therefore "reserved its position" on the Hungarian delegates' credentials, thereby allowing the United Nations to restore Hungary to full membership.[79] U Thant dutifully paid his respects in Budapest the following month, and the Hungarian question never reappeared on the agenda of the world organization. To further mark the end of their mini–cold war, Washington and Budapest agreed to curtail the mutual special restrictions on their diplomats, and later that year Hungary was allowed to purchase surplus wheat from the United States.[80] Peaceful engagement in the short-lived Kennedy era made some slight progress in other directions. In April 1963 the cultural exchange agreement with Rumania was renewed; three months later another agreement settling American claims and initiating cultural exchanges was signed in Sofia.[81] With regard to Yugoslavia, Kennedy endeavored to soften the impact of congressional hostility and welcomed Tito to the White House on the occasion of the latter's visit to the United Nations in October 1963. But such gestures seemed only to exacerbate a public opinion already out of tune with the theme of peaceful engagement.

Reaction among émigré groups to the pragmatic decision to normalize relations with Hungary was harsh and bitter. The Assembly of Captive European Nations (ACEN) had been campaigning assiduously against any recognition of the Kádár regime and the dropping of the Hungarian question from the United Nations' agenda, and had presented its case to members of Congress in a telegram dated May 16, 1963:

> We submit that approval of the credentials of the Hungarian Communist Delegation in the United Nations and especially the planned resumption of full diplomatic relations between the United States and the Kádár Régime are not justified for the following reasons: *First*, the concessions made by the Kádár Régime are spectacular, but slight, and do not substantially alleviate the lot of the Hungarian people. *Second*, the number of political prisoners actually released is still unknown since even two months after the promulgation of the amnesty decree, neither the number nor the identity of the released persons has been published by the régime. The amnesty obviously does not affect a substantial portion of individuals jailed for participation in the 1956 Revolt. *Third*, the fate of thousands of youths deported to the Soviet Union after the 1956 Revolt remains undisclosed (see U.N. Resolution 1127 of November 21, 1956). *Fourth*, the autonomy and basic rights of the Roman Catholic church have not even been partially restored. *Fifth*, the demands of the U.N. Resolutions for the withdrawal of foreign troops from Hungary and self-determination for the Hungarian people through free elections have not been implemented. There is no change in the institutional pattern of violations of basic human rights.[82]

Three weeks later, faced with the affirmative decision of the UN Credentials Committee, ACEN issued yet another statement warning that Washington's abstention would be "credibly represented to the captive peoples by communist propaganda as evidence that the *status quo* in East Central Europe has come to be accepted as final."[83] The Kennedy administration's dogged pursuit of détente, notwithstanding Cuba, the Wall, *et al.*, did not provide a hospitable atmosphere for such cold war rhetoric, and the émigré leaders were advised to tone down their denunciations. Yet the official attitudes themselves were somewhat schizophrenic, for Captive Nations Week was once again proclaimed in July 1963 and was widely celebrated across the nation and in Congress. That it simply symbolized a long-range moral aspiration was sorrowfully recognized even by ACEN, which refused "to accept the present Western policies toward our countries as final. Instead we persevere in our trust that the Western Powers will refrain from the fatal step of sanctioning the *status quo* in East-Central Europe and will take advantage of the present disarray in the Communist camp to press for an overdue solution of the East European problem."[84] But ACEN could offer no more of a solution to the dilemma of the satellites than could the original crusaders of liberation. Its positive recommendations more than ever avoided recourse to force and at the United Nations were limited to the pursuit of the chimera of self-determination. Otherwise, the émigrés warned on every possible occasion against nonaggression pacts and other political and economic agreements which would imply Western recognition of the finality of the *status quo*.[85] ACEN achieved one minor victory in 1963 when its protest against a UNESCO pamphlet which described the adhesion of the Baltic states to the Soviet Union as "voluntary" was endorsed by the United States and prompted a revision of UNESCO policies.[86]

In the face of such hostility President Kennedy and his associates tried to re-emphasize that their actions with regard to the satellites in no way detracted from their commitment to self-determination. "Too often our hands are tied by a rigid statutory perspective of the Communist world," declared Kennedy before a Pulaski Day audience in Buffalo during the 1962 congressional elections; "There are varying shades, even within the Communist world. We must be able to seize the initiative when the opportunity arises, in Poland in particular and in other countries as time goes on behind the Iron Curtain." But, he continued, "we must never—in any statement, declaration, treaty, or other manner—recognize Soviet domination of Eastern Europe as permanent."[87] One year later, Secretary of State Rusk confirmed the administration's hopeful view that a new day was dawning in East-Central Europe:

> The darkest night of Stalinist terror and oppression is past. Historic forces of nationalism are visibly at work. Gradually the smaller Communist nations of Eastern Europe seem to be finding for themselves a little more autonomy. They are taking steps to increase their trade and other contacts with the West—first, with countries of Western Europe, but also with the United States. And persistent pressures for more individual freedom are also evident, not only in the smaller Soviet bloc countries but within the Soviet Union itself. We would like to do what

we can to encourage these trends within the Communist world. We favor freer movements of information and of people between the bloc countries and the United States. On the whole, we think the trends toward nationalism and individual freedom are more likely to be furthered by a somewhat relaxed atmosphere than by an atmosphere of crisis or severe cold war.

As for self-determination in the satellites, Rusk said: "we shall try, by peaceful means, to help them move toward that goal. The world cannot rest while the wartime promises of the Allies and the goals of the United Nations remain unfulfilled in this great region of Europe."[88] This new myth of liberation, representing yet another adaptation of the original containment doctrine, was at least partly a rationalization of Kennedy's key concern with détente. The increasingly apparent rift between Moscow and Peking over ideological and territorial issues and the evidence of Rumania's economic nationalism may have encouraged him to believe that the Communist bloc was gradually succumbing to pluralistic pressures. Yet his entire foreign policy was oriented toward achieving a stable *modus vivendi* with the Soviet Union, and to this the question of liberation was necessarily subordinated.

Having overcome the Cuban missile challenge, stabilizing in the process both Cuba's status as a Soviet protectorate and West Berlin's links to the West, Kennedy proceeded to make a new plea for peace and détente in his address at American University on June 10. The negotiations he alluded to on that occasion shortly produced a test-ban treaty, as well as agreements on a Washington-Moscow "hot line" and cultural exchanges. Khrushchev thereupon tried to revive the idea of a nonagression pact to strengthen and legitimize what was in any case an impregnable Soviet position in East-Central Europe, and some of Kennedy's advisers felt that the resulting stabilization would allow for still greater liberalization in the satellites, but Adenauer's opposition to such initiatives continued to prevail. (When, along with the other satellites, the GDR signed the test-ban treaty, Washington had had to reassure Bonn that this implied no recognition of the Ulbricht regime.)[89] Much to Khrushchev's annoyance, the Western Allies shifted their attention to the problem of sharing nuclear weapons and the credibility of the American protective umbrella. Kennedy's tragic death in Dallas interrupted the momentum of his drive for détente, and his successor proved rather less capable of transcending the cold war's heritage of fearful mistrust. But Kennedy's pragmatic attempts to acknowledge the *fait accompli* of a Soviet sphere in East-Central Europe had already outpaced congressional and public attitudes, notwithstanding the popularity of the test-ban. The division of Europe had only been reaffirmed by Kennedy's determined stand on West Berlin and his acceptance of the

Wall, and the nuclear stalemate made the satellites more than ever inaccessible to direct American influence; indeed, despite the moral rectitude of the inflexible anticommunists, there was no realistic alternative to reviving America's links with the East Europeans. The Soviet Union's understanding of peaceful coexistence, however, did not preclude communist probes along less clearly defined stretches of the periphery, and the rapidly escalating conflict in Vietnam would only add to the difficulties of peaceful engagement, while the Czechoslovak experience in 1968 would shatter many dreams of inevitable evolutionary change in East-Central Europe.

BRIDGE-BUILDING BY LBJ

The mid-sixties saw the development of pluralistic tendencies in East-Central Europe, with the individual regimes adopting a variety of courses that were aimed at securing wider popular allegiance and reviving stagnant economies.[90] This new nationalism was most striking in the case of Rumania, where the party elite under Gheorgiu-Dej (succeeded in 1965 by Nicolae Ceausescu) was galvanized by the 1962 COMECON proposals for a "socialist division of labor" to reassert the country's economic independence and reject the relegation of Rumania to the role of a supplier of primary products. In subsequent years the regime attempted to pursue a semi-independent foreign policy by taking an ostensibly neutral stand in the Sino-Soviet debate and by developing closer economic and diplomatic contacts with the West (including the normalization of relations with West Germany in 1967, an act that contravened the general bloc policy of withholding recognition from Bonn until it recognized East Germany and the Oder-Neisse frontier). In the domestic sphere, however, the Bucharest regime made no move to liberalize its policies, relying instead on its externally directed nationalism to inspire the support of the masses. Against all expectations it was the Kádár regime that introduced the most radical domestic reforms. After a period of harsh repression and the completion of a brutal collectivization campaign, the regime finally took cognizance of the catastrophic state of the Hungarian economy and drew up plans for a major restructuring called the New Economic Mechanism, which, beginning in 1968, decentralized economic management and introduced new incentives in the interests of greater efficiency and productivity; these reforms were accompanied by a degree of tolerance in the social and cultural spheres that was unequaled in East-Central Europe. The Ulbricht and Novotný regimes also sought to improve economic management while, like Hungary, closely adhering to the foreign policies of the Soviet Union. In the case of East Germany, the now-captive labor force could at least draw comfort from having the highest standard of living in the Soviet bloc; in Czechoslovakia, as will be seen, the process of decompression took a more radical course. The Gomulka regime, on the other hand, failed to live up to its earlier promises in the spheres of economic modernization and political liberalization or in its foreign orientations. Factional disputes and the growing assertiveness of youth and the intelligentsia led the regime to consolidate its position in 1967 and 1968 by appealing to the nationalism and latent antisemitism of the working classes and by repressing student dissent.

In attempting to cope with their economic and social problems, the East European regimes all faced the dilemma of reconciling economic liberalization with the maintenance of party supremacy. An additional and ultimately dominant factor was the attitude of the Soviet leadership; Khrushchev, and, after his downfall in October 1964, Brezhnev and Kosygin, viewed these polycentrist tendencies with some alarm but, at least until the spring of 1968, appeared to condone the diverse nationalistic experiments in their client states. Public opinion in East-Central Europe also underwent certain changes in the mid-sixties. Although the United States was still the most popular foreign country among the masses (a preference somewhat less marked among the intellectuals, who were more susceptible to traditional feelings of cultural superiority), its failure to influence the course of events in the satellites—notably, on the occasion of the Hungarian revolution—led to an understandable decline of interest in its foreign policies. The satellite peoples no longer expected change through war, but they were equally skeptical about the chances of a meaningful reconciliation between the two superpowers. While in principle they favored closer relations with America, their interests took on a more exclusively European orientation.[91] This change coincided with the eastern initiatives of President de Gaulle and of the Kiesinger-Brandt coalition, and it represented a reassertion of traditional continental links, but it was no doubt also influenced by the absence of any tangible, as distinct from declaratory, evidence of American involvement in the fate of East-Central Europe. The East Europeans understood that improvements in their political, social, and economic life could come about only through an internal evolutionary process, and the behavior of at least some of their regimes in the mid-sixties seemed to indicate a refreshing responsiveness to their desires.

These pluralistic trends provided the inspiration for an address by Secretary of State Rusk on February 25, 1964. Denying that the Johnson administration had any illusions as to the hostile designs of the communists, Rusk explained that American policies aimed first to contain communist imperialism, second to reach specific agreements to reduce the danger of war, and third "to encourage evolution within the Communist world toward national independence, peaceful cooperation, and open societies." In his estimation, conditions in East-Central Europe were favorable to the pursuit of the third objective. Yugoslavia's "success in defending its independence made other peoples in Eastern Europe wonder why they could not do likewise." In Poland "a good deal of the national autonomy and domestic liberalization which the Poles won in 1956 persists." Rumania had "asserted a more independent attitude and has expanded its trade and other contacts with the West." Hungary had "turned to a more permissive policy of national conciliation." The United States, said Rusk, would encourage these trends and watch for similar developments in Czechoslovakia and Bulgaria.[92] Observed the secretary later that year, "It is not necessary to think of liberation as the result of some cataclysmic clash of nations; one can begin to think of liberation through change and through the reappearance of historic ties which lie deeply in the hearts of the peoples concerned."[93] Without abandoning the ultimate goal of liberation, then, the Johnson administration decided to carry on its predecessors' strategy of gradually Westernizing the satellites.

The pursuit of peaceful engagement in the hope of reviving East-Central Europe's links with the West aroused little controversy as a general proposition, but there was less of a consensus between the administration and Congress and the American public regarding the method of its implementation. If the ensuing debates over satellite policy lacked the partisanship of the late Truman years, they nevertheless reflected a cleavage that was only exacerbated by the deepening crisis in Vietnam. On the one hand, a number of experts and pundits castigated the administration for being too cautious in relaxing its cold war posture. One such advocate was George Kennan, whose frustration with Congress's obstruction of closer relations led to his resignation as ambassador to Belgrade. Arguing that the only rational approach was to encourage polycentrism, he charged that Washington was following two "wholly different and mutually contradictory foreign policies, one aiming at coexistence, the other at victory through confrontation," and complained that measures such as the Captive Nations Resolution "complicated the task of everyone in our government who has been working to avoid the catastrophe of war." Kennan deplored the West's firm opposition to military disengagement and a NATO–Warsaw Pact nonaggression treaty and argued that, if domestic political considerations prevented the United States from expanding its trade with the satellites, it should not impede the West Europeans from forging closer commercial links with their neighbors; a total blockade of the communist bloc would have no significant effect on their economies but would discourage the development of polycentrism. The monolithic view of communism, said Kennan, "still predominates in our public debates, and so deeply ingrained is it in our Congressional approaches that the slightest attempt to deviate from it raises instantaneous cries of anguish and indignation on the Hill."[94] Other critics argued that the communists had not abandoned their goal of world domination and that measures to normalize East-West relations could not affect the substance of the cold war. Hans Morgenthau reflected along these lines that the United States had been "unable to shed the illusion that civilized social intercourse among nations whose interests clash is somehow conducive to peace, and that the cold war could easily be ended if the antagonists would only treat each other in a more friendly and reasonable fashion."[95] Even if the Kremlin was irredeemably hostile to the West, however, the administration saw some merit in attempting to wean away its satellites, and the Johnson years brought repeated, if only marginally successful, efforts in that direction.

As in the Kennedy era, the main stumbling blocks were Congress and the popular suspicions mirrored on Capitol Hill. Undersecretary of State Averell Harriman and other State Department officials appeared before the Foreign Affairs Committee's Subcommittee on Europe in early 1964 to plead the case that Eastern Europe was no longer monolithic and that the administration's policy aimed to encourage the ongoing evolution "by using every kind of peaceful contact available."[96] The subcommittee reported in a rather less sanguine vein that "there is no indication that the process of change has altered the authoritarian nature of the Communist system, or appreciably undermined Communist Party control of the countries of the Soviet bloc" and warned that "overly optimistic interpretations of the significance and extent of change within the Soviet bloc, combined with the impact of the initial steps toward disarmament, can compound the problem by giving the United States a false sense of security." The United States, the report continued, should assist liberalization in the satellites by trade and exchanges but should also demand *quid pro quo* concessions, such as the lifting of travel restrictions and "electoral reforms."[97] The immediate reactions to Rusk's February address had not been unfavorable, however, and some prominent legislators—notably, Senator Fulbright—had endorsed its basic premises.[98] Moreover, there were indications that Western Europe's commercial offensive toward the East would prompt Congress to review its stand on the question of trade. In this conjuncture President Johnson decided to deliver a major public statement on U.S. policy toward the satellites. Speaking at the dedication ceremonies of the George C. Marshall Research Library at the Virginia Military Institute on May 23, the president declared:

> We will continue to build bridges across the gulf which has divided us from Eastern Europe. They will be bridges of increased trade, of ideas, of visitors, and of humanitarian aid. We do this for four reasons: First,

to open new relationships to countries seeking increased independence yet unable to risk isolation. Second, to open the minds of a new generation to the values and the visions of the Western civilization from which they come and to which they belong. Third, to give freer play to the powerful forces of national pride—the strongest barrier to the ambition of any country to dominate another. Fourth, to demonstrate that identity of interest and the prospects of progress for Eastern Europe lie in a wider relationship with the West.

As a sop to Bonn, where such overtures invariably aroused apprehensions about reunification, Johnson added that "wise and skillful development of relationships with the nations of Eastern Europe can speed the day when Germany can be reunited" and that the United States was unalterably committed to that goal.[99] Pursuing the theme of peaceful engagement, the president most notably omitted any requirement that the satellite regimes liberalize their domestic policies. This pragmatic omission and the unique stress on independence was no doubt influenced by the concurrent trade negotiations with the Rumanians, but it also reflected the more fundamental view that, if the United States was to court the East European governments, reminders of their internal shortcomings would be inopportune and possibly counterproductive.

By not imposing impossible demands on the satellites for internal change or outright secession, Johnson's bridge-building thesis managed to minimize adverse comment from the East. America's allies were even less disturbed, and Chancellor Ludwig Erhard proved to be rather more amenable than his predecessor would have been to President Johnson's explanation (on the occasion of the former's visit to Washington in June) that, although the United States was still committed in principle to Germany's reunification, the goals of security and stability in Europe and of improving relations with the East Europeans had first priority. A Soviet–East German treaty of friendship and cooperation, which restated the new orthodoxy that reunification could be achieved only through negotiations on an equal basis between the two sovereign German states, was announced coincidentally with Erhard's stay in Washington (the Russians having previously reassured Johnson that the agreement was not meant as a provocation), and it must have reinforced the president's advice to his guest that Bonn adopt a more flexible approach to the East. In the event, Adenauer's departure and Washington's bridge-building contributed to a reappraisal of Germany's foreign policy which led to the experimental *Ostpolitik* of the later sixties. Meanwhile, in the domestic political arena, the Johnson administration pursued its objective of peaceful engagement *sotto voce*, for fear of arousing the latent opposition to such initiatives, and, although Republican candidate Barry Goldwater thundered about the

Democrats' defeatism, neither presidential aspirant made an issue of satellite policy in the 1964 campaign. Following his lopsided victory, President Johnson turned to the implementation of the bridge-building policy, and declared in his 1965 State of the Union message: "In Eastern Europe, restless nations are slowly beginning to assert their identity. Your government, assisted by leaders in labor and business, is now exploring ways to increase peaceful trade with these countries and with the Soviet Union."[100] Once again, however, efforts to achieve that goal would prove to be an exercise in futility.

The expansion of America's trade with the communist bloc was subject to a number of statutory limitations that antedated Johnson's declaration of intent. Trade in items of strategic significance had originally been curtailed by the Mutual Defense Assistance Control (Battle) Act of 1951 and remained thereafter under the multilateral supervision of the Coordinating Committee, which had periodically reviewed and reduced the embargo lists. The European participants in the Coordinating Committee became increasingly reluctant to hinder the development of their commercial relations with the East, but, although the Battle Act provided for sanctions against recalcitrant allies, President Johnson's use of his discretionary power had avoided any termination of American aid on these grounds. The Mutual Security Act of 1954 had imposed an embargo on trade in military matériel with the communists, a restriction that had little bearing on bridge-building. As noted earlier, an amendment to the Foreign Assistance Act of 1961 made specific presidential assurances a prerequisite for American aid (in passing the Food for Peace Act of 1966 Congress insisted on the extension of similar limitations to countries trading with Cuba and North Vietnam), and Section 231 (a) of the Trade Expansion Act of 1962 instructed the president to withdraw trade concessions from communist states, although the subsequently approved Section 231 (b) in effect allowed the restoration of most-favored-nation treatment to Poland and Yugoslavia.[101] Finally, a 1962 amendment to the Export Control Act set criteria for the licensing of exportable goods not on the international embargo lists; the ambiguity of these criteria, however, led initially to a marked caution on the part of Commerce Department administrators in granting licenses for shipments to communist countries.

Although in 1964 President Johnson had succeeded in implementing Kennedy's wheat deal with the Russians and had received encouragement from a number of senators and businessmen, his long political experience told him that very careful preparation would have to precede a formal proposal for the revision of the abovementioned restrictions. On February 16, 1965, he announced the formation of a special presidential committee on East-West trade headed by J. Irwin Miller, chairman of the board of the Cummins Engine Company, and a little more than two months later the committee duly presented its report. Presidential committees tend to mirror their patron's philosophy, and the Miller committee was no exception. It asserted that the Soviet Union's ties with the satellites were weakening, that the forces of nationalism were growing in the latter, and that "trade with the European Communist countries is politics in the broadest sense—holding open the possibility of careful negotiation, firm bargaining, and constructive competition. In this intimate engagement men and nations will in time be altered by the engagement itself." The report acknowledged that the nonconvertibility of East European currencies and those nations' limited potential exports to the United States did not foreshadow a vast increase in trade, but it argued that the satellites coveted American machinery, equipment, and technical data and that this advanced technology could provide the United States with "bargaining leverage." In any event, the commercial significance of trade was "dwarfed by political considerations," and the "case for expanding peaceful trade comes down to the proposition that we can use trade to influence the internal evolution and external behavior of Communist countries." The report recommended more flexible export licensing and, most important, the granting to the president of discretionary power to extend and withdraw most-favored-nation treatment. In the matter of credits the committee took a more cautious stand. By the Berne Convention of 1961 the seven largest Western creditor nations had agreed not to extend credits for periods of more than five years, but by 1964 Britain and France had technically contravened this agreement in extending or promising to extend longer credits to Czechoslovakia and Rumania. The trade report warned that "permitting these countries to pile up long-term debt could enable them to put their creditors under substantial pressure to accept unwanted commodities in lieu of defaults and could amount to a subsidy for their economies" and urged adherence to the original convention.[102]

In receiving the Miller committee's report, President Johnson indicated that he would submit recommendations to Congress after consultations with the West Europeans, but it was mainly the evidence of growing domestic opposition that delayed his initiative. Finally, in May 1966, the draft of the "East-West Trade Relations Act of 1966" was transmitted to Congress; it proposed to empower the president to enter into three-year, renewable commercial agreements with the communists and to extend most-favored-nation treatment, but it did not specifically modify the Export Control Act or Battle Act restrictions on strategic goods.[103] In his letter of transmittal, Secretary of State Rusk claimed there was "abundant evidence that without the authority this legislation would provide, we are losing and will continue to lose significant opportunities to influence the course of events in Eastern Europe" and assured Congress that "no agreement will be made under this authority except in return for benefits of equal importance to the United States." At the same time, he noted that these benefits would materialize only in the long run.[104] The Democratic chairman of the House Ways and Means Committee, Wilbur Mills, was unimpressed; he announced that his committee would not even hold hearings on the proposed bill during the current session.[105] The stalemate resulting from Mills's decision to table the bill without discussion reflected the nature of the American system of checks and balances, but the decision itself was not purely idiosyncratic, for the prevailing political climate was decidedly inhospitable to détente with the satellites.

Support for the administration's efforts to relax trade restrictions came principally from businessmen envious of the West Europeans' commercial forays into the Soviet sphere and from certain senators. The Committee on Foreign Relations had held hearings on East-West trade early in 1964 and again a year later, and under the chairmanship of Senator Fulbright the tone of the hearings had not been entirely unfavorable to the administration. Some committee members did express reservations. Senator Lausche wondered whether increased trade would not imply U.S. acceptance of the regimes, and Senator Mundt complained to Undersecretary of State George Ball that "we have written in restrictions every year to Communist countries and you have found a way to get around them. The attitude of Congress is certainly not one to encourage trade with Communist countries."[106] But Fulbright insisted that Americans had to overcome the myth that trade with the satellites was a "compact with the Devil."[107] Moreover, a Foreign Relations Committee survey of the views of 125 businessmen and 20 bankers found that a majority supported trade expansion and Export-Import Bank guarantees, while in February 1967 five of six members of the committee's Special Study Mission to Europe reported in favor of more trade with Eastern Europe. Similar endorsements came in the early months of 1967 from the U.S. Council of the International Chamber of Commerce, from the Action Committee on Export Promotion in its report to the National Export Expansion Council, from the Bankers Association for Foreign Trade, and from participants in the National Foreign Trade Convention and the Thirty-first American Assembly. Already in 1964 the U.S. Chamber of Commerce had reversed its earlier opposition to expanded trade relations, and a study sponsored by the National Association of Manufacturers reached similar conclusions.[108] Yet even with the backing of these powerful interest groups the administration failed to convert or prevail over organized grass-roots opposition and its strategically situated spokesmen in Congress.

Congress and the public have had "difficulty in reconciling a policy of United States initiatives to improve East-West relations with the involvement of Communist countries in Viet-Nam," understated the Battle Act report for 1967.[109] Indeed, large sections of the American public reasoned that any friend of the Vietnamese communists was no friend of the United States, and that trading with satellites providing aid for Ho Chi Minh amounted to trading with the enemy. Such arguments may have been logically unexceptionable, but they ignored the mitigating factor that the East European regimes had little choice but to follow Moscow's lead in providing at least token assistance to North Vietnam. Trade with Cuba also was considered by the public to be an unfriendly act, and Congress responded by applying restrictions in the Food for Peace Act of 1966, restrictions that forced the administration to cancel a major wheat sale to Yugoslavia. Much of American big business stood with the administration on the East-West trade issue, but the American Legion, the Young Americans for Freedom, and other organizations ranging from the political middle to the far right took a vocal and diametrically opposite view. Big labor, motivated by a fear of dumping and by its anticommunism, also objected to trade expansion; the one dissenting postscript to the Miller report had been appended by the AFL-CIO's director of research. Starting from the basic premise that trade with the satellites was trade with the enemy, this opposition argued that in such circumstances there were no nonstrategic goods and it mounted a massive campaign to prevent the administration from liberalizing statutory restrictions and to stop individual companies from trading with the East.

In the first instance the campaign was successful, thanks to congressional support, particularly in the House of Representatives; in its second orientation the campaign also achieved success—notably, in 1965, when the Firestone Tire and Rubber Company was persuaded to abandon its plans to build a synthetic rubber plant in Rumania.[110] Concurrently, boycotts were organized by the Committee to Warn of the Arrival of Communist Merchandise on the Local Business Scene, which published an index of such goods "to combat, sidetrack and eventually wreck the economic efforts of the Communists to bleed and destroy our Nation."[111] The boycotts were by no means the inconsequential efforts of a lunatic fringe; they were endorsed by numerous municipalities and citizens' groups who greeted the arrival of Polish hams with righteous indignation. The administration's concerned reaction testified to the extent of this opposition. Secretaries Rusk, McNamara, and Connor wrote an open letter to the American cigarette manufacturers, commending them for their resistance to pressures to boycott Yugoslav tobacco and declaring that "any individuals or groups that seek to intimidate, boycott, blacklist, use or threaten economic reprisals against . . . American enterprises for carrying on lawful trade with Eastern European countries act harmfully and irresponsibly." Undersecretary of State Ball declared on the program "Face the Nation" that it was "absolutely unacceptable that right wing or left wing or any other kind of group should by intimidation or by threat of boycott try to subvert or to undermine the foreign policy of the United States"—harsh words that testified to the administration's determination to abandon cold war tactics vis-à-vis the satellites.[112] The State Department went so far as to publish in September 1966 a pamphlet entitled *Private Boycotts versus the National Interest*. But neither entreaties nor warnings could erase the frustrations of the Vietnam war and the dogmatic anticommunism that it induced in the minds of many American citizens.

On October 7, 1966, in a major address delivered before the National Conference of Editorial Writers in New York City, President Johnson returned to the theme of bridge-building. Observing that he was still committed to the proposed East-West Trade Relations Act, he announced a number of new steps, including the removal of export controls on hundreds of nonstrategic items, permission for the Export-Import Bank to guarantee commercial credits to Poland, Hungary, Bulgaria, and Czechoslovakia, and consideration of the expenditure of America's Polish currency holdings in Poland itself so as to ease the burden of Polish debt. The President also announced that the Export-Import Bank was prepared to finance U.S. exports for the projected Fiat automobile plant in the Soviet Union and that he would ask for early action by Congress on a Soviet-American consular agreement. In his quest for détente he even implicitly endorsed the objectives of Moscow's own campaign for a European security conference: "Hand in hand with these steps to increase East-West ties must go measures to remove territorial and border disputes as a source of friction in Europe. The Atlantic nations oppose the use of force to change existing frontiers."[113] The president's speech thus forcefully reiterated the basic philosophy of bridge-building—to stabilize the European *status quo* and to slowly Westernize the satellite regimes. But such policy statements and exercises of executive powers could not resolve the legislative stalemate or nullify the impact of popular resistance. Throughout 1966 and 1967, government officials would fruitlessly pursue the task of persuasion, arguing that blanket protests against trade with the communists were reactions to the facts of the last decade and that an expansion of trade would have "no material relationship" to the communist effort in Vietnam but was rather in the economic and political interests of the United States.[114] Speaking in Madison, Wisconsin, in the fall of 1967, Johnson's hand-picked ambassador to Warsaw, John A. Gronouski, concluded regretfully that the entire bridge-building program "ran into deep trouble under the sustained attack of those to whom peaceful engagement is being 'soft on communism' "; he noted that the president's trade bill was "in danger of congressional extinction," that the decision to extend government credit to companies participating in the Fiat plant was "under serious attack," and that Congress had killed a $10 million program for the purchase of U.S. publications and films in Poland and was threatening once again to remove Poland's most-favored-nation status.[115]

How much Johnson's bridge-building actually achieved in tangible terms is difficult to estimate. The administration did exercise its discretion to relax export licensing procedures in response to complaints from business interests that America's allies were unfairly advantaged in the East European markets; indeed, France, Britain, and Japan in particular were inclined to make liberal use of the "special national interest or hardship" escape clause in the informal Coordinating Committee embargo agreement.[116] Accordingly, the 1962 amendment to the Export Control Act prohibiting trade in goods that might strengthen the economic potential of the satellites was increasingly interpreted not to exclude items already supplied by other friendly countries. Observed a Commerce Department official, "It obviously does not contribute to the building of bridges of peaceful trade if we limit our potential East European customers to those U.S. products which are no better than those they can obtain in Western Europe"; he admitted, however, that "it is often difficult and time consuming to determine whether the shipment of a commodity is likely to make a significant contribution to the military or economic potential of a bloc country which would prove detrimental to the national security and welfare of the United States."[117] In the event, by 1967 some 400 nonstrategic items had been removed from U.S. embargo lists, many of them representing technical data rather than manufactured products. In retrospect the Western embargo in the postwar period did not significantly affect the economic development of the satellites and it influenced their policies even less; on the other hand, it gave rise to unnecessary frictions among the Allies, particularly when American subsidiaries were compelled to observe U.S. restrictions.[118] That the easing of these restrictions did not result in a major upsurge in America's trade with the satellites was due to the latter's lack of most-favored-nation status, as well as to certain secular limitations; after a high of $195 million in 1964, the total value of U.S. exports to the satellites (not including Yugoslavia) fell to less than $94 million the following year as wheat sales to Poland were curtailed, and by 1967 it had risen to only $134 million (see Table 1). Indeed, indications are that the economic basis for a greatly expanded trade with the East European states simply does not exist, for few of the latter's products are suitable for the American market, and therefore a big increase in U.S. exports would require long-term credits or aid which at least in the mid-sixties had no chance of gaining congressional support.[119] The

Table 1. U.S. Trade with East-Central Europe, 1961–1967

	Exports (in thousands of dollars)							Imports (in thousands of dollars)						
	1961	1962	1963	1964	1965	1966	1967	1961	1962	1963	1964	1965	1966	1967
Albania	—	—	—	18	8	166	56	74	123	117	102	113	109	335
Bulgaria	47	33	137	4,819	3,613	3,631	4,219	1,248	1,136	1,195	1,177	1,666	2,529	2,814
Czechoslovakia	7,385	7,172	9,790	11,334	27,685	37,336	19,155	9,286	9,989	10,370	12,706	16,741	27,695	26,241
East Germany	2,775	1,698	6,403	20,211	12,413	24,864	26,330	2,529	3,096	3,158	6,686	6,537	8,194	5,647
Hungary	1,349	836	17,280	13,654	9,327	10,053	7,570	2,024	1,183	1,585	1,693	2,092	2,985	3,884
Poland	74,791	94,454	108,897	138,030	35,417	52,988	60,827	41,316	45,836	43,119	54,202	65,861	82,948	90,960
Rumania	1,404	802	1,249	5,155	6,385	27,057	16,796	1,362	626	789	1,272	1,836	4,655	6,176
Estonia, Latvia, and Lithuania	2,911	4,888	2,687	1,807	—	—	—	2	1	831	518	58	139	121
Totals	90,662	109,883	146,443	195,028	94,848	156,095	134,953	57,841	62,620	61,164	78,356	94,094	129,254	136,178

Sources: U.S., Department of Commerce, *Trade of United States with Communist Areas in Eastern Europe and Asia, 1963–65*, Overseas Business Report Series, August 1966, and *ibid, 1965–67*, September 1968.

marketability of certain satellite products (primarily foodstuffs) in Western Europe explains at least in part the more rapid development of trade between these two regions. Only in the later sixties would certain East European regimes resort to joint industrial development projects as a method of importing technological knowhow without upsetting their balance of trade with the West.

While in the days of Dulles and liberation psychological warfare had served as an integral part of official policy, propaganda in the era of peaceful engagement and bridge-building necessarily became an anomalous, if not anachronistic, tool. The process of adjustment varied from outlet to outlet, for, as the director of the Voice of America pointed out to a congressional subcommittee, fundamental distinctions had to be kept in mind: "VOA is the official voice of the United States, its people and its leaders, speaking to the target areas, while RFE is the voice of free East Europeans speaking to their captive homelands."[120] In the case of VOA this description was only partly accurate, for it by-passed the problem of reconciling potentially conflicting viewpoints between the administration and other Americans, and the report of the same subcommittee in 1963 testified to this effect:

> There is a lack of knowledge, and confusion, behind the Iron Curtain about the U.S. position on the captive European nations. That policy is not clearly understood even in the United States. This tends to undermine the spirit of resistance to communism in the captive nations, and should have been remedied long ago. Indicative of the attitude of executive agencies toward this issue is the failure of the Voice of America to give news coverage to the hearings of this committee on the captive nations even though responsible officials of that very Agency stated that it was obviously important for the people behind the Iron Curtain to be made aware of the continuing U.S. concern about their welfare.[121]

Testifying that same year before another subcommittee, a Polish-speaking congressman complained that, whereas on RFE he was allowed to discuss the anticommunist activities of Polish-American groups, on VOA he had to limit himself to innocuous subjects such as folk dancing in the Midwest.[122] Despite such criticisms, however, the Voice of America's programming followed the philosophy of peaceful engagement and refrained from the crusading tones of earlier years; this change was reflected in the reduction of broadcasts specifically aimed at East-Central Europe (as distinct from its general service) from a high of 538.0 weekly hours in 1956 to 178.5 hours in 1967.[123]

Radio Free Europe also adjusted its sails to the new winds in Washington and in the satellites. Having abandoned its earlier role as an agent of rollback, it no longer attempted to crystallize occasional official or unofficial statements into a policy of liberation; instead, it concentrated on cross-reporting internal developments in the communist bloc so as to educate its listeners about the possibilities of domestic reform and laid increased stress on the prospects for a gradual reintegration of the satellite peoples into a European community.[124] Its programming also took on a less overwhelmingly political character, with music programs such as "Teenager Party" being tailored to the younger listeners' taste for Western pop culture. At the same time, RFE continued to fulfill the useful function of providing immediate and accurate information, and this has gradually compelled the East European media to upgrade their standards of reporting within the limitations of official policy. According to Radio Free Europe's own surveys, its new style did not alienate its listeners. In most satellites, listening to Radio Free Europe is still officially frowned upon, but the regimes gradually came to the conclusion that the language of peaceful liberation no longer presented a direct threat to their survival, even if spoken by émigrés; the costly efforts at jamming were abandoned by the Poles in 1956, by the Rumanians in 1963, and by the Hungarians in 1964.[125]

With a staff of fifteen hundred and an annual budget (in the mid-sixties) of around $12 million, Radio Free Europe was a sizable enterprise, and, in the wake of revelations in 1967 regarding secret CIA subsidies to student and other organizations, its financing came under public scrutiny. By its own account RFE was financed through private contributions, but its reliance on a government subsidy channeled through the CIA had long been an open secret. Nevertheless, in February 1967 General Clay was returned to the chairmanship of FEC in order to refurbish its public image. The administration felt bound to carry out an investigation, and the president accordingly appointed a special committee headed by Undersecretary of State Katzenbach to look into the matter of secret subsidies. Katzenbach reportedly favored their curtailment, but he ultimately agreed to maintain support for RFE and Radio Liberty in view of their continuing compatibility with U.S. foreign policy.[126] Thus the covert method of financing RFE was maintained, although it would once again come under congressional attack in 1971. President Johnson himself had given the seal of approval to RFE on the occasion of a meeting with some of its administrators in December 1964: "When the peoples of Eastern Europe are again able to enjoy radio broadcasting from their own capitals which tells them as much as Radio Free Europe does, then Radio Free Europe will have finished its job. Until then, RFE has work ahead of it, day in and day out, year in year out."[127] Moreover, the president did not discontinue the annual practice of proclaiming Captive Nations Week;

while the State Department was manifestly unhappy with such a leftover from the cold war, its cancellation would have unnecessarily aroused political passions among émigrés and other Americans, and its proclamation was no longer likely to create dangerous illusions in East-Central Europe. When the Polish ambassador lodged an official complaint about a speech in which Arthur Goldberg censured the Warsaw government for its repression of religious freedom, Secretary of State Rusk allegedly told him: "Mr. Ambassador, could you perhaps allow us some fifteen per cent of our speech-making for domestic purposes? We allow a much larger percentage for yours."[128] This was not so much a diplomatic reassurance as a candid reflection on the constraints of American politics.

The task of building bridges to the individual satellites was hampered in the mid-sixties not only by domestic resistance but also by the Vietnam war. Relations took a turn for the worse after the first bombing of the Hanoi-Haiphong area in June 1966, and Moscow's reply to the Johnson speech of October 7, that détente must await American disengagement from Vietnam, was faithfully echoed in the satellite press. But, if the satellite regimes paid obeisance to the Kremlin by occasionally denouncing bridge-building as a tool of American imperialism, they at the same time eagerly courted Washington in the expectation of gaining credits and expanded trade. For a time Rumania appeared to be the prime candidate for bridge-building. As early as 1963 the Department of Commerce granted a license to an American firm to build a steel mill for the giant Galati metallurgical complex, and, when the Soviet Union failed to express grave displeasure, the Rumanians sent a high-level delegation headed by Gheorghe Gaston-Marin, chairman of the State Planning Committee, to negotiate further economic concessions. In a joint communiqué issued on June 1, 1964, the United States agreed to establish a general licensing procedure under which most commodities would not require individual licenses and to grant licenses for a number of industrial installations, private credits for which would be guaranteed by the Export-Import Bank; in turn, the Rumanians agreed not to trans-ship or re-export goods without the consent of the United States. In addition, trade and tourist facilities would be mutually expanded and the level of diplomatic missions would be raised from legations to embassies.[129] Later that same year the Rumanian government announced the purchase of a catalytic cracking plant from an American firm, to be financed by a $16 million credit repayable over seven years (an agreement by which the United States contravened the Berne Convention), and a proposal to buy a complete rubber plant from the Firestone Company. Gaston-Marin even issued a tentative invitation to American firms to set up production facilities in Rumania, but this turned out to be too radical an idea for the party to swallow and he was dismissed from his post in August 1965.[130] In the event, the Rumanians soon discovered that a great hiatus existed between President Johnson's bridge-building speeches and the realities of U.S. trade policy. Most-favored-nation treatment was not granted, licensing for most of the items they had expressed an interest in turned out to be an interminable process, and the Firestone deal fell through because of public pressure. The volume of U.S.-Rumanian trade tripled between 1964 and 1967, but it was still less than that of Poland, East Germany, and Czechoslovakia with the United States, and it remained marked by a sizable imbalance in the Americans' favor. Foreign Minister Corneliu Manescu was the only East European in attendance at the UN General Assembly in October 1966 who was invited by Rusk to a dinner conference. Moreover, the U.S.-Rumanian cultural exchange program was renewed in 1967. But such gestures could not overcome the Rumanians' disappointment at the Johnson administration's failure to follow through its promises of closer commercial relations. The maintenance of an independent stance in foreign policy by the Ceausescu regime owed little to the policy of bridge-building.

In the case of Poland, the administration tried to keep alive the special relationship that had materialized after 1956, but its efforts were hindered both by Gomulka's close adherence to Soviet foreign policy and by some of the same limitations on trade that applied to the other satellites. In 1964 Gomulka once again revived the Rapacki Plan in the hope of preventing West Germany's participation in the multilateral nuclear force then under discussion by the NATO allies, and the necessarily procommunist bias of the Polish members of the international observation commissions in Laos and Vietnam further annoyed the United States. Nevertheless, Johnson attempted to improve relations by appointing a Polish-American, Postmaster-General John A. Gronouski, as ambassador to Poland, and, in a speech on May 3, 1966, marking the Polish national millenium, the president noted that in the foregoing two years the United States had dedicated an American-financed children's hospital in Krakow, increased its support for CARE and other relief programs, fostered an understanding between the two nations' academies of science on an exchange program, and expanded cultural exchanges and the sale of U.S. printed matter and films in Poland.[131] Thanks to Poland's most-favored-nation status, the volume of her trade with the United States was as great as that of all the other satellites combined, even though in 1964 Congress had ruled that Poland would have to pay for food imports in dollars on five-year credit terms and had thereby effectively terminated the sale of surplus wheat; in 1967 the United States exported more than $60 million worth of goods to Poland and imported close to $91 million.

Relations with Hungary improved only marginally in the Johnson years. Although upon occasion Kádár would complain of U.S. economic discrimination, little progress was made on the settlement of American claims, and trade between the two countries actually declined between 1963 and 1967. An additional irritant was the presence of Cardinal Mindszenty in the U.S. legation in Budapest. The aging prelate adamantly refused to leave his refuge until the Hungarian government recognized his title as spiritual leader of the Catholic church; the regime was willing to grant him safe passage out of the country but would not allow him to resume his functions in Hungary. The Johnson administration nevertheless recognized that in the domestic sphere, particularly in economic management, Kádár had manifested a remarkable degree of pragmatism and tolerance, and in late 1966 mutual agreement was reached to raise diplomatic representation to the ambassadorial level; this agreement was implemented with some embarrassment to the Hungarian government, however, for in May 1967 its chief negotiator and chargé d'affaires, János Radványi, defected to the United States.[132]

The show trial in December 1963 of a Bulgarian accused of spying for the United States and an organized demonstration at the U.S. legation in Sofia, ostensibly a protest against American involvement in the Congo, were symptomatic of generally cool relations between the United States and Bulgaria, but American firms continued to exhibit at the biennial Plovdiv fair. Closer to home, Bulgaria concluded an agreement with Greece in 1964 which reduced the amount of reparations owed by the former and opened the way for closer links between the two traditionally hostile Balkan neighbors. Relations with Czechoslovakia also improved in the mid-sixties, despite the mutual expulsion of diplomats in July 1966 following U.S. charges that the Czechoslovak embassy had attempted to recruit a spy, and American firms showed an increasing interest in exhibiting at Czech industrial fairs. Indeed, U.S. companies took advantage of the more permissive atmosphere of bridge-building by participating either directly or through their European subsidiaries in a number of East European fairs at Poznań, Plovdiv, and Budapest, as well as at Leipzig in East Germany, where in March 1966 some forty American firms were represented. When that same month the Ulbricht regime submitted an application for membership in the United Nations, Britain, France, and the United States rejected the proposal by maintaining that the German Democratic Republic was not a state. While this opposition was, as before, predetermined by Bonn's attitude toward East Germany, it contrasted strangely with the steady growth in the West's trade with that country, third highest of all trade with the satellites in the case of the United States; the Allies had opted for this admittedly schizophrenic approach, pending a bilateral rapprochement between the two German governments.

In sum, the changes that occurred in East-Central Europe in the mid-sixties could not really be attributed to the largely rhetorical, fractionally implemented policy of bridge-building. The chief recipient of U.S. aid, Poland, moved toward a more orthodox ideological position, while Hungary, despite its strained relations with Washington, acquired the most liberal economic and sociopolitical system in the bloc. The most remarkable development in this period was not the American version of peaceful engagement but rather the mutual rediscovery of East and West Europeans. This peaceful engagement in a strictly European context had the blessing of the United States, but it also reflected the West Europeans' perception that in an age of test bans and mutual deterrence the division of Europe could be attenuated only through a gradual process of continental integration, the progress of which depended on themselves rather than on the policies of a distant superpower with global responsibilities. In forging closer links with the satellites the West Europeans enjoyed numerous advantages over the United States; they were geographically more proximate, shared a common history, had traditional patterns of trade which had been dislocated only as a result of Soviet hegemonic policy, and, last but not least, lacked the domestic opposition that had so effectively impeded the efforts of the Kennedy and Johnson administrations at bridge-building.[133] Furthermore, the anti-American nationalism voiced most openly by President de Gaulle materialized at the very moment when the East European regimes began to exhibit nationalistic tendencies of their own. Already in the fall of 1958 Adenauer and de Gaulle had hinted at a wider all-European federation, and the French president would return time and again to the theme of a *"Europe des patries"* stretching from the Atlantic to the Urals.[134] France subsequently mounted a diplomatic offensive toward the East in pursuit of de Gaulle's strategy of *"détente, entente, et coopération."* The General's visits to Moscow and Warsaw and the travels of Foreign Minister Couve de Murville to East European capitals in the course of 1966 testified to this new orientation and to the underlying hope that the Soviet Union would allow its satellites to become more closely integrated with their Western neighbors. De Gaulle found encouragement in the Warsaw Pact's Bucharest Declaration of 1966, which revived the oft-repeated proposal for a European security conference that would legitimize the *status quo* and replace existing alliances with an all-inclusive security system, but the proposal was once again dropped at the Karlovy Vary conference the following spring. This ambivalence on the part of the Russians was inspired less by de Gaulle's symbolic forays than by the reversal of Germany's long-standing posture of isolation from the East. Having come into office in December 1966, the

Kiesinger-Brandt "Grand Coalition" elaborated on the earlier overtures of Chancellor Erhard and tacitly abandoned the Hallstein Doctrine in favor of a more flexible *Ostpolitik*, which entailed the pursuit of closer diplomatic and economic relations with Germany's traditional sphere of influence in East-Central Europe.[135] The new government admitted that the Munich agreement was null and void (not *ab initio*, as the communists insisted, but because of Hitler's subsequent occupation of Czechoslovakia), ceased to insist on the legitimacy of Germany's prewar frontier with Poland but noted that the matter had to be settled by a peace treaty, offered to upgrade contacts with the East Germans, and implicitly dismissed reunification as a distant and secondary objective. With the exception of Ulbricht and Gomulka, the satellite regimes responded favorably to these overtures, and a rift appeared in the communist bloc between the former—Ulbricht fearing that the resulting détente would lead to his isolation, Gomulka concerned that, if the bogey of German revanchism waned, popular support for his Soviet-supported regime might follow suit[136]—and the latter, which looked upon West Germany as a promising trading partner. In the event, the Rumanians established diplomatic relations with Bonn, but the apprehensive Russians succeeded in dissuading the other regimes from doing likewise.

While governments on both sides of the apparently shaky Iron Curtain debated the merits of *Ostpolitik* and a European security conference, the commercial relations of Eastern and Western Europe continued to develop at a rapid rate and overshadowed the faltering efforts of the Johnson administration to build trade bridges to the satellites. Western Europe's $3 billion of exports to the satellites in 1966 contrasted strikingly with the corresponding figure of $156 million for the United States. Without abandoning its pursuit of more flexible trade legislation, the administration viewed with approval and perhaps a touch of envy the Europeans' appropriation of its own policy. Professor Brzezinski, who served in 1967 as a member of the State Department's Policy Planning Council (PPC), continued to urge that the United States take cognizance of the altered nature of the East European systems. Observing that the satellites were gradually moving from an international revolutionary orientation to a new, "parochial conservative nationalism with a Communist tinge," he argued that "economic multilateral cooperation in the long run runs counter to centralized direction of individual Communist states" and that, if such cooperation were fostered, the satellite societies could evolve into "semi-dictatorships of increasingly Socialistic character (and of less Communist dictatorial kind), including more internal social pluralism." In stressing evolutionary change, Brzezinski differed from earlier policies by rejecting even more categorically the prospect of liberation in the sense of genuine national self-determination: "I am convinced that it would be idle, and probably counterproductive to concentrate on stimulating East European nationalism, or hostility to the Soviet Union. . . . Some East European countries can act as transmission belts by moving ahead of the Soviet Union, but not for the purpose of separating themselves entirely from the Soviet Union, but rather for the purpose of promoting a different kind of East-West relationship."[137] Wider economic cooperation required that the European *status quo* be stabilized even further, and, upon retiring from the PPC in December, Brzezinski made a public plea for direct talks between the two military alliances to end the twenty-year-old confrontation and pave the way for a reconciliation of Europeans East and West.[138] Desperately trying to extract himself from the quicksand of Vietnam and eager to regain some prestige by championing a Soviet-American détente, President Johnson in all likelihood shared these perceptions and expectations. Indeed, as 1967 drew to a close, there was a great deal of optimism in the administration about the ongoing liberalization in East-Central Europe. Perhaps the policy of peaceful engagement, even if implemented by proxy by America's allies, would bring to the satellite peoples the degree of freedom they and anyone else might hope for in a world of superpowers.

DÉTENTE AND THE BREZHNEV DOCTRINE

As the Johnson administration moved into its final year, the prospects for détente and peaceful change in East-Central Europe appeared to be ascending. Agreement on a nonproliferation treaty seemed assured, and feelers were sent out for talks on the limitation of strategic armaments. Meanwhile, the progress of Bonn's *Ostpolitik* and the apparent stability of the European *status quo* gave rise to the view in certain parts of Congress that the moment had come to reduce America's military commitment to NATO. With the growing unpopularity of the war in Vietnam, opposition to trade with the communist bloc also appeared to be wavering, and the administration prepared to reintroduce its East-West Trade Relations bill. In East-Central Europe, the winds of liberalization were blowing unevenly but stronger than at any time since the 1956 upheavals. The Kádár regime's New Economic Mechanism, which embodied certain aspects of a market economy, went into operation on January 1, 1968; the regime had for some years been relaxing its restrictions on travel and freedom of expression, while in the external field it had been accelerating its drive for more trade with the West and had even toyed with the idea of greater regional cooperation in the Danubian Basin, including Austria and Yugoslavia, all without reducing its dutiful support for Soviet foreign policy. The Rumanians were persisting in their independent stance in external

relations and economic and trade policy, while the Bulgarians were continuing their drift toward closer relations with Greece and, in 1968, with
Turkey. At the Karlovy Vary conference in the spring of 1967, all the
satellites had agreed (in the notable absence of Rumania) to withhold
recognition from Bonn, pending an alteration in West Germany's policy
regarding the Pankow regime, but the agreement reflected only Gomulka's
and Ulbricht's apprehensions, for the others had seemed eager to respond
at least to Bonn's economic overtures.

In Czechoslovakia, however, long one of the most docile satellites, the
forces of reform would rise to the surface in most dramatic fashion and
threaten the incipient détente.[139] Under the guidance of Antonin
Novotný, who held both the office of president and the post of first
secretary, the country's economy had undergone such a disastrous decline
that by 1967 the regime was compelled to initiate open discussions of
alternative methods of planning and management. In the intellectual
sphere a certain relaxation had taken place in the mid-sixties, but resistance to the official pro-Arab line in the wake of the six-day Arab-Israeli
war led to the closing of the Writers' Union magazine in 1967. Meanwhile,
Novotný's anti-Slovak policies were arousing opposition within the
Slovakian party. These varied sources of elite and popular dissatisfaction
gradually coalesced into an anti-Novotný movement, which gathered such
momentum that in December 1967 Brezhnev was forced to visit Prague to
look into the question of succession. Concerned about the effects of Bonn's
Ostpolitik and with the need to consolidate the Warsaw Pact's "northern
tier" of Poland, East Germany, and Czechoslovakia, the Russians saw no
need to cling to a satrap who in any case defied the new orthodoxy of
collective leadership; on January 5 Novotný was replaced as first secretary
by a veteran communist who had held the same post in the Slovakian
party, Alexander Dubček. The latter's appointment immeasurably
strengthened the hand of the reformers in the party, whose efforts were in
turn welcomed and encouraged with growing enthusiasm by the mass
public. Dubček and his like-minded colleagues proceeded to remove a
number of Novotný supporters from high office, and, when in February a
certain General Sejna defected to the United States and the news spread
that he had plotted to intervene with force on behalf of Novotný prior to
the latter's demotion, the clamor for an investigation led to further dismis-
sals and to Novotný's own resignation on March 22. Meeting between
March 28 and April 5, the Central Committee proceeded to expel
Novotný and his supporters from the Party Presidium and to compose a
radical manifesto known as the "Action Program."[140] The program aimed
at the creation of what Dubček called "socialism with a human face"; it
involved a policy of democratization which stressed socialist legality (in-

cluding the rehabilitation of victims of the Stalinist period), a federal structure more responsive to the needs of the Slovaks, and a broader application of the New Economic Model, tentatively introduced under Novotný, so as to decentralize and secularize economic management, revive the profit motive, and modernize industry to make its products once again competitive on the international market. While affirming Czechoslovakia's undying loyalty to the socialist bloc, the Action Program indicated the need to seek credits from, and expand trade with, all interested countries, including those in the West; in the domestic political sphere, the document cautiously emphasized the leading role of the party, but implied the possibility of greater pluralism under the umbrella of the communist-dominated National Front.

Viewed in the light of concurrent trends in Hungary and Rumania, the reforms advocated in the Action Program were far from revolutionary, but they manifestly intensified the apprehensions of the conservative regimes in East Germany and Poland. In March, Gomulka had resorted to the police and workers' brigades to quell student demonstrations in Warsaw and Kraków. The unrest among students and intellectuals had been exacerbated by the curtailment in January of the performance of a classical play with anti-Russian overtones, but Gomulka's forceful reaction was aimed principally at repelling certain threatening factions within the party (notably, that of the conservative-nationalist minister of the interior, General Moczar); above all, the Polish leader feared the spread of the spirit of democratization that prevailed in Prague. As the most dogmatic and internationally, if not domestically, insecure of all satellite leaders, Ulbricht similarly abhorred the individual freedoms envisaged by the Action Program, but his chronic worry was that the other satellites might take the bait of Bonn's *Ostpolitik* without waiting for Western recognition of his regime's legitimacy and thereby leave East Germany an isolated anachronism. The disapprobation of these two neighbors of Dubček became more hysterical as the months went by, but the decisive judgment on his policy of "humane socialism" had to come from the Kremlin, and there the confluence of forces did not appear to favor such experimentation in the early months of 1968. When the CPSU's Central Committee met in plenary session in March, the hard-liners reportedly criticized Kosygin's economic policies and their potential political consequences and complained that the Soviet Union's flirtation with détente had produced a rift with China and Albania, allowed setbacks over Cuba and in the Middle East, and invited the West's, particularly West Germany's, bridge-building offensive.[141] Subjected to these domestic and satellite pressures, the Soviet leadership became even more concerned after the publication of the Action Program and after receiving news of the tentative consultations between Czechoslovakia and West Germany over the possible granting of private credits; Czech Foreign Minister Hajek stressed that there was no question of diplomatic recognition, but even the hint of a Bonn-Prague rapprochement was enough to arouse feelings of insecurity in the Kremlin and in Pankow.

From the beginning of May, a rash of bilateral and multilateral conferences took place in the communist bloc, with the roles of the individual actors being fairly well defined: Gomulka and Ulbricht recommended the curtailment of the Czechoslovak experiment; Kádár attempted to act as a moderate intermediary (Ceausescu was sympathetic but was ignored by Moscow); and Dubček and his associates persevered in their reforms while reassuring the Russians of their loyalty and fundamental orthodoxy. The Dubček regime had to agree to the holding of Warsaw Pact exercises in Czechoslovakia in June, but it remained reasonably confident of its freedom to democratize on the basis of the Action Program. Said Joseph Smrkovsky, president of the National Assembly, in May: "We must understand the fears of the Soviet Union, which has in mind not only Czechoslovakia but the security of the whole socialist camp. Even so, the Soviet comrades have declared that they do not want to, and will not, interfere in Czechoslovakia's internal affairs."[142] In Prague, the Central Committee met to schedule an Extraordinary Congress of the party for September 9 and to set up study groups to prepare a new federal constitution and consider a variety of alternatives for political and economic reform. On June 20, as the Warsaw Pact forces were beginning their military exercises, the government announced the abolition of advance censorship, and a week later newspapers published the famous "Two Thousand Words" manifesto, issued by a group of leading intellectuals, which urged a more rapid pace of democratization and recommended firm and, if necessary, armed resistance to foreign interference. The atmosphere now became even more threatening to the reformers as Soviet troops lingered on while the Soviet, Polish, and East German presses attacked the manifesto. Party leaders from Moscow, Sofia, Warsaw, Budapest, and Pankow met in the Polish capital on July 15 (the Czechoslovaks having declined to appear before what amounted to a tribunal), and sent a letter to Prague voicing deep disturbance over counter-revolutionary manifestations and the weakening of the party's leading role and demanding that remedial measures be taken.[143] The increasingly apprehensive reformers in Prague requested bilateral negotiations and finally met the full Soviet Politburo at Cierna-nad-Tisou in eastern Slovakia on July 29. This turned out to be a climactic confrontation, with the most violent denunciations reportedly coming from Ukrainian party head Piotr Shelest, who was concerned about the impact of Czech radio reports on the democratization program among his already restive constituents. The reformers stood firm, and the Cierna meeting produced an agreement to end all public attacks by either side; five days later the Warsaw five met with the Czechoslovaks at Bratislava to ratify the Cierna accord. Displays of grudging harmony could not, however, overcome the progressive polarization of the two sides. The two communist outsiders, Tito and Ceausescu, were greeted effusively when they visited Prague early in August, while Ulbricht made an abortive and unhappy visit to Karlovy Vary. On August 10 new party statutes were published allowing for secret voting and the tolerance of factions, and a few days later the old Social Democratic party began to reorganize. Dubček and his liberal colleagues were riding on an unprecedented ground swell of popular support.

It is not yet clear what prompted the final act of intervention by the Warsaw five or to what extent the Cierna and Bratislava agreements had represented a genuine disposition to compromise.[144] A military build-up in Western Russia and the Ukraine had been going on for more than a month in preparation for such an eventuality, and all that the potential invaders now lacked was the pretence of legality which Kádár had provided in 1956. The Soviet Central Committee met in emergency session on August 19, and Brezhnev dispatched a letter to Dubček accusing him of reneging on their earlier agreements. The Russians apparently expected that Dubček would read the letter to his party's Presidium meeting on the evening of August 20, whereupon one of the remaining Czech hard-liners, perhaps Alois Indra, would propose new measures and invite foreign support. In the event, Indra's resolution was rejected by the Presidium and Soviet Ambassador Chervonenko waited in vain (along with the presses of the Warsaw five) for the gratuitous invitation.[145] That night some 600,000 troops from the five countries occupied Czechoslovakia and the Presidium issued a terse statement warning the population not to resist and declaring that the invasion was "contrary not only to the fundamental principles of relations between socialist states but also . . . a denial of fundamental norms of international law."[146] The subsequent ill-fated attempts of President Svoboda and the other reformers to salvage something of their program and freedom of action lie beyond the scope of this study. They and the people of Czechoslovakia demonstrated exemplary unity and resourcefulness in facing up to the intimidation of their supposed allies, and the appointment of the relatively moderate Gustav Husak to replace Dubček, as well as the absence of mass arrests such as those which followed the Hungarian revolution, allowed for some momentary optimism in the immediate aftermath of the invasion; despite mass passive resistance, however, the promised reforms of that euphoric Prague spring were destined to disappear without a trace.

As in the case of earlier disturbances in the satellites, the Soviet Union tried to implicate the West, and the news agency *Tass* announced on August 21 that the Warsaw Pact intervention had been requested by unnamed party and government leaders to counter the "threat emanating from the counter-revolutionary forces which have entered into a collusion with foreign forces hostile to socialism." Two months earlier, an alarmist East German press had reported the presence of American tanks in Prague, but these turned out to be props for a film being shot in the capital. On July 19 *Pravda* reported the discovery of U.S.-made arms and a secret U.S. Army document on cooperation with East European insurgent elements near Karlovy Vary, which led Secretary of State Rusk to issue a formal protest against such allegations of complicity. Following the invasion, the Soviet-sponsored Radio Vltava would charge that counter-revolutionaries had been trained by U.S. Special Forces and abetted by the CIA. While it is conceivable that a few Czechoslovaks might have returned from the West to join the reform movement, there is no objective evidence of any systematic Western effort at subversion; even Radio Free Europe had lost much of its audience after the liberation of the Czechoslovak mass media from complete party control. Indeed, such allegations of Western interference were intended primarily for domestic consumption. Determined to avoid their mistake of 1956 and to share the inevitable opprobrium by moving in with their allies, the Russians were compelled by the peaceful nature of the reform movement to revive the convenient specter of imperialist aggression and thereby justify the mobilization of the Warsaw Pact. Even so, the main butt of communist attacks would be Bonn, not Washington, partly because the Russians perceived that the *Ostpolitik* was proving far more effective than Johnson's bridge-building in drawing the economically beleaguered satellite regimes' eyes westward, and partly because they hoped to isolate the crisis in Czechoslovakia from the ongoing efforts to achieve détente with the United States.

In the eyes of the Johnson administration, the invasion of Czechoslovakia could not have come at a worse time, for it not only cast a pall over the whole policy of peaceful engagement but also blocked the president's path to a summit conference. As the reform movement in Prague gathered steam in the early months of 1968, Washington exhibited a caution that bordered on paralysis. The State Department's only official comment, issued on May 1, was that the administration was "watching with interest and sympathy recent developments in Czechoslovakia, which seem to represent the wishes and needs of the Czechoslovak people. We hope that these developments will lead to an improvement of relations between Eastern and Western Europe and between Czechoslovakia and the United States."[147] At the same time, the State Department invited the Prague regime to reopen negotiations on the questions of Czechoslovak gold and American claims. The return of $20 million in gold bullion, in U.S. safe-keeping since the war, had been made contingent upon compensation for nationalized American property, and a tentative agreement reached in 1961 had subsequently been rejected in Washington when it appeared that the Czechoslovak offer (of $2 million, against a total U.S. claim of $110 million) would not be acceptable either to private and corporate claimants or to Congress; the new overture asked for a reply to an American proposal made in November 1967. Within a week U.S. Ambassador Jacob D. Beam called on Foreign Minister Hajek to reopen talks on these and commercial matters; the Czechoslovaks' most pressing need, however, was for credits to revive their faltering economy, and the administration, mindful of congressional resistance, had to advise them that it was not prepared "at present" to accede to their request for a $500 million loan.[148] The most that Washington could do was to relax export licensing procedures in the Department of Commerce and to release to residents of Czechoslovakia some $5 million in previously blocked social security and other retirement benefits.[149] Certain members of Congress did try to respond to the changed situation in Prague. Congressman Paul Findley (Rep., Ill.) introduced an amendment to the Foreign Assistance Act which would enable the president to grant most-favored-nation treatment to countries that became members of GATT (of which Czechoslovakia was in fact a founding member), while, in the Senate, Walter Mondale (Dem., Minn.) introduced a Czechoslovak trade bill and with thirteen other senators sponsored a joint resolution to modify the Export-Import Bank's financing restrictions and the regulations of the Export Control Act. But the legislative process was far too ponderous and congressional resistance to bridge-building was too deeply entrenched to allow for swift reaction to the Dubček experiment. When Senator Claiborne Pell (Dem., R.I.) returned from a visit to Prague with the suggestion that President Johnson name a high-level federal mediator to break the deadlock in the financial negotiations, State Department sources commented sourly that Pell should exert his pressure on Capitol Hill instead.[150]

The administration was inhibited from responding more vigorously to requests for credits and other economic concessions not only by domestic political constraints but also by a well-founded fear that any American initiative would harm the Dubček regime's chances of survival. The old problem of assuring East European reformers of American sympathy and support without strengthening the proponents of repression in the Kremlin remained as insoluble as ever, and the Johnson administration opted for what was perhaps the easiest alternative, to defer vocal and material encouragement until the reform movement had managed to consolidate itself; while this passive attitude alienated many Czechoslovaks who hoped for some sympathetic gesture, it in no way weakened popular support for the Dubček regime. Furthermore, American policy makers had been lulled by their own strategy of peaceful engagement into an optimistic frame of mind and were rather too ready to discount the likelihood of Soviet intervention.[151] Their anticipation of détente carried with it the assumption that the Soviet leadership felt secure enough in Europe to allow a degree of diversity in its satellites, and experts in Washington calculated that the national particularism exhibited by the Czechoslovak reformers did not clash with the irreducible interests of the Kremlin. As the pace of democratization quickened, the rumblings in Moscow, Warsaw, and Pankow became increasingly ominous, but the Johnson administration gave no public sign of its concern. At his press conference on July 30, Secretary of State Rusk revealed that he had made an oral representation to Soviet Ambassador Anatoli Dobrynin regarding Czechoslovakia but declined to elaborate, in view of the ongoing negotiations at Cierna.[152] According to East European sources, Rusk had told Dobrynin that Washington would strongly deplore the use of force to impose alternative policies on the Prague regime, but had left the ambassador with the impression that the United States would not intervene militarily on behalf of Czechoslovakia. Whatever the tenor of Rusk's remarks, however, the Russians needed little reassurance on that score, and shortly after the secretary's press conference U.S. Ambassador Llewellyn Thompson reported from Moscow that Soviet military preparations pointed to a high probability of invasion. In his memoirs President Johnson notes that the Czechs themselves had indicated they would offer no military resistance nor welcome Western offers of assistance, and he concludes, "We could only try to avoid any action that would further inflame the situation."[153]

The posture of subdued optimism adopted by official Washington in the weeks preceding the invasion was influenced by concurrent negotiations that took priority over the problems and prospects of East-Central Europe. Earlier in the year President Johnson had intimated to the Russians that the time might be opportune to reaffirm their mutual desire for détente; he was inspired to suggest a summit meeting not only by the intrinsic merits of détente but also by the need to refurbish a domestic image badly tarnished by the Vietnam war and to enhance the Democratic party's chances in the upcoming election. Such a meeting was all the more timely because there were rumblings of discontent in Congress over the costs of maintaining America's substantial military commitment to NATO. Senator Mansfield had launched a campaign to reduce the size of the U.S. contingent in Europe, and NATO meetings in May and June had produced recommendations for the initiation of negotiations over mutual and balanced force reductions by the two alliances.[154] Therefore, when on August 19 Ambassador Dobrynin delivered Kosygin's invitation to a summit conference in Moscow in October, Johnson promptly grasped the opportunity to become the second American president (after Roosevelt) to visit the Soviet Union. The meeting and the initiation of talks on the limitation of strategic weapons were to be announced simultaneously in Washington and Moscow, the White House press corps being notified of an important briefing to be held at 9:30 A.M. on August 21. It remains an open question whether the Soviet leaders had so overestimated Johnson's determination to achieve a spectacular and personally prestigious breakthrough in East-West relations that they genuinely expected him to persevere regardless of what happened to Czechoslovakia.

In the event, when shortly after 8:00 P.M. on August 20 Dobrynin presented himself at the White House to advise the president that the "rendering of direct assistance" to Czechoslovakia was under way, the latter had already guessed the purpose of his visit. The Soviet message insisted that the "current events should not harm Soviet-American relations," and concurrently the Kremlin's envoys made similar *démarches* in other Western capitals to assure the powers that the intervention in Czechoslovakia was purely a family affair within the socialist camp and should not be interpreted as a hostile act.[155] Secretary of State Rusk was testifying before the Democratic Platform Committee when its chairman, Congressman Hale Boggs, interrupted the proceedings to read a message giving news of the invasion. Observing that he ought to see what it was all about, the secretary repaired to the White House, where President Johnson had convened the National Security Council in emergency session.[156] Rusk was instructed to call Dobrynin and to advise him that the imminent announcement of the summit meeting would not be made, but otherwise it was a foregone conclusion that the administration would do no more than express displeasure and unofficially proclaim a brief period of mourning for the failure of the latest East European attempt at national self-determination. "The tragic news from Czechoslovakia shocks the conscience of the world," declared the president in a radio-television address on August 21. "The excuses offered by the Soviet Union are patently contrived. . . . The action of the Warsaw Pact allies is in flat violation of the United Nations Charter. We are consulting urgently with others to consider what steps should be taken in the United Nations. . . . Meanwhile, in the name of mankind's hope for peace, I call on the Soviet Union and its associates to withdraw their troops from Czechoslovakia. . . . It is never too late for reason to prevail."[157]

The Western Allies had deliberately adopted a low profile regarding the Czechoslovak gambit in order to avoid giving the Russians a pretext for intervention, and the swiftness and efficiency of the operation came as an unpleasant surprise to NATO headquarters.[158] The West thereupon imposed a moratorium on further bridge-building initiatives and resorted to the UN Security Council to voice its disapprobation. The request for a Council meeting was signed by Canada, Denmark, France, Paraguay, the United Kingdom, and the United States, and then, by a vote of 13 to 2, the Soviet Union and Hungary were overruled and the Council took up the issue of Czechoslovakia late in the night of August 21. U.S. delegate George Ball drew attention to the grim parallel between Budapest in 1956 and Prague in 1968, asking rhetorically, "who among us has not hoped against hope that these 12 years had worked a change for the better in the minds of the Soviet leadership?" For his part, the French delegate felt compelled to voice the Gaullist view that the invasion was a consequence of the "policy of blocs which unfortunately had been imposed on Europe by the Yalta agreements." Predictably, Soviet Ambassador Jakob Malik castigated the United States for its imperialistic activities in Vietnam and read to the Security Council an appeal for assistance which had originated with an anonymous Czechoslovak group. The following day the United States and six other members introduced a draft resolution which affirmed the sovereign political independence and territorial integrity of Czechoslovakia, condemned the intervention and called upon its perpetrators to withdraw, requested members of the United Nations "to exercise their diplomatic influence" to achieve this, and instructed the secretary-general to investigate and report on the implementation of the resolution. Meanwhile, the permanent mission of Czechoslovakia to the United Nations had advised the Security Council of President Svoboda's qualification of the intervention as illegal and had appealed for world support. At 4:00 A.M. on the twenty-third Malik vetoed the resolution, then dismissed a new proposal by the Canadian delegate that the secretary-general send a special representative to Prague to assure the safety of Czechoslovakia's leaders as a "new trick of the NATO countries in this dirty, shoddy business." Foreign Minister Hajek addressed the Council on the twenty-fourth, denying charges that socialism in his country had been threatened by outside or counter-revolutionary forces, but he and his colleagues understood that these deliberations would not help their case at the on-going negotiations in Moscow, and three days later they requested that the Czechoslovak item be withdrawn from the Security Council's agenda. Having recorded their displeasure, the Western powers willingly agreed to postpone further consideration of the matter, pending clarification of the Soviet-Czech talks; the precedent of Hungary loomed large in their minds and discouraged any quest for further UN action.[159] Queried in November about the prospects of the issue being revived, the U.S. representative to the United Nations allowed that "circumstances have not recommended themselves yet to convince the powers who are unhappy about it to think the General Assembly could successfully take cognizance of it, as a practical matter."[160] Secretary-General U Thant had issued a statement on August 21 deploring the effect of the invasion on international morality, but he never carried through a tentative plan to visit Prague, and by September he had reverted to his peculiar double standard by criticizing the American bombing of North Vietnam while referring cryptically to the "contractual obligations" of the Warsaw Pact countries.

The perfunctoriness of the West's expressions of sympathy may have offended the average Czechoslovak, but his leaders understood the constraints of the bipolar system as well as the Russians—to their advantage—and the Americans. Secretary of State Rusk noted at a press conference on August 22 that the Prague regime had "made clear to us both in Washington and New York City and by its own broadcasts what its own view of this situation is. They have not asked us for any specific action or steps as far as we are concerned."[161] While the West's reaction to the invasion had a flair of capitulation, it only reflected the absence of reasonable alternatives. The placing of U.S. forces in Germany on alert, or, as George Kennan later suggested, the expedition of 100,000 additional troops to West Germany with the understanding that they would not be withdrawn until the Warsaw Pact forces had evacuated Czechoslovakia, would have increased tensions in Europe without deflecting the Russians from their chosen path; neither ringing declarations of concern nor proposals for some European security conference could have altered the Soviet Union's determination to preserve its direct influence over Czechoslovakia.[162] Washington's impotence nevertheless led to the revival of the hoary accusations of Soviet-American complicity in the division of Europe. The most prestigious proponent of this conspiratorial thesis was President de Gaulle, who was obviously miffed at the failure of his Eastern policy and found it convenient to blame the participants in a wartime conference from which he had been ignominiously excluded.[163] (Among the more fantastic rumors circulating in France at the time of the invasion was that of a secret Moscow-Washington deal whereby the Soviet Union would instruct the French Communist party to assist de Gaulle by staying aloof from the May disturbances in exchange for American noninterference in Czechoslovakia.) Secretary of State Rusk felt compelled to acknowledge the allegations that "there must have been some 'spheres of influence' agreement between us, that perhaps there was 'an arrangement' made at the Yalta Conference, that perhaps the Soviets acted in Czechoslovakia with some 'carte blanche' from the United States, that we concurred or connived in that aggression," but to deny that the U.S. had entered into any such agreements. On the other hand, Rusk observed, "we recognize the reality of the Soviet military position and the existence of the Warsaw Pact. President Johnson, like President Eisenhower, recognized that there was little we could do, through the use of military force, to assist any of those countries without automatically engaging in general war with the Soviet Union." He went on: "Nor did we in any way indicate that we would ignore an invasion of Czechoslovakia by the Soviet and other Warsaw Pact forces. On the contrary, ahead of time, through Soviet Ambassador Dobrynin, I strongly protested the Soviet charges of 'complicity' by the United States in any endeavor to overthrow socialism in Czechoslovakia. For it seemed to be a charge that could be used as a pretext for a military move against that country." The secretary also dismissed the suggestion that perhaps the Vietnam war impeded U.S. action over Czechoslovakia, noting that since no one suggested open war over that country this could not be a military argument, whereas in purely political terms the United States was seeking freedom equally in Vietnam and in East-Central Europe.[164]

The Johnson administration was nevertheless sensitive to accusations that it had not done all in its power to deter the Russians from invading Czechoslovakia, and it would try to repair the damage in subsequent months. The Tito and Ceausescu regimes had not minced words in denouncing the invasion (which led commentators to draw a parallel with the prewar Little Entente), and there was some apprehensive speculation that the Soviet leaders might decide to use force to repress their heresy as well. When, in the last week of August, intelligence reports reached Washington indicating that Soviet troops were massing on Rumania's borders, President Johnson issued a public warning against anyone unleashing the dogs of war.[165] Then on September 26 an article appeared in *Pravda* arguing in defense of the Warsaw Pact's right of collective intervention that the sovereignty of each socialist country cannot be opposed to the interests of the socialist camp and of the world revolutionary movement; the so-called Brezhnev Doctrine of a socialist commonwealth was restated authoritatively by Foreign Minister Andrei Gromyko before the U.N. General Assembly on October 3. The threatening implications of this doctrine did not escape President Tito, who proceeded to alert his military forces against a possible attack, while Washington dispatched Undersecretary of State Katzenbach to Belgrade to offer at least moral support. The nature of potential Western assistance was never specified, but the North Atlantic Council warned the Soviet Union in November that further interventions would create an international crisis with grave consequences. As Secretary of State Rusk said in an interview on December 1: "I don't have the impression that the Soviet Union is seeking a major confrontation, but what they are asking us to accept is that in this 'Socialist commonwealth' the Soviet Union has the right to use its armed forces to determine what happens inside independent countries, and that is very difficult for the rest of us to accept." Queried about reports that at the NATO conference in November he had privately argued that Soviet intervention in Rumania, Yugoslavia, or Austria should be interpreted as a threat to the West, Rusk responded with some annoyance by drawing a distinction between an expansion of NATO's commitments and "recognition of the fact that things that happen in Central Europe and in the Mediterranean, for example, can directly involve the security interests of NATO." In terms of the proposed SALT talks, he added that an invasion of Rumania would be "perhaps an even more serious setback" than the occupation of Czechoslovakia.[166] Whether the Soviet leaders were deterred by such ambiguous warnings or by other considerations is not clear, but, in the event, the threat of further interventions in East-Central Europe gradually receded. At Budapest in October a preparatory committee announced the postponement of the world summit conference of communist parties, which the Russians had long sought in order to reassert their ideological primacy in the face of Chinese attacks; instead the Soviet Union directed its efforts toward the reorganization and strengthening of the Warsaw Pact's northern tier and toward the extension of its military presence in the Mediterranean.

While the Kremlin was trying to divert attention from the Czechoslovak affair by making aggressive noises in other directions, the Western allies proceeded to appraise the invasion's significance in terms of the European *status quo*. That *status quo* had been altered, noted the State Department, by the presence of Soviet forces in a country which had been free of foreign troops since the end of World War II;[167] in the Moscow agreements of August 27 the Czechoslovaks had reluctantly sanctioned the stationing of Soviet units on the West German border. Meanwhile, the Russians were busily propagating the myth that the invasion had been necessitated by the "perfidious plans of NATO warmongering circles" and that according to these plans West Germany was to be the "striking force of world imperialism in the attack on the position of the socialist world."[168] Already in July the Kremlin had denounced Bonn's *Ostpolitik* and its positive stand on the mutual renunciation of the use or threat of force. When the Soviet Union subsequently claimed the residual right to intervene in West Germany's political affairs under Articles 53 and 107 of the UN Charter ("against renewal of aggressive policy by a former enemy state"), the United States declared on September 17 that such intervention would be met by "immediate allied response."[169] It is conceivable that the Russians had been worried all along about the prospect that, as the United States reduced its military presence in Europe, the *Bundeswehr* would be redeployed along a weakly defended Czechoslovak border, but it soon became clear that, once the military defense of the northern tier was consolidated and the Czechoslovak situation normalized, Moscow would abandon its tactical threats against Bonn and revert to its more long-run strategy of trying to weaken NATO. One immediate effect of the invasion was to still congressional voices urging U.S. withdrawal; as Secretary of Defense Clark Clifford remarked in September, the events in East-Central Europe had "demonstrated that a significant American military presence in Western Europe is still needed."[170]

Although the Czechoslovak affair prompted both sides to reappraise their collective defense strategies, the reassertion of Soviet influence in that country did not fundamentally alter the developing East-West consensus in favor of détente. Indeed, Washington's commiseration with the unfortunate Dubček was at least privately tempered by regret at his failure to pacify the apprehensive Russians; the invasion and the public revulsion it occasioned in the West dashed Johnson's hopes for a summit conference, for Soviet assistance in securing a negotiated peace in Vietnam, for early ratification of the nonproliferation treaty, and for talks on the limitation of strategic armaments. These goals, rather than any political alteration in the European *status quo*, were what the administration meant by détente; the East Europeans, in Washington's view, should rest content with whatever rate of liberalization was tolerable to the Soviet Union. One day after the invasion, the administration's senior consultant on Soviet and satellite affairs, Professor Brzezinski, recommended that the West's outrage ought not to detract from its long-term policy of building bridges, and even claimed somewhat ambiguously that "it was the success of this policy that forced the Soviet Union into this criminal act."[171] But the rationale of bridge-building was inevitably weakened by renewed evidence that the Kremlin would not shrink from using force to curtail liberalization; as Katzenbach told the Assembly of the Western European Union in Paris on October 15: "We must not make the mistake of looking on the Czech adventure as an 'aberration' in Soviet policy. Rather, it was true to type."[172] Recognizing that there was no realistic alternative to the pursuit of détente, the administration opted for the briefest possible period of mourning, complete with denunciations of the Brezhnev Doctrine and of Soviet brutality, before reverting to its earlier course. Reflecting on the Senate's decision to delay giving its consent to the nonproliferation treaty, Secretary of State Rusk argued that a "major interruption to East-West relations is a price which the Soviets cannot feel is in their interests in the long run" and noted that he was "very sorry indeed to see a development like Czechoslovakia that would create an atmosphere in which the Nonproliferation Treaty gets into trouble."[173] Such pragmatic perspectives did not, however, entirely allay suspicions that President Johnson's unseemly haste to reopen negotiations on a summit were motivated more by partisan politics than by some noble vision of reconciliation between East and West.[174]

Although the American public reacted in righteous horror to the invasion, it did so without the guiltful soul-searching that had followed the repression of the Hungarian revolution, and this moderation testified at least to the greater realism of the policies pursued by the various administrations in the intervening years. The effect of Czechoslovakia on the U.S. presidential race of 1968 is rather more difficult to ascertain, for none of the candidates—for nomination or for election—chose to make an issue of American policy toward the satellites. Senator Eugene McCarthy's offhand remark that the invasion was "not a major crisis" might have been factually accurate, but it was also a model of tactlessness and political insensitivity and doubtless hurt the image of the Democratic "peace group"; conversely, Czechoslovakia strengthened the position of the more hard-line supporters of Vice-President Humphrey on the Platform Committee.[175] It is nevertheless questionable whether either Humphrey's nomination at the convention that opened in Chicago five days after the invasion or his subsequent defeat at the hands of Richard Nixon was significantly affected by developments in the Soviet bloc. The publicists on Nixon's team were delighted by this fortuitous demonstration of their candidate's thesis that the Russians had not really mellowed with the years. One of them, Frank Shakespeare, later appointed by Nixon to head the USIA, exulted on the morning of the invasion: "What a break! This Czech thing is just perfect. It puts the soft-liners in a hell of a box!" He then proceeded to cut Nixon's acceptance speech reference to "the era of negotiation" from the Republicans' latest television commercial.[176] In Vice-President Humphrey's estimation the invasion and the postponement of Johnson's summit meeting with Premier Kosygin definitely damaged his prospects: "When I heard the news of the invasion, it immediately dawned on me that the whole political atmosphere of the campaign had become more turbulent and more difficult—for me and for the Democratic party."[177] The Czechoslovak episode did not inspire debate on satellite policy, however, and the two presidential aspirants differed only marginally in their proposed policies toward the Soviet Union; Nixon would advocate rhetorically a shift from the era of confrontations to the era of negotiations, while Humphrey would similarly urge a shift from policies of confrontation and containment to policies of reconciliation and peaceful engagement. In view of the narrowness of Nixon's victory, it is nevertheless conceivable that a successful summit and top-level disarmament negotiations might have altered the outcome of the campaign.

The prospects of bridge-building appeared to be favorable until the Czechoslovak setback. In his economic report in February, President Johnson had once again asked Congress for authority to expand trade with East-Central Europe,[178] and administration officials returned to the attack in various congressional committee hearings. Deputy Undersecretary of State for Political Affairs Charles E. Bohlen told the House Subcommittee on Europe that it was in the interests of the United States to stimulate by trade a diversification in the economic life of the satellites which in turn would "weaken the overall control, the monolithic control, of the Communist Party over all phases of national life"; he would argue further that trade in peaceful goods was not related to satellite aid for the North Vietnamese.[179] Sponsored by Senator Mondale *et al.*, a joint resolution favoring trade in peaceful goods with the East Europeans led to hearings before the Banking and Currency Committee's Subcommittee on International Finance. After outlining the more liberal trade policies of other noncommunist countries, Philip H. Trezise, U.S. representative to the Organization for Economic Cooperation and Development (OECD), told the same subcommittee that the United States was "virtually a nonparticipant" in trade with Eastern Europe (accounting for about 16 per cent of the world's exports but only three-tenths of 1 per cent of the exports to Eastern Europe) and noted that "our national policy is hampered by public misconceptions about East-West trade."[180] Satellite aid to Vietnam continued to be a major psychological stumbling block, and right-wing pressure groups carried on their campaigns (the John Birch Society gathered more than 1,500,000 signatures to a petition against aid and trade with the communists,)[181] but the progress of liberalization in Czechoslovakia in the early months of 1968 helped the case for bridge-building, as did President Johnson's initiatives for détente. Meanwhile, the East Europeans continued to press for credits and tariff concessions (a Bulgarian trade mission visited the United States in May) while taking advantage of the relaxation of export controls;[182] in a barter arrangement early in 1968, Hungary agreed to supply industrial explosives and canned foodstuffs in exchange for technical assistance and ingredients from the Coca Cola Company. Then, with the Warsaw Pact invasion of Czechoslovakia, efforts at building commercial bridges to the East were again hindered. "We would not expect," said Secretary of State Rusk in a masterly understatement on August 22, "that the East-West trade suggestions put forward by the President would be acted upon promptly by

Congress."[183] The Rumanians were rewarded for their denunciation of the invasion by new agreements on cultural and other exchanges, but similar initiatives with the other satellites were postponed. In September the United States canceled the projected visit of a college band to the Soviet Union and participation in the Plovdiv trade fair, but it pointedly advised Czechoslovakia that it would participate in the Brno fair.[184] Such symbolic discrimination was a far cry from the earlier promises of bridge-building.

If the invasion of Czechoslovakia did not represent a major international crisis and did not increase the risk of East-West conflict, it did necessitate a reappraisal of the basic premises of détente. Washington's bridge-building, Bonn's *Ostpolitik*, and de Gaulle's vision of an independent Europe from the Atlantic to the Urals were predicated on the assumption of an irreversible process of domestic liberalization in the Soviet bloc; détente, then, would involve a Soviet-American stabilization of the international system to prevent war and allow for evolutionary change. The Soviet Union, however, demonstrated that it would act without any pretense of legality to curtail internal change in a satellite even when the latter did not threaten to secede as Hungary had done in 1956. When at the second Moscow meeting the Czechs referred to the sympathetic statements of some Western Communist parties, Brezhnev reportedly retorted: "They have gone over to reformism. We are not interested in what they say. There is no hope of revolution in the West. We must consolidate the Socialist Commonwealth."[185] This rigid posture of retrenchment ruled out any hope of liberalization and convergence through détente and of the ultimate liberation of the East Europeans from Soviet suzerainty, but it did not deter the Western powers from seeking to stabilize the arms race and normalizing East-West relations. France condemned the invasion, but as Foreign Minister Michel Debré observed, "a car crash on a road is no reason for banning traffic on that road."[186] Secretary of State Rusk advised the Kremlin that the road to détente was the road of the UN Charter, but no one seriously proposed to make détente conditional on an even partial liberation of East-Central Europe. For their part, the Russians strove to persuade the West that domestic squabbles within their sphere should in no way obstruct the road to peaceful coexistence.[187]

President Johnson waited until November before reviving his proposal for a summit, but by then the Russians had shifted their focus to his putative successor, and the latter was apparently cool to the idea. Then, in his last State of the Union message, Johnson noted the postponement of SALT as a consequence of the Czechoslovak invasion.[188] The promise of evolutionary liberation implicit in the policies pursued by the various administrations since 1956 rang hollow after the invasion, but, though the bridge-building strategy was momentarily discredited, no one, including the Nixon administration, could devise a meaningful alternative capable of challenging the reality of Soviet power and rule in East-Central Europe.

VII
SPHERES
AND INFLUENCE

The history of East-Central Europe is marked by the flux and reflux of great empires on its periphery. Situated at the crossroads of the Continent, economically weak, divided by ethnic and historical rivalries, the East Europeans time and again fell prey to the dynastic ambitions of Habsburgs, Hohenzollerns, and Romanovs, as well as to the expansionary drive of the Sublime Porte. For much of the nineteenth century the Concert of Europe managed to preserve a stable balance of power and to overcome both the burgeoning nationalism that led to the rebellions of 1848 and the dangers of a power vacuum in the Balkans that resulted from the decline of Turkish influence. By 1914 these factors, added to the rapidly rising power of Germany and the inherent weakness of the Habsburg imperial system, had produced a disequilibrium that impelled the more adventurous states to test their strength on the battlefield. Initially, the goals of the protagonists in this war to end all wars did not entail a major restructuring of the European system. As the conflict progressed to a bitter and incredibly bloody deadlock, however, the voices advocating a more lasting, Kantian solution to the problem of interstate war acquired a new urgency. On the side of the Central Powers, Pastor Naumann, among others, took up the cry for a multi-ethnic federation to replace the old imperial order in Eastern Europe, but nationalistic passions and the requisites of war precluded much of a positive response. At first there was little concern with the consequences of peace among the Entente powers, but when the unexpected elusiveness of victory made the participation of the United States imperative, their mission acquired an ideological façade that was largely inspired by the political philosophy of President Wilson.

While the United States had hitherto remained aloof from the affairs of the Old World, as a nation created by refugees from political oppression and economic want, it would upon occasion manifest sympathy for the nationalistic strivings of the East Europeans. Having gained independence through a revolution that produced at least two heroes of East European origin in the persons of Pulaski and Kosciuszko, the Americans espoused with unbridled enthusiasm the cause of Louis Kossuth and the Hungarian revolution of 1848. This support was of no material consequence, but, as vast waves of East European immigrants reached the New World toward the end of the century, concern for the fate of their compatriots, many of whom remained under foreign rule, became part of the American political ethos. Organizations of Polish and Czech émigrés and their descendants, as well as prominent advocates such as Paderewski and Tomas Masaryk, mounted campaigns in the course of the Great War with a view to securing the national independence of their homelands. President Wilson, who had originally favored preservation of the Austro-Hungarian empire, proved susceptible to these pressures, and all the more so because they harmonized with his idealistic world view of a peaceable society of national and democratic states. The Paris treaties which created roughly the present configuration of East European states turned out to be a travesty of Wilson's principles of ethnic self-determination and "open covenants openly arrived at," however, not because of some duplicity on the part of the president, but rather because of a combination of the region's complex ethnic mosaic, tactical wartime promises to certain East European factions, and the security requirements of the European victors, most notably of the French. As a result, Austria, Hungary, and Bulgaria found themselves ethnically and territorially truncated. The Poles regained national sovereignty after close to two centuries of servitude. Rumania was enlarged by the annexation of Bessarabia from the Soviet Union as well as of formerly Hungarian Transylvania. Czechs and Slovaks merged with German, Hungarian, and Ruthenian minorities into a newly formed republic, while the southern Slavs became reluctantly united under a Serbian king. None of the new states turned out to be ethnically homogeneous, and their postwar political systems, with the possible exception of that of the Czechs, fell short of Wilson's democratic model. Instead, the peace treaties created a highly unstable regional system divided between revisionist and *status quo* states whose manifest weakness found compensation only in nationalistic rhetoric and the search for powerful allies.

If World War I represented the breakdown of the nineteenth-century European balance of power, the eventual victors made little attempt to restore that balance, resorting instead to a punitive peace which stood in sharp contrast to the prudent restoration effected at the Congress of Vienna. The powerful disintegrative force of national particularism, the profound feeling of insecurity among the French, and the resentment of the Germans at being collectively branded with the opprobrium of war guilt all conspired against such a restoration. When, after tantalizing the Europeans with President Wilson's prescription for perpetual peace, the United States beat a hasty retreat from the Old World, it devolved upon the latter to belatedly devise a new balance of power at Locarno, but the basic prerequisites for its success were soon found to be lacking, for no amount of diplomacy could conjure back the homogeneity of the early nineteenth-century system. In such initiatives as the Dawes Plan and the Kellogg-Briand Pact the United States manifested a limited interest in the affairs of Europe, but Washington's dominant orientation remained one of isolationism, and its abstention from the League of Nations only weakened that organization's capacity to cope with the disharmonies of the *status quo* negotiated and codified at Versailles.

Of even greater consequence than Wilson's abortive foray into international politics was the Bolshevik coup in Russia. The impulse toward national self-determination fragmented the old European system, but the entrenchment of a revolutionary and transnational ideology in the Soviet Union proved to be even more inimical to the restoration of international stability. Indeed, since 1917 the world has been in the grips of an international civil war. In the interwar period the Western powers' determination to contain the Bolshevik infection hampered their efforts to cope with the additional threat of nazism. Hostile to both ideologies, but most fundamentally to that of Marxism-Leninism, the United States nevertheless remained in the wings until directly attacked, and it thereafter directed its energies to the pursuit of military victory. That single-minded quest subsumed the destruction of nazism, but it also reflected a pragmatic and ultimately disastrous disregard for the underlying ideological and strategic ambitions of the Soviet Union. By isolating itself from the affairs of Europe in the interwar period, the United States had indirectly contributed to the rise of Hitler; by a fastidious avoidance of any consideration of the territorial and political consequences of victory, the Roosevelt administration allowed its Soviet ally to press its advantage with impunity. The rationale for this policy, that spheres of influence were a discredited and outdated European concept, rang somewhat hollow in light of Washington's unaltered insistence on the inviolability of an American sphere of interest in the Western Hemisphere. Moreover, the prospects of the Rooseveltian alternative, an international organization dedicated to the peaceful preservation of the new *status quo*, were jeopardized by an apolitical military strategy that paid scant attention to the eventual territorial distribution of power and by the unrealistic expectation that the momentarily dormant ideological contest would somehow become subordinated to a consensual allegiance to the UN Charter. In such an operational context the reiteration of principles of democratic self-determination was counterproductive to the extent that it implied an American commitment to the implementation of those principles.

The principal victims of this asymmetry in the wartime policies of the United States were, of course, the East Europeans. For a few years after the war the United States possessed the power to repair the earlier strategic mistakes and compel a Soviet retreat from East-Central Europe. War-weariness and inertia, the inherent political inability of a great democracy to launch such a crusade, and remnants of the hope that perhaps Stalin would tolerate a modicum of independence and diversity among his small neighbors combined to preclude this alternative. Instead, the Truman administration rapidly divested itself of any Wilsonian illusions regarding the United Nations and opted for a pragmatic balance-of-power strategy, containment, which, as one scholar observed, "curiously combined a Realist preoccupation with power and a Utopian expectation of the 'withering away' of the Soviet challenge."[1] Despite a declaratory dimension that paid lip service to the long-term revisionist goals of the United States, containment was in essence a policy of the *status quo*. Its paramount function was to build up the military and economic strength of the United States and its allies to a level of impregnable supremacy, and all other interests and diplomatic devices were subordinated to this end. The disastrous consequences of Hitler's appeasement had undoubtedly conditioned official Washington against making the same mistake in the face of what was seen as an equally irreconcilable foe. Thus, the third alternative, to frankly recognize Stalin's newly acquired sphere of influence, would have represented a repudiation of deeply rooted and oft-proclaimed principles of U.S. foreign policy without, for all that, erasing the reality of the global confrontation between Soviet communism and the capitalistic democracies.[2] Moreover, Stalin's sphere was in reality one less of "influence" than of unpalatable, brutal dominance. The goals of Soviet security and the diffusion of communism were inextricably entwined in Stalin's mind, and the East Europeans bore the brunt of the resulting historical shift in the continental balance of power. Having failed to prevent this shift, the United States had little option but to resort to the compromise of containment, which refused to legitimize the new Soviet sphere while tacitly recognizing its existence.

From 1948 onward, the East European sector of the Soviet empire evolved independently of the vagaries of American foreign policy, for neither the policy of liberation nor that of peaceful engagement could materially affect the status of the satellites. The former, by forcefully reasserting America's commitment to the objectives of the Declaration on Liberated Europe, aroused certain expectations of Western assistance. By the time the rigors of Stalinism had driven the East Germans, then the Poles and the Hungarians, to revolt, such assistance was seen in Washington as entailing unacceptable risks. Once the avoidance of nuclear confrontation had become the irreducible national interest of the United States, the fate of the East Europeans became impervious to Western influence. To rule out direct intervention was far easier, however, than to accept the permanence of Soviet hegemony, and succeeding administrations searched for some new nonviolent formula by which to weaken the links that bound the satellites to Moscow. But neither propaganda and economic embargoes nor trade and cultural exchanges altered or compensated for the dominant factor of the Soviet Union's unwavering determination to preserve its sphere by any means at its disposal.

Rooted in impotence, Washington's policies toward East-Central Europe varied more in their declaratory forms than in their operational forms, for the basic premises of containment had become an orthodoxy. The variations in rhetoric owed as much to the personalities of politicians as to the requisites of domestic politics. John Foster Dulles read Stalin's *Problems of Leninism* in 1946 and never deviated thereafter from his conviction that the two systems were morally and politically irreconcilable and that the United States was predestined to be the leader of a crusade to liberate the world from godless communism. But the dour and adamantine cold-warrior could not conjure up the power to launch his crusade and veered instead into the frustrating fantasy world of political warfare. The propaganda of liberation waned after 1956, but the myth of liberation as a sacred goal lingered on, so deeply entrenched in the American psyche that later administrations would continue to pay obeisance to it by symbolic gestures such as the annual proclamation of Captive Nations Week.[3] While the policy of liberation could be faulted for its occasional propagandistic excesses, and though it undoubtedly exacerbated the cold-war posturings of the two superpowers in the 1950s, charges that it retarded accommodation with the Soviet Union rest on the rather shaky assumption that the status of East-Central Europe represented the substance, rather than a single and increasingly symbolic aspect, of Soviet-American discord.

After the Hungarian tragedy there arose the new orthodoxy of peaceful engagement, which was aimed at marginal and gradual accretions to the East Europeans' welfare and independence without inspiring serious unrest and without destabilizing the continental *status quo*. The relative failure of this new approach was due only superficially to the domestic opposition it encountered. Throughout the postwar period, the predominant mood in Congress and among the public was consistently more uncompromising (without, for all that, favoring a military solution) than that of the incumbent administrations, and this asymmetry became most marked in the Kennedy and Johnson years. Popular and congressional abhorrence of "trade with the enemy" was understandable as an emotional reaction, particularly in light of East European aid to North Vietnam, but it made little sense in terms of economics. Long-term credits could be legitimately ruled out on the grounds that they might allow individual regimes to postpone necessary economic reforms, but normal commercial relations and most-favored-nation status would provide a useful alternative to the East Europeans' dependence on intrabloc trade and technology. Nevertheless, even if the Johnson administration had prevailed over domestic opposition and had implemented its intrinsically unexceptionable policy of bridge-building, the ultimate success of that strategy would have been dependent on the corresponding policies of the Soviet Union. These, as demonstrated most recently in Czechoslovakia, imposed a definite ceiling on political decompression and liberalization, the virtually inevitable byproducts of economic reforms, which are, in turn, the prerequisites for effective East European participation in world trade.

Without reverting to the hard line he had exhibited in earlier years, President Nixon drew his conclusions from the domestic and Soviet constraints on bridge-building and eschewed any major American initiative in that direction. He did become the first president to visit East-Central Europe when he made a brief stopover in Bucharest in August 1969, and he repeated the performance by meeting with Tito in September of the following year. The Russians denounced this "diplomacy of smiles" and charged that the Americans were "continuing with their perfidious tactic of 'building bridges' aimed at undermining the solidarity of socialist countries and driving a wedge between them," but, though the Nixon visits symbolized approval of the more or less independent foreign policies of his hosts without regard for the domestic merits or shortcomings of the regimes, they carried no implication of intensified bridge-building. In the realm of trade expansion, the administration adopted the pace of Congress, which under the pressure of business interests passed in 1969 a new Export Control Act which further liberalized licensing procedures. Subsequently, the administration removed the remaining restrictions on the export of American grain to the Soviet bloc, supported the relaxation of legislative restraints on Export-Import Bank credits for exports to the bloc, facilitated Rumania's access to GATT, and actively sought congressional approval for granting most-favored-nation status to that country. The Coordinating Committee meanwhile persevered in the gradual reduction of the lists of prohibited "strategic goods."

Such progress as was made in normalizing relations with East-Central Europe owed less to forceful leadership from the White House than to an alteration in the mood of Congress. Disengagement from Vietnam, a loss of confidence in America's moral superiority and omnipotence, and Nixon's reorientation of American foreign policy away from the simple equations of bipolarity have tended to relegate the myth of liberation to the limbo of battles fought and lost. The increasingly precarious status of the "private" propaganda organs is a case in point. The CIA's sponsorship of Radio Free Europe and Radio Liberty lost its last veils of secrecy when in January 1971 Senator Clifford Case publicly deplored the practice of covert funding without congressional supervision. The Nixon administration moved to save the stations by endorsing a bill to create an overtly federally funded, privately directed corporation, only to hear Senator Fulbright, chairman of the Foreign Relations Committee, denounce RFE and Radio Liberty as "relics of the cold war" and demand their demise.[4] Radio Free Europe's predicament was not without irony, for the station had long ago abandoned the language of liberation while remaining a popular alternative to the state media in East-Central Europe, particularly in Czechoslovakia after the 1968 invasion. In the event, on June 6, 1972, the Foreign Relations Committee overrode its chairman and approved the administration's compromise request for a further year's funding of the stations. The committee's recommendation that the European allies be invited to share in the future financing of these propaganda operations testified to the altered domestic and international political climates.

While the innovative spirit of the Nixon foreign policy has been most evident in other areas—notably, with regard to Peking—it was manifested more modestly in the candid admission that the East European *status quo* was impervious to any American-inspired alteration. As the president reported to Congress in February 1970:

> It is not the intention of the United States to undermine the legitimate security interests of the Soviet Union. The time is certainly past, with the development of modern technology, when any power would seek to exploit Eastern Europe to obtain strategic advantage against the Soviet Union. It is clearly no part of our policy. Our pursuit of negotiation and détente is meant to reduce existing tensions, not to stir up new ones.
>
> By the same token, the United States views the countries of Eastern Europe as sovereign, not as parts of a monolith. We can accept no doctrine that abridges their right to seek reciprocal improvement of relations with us or others. We are prepared to enter into negotiations with the nations of Eastern Europe, looking to a gradual normalization of relations. We will adjust ourselves to whatever pace and extent of normalization these countries are willing to sustain.[5]

The message remained unaltered two years later: "We do not want to complicate the difficulties of East European nations' relations with their allies; nevertheless there are ample opportunities for economic, technical, and cultural cooperation on the basis of reciprocity. The Eastern European countries themselves can determine the pace and scope of their developing relations with the United States."[6] In practice, the administration fell back on its last alternative, one which had in any case been gaining ground ever since the West Germans abandoned the Hallstein Doctrine. According to the president's adviser for national security affairs, Henry Kissinger, "the major initiatives to improve relations between Western and Eastern Europe should originate in Europe, with the United States in a reserve position." This perhaps inevitable transfer of responsibility required better coordination among the Allies than had prevailed in the past, but, added Dr. Kissinger, "in any event, no Western policy can guarantee a more favorable evolution in Central Europe; all it can do is to take advantage of an opportunity if it arises."[7] Thus, after pursuing the elusive goal of liberation for some twenty years, American policy makers finally acknowledged their impotence and passed the torch to their allies.

The East Europeans have long faced the alternatives of German and Russian spheres of influence. With memories of the Nazi era still alive in their neighbors' minds, particularly among the Poles and the Czechs, the West Germans were at first glance ill-suited to take over the task of bridge-building. Yet this is precisely what occurred when, after his election in late 1969, Chancellor Willy Brandt launched his *Ostpolitik* with renewed vigor.[8] The gamble was a bold one, and the pace of its execution spectacular. Within a year, Brandt negotiated the Treaty of Moscow, by which Bonn renounced the use of force and accepted the existing borders in Eastern and Central Europe; concluded a similar treaty with Poland renouncing Germany's claims to territories lying east of the Oder-Neisse frontier; and conferred at length with his East German counterpart. A less "atmospheric" and more substantive agreement was reached by the four occupying powers regarding the status of West Berlin in September 1971. Having demonstrated by force in 1968 the permanence of its hegemonic claims, the Soviet Union reverted to the pursuit of détente for two apparent reasons. By courting the West Germans, it hoped to weaken NATO and thereby consolidate its western flank at a time when it was threatened by China in the East; it also hoped to approach its long-term objective of becoming the unchallenged preponderant power on the continent of Europe. Similarly, concurrent Soviet proposals for an all-European security conference were aimed at the final legitimization of its sphere and at the erosion of U.S. influence in Europe. As for Bonn's calculations, they followed the optimistic model of bridge-building: that a more relaxed political atmosphere, bought at the price of symbolic concessions, would in the long run facilitate its economic penetration of East-Central Europe and the reintegration of the Soviet dependencies into a European community.

Whatever the intrinsic merits of détente—an elusive and dangerously subjective concept—neither the overdue recognition of the German Democratic Republic, nor some balanced reduction of forces by the two alliances, nor expanded trade, either directly or by the intermediary of America's allies, is likely to alter the Soviet Union's self-arrogated role as ultimate arbiter of developments in its sphere.[9] That sphere continues to serve a number of functions that make it indispensable in the eyes of the men in the Kremlin. It is a strategic buffer zone, a protected trading area, an intermediary for Third World aid, and tangible evidence of the exportability of the Soviet model. Influence, of course, is a matter of degree, and closer contacts can only benefit the mass of satellite peoples, many of whom still look upon the Western democracies as preferable, if imperfect, economic and political models. Through some East-West agreement a reduction of the Soviet military presence in Eastern Europe might have a positive psychological effect, without arousing illusions of independence, particularly in light of the Czechoslovak experience. Relatively little space in the present study has been devoted to the foreign policy process within the communist states of East-Central Europe because of the obscurity of its mechanics and the infrequency of policies that diverge noticeably from Soviet orthodoxy. Perhaps the next generation of East European communist leaders will perceive with greater clarity that they are not the participants in an ideological crusade whose victory is a historical inevitability but are rather the subjects of a hegemonic power which in many respects is more backward than themselves. Nevertheless, the prospects for a stable, gradual, and internally generated evolution, which is what the United States and its allies hope for, are dim, for the satellite regimes are caught between the often conflicting demands of their constituents and of the Kremlin and are hard put to satisfy one without provoking the other. The masses' yearning for social, economic, and political reform is as ineradicable as their nationalism and will unavoidably lead to clashes between the popular will and an unresponsive Soviet-style authority, as occurred once again in Poland in December 1970. At the beginning of the seventies the most notable examples of satellite voluntarism were manifested in Hungary and Rumania. The Kádár administration acquired an enviable record of liberalization in the economic and cultural spheres, remaining all the while a dutiful mouthpiece of Soviet foreign policy, whereas the Ceausescu regime pursued the reverse strategy by acting as the bloc's maverick in foreign policy matters and keeping domestic liberalization to a minimum. One facile conclusion might be that the Kremlin is willing to tolerate a degree of voluntarism in either the domestic or the foreign policy sphere, but never in both simultaneously. Such calculations can be only tentative, however, for, as the East Europeans have unhappily learned, liberalization under Soviet suzerainty is a far-from-irreversible process.

While observing from afar the progress of *Ostpolitik*, the Nixon administration faces dilemmas that are as old as the cold war, for, if détente in Europe signifies merely a formal recognition of the inviolability of the Soviet sphere—and this appears to be the Kremlin's interpretation—it represents not a mutual compromise but empty appeasement. Few still fear a Soviet military incursion into Western Europe, but, on the other hand, there is no indication that the Soviet Union covets any concession (in the sphere of arms control for instance) sufficiently that it could serve in a *quid pro quo* understanding allowing for substantially greater national independence in East-Central Europe. The status of those countries, as Washington long ago learned but for moral and political reasons is reluctant to acknowledge, is non-negotiable. As Secretary of State William Rogers correctly insisted in late 1971, a European security conference should encourage the reconciliation of sovereign European states, not confirm their division.[10] The temptation is nevertheless strong, in a post-Vietnam era of domestic demoralization and of pragmatic adjustments to a changing global balance of power, to overcompensate for earlier moralistic excesses by retrenching to a posture of neoisolationism disguised as *Realpolitik*. When a veteran diplomat such as George Ball writes, "not only do we still depend on the time-honored device of the balance of power . . . but we tacitly claim and recognize other hoary concepts as, for example, 'spheres of influence' or, more accurately, 'spheres of interest,' " he may be engaging in a salutary exercise of demystification.[11] But acknowledgment of the historical truism that great powers tend to claim such spheres does not necessarily detract from the moral validity of American revisionism in the face of Soviet oppression. Moreover, to recognize a state's sovereignty diplomatically implies no approval of its domestic regime or of any hegemonic constraints on its foreign policy.

In terms of concrete policy regarding East-Central Europe, the twin legacies of the Bolshevik Revolution and World War II represent a challenge and a conundrum whose early solution lies beyond the capacity of the United States. The historical record is one of dismal failures only partially relieved by the maintenance of Yugoslavia's nonalignment. While the concept of national interest defies unimpeachable definition, it can certainly be argued that the long-range interests of the United States were as ill-served by its wartime tactical concessions as by the hortatory excesses of psychological warfare. Neither presidents nor secretaries of state nor congressmen proved to be immune to misperception and misjudgment; as for the professionals in the State Department, their generally superior expertise was frequently nullified by their traditionally subordinate role. The inaccuracy of the decision-makers' assessments of prevailing circumstances and their misleading reiteration of principles can be attributed to weakness of intellect as well as to the immense complexity of their task. Yet in an international system marked by the clash of fundamentally irreconcilable ideologies it would be an abject abdication of responsibility on the part of the world's most powerful democracy—which incidentally bears some blame for the involuntary subjection of the East Europeans—to abandon all pretense at revisionism. Tocqueville observed more than a century and a half ago that, once Americans have taken up an idea, nothing is more difficult than to eradicate it from their minds, and the goal of liberation may yet prove to have roots deep enough to withstand the winds of ideological relativism. For the foreseeable future, the basic premise of containment, however unpalatable, retains its validity: change will likely come about only through the internal transformation of the Soviet system. But that flawed and often inhuman system has demonstrated a capacity for endurance and resistance to change which drives the East European man in the street to seek salvation from hegemony in some hypothetical Sino-Soviet conflagration. Meanwhile, the United States, remaining loyal in principle to the prescriptions of the Atlantic Charter, must look upon East-Central Europe as a living testimony to the limits of its power.

NOTES

CHAPTER I

1. John F. Montgomery, *Hungary: The Unwilling Satellite* (New York, 1947), pp. 20, 116.

2. Arthur H. Vandenberg, Jr., ed., *The Private Papers of Senator Vandenberg* (London, 1953), p. 32 (hereinafter cited as *The Vandenberg Papers*); U.S., Congress, Senate, Committee on Foreign Relations and Department of State, *A Decade of American Foreign Policy: Basic Documents, 1941–1949* (Washington, D.C., 1950), p. 481. Declarations of war by the pro-German regimes of Father Tiso in Slovakia and Ante Pavelich in Croatia were not acknowledged by the United States, on the implicit grounds that they did not come from sovereign states. On the Hungarian government's constrained ambivalence in noting the existence of a "state of war," see Montgomery, *op. cit.*, pp. 152–55.

3. Quoted in Alan Palmer, *The Lands Between* (London, 1970), p. 251. See also James MacGregor Burns, *Roosevelt: The Soldier of Freedom* (New York, 1970), p. 65.

4. John J. McCloy, *The Challenge to American Foreign Policy* (Cambridge, Mass., 1953), p. 36.

5. See U.S., Department of State, *Foreign Relations of the United States: Diplomatic Papers, 1941*, vol. 1 (Washington, D.C., 1958), pp. 170–72, 345–54, 759–61.

6. *Department of State Bulletin*, August 16, 1941, p. 125. For details of the genesis of the Atlantic Charter, see Theodore A. Wilson, *The First Summit: Roosevelt and Churchill at Placentia Bay, 1941* (Boston, 1969), pp. 174–207.

7. See Robert E. Sherwood, ed., *The White House Papers of Harry L. Hopkins*, 2 vols. (London, 1948–49), 1:363–64.

8. Great Britain, *Parliamentary Papers*, "Report of Proceedings, Inter-Allied Meeting Held in London at St. James's Palace on September 24, 1941," Cmd. 6315, 1941; Winston Churchill, *The Hinge of Fate* (Boston, 1950), p. 327.

9. Anthony Eden, *The Reckoning* (Boston, 1965), p. 296; Winston Churchill, *The Grand Alliance* (Boston, 1950), pp. 630–31.

10. Milovan Djilas, *Conversations with Stalin* (New York, 1962), p. 114.

11. Robert E. Sherwood, *Roosevelt and Hopkins* (New York, 1948), p. 748.

12. Robert I. Gannon, *The Cardinal Spellman Story* (New York, 1962), pp. 222–23.

13. William C. Bullitt, "How We Won the War and Lost the Peace," *Life*, August 30, 1948, p. 94. "Of one thing I am certain, Stalin is not an imperialist," said Roosevelt on one occasion to the Polish émigré leader Stanislaw Mikolajczyk (Mikolajczyk, *The Rape of Poland: Pattern of Soviet Aggression* [New York, 1948], p. 59).

14. Cordell Hull, *The Memoirs of Cordell Hull* (New York, 1948), p. 1314.

15. Sherwood, *Roosevelt and Hopkins*, p. 674.

16. See John Ehrman, *Grand Strategy*, vol. 5 (London, 1956), p. 95.

17. Herbert Feis, *Churchill, Roosevelt, Stalin: The War They Waged and the Peace They Sought* (Princeton, 1957), p. 218.

18. John R. Deane, *The Strange Alliance* (New York, 1947), pp. 42ff.

19. Elliott Roosevelt, *As He Saw It* (New York, 1946), p. 184.

20. Lord Moran, *Churchill* (London, 1966), p. 144.

21. Field Marshal Earl Alexander of Tunis, *The Alexander Memoirs, 1940–1945* (London, 1962), p. 138; Harold Macmillan, *The Blast of War, 1939–1945* (London, 1967), pp. 502–11; Winston Churchill, *Triumph and Tragedy* (Boston, 1953), p. 151. In an astonishing reversal of his earlier stand at Teheran, Stalin now endorsed Churchill's initiative, even though he knew that Tito was adamantly opposed to Allied operations in his country; one can only speculate that, far from expecting the British and the Americans to precede him in Vienna or in western Hungary, the Soviet leader anticipated that a Balkan operation would draw German troops away from his fronts and only accelerate the Red Army's advance into Central Europe. See Feis, *op. cit.*, p. 445; and Vladimir Dedijer, *Tito* (New York, 1953), p. 234.

22. Quoted in Burns, *op. cit.*, pp. 478–79.

23. Eden, *op. cit.*, p. 467. Macmillan records that this American opposition was a "bitter blow" to Churchill: "A break through the Ljubljana Gap and a march into Austria might have altered the whole political destinies of the Balkans and Eastern Europe. In his arguments against this bold concept, Roosevelt had insisted on the fact that Stalin had been told about the landings in southern France at Teheran, a year before" (Macmillan, *op. cit.*, p. 511).

24. See Chester Wilmot, *The Struggle for Europe* (London, 1952), p. 630 and *passim*; and Hanson W. Baldwin, *Great Mistakes of the War* (London, 1950),

pp. 14–53. Wrote General Mark Clark after the war: "Not alone in my opinion, but in the opinion of a number of experts who were close to the problem, the weakening of the campaign in Italy in order to invade Southern France, instead of pushing on into the Balkans, was one of the outstanding political mistakes of the War. . . . American top-level planners were not interested. . . . I later came to understand, in Austria, the tremendous advantages that we had lost by our failure to press on into the Balkans. . . . Had we been there before the Red Army not only would the collapse of Germany have come sooner, but the influence of Soviet Russia would have been drastically reduced" (Mark Clark, *Calculated Risk* [London, 1951], pp. 348–51).

25. See Michael Howard, *The Mediterranean Strategy in the Second World War* (London, 1968), pp. 66–67 and *passim*.

26. See Alan Clark, *Barbarossa: The Russian-German Conflict, 1941–45* (New York, 1965), pp. 401–3; and Adam B. Ulam, *Expansion and Coexistence* (New York, 1968), pp. 363–64.

27. U.S., Department of State, *Foreign Relations of the United States: Diplomatic Papers, 1943*, vol. 3 (Washington, D.C., 1963), pp. 16, 23–24 (hereinafter cited as *Foreign Relations of the United States, 1943*). Roosevelt also observed at the meeting that, if the Western Allies raised no objection to the incorporation of the Baltic states into the Soviet Union, Stalin might feel inclined to make reciprocal concessions in other areas.

28. Churchill, *Triumph and Tragedy*, p. 366.

29. Edward J. Rozek, *Allied Wartime Diplomacy: A Pattern in Poland* (New York, 1958), p. 39.

30. See W. W. Kulski, "The Lost Opportunity for Russian-Polish Friendship," *Foreign Affairs*, 25 (July 1947): 676; David J. Dallin, *Soviet Russia's Foreign Policy, 1939–1942* (New Haven, 1942), p. 399; Feis, *op. cit.*, pp. 33–34.

31. Churchill, *The Hinge of Fate*, p. 327.

32. See Jan Ciechanowski, *Defeat in Victory* (New York, 1947), pp. 149–57; and Burns, *op. cit.*, p. 365.

33. Churchill, *The Hinge of Fate*, p. 759.

34. U.S.S.R., Ministry of Foreign Affairs, *Correspondence between the Chairman of the Council of Ministers of the U.S.S.R. and the Presidents of the U.S.A. and the Prime Ministers of Great Britain during the Great Patriotic War of 1941–1945*, 2 vols. (Moscow, 1957), 2:61 (hereinafter cited as *Stalin Correspondence*). For details of the Katyn affair, see U.S., Congress, House, *Hearings before the Select Committee to Conduct an Investigation of the Facts, Evidence, and Circumstances of the Katyn Forest Massacre*, 82nd Cong., 2nd sess., 1952; and J. K. Zawodny, *Death in the Forest* (Notre Dame, Ind., 1962).

35. Hull, *The Memoirs of Cordell Hull*, p. 1266.

36. *Foreign Relations of the United States, 1943*, 3:337, 469–70.

37. Sherwood, *Roosevelt and Hopkins*, p. 796. See also Burns, *op. cit.*, pp. 412–13.

38. General Sikorski Historical Institute, *Documents on Polish-Soviet Relations, 1939–1945*, 2 vols. (London, 1967), 2:159–60 (hereinafter cited as *Documents on Polish-Soviet Relations*).

39. Hull, *The Memoirs of Cordell Hull*, p. 1442. See also *Documents on Polish-Soviet Relations*, pp. 250–56; *Stalin Correspondence*, 2:120–21, 133, 146–48; Arthur Bliss Lane, *I Saw Poland Betrayed* (Indianapolis, 1948), p. 58; Mikolajczyk, *op. cit.*, pp. 58ff.; and Ciechanowski, *op cit.*, p. 146.

40. See Tadeusz Komorowski, *The Secret Army* (New York, 1951), pp. 201-5; and *Documents on Polish-Soviet Relations*, pp. 276-77, 308.

41. *Stalin Correspondence*, 2:157. On August 2 Stalin had advised Roosevelt that the Polish question hinged on the émigrés' ability to cooperate with the Committee of National Liberation, "which is already functioning in Poland and to which the democratic forces of Poland are rallying more and more" (*ibid.*, pp. 153-54).

42. George F. Kennan, *Memoirs, 1925-1950* (Boston, 1967), pp. 210-11.

43. Feis, *op. cit.*, p. 386.

44. See Churchill, *Triumph and Tragedy*, p. 141.

45. Kennan, *op. cit.*, p. 211.

46. See Eduard Beneš, *Memoirs* (London, 1954), pp. 186, 240-63.

47. See *Foreign Relations of the United States, 1943*, 3:670n, 719, 728-33.

48. U.S., Department of State, *Foreign Relations of the United States: Diplomatic Papers, 1944*, vols. 3 and 4 (Washington, D.C., 1965-66), 3:521-23 (hereinafter cited as *Foreign Relations of the United States, 1944*).

49. R. Harris Smith, *OSS: The Secret History of America's First Central Intelligence Agency* (Berkeley, 1972), pp. 104-5; and Florimond Duke, *Name, Rank, and Serial Number* (New York, 1969), p. 46. For further details of the peace feelers, see Nicholas Kállay, *Hungarian Premier* (London, 1954), pp. 9, 360-70, 373ff., 386-87; Sir Llewellyn Woodward, *British Foreign Policy in the Second World War* (London, 1962), p. 480; John A. Lukacs, *The Great Powers & Eastern Europe* (New York, 1953), pp. 489, 494-95, 623; and *Foreign Relations of the United States, 1944*, 4:186.

50. *Department of State Bulletin*, October 29, 1944, p. 492.

51. *Ibid.*, September 17, 1944, p. 289.

52. See *Foreign Relations of the United States, 1944*, 4:157-61.

53. Hull, *The Memoirs of Cordell Hull*, p. 1461.

54. *Foreign Relations of the United States, 1944*, 4:236; Hull, *The Memoirs of Cordell Hull*, p. 1461.

55. *Foreign Relations of the United States, 1944*, 4:223, 230.

56. Feis, *op. cit.*, p. 548. Secretary of War Stimson wrote in his diary on October 23 that the United States ought to prevent the Soviets from introducing their secret police system "into the countries which they are now invading, particularly Hungary. Hungary has not a Slavic population and I do not believe would willingly accept the methods of the OGPU. We should not allow them to be driven by the Russians into doing it" (Henry L. Stimson and McGeorge Bundy, *On Active Service in Peace and War* [New York, 1948], p. 607). As will be seen, he would on other occasions argue categorically against American involvement.

57. Kennan, *op. cit.*, p. 235.

58. World Peace Foundation, *Documents on American Foreign Relations, 1944-1945* (Princeton, 1947), pp. 244-50 (hereinafter cited as *Documents on American Foreign Relations, 1944-1945*). See also *Foreign Relations of the United States, 1944*, 3:887, 890, 915-18, 952.

59. See *Foreign Relations of the United States, 1944*, 4:1334-55, 1372, 1411, 1415-16.

60. *Ibid.*, p. 1387. See also *ibid.*, p. 1444; and U.S., Department of State, *Foreign Relations of the United States, 1945: The Conferences at Malta and Yalta* (Washington, D.C., 1955), pp. 256-57, 264 (hereinafter cited as *The Conferences at Malta and Yalta*). Back in September 1943, Roosevelt had expressed to Archbishop Spellman his

opposition to the resurrection of prewar Yugoslavia, favoring instead independent Croat and Slovene states (Gannon, *op. cit.*, p. 224). Perhaps the president was responding ingenuously to Spellman's concern for these Catholic nations; in any case the growing predominance and independence of Tito's multi-ethnic movement soon made such speculations irrelevant.

61. See Dedijer, *op. cit.*, p. 233.

62. Hull, *The Memoirs of Cordell Hull*, p. 1452.

63. *Ibid.*, pp. 1454-55.

64. Churchill, *Triumph and Tragedy*, pp. 234-35.

65. *Ibid.*, p. 208.

66. Sherwood, *Roosevelt and Hopkins*, p. 834.

67. Churchill, *Triumph and Tragedy*, p. 227; cf. Hull, *The Memoirs of Cordell Hull*, p. 1458.

68. Eden, *op. cit.*, p. 483; *Foreign Relations of the United States, 1944*, 3:452.

69. Churchill, *Triumph and Tragedy*, pp. 227-28.

70. Rozek, *op. cit.*, p. 283. See also Mikolajczyk, *op. cit.*, pp. 97-98.

71. Churchill, *Triumph and Tragedy*, pp. 233-34. While in Moscow, Churchill drafted a note to Stalin explaining: "there exists in all these countries the ideological issue between totalitarian forms of government and those we call free enterprise controlled by universal suffrage. We are very glad that you have declared yourselves against trying to change by force or by Communist propaganda the established systems in the various Balkan countries. Let them work out their own fortunes during the years that lie ahead." Happily for the Soviet leader's blood pressure, the note was never transmitted (*ibid.*, p. 232).

72. *The Memoirs of Cordell Hull*, p. 1461.

73. Kennan, *op. cit.*, pp. 222-23.

74. *The Conferences at Malta and Yalta*, pp. 64-66.

75. Kennan, *op. cit.*, p. 171.

76. Churchill, *Triumph and Tragedy*, p. 393.

77. On the military setting of Yalta, see Diane Shaver Clemens, *Yalta* (New York, 1970), pp. 63-95.

78. *The Conferences at Malta and Yalta*, pp. 217-25; *Stalin Correspondence*, 2:175, 180-84.

79. See *The Conferences at Malta and Yalta*, pp. 240-42; and *Foreign Relations of the United States, 1944*, 3:435-36, 481-96.

80. See *Foreign Relations of the United States, 1944*, 4:255-59.

81. *Ibid.*, p. 281.

82. *Ibid.*, 3:910-11.

83. Churchill, *Triumph and Tragedy*, p. 341; Council on Foreign Relations, *The United States in World Affairs, 1945-1947* (New York, 1947), p. 55.

84. One notable skeptic was Senator Vandenberg, who told Hull: "The peace will create a new *status quo* in the world. The new 'League' will defend this new *status quo*. It is my position that the United States cannot subscribe to this defense, no matter how hedged about, unless and until we know more about what the new *status quo* will be" (*The Vandenberg Papers*, p. 96).

85. *Foreign Relations of the United States, 1944*, 4:1025-26.

86. See, for instance, Gabriel Kolko, *The Politics of War* (New York, 1968), pp. 169-70. Although in this period the British were supporting the Papandreou government in Greece against leftist guerrillas and were taking an active interest in the

internal politics of Belgium and Italy, in none of these countries did the communists attract anywhere near majority support. See Martin F. Herz, *Beginnings of the Cold War* (New York, 1969), pp. 127-29.

87. *The Conferences at Malta and Yalta*, pp. 94-95, 103, 105, 230.

88. *Ibid.*, pp. 242-45.

89. U.S., Department of State, *Postwar Foreign Policy Preparation, 1939-1945* (Washington, D.C., 1949), pp. 372-73, 655-57; Edward R. Stettinius, Jr., *Roosevelt and the Russians: The Yalta Conference* (New York, 1950), pp. 68, 87.

90. Stettinius, *op. cit.*, pp. 42 and 88-89.

91. *Ibid.*, p. 113; James Byrnes, *Speaking Frankly* (New York, 1947), p. 31; *The Conferences at Malta and Yalta*, pp. 677-81.

92. *The Conferences at Malta and Yalta*, pp. 716-21.

93. John L. Snell, ed., *The Meaning of Yalta* (Baton Rouge, 1956), p. 123.

94. *The Conferences at Malta and Yalta*, pp. 973-74.

95. Byrnes, *op. cit.*, pp. 32, 33; William D. Leahy, *I Was There* (New York, 1950), pp. 315-16.

96. *The Conferences at Malta and Yalta*, pp. 908-9.

97. Interview by Tad Szulc of the *New York Times*, *The Globe and Mail* (Toronto), February 13, 1970. Molotov had insisted that the reference in the original American draft to the establishment of "appropriate machinery," if necessary to implement the declaration, be deleted, an amendment the Americans could scarcely cavil after Roosevelt's rejection of the emergency high commission. See *The Conferences at Malta and Yalta*, pp. 863, 873.

98. *Documents on American Foreign Relations, 1944-1945*, pp. 352-53.

99. *Ibid.*, pp. 24-25.

100. Churchill, *Triumph and Tragedy*, pp. 400-401.

101. *Documents on Polish-Soviet Relations*, pp. 309, 523; *The Vandenberg Papers*, p. 150. Motions were also introduced in the U.S. House and Senate deploring the Yalta agreement on the Curzon line (79th Cong., 1st sess., 1945, H. Con. Res. 31).

CHAPTER II

1. U.S., Department of State, *Foreign Relations of the United States: Diplomatic Papers, 1945*, vols. 4 and 5 (Washington, D.C., 1967-68), 5:478 (hereinafter cited as *Foreign Relations of the United States, 1945*).

2. The new government included a token right-winger in the person of former Prime Minister Gheorghe Tatarescu (see Henry L. Roberts, *Rumania* [New Haven, 1951], p. 271). An OSS detachment had reached Bucharest in September 1944, and one of its members claims to have played an influential role with the Rumanian government, but it was expelled by the Russians in 1945 (see R. Harris Smith, *OSS: The Secret History of America's First Central Intelligence Agency* [Berkeley, 1972], pp. 30, 108).

3. *Foreign Relations of the United States, 1945*, 5:511 ff.

4. James Byrnes, *Speaking Frankly* (New York, 1947), pp. 52-53. Eden observed that after this coup the British and the Americans "had not the power to deny Soviet action in the greater part of the Balkans, where the Russians could claim to be setting up their own security system against Germany. It was better to reserve our arguments for areas where we had special interests and the means to back them" (Anthony Eden, *The Reckoning* [London, 1965], p. 523).

5. George F. Kennan, *Memoirs, 1925-1950* (Boston, 1967), p. 254.

6. Winston Churchill, *Triumph and Tragedy* (Boston, 1953), p. 372.

7. Herbert Feis, *Churchill, Roosevelt, Stalin: The War They Waged and the Peace They Sought* (Princeton, 1957), p. 575; U.S.S.R., Ministry of Foreign Affairs, *Correspondence between the Chairman of the Council of Ministers of the U.S.S.R. and the Presidents of the U.S.A. and the Prime Ministers of Great Britain during the Great Patriotic War of 1941-1945*, 2 vols. (Moscow, 1957), 2:202-3 (hereinafter cited as *Stalin Correspondence*).

8. See *Stalin Correspondence*, 2:206-7; and Martin F. Herz, *Beginnings of the Cold War* (New York, 1969), pp. 87-88.

9. W. Millis and E. S. Duffield, eds., *The Forrestal Diaries* (New York, 1951), p. 40 (hereinafter cited as *The Forrestal Diaries*).

10. *Stalin Correspondence*, 2:211-12.

11. Harry S. Truman, *Memoirs by Harry S. Truman:* vol. 1, *Years of Decisions*; vol. 2, *Years of Trial and Hope* (Garden City, N.Y., 1955-56), 1:15.

12. *Stalin Correspondence*, 2:215-17.

13. *Foreign Relations of the United States, 1945*, 5:231-33.

14. For details of this meeting, see Truman, *op. cit.*, 1:77-79; Henry L. Stimson and McGeorge Bundy, *On Active Service in Peace and War* (New York, 1948), p. 609; *The Forrestal Diaries*, p. 50; and *Foreign Relations of the United States, 1945*, 5:252-55.

15. Truman, *op. cit.*, 1:82.

16. *Stalin Correspondence*, 2:219-20.

17. See Philip E. Mosely, "The Occupation of Germany: New Light on How the Zones Were Drawn," *Foreign Affairs*, 28, no. 4 (1950): 580-604.

18. Forrest C. Pogue, "Why Eisenhower's Forces Stopped at the Elbe," *World Politics*, 4, no. 3 (1952): 360-65.

19. Churchill, *Triumph and Tragedy*, p. 503.

20. *Foreign Relations of the United States, 1945*, 4:444-45. See also Sir Alexander Cadogan, *The Diaries of Sir Alexander Cadogan, 1938-1945*, ed. D. Dilks (London, 1971), pp. 728, 735-36; and Pogue, *loc. cit.*, pp. 365-67.

21. Churchill, *Triumph and Tragedy*, pp. 569-70, 573.

22. Arthur Krock, *Memoirs* (New York, 1968), p. 234.

23. See Herz, *op. cit.*, pp. 153-69.

24. U.S., Department of State, *Foreign Relations of the United States, 1945: The Conferences at Malta and Yalta* (Washington, D.C., 1955), pp. 313, 324 (hereinafter cited as *The Conferences at Malta and Yalta*).

25. Arthur Schlesinger, Jr., "Origins of the Cold War," *Foreign Affairs*, 46, no. 1 (1967): 49.

26. *New York Times*, December 6, 1945.

27. Gabriel Kolko, *The Politics of War* (New York, 1968), p. 177.

28. *Stalin Correspondence*, 2:227.

29. Kennan, *Memoirs*, p. 212.

30. U.S., Department of State, *Foreign Relations of the United States, 1945: The Conference of Berlin*, vols. 1 and 2 (Washington, D.C., 1960), 1:24ff. (hereinafter cited as *The Conference of Berlin*).

31. Truman, *op. cit.*, 1:245. Claims that Truman used the A-bomb not so much to defeat Japan as to intimidate Stalin (namely, Gar Alperowitz, *Atomic Diplomacy: Hiroshima and Potsdam* [New York, 1965], p. 242) strike this writer as fanciful.

32. Walt W. Rostow, *The United States in the World Arena* (New York, 1960), p. 144. Vandenberg made a similar recommendation in a speech to the Senate on January 10; see Arthur Vandenberg, Jr., ed., *The Private Papers of Senator Vandenberg* (London, 1953), pp. 136-37 (hereinafter cited as *The Vandenberg Papers*).

33. See Rostow, *op. cit.*, p. 179. Stalin, meanwhile, wasted no time in erasing memories of Soviet-American collaboration; by June 1945, intelligence sources in the Soviet Union reported that party agitators in the factories had shifted to a new, anti-American line (Christopher Felix [pseud.], *A Short Course in the Secret War* [New York, 1963], p. 23).

34. *Stalin Correspondence*, 2:242.

35. *The Conference of Berlin*, 1:201, 317, 399-400.

36. *Ibid.*, pp. 258-59.

37. Byrnes, *op. cit.*, p. 71.

38. *The Conference of Berlin*, 2:644.

39. Byrnes, *op. cit.*, p. 73.

40. *Ibid.*, p. 74.

41. Philip E. Mosely , *Face to Face with Russia* (New York, 1948), p. 23.

42. William D. Leahy, *I Was There* (New York, 1950), p. 485.

43. *The Conference of Berlin*, 1:1492.

44. *Ibid.*, pp. 1494-95.

45. See George H. Blakeslee, "Negotiating to Establish the Far Eastern Commission, 1945," in *Negotiating with the Russians*, ed. Raymond Dennett and Joseph E. Johnson (Boston, 1951), p. 131.

46. Byrnes, *op. cit.*, p. 85.

47. Ibid., pp. 80-81; *The Conference of Berlin*, 2:1491-92.

48. *The Conference of Berlin*, 2:1481-87, 1495-96.

49. *Department of State Bulletin*, August 12, 1945, p. 211.

50. Byrnes, *op. cit.*, p. 105.

51. *Ibid.*, pp. 98-99.

52. *Department of State Bulletin*, November 6, 1943, p. 310.

53. *Ibid.*, December 30, 1945, p. 1034. See also Stephen D. Kertész, "The Methods of Communist Conquest: Hungary, 1944-47," *World Politics* 3 (1950): 40.

54. *Department of State Bulletin*, August 19, 1945, p. 274.

55. Mark Ethridge and C. E. Black, "Negotiating on the Balkans, 1945-1947," in *Negotiating with the Russians*, ed. Raymond Dennett and Joseph E. Johnson (Boston, 1951), p. 190.

56. C. L. Sulzberger, *A Long Row of Candles* (New York, 1969), p. 267.

57. Ethridge and Black, *loc. cit.*, p. 193.

58. *Department of State Bulletin*, December 30, 1945, p. 1034.

59. *Ibid.*, August 26, 1945, p. 280.

60. Ethridge and Black, *op. cit.*, pp. 197-98; Ferenc Nagy, *The Struggle Behind the Iron Curtain* (New York, 1948), p. 400.

61. Byrnes, *op. cit.*, p. 108.

62. Ethridge and Black, *loc. cit.*, p. 201.

63. Byrnes, *op. cit.*, pp. 115-21.

64. Kennan, *Memoirs*, pp. 284, 287.

65. Truman, *op. cit.*, 1:552; cf. Byrnes, *op. cit.*, pp. 238-39. Truman was also convinced that the Russians intended to invade Turkey.

66. U.S., Department of State, *Making the Peace Treaties* (Washington, D.C., 1947), p. 20 (hereinafter cited as *Making the Peace Treaties*); Byrnes, *op. cit.*, p. 255.

67. See U.S., Department of State, *Foreign Relations of the United States: Diplomatic Papers, 1946*, vol. 6 (Washington, D.C., 1969), pp. 658–66 (hereinafter cited as *Foreign Relations of the United States, 1946*). See also *Department of State Bulletin*, June 9, 1946, p. 1007; June 16, 1946, p. 1048; and December 8, 1946, p. 1057.

68. *Department of State Bulletin*, August 3, 1947, p. 229.

69. *Foreign Relations of the United States, 1946*, 6:56–58. Harriman added that recognition of a Bulgarian regime that flouted the Moscow decisions might have a "disastrous effect" on the inclination of the neighboring Groza government to resist communist and Soviet pressures.

70. *Ibid.*, pp. 74–75. The U.S. representative in Sofia, Maynard Barnes, was pleased with this protest, but added pessimistically that "our experience to date leads us to anticipate no improvement as result of representations couched in language of one gentleman to another" (*ibid.*, p. 77).

71. See Isaac A. Stone, "American Support of Free Elections in Eastern Europe, I" *Department of State Bulletin*, August 17, 1947, pp. 316–17.

72. *Foreign Relations of the United States, 1946*, 6:174–75.

73. *Ibid.*, pp. 696–709. See also the supporting view of former Soviet Foreign Minister Maxim Litvinov, *ibid.*, p. 763.

74. *The Forrestal Diaries*, pp. 158–59. Forrestal observed that, at the time, the Western Allies would have been "totally incapable" of resisting a Russian thrust westward.

75. Kennan, *Memoirs*, p. 255; *Foreign Relations of the United States, 1945*, 4:456–509. Already at the San Francisco conference in April a British observer had noted that Jan Masaryk "is completely a prisoner of the Russians. Benes and most of his Govt. being held by Joe in Moscow, and he has to say what he's told. He's very apologetic about it, but I tell him that we all understand his position and sympathize" (Cadogan, *The Diaries of Sir Alexander Cadogan*, pp. 734–35). See also Josef Korbel, *The Communist Subversion of Czechoslovakia, 1938–1948* (Princeton, 1959), pp. 119ff.

76. *Foreign Relations of the United States, 1946*, 6:178–80.

77. *Ibid.*, p. 178.

78. *Ibid.*, pp. 204–5.

79. *Ibid.*, p. 213.

80. *Ibid.*, pp. 233–234, 239–40.

81. See *Foreign Relations of the United States, 1945*, 4:1154–60.

82. *Stalin Correspondence*, 1:340; Churchill, *Triumph and Tragedy*, p. 560.

83. *Department of State Bulletin*, December 23, 1945, p. 1020.

84. See *Foreign Relations of the United States, 1946*, 6:868, 931.

85. See *ibid.*, pp. 920–21, 959–61.

86. Stephen D. Kertész, *Diplomacy in a Whirlpool* (Notre Dame, Ind., 1953), p. 106.

87. Nagy, *op. cit.*, p. 134.

88. *Foreign Relations of the United States, 1946*, 6:275.

89. *Ibid.*, pp. 293, 361.

90. *Ibid.*, pp. 297–98. See also Nagy, *op. cit.*, p. 182.

91. H. F. A. Schoenfeld, "Soviet Imperialism in Hungary," *Foreign Affairs*, 26, no. 3 (1948):557.

92. See Kertész, *Diplomacy in a Whirlpool*, pp. 156ff.

93. *Department of State Bulletin*, August 4, 1946, pp. 229–32; and October 6, 1946, pp. 638–39.

94. Kertész, *Diplomacy in a Whirlpool*, p. 122. See also Korbel, *op. cit.*, p. 161; and *Foreign Relations of the United States, 1946*, 6:361-73.

95. Nagy, *op. cit.*, pp. 209-10; cf. Korbel, *op. cit.*, pp. 179-80. Meanwhile, in February, Hungary and Czechoslovakia had signed an agreement for a limited exchange of population.

96. Nagy, *op. cit.*, p. 219; *Foreign Relations of the United States, 1946*, 6:301-2. For further American views on the Transylvanian question, see *ibid.*, pp. 281-82, 298-99, 302-3, 307-10, 316-17.

97. *Ibid.*, pp. 306-14; Nagy, *op. cit.*, pp. 225-37.

98. *Foreign Relations of the United States, 1946*, 6:272-73.

99. Byrnes, *op. cit.*, p. 160.

100. *Ibid.*, p. 137.

101. *Making the Peace Treaties*, p. 112.

102. See Philip E. Mosely, "Peace-Making, 1946" *International Organization*, 1, no. 1 (1946): 22-32. American documentation relative to the Paris peace conference can also be found in U.S., Department of State, *Foreign Relations of the United States, 1946: The Paris Peace Conference*, vols. 3 and 4 (Washington, D.C., 1970).

103. *Foreign Relations of the United States, 1946*, 6:216. See also Byrnes, *op. cit.*, pp. 143-44.

104. See Hungary, Ministry of Foreign Affairs, *La Hongrie et la Conférence de Paris* (Budapest, 1947), vols. 1, 2, and 4; and Michael Hogye, *The Paris Peace Conference of 1946: Role of the Hungarian Communists and of the Soviet Union* (New York, 1954).

105. Harold Nicolson, "Peacemaking in Paris: Success, Failure, or Farce?" *Foreign Affairs*, 25, no. 2 (1947):198.

106. Amelia C. Leiss, ed., *European Peace Treaties after World War II* (Boston, 1954), pp. 97-98.

107. *Ibid.*, pp. 88-92.

108. *Ibid.*, pp. 123-29.

109. U.S., Department of State, *Paris Peace Conference, 1946: Selected Documents* (Washington, D.C., 1947), pp. 1063-64; Leiss, *op. cit.*, pp. 101-3.

110. Leiss, *op. cit.*, pp. 93-96. Cf. Hogye, *op. cit.*, pp. 19-30; and Maurice A. Pope, *Soldiers and Politicians* (Toronto, 1962), pp. 316-18.

111. *Making the Peace Treaties*, p. 127; John C. Campbell, "The European Territorial Settlement," *Foreign Affairs*, 26, no. 1 (1948): 214.

112. Leiss, *op. cit.*, pp. 121-22.

113. For the texts of the Bulgarian, Hungarian, and Rumanian draft treaties, see *ibid.*, pp. 251-321.

114. Sulzberger, *op. cit.*, p. 340.

115. *Making the Peace Treaties*, pp. 144-45, 150.

116. Byrnes, *op. cit.*, pp. 256 and 234-36.

117. *The Forrestal Diaries*, pp. 296-97.

118. Hans J. Morgenthau, *American Foreign Policy: In Defense of the National Interest* (London, 1952), p. 91.

119. Walter Bedell Smith, *My Three Years in Moscow* (Philadelphia, 1950), p. 196.

120. World Peace Foundation, *Documents on American Foreign Relations, 1947* (Princeton, 1949), p. 2 (hereinafter cited as *Documents on American Foreign Relations, 1947*).

121. U.S., Congress, Senate, Committee on Foreign Relations, *Hearings on the Treaties of Peace with Italy, Rumania, Bulgaria, and Hungary*, 80th Cong., 1st sess., 1947, p. 174.

122. *Documents on American Foreign Relations, 1947*, p. 641.

123. See *Foreign Relations of the United States, 1946*, 6:318-20.

124. *Ibid.*, pp. 332-33.

125. *Documents on American Foreign Relations, 1947*, p. 641.

126. Schoenfeld, *loc. cit.*, p. 563.

127. *New York Times*, March 11, 1947.

128. *Department of State Bulletin*, March 16, 1947, p. 495; and March 30, 1947, pp. 583-84.

129. Nagy, *op. cit.*, p. 387.

130. *New York Times*, June 6, 1947. See also *Department of State Bulletin*, June 15, 1947, p. 1161; and June 22, 1947, pp. 1214-16.

131. *New York Times*, June 5, 1947.

132. *Ibid.*, June 11, 1947.

133. Hungary, Ministry of Information, *Fehér Könyv: A magyar köztársaság és a demokrácia elleni összeesküvés* (Budapest, 1947); for the account of the resident U.S. intelligence operative, see Felix [pseud.], *op. cit.*, pp. 217-36.

134. Byrnes, pp. *op. cit.*, pp. 304-5.

135. *New York Herald Tribune*, August 7, 1947.

136. *Department of State Bulletin*, August 24, 1947, p. 392; Felix [pseud.], *op. cit.*, pp. 248ff. The Central Intelligence Group had been organized to replace the wartime Office of Strategic Services and was itself superseded by the Central Intelligence Agency in 1947.

137. See *Foreign Relations of the United States, 1946*, 6:448-50.

138. For U.S. protests regarding political abuses in Poland, see *ibid.*, pp. 419-20, 425-28.

139. *Ibid.*, p. 483.

140. *Ibid.*, pp. 494-95.

141. See *ibid.*, pp. 485-87, 517, 544-55; and *Department of State Bulletin*, February 9, 1947.

142. Arthur Bliss Lane, *I Saw Poland Betrayed* (Indianapolis, 1948), p. 7.

143. *Department of State Bulletin*, February 16, 1947, p. 299.

144. *New York Times*, March 13, 1947.

145. Dean Acheson, *Present at the Creation* (New York, 1969), p. 225.

146. See, for instance, David Horowitz, *The Free World Colossus* (New York, 1965), pp. 92-95.

147. Harry B. Price, *The Marshall Plan and Its Meaning* (Ithaca, N.Y., 1955), p. 4.

148. Max Beloff, *The United States and the Unity of Europe* (Washington, D.C., 1963), pp. 14-16.

149. Kennan, *Memoirs*, pp. 333-41.

150. Price, *op. cit.*, p. 24; Kennan, *Memoirs*, p. 342.

151. *Documents on American Foreign Relations, 1947*, pp. 9-11.

152. Price, *op. cit.*, p. 28.

153. See Stephen D. Kertész, ed., *The Fate of East-Central Europe* (Notre Dame, Ind., 1956), p. 239.

154. Korbel, *op. cit.*, p. 182.

155. Kennan, *Memoirs*, p. 341.

156. "The Sources of Soviet Conduct," reprinted in George F. Kennan, *American Diplomacy, 1900-1950* (New York, 1963), pp. 95-105.

157. Kennan, *Memoirs*, pp. 356-65.

158. Winston Churchill, *Europe Unite* (London, 1953), p. 415; *New York Herald Tribune* (European ed.), May 29-30, 1965.

159. Kennan, *Memoirs*, p. 403.

160. Dana Adams Schmidt, *Anatomy of a Satellite* (Boston, 1952), p. 110.

161. For details of the coup, see Paul E. Zinner, *Communist Strategy and Tactics in Czechoslovakia, 1918-1948* (New York, 1963), pp. 196-223; and Hubert Ripka, *Le coup de Prague* (Paris, 1949).

162. See Kennan, *Memoirs*, pp. 400ff.

163. See Arthur Krock's commentary in the *New York Times*, August 5, 1948.

164. Kennan, *Memoirs*, pp. 421-24, 443-44; Acheson, *op. cit.*, p. 291.

165. See Jean Edward Smith, *Germany beyond the Wall* (Boston, 1969), pp. 212-13.

166. See Acheson, *op. cit.*, pp. 341-42.

167. See Royal Institute of International Affairs, *Documents on International Affairs, 1951* (London, 1954), p. 279; and J. E. Smith, *op. cit.*, 216-17.

168. *Department of State Bulletin*, April 7, 1952, pp. 551-52.

169. Acheson, *op. cit.*, p. 630.

170. *Department of State Bulletin*, April 7, 1952, pp. 530-31; Royal Institute of International Affairs, *Documents on International Affairs, 1952* (London, 1955), pp. 105-13.

171. J. E. Smith, *op. cit.*, p. 218. Pieck and Grotewohl had apparently been told by Stalin that their regime would have to be liquidated in the interests of a reunited Germany and that the SED would have to "follow the Italian example" and become a minority party. See Harrison Salisbury's report in the *New York Times*, 16 March 1963; and Adam B. Ulam, *Expansion and Coexistence* (New York, 1968), pp. 506-38.

172. Acheson, *op. cit.*, p. 291.

173. See "Soviet Violations of Treaty Obligations: Document Submitted by the Department of State to the Senate Committee on Foreign Relations," *Department of State Bulletin*, June 6, 1948, pp. 738-44.

174. *Ibid.*, March 27, 1949, p. 391.

175. *Ibid.*, June 12, 1949, pp. 756-58.

176. UN General Assembly Resolution 272, April 30, 1949.

177. UN General Assembly Resolution 294, October 22, 1949.

178. UN Document A/1486.

179. Council on Foreign Relations, *The United States in World Affairs, 1949* (New York, 1950), p. 275; The Brookings Institution, *Major Problems of United States Foreign Policy, 1949-1950* (Washington, 1949), p. 105.

180. See Yugoslavia, Ministry of Foreign Affairs, *Conférence Danubienne, Beograd, 1948: Recueil des Documents* (Belgrade, 1949).

181. See John C. Campbell, "Diplomacy on the Danube," *Foreign Affairs*, 27, no. 2 (1949): 315-37.

182. "Suspension of Austrian Treaty Negotiations," *Department of State Bulletin*, June 6, 1948, pp. 746-47. According to the Potsdam protocol, no reparations were to be exacted from Austria (*The Conference of Berlin*, 2:1490).

183. See U.S., Department of State, *American Foreign Policy, 1950–1955* (Washington, D.C., 1957), pp. 2117–21 (hereinafter cited as *American Foreign Policy, 1950–1955)*; and Hungary, Ministry of Foreign Affairs, *Documents on the Hostile Activity of the United States Government against the Hungarian People's Republic* (Budapest, 1951), pp. 153–87.

184. *Department of State Bulletin*, July 16, 1951, p. 94.

185. *American Foreign Policy, 1950–1955*, pp. 2122–23.

186. *Department of State Bulletin*, January 7, 1952.

187. *Ibid.*, March 6, 1950, pp. 351–56, 381.

188. *New York Times*, February 25, 1950.

189. *Ibid.*, February 17, 1950.

190. *Ibid.*, March 17, 1950.

191. *Department of State Bulletin*, October 6, 1952, pp. 521–22. See also Bogdan C. Novak, *Trieste, 1941–1954* (Chicago, 1970).

192. See John C. Campbell, *Tito's Separate Road* (New York, 1967), pp. 14–29.

193. *New York Times*, December 24, 1949.

194. Council on Foreign Relations, *The United States in World Affairs, 1948–1949* (New York, 1949), 201 (hereinafter cited as *The United States in World Affairs, 1948–1949)*.

195. Mutual Defense Assistance Control Act of 1953, Public Law 213, 82nd Cong., 1st sess., October 26, 1951. See U.S., Foreign Operations Administration, *The Revision of Strategic Trade Controls* (Washington, D.C., 1954); and U.S., Department of State, International Cooperation Administration, *The Strategic Trade Control System, 1948–1956* (Washington, D.C., 1957).

196. *New York Times*, February 25, 1950.

197. *The United States in World Affairs, 1948–1949*, pp. 23–24.

198. John Foster Dulles, *War or Peace* (New York, 1950), p. 249.

199. Robert T. Holt, *Radio Free Europe* (Minneapolis, 1958), p. 10.

200. *New York Times*, May 3, 1951, and November 25, 1951.

201. Brutus Coste, "Propaganda to Eastern Europe," *Public Opinion Quarterly*, 14 (Winter 1950/51): 643–58.

202. Holt, *op. cit.*, p. 238n.

203. *Ibid.*, p. 5.

204. Imre Kovács, ed., *Facts about Hungary: The Fight for Freedom* (New York, 1966), pp. 302–3.

205. *New York Times*, June 13, 1952.

206. This account is based on Bruce Page *et al.*, *The Philby Conspiracy* (Garden City, N.Y., 1968), pp. 197–202; and Kim Philby, *My Silent War* (New York, 1968), pp. 191–98. See also Sulzberger, *op. cit.*, p. 498; and Felix [pseud.], *op. cit.*, pp. 55–56, 139–40.

207. See Isaac A. Stone, "American Support of Free Elections in Eastern Europe, II," *Department of State Bulletin*, August 31, 1947, pp. 109–10; and *Foreign Relations of the United States, 1946*, 6:1–45.

208. Sulzberger, *op. cit.*, p. 750.

CHAPTER III

1. Francis H. Russell, quoted in James Burnham, *Containment or Liberation* (New York, 1953), p. 54.

2. Walter Lippmann, *The Cold War* (New York, 1947), p. 8.

3. Burnham, *op. cit.*, pp. 42-43.

4. Lippmann, *op. cit.*, p. 9.

5. Burnham, *op. cit.*, p. 39.

6. John W. Spanier, *American Foreign Policy since World War II*, 3rd rev. ed. (New York, 1968), p. 101.

7. Burnham, *op. cit.*, p. 35.

8. Lippmann, *op. cit.*, pp. 11, 14.

9. Burnham, *op. cit.*, p. 70.

10. See, for instance, Senator Robert Taft's advocacy of subversion as a means of fostering East European oppositional elements, in *A Foreign Policy for Americans* (New York, 1951), pp. 118ff.

11. U.S., Congress, *Congressional Record*, 82nd Cong., 1st sess., 1951, 96: A7975-77, "Penetration Program against Communism," extension of remarks made by the Hon. Alexander Wiley in the Senate on January 2, 1951.

12. U.S., Congress, House, Committee on Foreign Affairs, *The Mutual Security Program: Hearings*, 82nd Cong., 1st sess., 1951, pp. 1106-9.

13. Public Law 164, sec. 101 (a).

14. U.S., Congress, *Congressional Record*, 82nd Cong., 1st sess., 1951, 97:13951, A6950-51.

15. *Department of State Bulletin*, December 3, 1951, pp. 910-11.

16. *Ibid.*, December 31, 1951, p. 1056.

17. Council on Foreign Relations, *The United States in World Affairs, 1951* (New York, 1952), p. 399.

18. World Peace Foundation, *Documents on American Foreign Relations, 1951* (Princeton, 1953), p. 141.

19. *Department of State Bulletin*, January 7, 1952, p. 31.

20. *Soviet News*, January 16, 1952; *New York Times*, January 26, 1952.

21. *Department of State Bulletin*, January 7, 1952, p. 32.

22. U.S., Congress, Senate, Committee on Foreign Relations, *The Mutual Security Act of 1953*, 83rd Cong., 1st sess., 1953, S. Rept. 61.

23. *New York Times*, January 18 and March 24, 1952. See also Murray Sayle, "The Green Berets," *The Sunday Times Magazine*, November 9, 1969, pp. 53-54.

24. Alexander Boray [pseud.], "Should We Stir Up Resistance behind the Iron Curtain Now?" *The Reporter*, October 14, 1952, p. 17. The author went on to quote the exiled Polish general Bor-Komorowski as being opposed to the creation of resistance groups on the grounds that the risks would be too great, the secret police in the satellites being both ubiquitous and ruthless.

25. Bernard Brodie, "Unlimited Weapons and Limited War," *ibid.*, November 18, 1954.

26. See Coral Bell, *Negotiation from Strength* (New York, 1963), p. 20.

27. See Hanson Baldwin, *The Price of Power* (New York, 1948) pp. 297-99.

28. *New York Times*, January 10, 1952.

29. *Time*, February 26, 1951, p. 17.

30. Thomas R. Phillips, "An End to Containment," *The New Republic*, January 21, 1952, p. 16.

31. *Le Populaire*, June 26, 1953.

32. *New York Times*, August 14, 1952.

33. Paul H. Nitze, *U.S. Foreign Policy, 1945-1955* (Washington, D.C., 1956), p. 48.

34. *Le Monde*, February 10, 1953; *L'Humanité*, February 10, 1953.

35. Burnham, *op. cit.*, p. 138.

36. *Ibid.*, p. 223.

37. *Ibid.*, p. 242.

38. *Ibid.*, p. 237.

39. William Henry Chamberlin, *Beyond Containment* (Chicago, 1953), p. 357.

40. Cf. Gordon A. Craig, *War, Politics, and Diplomacy* (New York, 1966), pp. 271–72.

41. *New York Times*, December 14, 1949.

42. John Foster Dulles, *War or Peace* (New York, 1950), p. 175.

43. *Ibid.*, p. 247.

44. John Foster Dulles, "A Policy of Boldness," *Life*, May 19, 1952, pp. 146–60.

45. *Ibid.*, p. 146.

46. *Ibid.*, pp. 152, 154.

47. *Ibid.*, p. 154.

48. *Ibid.*, pp. 154, 157.

49. *Ibid.*, p. 157.

50. *Ibid.*, p. 160.

51. See Louis L. Gerson, *John Foster Dulles*, (New York, 1967), pp. 74–75; and Dwight D. Eisenhower, *Mandate for Change* (New York, 1963), p. 23.

52. C. L. Sulzberger, *A Long Row of Candles*, p. 750. See also Gerson, *John Foster Dulles*, p. 76.

53. Walter Millis and E. S. Duffield, eds., *The Forrestal Diaries* (New York, 1951), p. 520.

54. Sulzberger, *op. cit.*, p. 767.

55. Republican National Committee, *Official Report of the Proceedings of the Twenty-fifth Republican National Convention, 1952* (n.p., n.d.), p. 143.

56. Council on Foreign Relations, *Documents on American Foreign Relations, 1952* (New York, 1953), pp. 80–83 (hereinafter cited as *Documents on American Foreign Relations, 1952*).

57. Louis L. Gerson, *The Hyphenate in Recent American Politics and Diplomacy* (Lawrence, Kan., 1964), p. 183. See also *ibid.*, pp. 184ff.; Athan G. Theoharis, *The Yalta Myths: An Issue in U.S. Politics, 1945–1955* (Columbia, Mo., 1970), pp. 147–48; D. F. Fleming, *The Cold War and Its Origins* (London, 1961), p. 807; and Richard Goold-Adams, *A Time of Power* (London, 1962), p. 302.

58. Gerson, *The Hyphenate*, pp. 189–91.

59. *New York Times*, August 14, 1952. See also Theoharis, *op. cit.*, p. 145.

60. *Ibid.*, August 26, 1952.

61. Emmet John Hughes, *The Ordeal of Power* (New York, 1963), p. 30.

62. "Notes for a Foreign Policy Discussion," August 21, 1952, Dulles Papers.

63. *New York Times*, August 28, 1952.

64. *Ibid.*

65. Gerson records that this was one of the two occasions on which Eisenhower was vexed by Dulles, the other being the Suez episode (*John Foster Dulles*, p. 88). See also Sherman Adams, *Firsthand Report* (New York, 1961), p. 88; and Hughes, *op. cit.*, p. 70.

66. *Documents on American Foreign Relations, 1952*, p. 92; statement released September 4, 1952, Dulles Papers.

67. Dulles to Richard Rovere, quoted in John R. Beal, *John Foster Dulles, 1888–1959* (New York, 1959), p. 132.

68. *New York Times*, May 29 and June 16, 1952.

69. *Ibid.*, August 26, 1952. See also Adlai Stevenson, *Major Campaign Speeches, 1952* (New York, 1953), pp. 74, 92, 119.

70. *New York Times*, September 3, 1952.

71. Quoted in Norman A. Graebner, *The New Isolationism* (New York, 1956), p. 104.

72. *Department of State Bulletin*, September 22, 1952, pp. 423–27.

73. *New York Herald Tribune*, September 13, 1952.

74. *New York Times*, October 5, 1952.

75. *Ibid.*, October 11, 1952.

76. *Documents on American Foreign Relations, 1952*, p. 101.

77. *New York Times*, May 16, 1952.

78. *Life*, September 22, 1952, p. 30.

79. *The Economist*, August 30, 1952, p. 488; and October 18, 1952, p. 137. The chief of staff of Allied Headquarters seemed to agree with this view of liberation. In the course of an interview in September, General Gruenther said that it was absolutely necessary to keep up the hope of the captive peoples, but he warned: "I do not believe that we could liberate them without war. There is no question of launching such a war" (*New York Times*, September 12, 1952).

80. *New York Times*, September 7, 1952.

81. *Washington Post*, November 9, 1952.

82. Quoted in Roscoe Drummond and Gaston Coblentz, *Duel at the Brink* (London, 1961), p. 18.

83. Quoted in Stephen D. Kertész, ed., *The Fate of East Central Europe* (Notre Dame, Ind., 1956), p. 89.

84. *New York Times*, September 9, 1952.

85. *Life*, September 22, 1952, p. 30.

86. See Gerson, *The Hyphenate*, pp. 198–99; and Theoharis, *op. cit.*, pp. 149, 238–43.

87. Herman Finer, *Dulles over Suez* (Chicago, 1964), p. x.

88. Hans J. Morgenthau, *American Foreign Policy: In Defense of the National Interest* (London, 1952), p. 113.

89. Statement released November 5, 1952, Dulles Papers.

90. See Drummond and Coblentz, *op. cit.*, p. 302.

91. Charles C. V. Murphy, "The Eisenhower Shift—Part I," *Fortune*, January 1956, pp. 86–87.

92. Charles C. V. Murphy, "The Eisenhower Shift—Part III," *Fortune*, March 1956, p. 112.

93. *New York Times*, January 1, 1953.

94. Council on Foreign Relations, *Documents on American Foreign Relations, 1953* (New York, 1954), p. 20 (hereinafter cited as *Documents on American Foreign Relations, 1953*). In a final affirmation of the validity of the containment doctrine, Truman told Congress on January 7 that, "if the communist rulers understand they cannot win by war, and if we frustrate their attempts to win by subversion, it is not too much to expect their world to change its character, moderate its aims, become more realistic and less implacable, and recede from the cold war they began" (*ibid.*, pp. 16–17).

95. S. Adams, *op. cit.*, p. 88.

96. Hughes, *op. cit.*, p. 207.

97. S. Adams, *op. cit.*, p. 87.

98. *Department of State Bulletin*, February 9, 1953, pp. 212–16. However, in order to counter some extreme interpretations and conciliate the opposition, Dulles now emphasized that the United States had "from the beginning stood for liberation."

99. U.S., Congress, Senate, Committee on Foreign Relations, *Nomination of John Foster Dulles*, 83rd Cong., 1st sess., 1953, p. 6.

100. *Ibid.*

101. U.S., Congress, *Congressional Record*, 83rd Cong., 1st sess., 1953, 99:67, 68, 318, 435, 756.

102. *Documents on American Foreign Relations, 1953*, p. 188.

103. *Department of State Bulletin*, March 2, 1953, p. 330.

104. See Hughes, *op. cit.*, p. 87.

105. Dulles Papers.

106. Eisenhower, *op. cit.*, p. 211.

107. Letter dated March 2, 1953, Dulles Papers.

108. U.S., Congress, House, Committee on Foreign Affairs, *Hearings on House Joint Resolution 200: Joining with the President of the United States in a Declaration regarding the Subjugation of Free Peoples by the Soviet Union*, 83rd Cong., 1st sess., 1953, pp. 3–22.

109. See Theoharis, *op. cit.*, pp. 160–61. Meanwhile, on February 27, the Senate had unanimously adopted a humanitarian- rather than a liberation-oriented resolution denouncing the persecution of religious and ethnic groups by the communist regimes and urging the president to take the matter before the United Nations (U.S., Congress, Senate Resolution 84, 83rd Cong., 1st sess., 1953).

110. S. Adams, *op. cit.*, p. 93; Theoharis, *op. cit.*, p. 160.

111. Account of telephone conversation, March 28, 1953, Dulles Papers.

CHAPTER IV

1. Quoted in Emmet John Hughes, *The Ordeal of Power* (New York, 1963), p. 109.

2. *Ibid.*

3. Council on Foreign Relations, *Documents on American Foreign Relations, 1953* (New York, 1954), p. 33 (hereinafter cited as *Documents on American Foreign Relations, 1953*).

4. *New York Times*, April 19, 1953. Columnist David Lawrence offered a variation on this theme in the *New York Herald Tribune*, April 17, 1953: "If the Soviet leaders spurn the hand of peace as offered by America, speaking for the free world, the pressure inside the Iron Curtain to realize the Eisenhower terms will intensify as the crusade for self-liberation begins among the oppressed people of Europe and Asia."

5. *New York Times*, April 26, 1953. Taking its cue from *Pravda*, the Hungarian party organ *Szabad Nép* asserted, "We don't feel the least enthusiasm for the aid proffered by President Eisenhower," and it attacked the United States for blocking Hungary's admission to the United Nations (*New York Times*, April 28, 1953).

6. Konrad Adenauer, *Memoirs, 1945-53* (London, 1965), pp. 442–44.

7. U.S., Congress, Senate, Committee on Foreign Relations, *Documents on Germany, 1944-1959*, 86th Cong., 1st sess., 1959, pp. 107–10 (hereinafter cited as *Documents on Germany, 1944-1959*).

8. Royal Institute of International Affairs, *Documents on International Affairs, 1953* (London, 1956), pp. 57-65.

9. Quoted in Eugene Davidson, *The Death and Life of Germany* (New York, 1959), pp. 332-33. See also Stefan Brant [pseud.], *The East German Rising* (London, 1955); and Arnulf Baring, *Der 17. Juni 1953* (Bonn, 1958).

10. Baring, *op. cit.*, p. 38.

11. See Brant [pseud.], *op. cit.*, pp. 168-74; and Baring, *op. cit.*, p. 68.

12. For Ulbricht's statement, see the quote from *Neues Deutschland* (November 28, 1961) in Melvin Croan, "East Germany: Lesson in Survival," *Problems of Communism*, 11 (1962): 8. See also Harrison E. Salisbury's account in the *New York Times*, March 16, 1963.

13. *New York Times*, August 24, 1953.

14. James B. Conant, *My Several Lives* (New York, 1970), p. 557.

15. Edmond Taylor, "RIAS: The Story of an American Psywar Outpost," in *A Psychological Warfare Casebook*, ed. William E. Daugherty (Baltimore, 1958), p. 145.

16. Brant [pseud.], *op. cit.*, pp. 67-68.

17. Taylor, *loc. cit.*, pp. 145-50.

18. Davidson, *op. cit.*, p. 334.

19. Quoted in *ibid.*, p. 341.

20. See the Alsops' account in the *New York Herald Tribune*, June 28, 1953; cf. Council on Foreign Relations, *The United States in World Affairs, 1953* (New York, 1955), pp. 142-43.

21. Conant, *op. cit.*, p. 601.

22. *Documents on American Foreign Relations, 1953*, pp. 170-76.

23. *Department of State Bulletin*, July 13, 1953, p. 40.

24. Quoted in Hughes, *op. cit.*, p. 147.

25. *Documents on Germany, 1944-1959*, pp. 110-12.

26. U.S., Congress, Senate, Concurrent Resolution 36, 83rd Cong., 1st sess., August 3, 1953.

27. Quoted in Taylor, *loc. cit.*, p. 148.

28. This was the view held by, among others, Charles Bohlen, U.S. ambassador to Moscow; see C. L. Sulzberger, *A Long Row of Candles* (New York, 1969), pp. 914-15. Cf. Hugh Seton-Watson, "Can We Free Eastern Europe Now?" *Commentary*, 16, no. 5 (1955): 404.

29. In his memoirs, Adenauer quotes without comment an article from the *Neue Zürcher Zeitung* (June 16, 1963) which argued that the East Germans had been encouraged by Eisenhower's victory on the liberation platform, but the fact remains that at the time of the uprising the chancellor behaved most cautiously and in no way blamed the Americans for their inaction. (See Konrad Adenauer, *Erinnerungen, 1953-1955* [Stuttgart, 1966], p. 221).

30. S. Kracauer and P. L. Berkman, *Satellite Mentality* (New York, 1956), p. 153. While émigrés in general are prone to exaggerate the negative aspects of their former environment, subsequent events in the satellites tend to corroborate the evidence presented in this survey.

31. U.S., Department of State, *Program Test of Voice of America's New York and Munich Output in Hungarian*, prepared by the Institute of Communications Research, Inc. (Washington, D.C., 1953).

32. Council on Foreign Relations, *Diplomacy and the Communist Challenge: A Report on the Views of Leading Citizens in Twenty-five Cities*, ed. Joseph Barber

(New York, 1954), pp. 8, 37.

33. See U.S., Congress, Senate, Committee on Foreign Relations, *Hearings on the Mutual Security Act of 1952*, 82nd Cong., 2nd sess., 1952, pp. 501–21.

34. See Murray Sayle, "The Green Berets," *Sunday Times Magazine*, November 9, 1969, pp. 53–54.

35. Assembly of Captive European Nations, *Organization, Resolutions, Reports, Debate*, 1st sess., September 20, 1954–February 11, 1955 (New York, 1955), pp. 12, 45–46, 57–59, 89–92, and *passim*.

36. Quoted in Coral Bell, *Negotiation from Strength* (New York, 1963), p. 105.

37. Louis L. Gerson, *The Hyphenate in Recent American Politics and Diplomacy* (Lawrence, Kan., 1964), p. 213.

38. See *New York Times Magazine*, December 5, 1954, pp. 13ff.

39. *New York Times*, August 10, 1954.

40. *Ibid.*, January 3, 1955.

41. U.S., Congress, Senate, Committee on Foreign Relations, *Tensions within the Soviet Captive Countries*, pt. 7: *Hungary*, 84th Cong., 1st sess., 1955.

42. Charles C. V. Murphy, "The Eisenhower Shift—Part III," *Fortune*, March 1956, p. 232.

43. *Documents on American Foreign Relations, 1953*, p. 40.

44. *Ibid.*, p. 217.

45. Quoted in Roscoe Drummond and Gaston Coblentz, *Duel at the Brink* (London, 1961), p. 92.

46. Council on Foreign Relations, *Documents on American Foreign Relations, 1954* (New York, 1955), p. 22. Wrote Dulles in a private letter to Alfred Kohlberg dated October 14, 1953: "I am alert to the importance . . . of avoiding anything which might seem to sanctify Soviet rule over the satellite peoples" (Dulles Papers).

47. *Department of State Bulletin*, February 23, 1953, pp. 304–5; March 2, 1953, pp. 333–35; March 16, 1953, pp. 409–11; April 13, 1953, pp. 539–41.

48. *Der Tagesspiegel*, March 26, 1954.

49. See Harold Stassen's report, *World-Wide Enforcement of Strategic Trade Controls: Mutual Defence Assistance Control Act of 1951 (The Battle Act)—Third Report to Congress, First Half of 1953* (Washington, D.C., 1953).

50. "Special Guidance for Broadcasts on Liberation," September 2, 1952, quoted in Robert T. Holt, *Radio Free Europe* (Minneapolis, 1958), p. 24.

51. See, for instance, his letter to Henry Ford II, March 25, 1954, Dulles Papers.

52. Robert T. Holt and Robert W. Van De Welde, *Strategic Psychological Operations and American Foreign Policy* (Chicago, 1960), pp. 208–9.

53. *Ibid.*, pp. 210–23.

54. Holt, *op. cit.*, p. 162.

55. *Department of State Bulletin*, June 7, 1954, p. 881; January 3, 1955, pp. 14–16.

56. Taylor, *loc. cit.*, p. 150.

57. Kracauer and Berkman, *op. cit.*, p. 124.

58. Raymond Swing, quoted in *ibid.*, p. 180.

59. Thomas I. Cook and Malcolm Moos, *Power through Purpose: The Realism of Idealism as a Basis for Foreign Policy* (Baltimore, 1954), p. 147.

60. *New York Times*, March 16, 1955; *The Observer*, May 3, 1953.

61. Charles O. Lerche, *Foreign Policy of the American People*, (Englewood Cliffs, N.J., 1967), pp. 319–20.

62. James Reston, "An Inquiry into Foreign Policy," *New York Times Magazine*, January 16, 1955, p. 62.

63. Quoted in Stephen D. Kertész, ed., *The Fate of East Central Europe* (Notre Dame, Ind., 1956), pp. 427-28. Writing of the Eisenhower administration in the spring of 1955, an American journalist observed that "it is not unreasonable to say that it has long since been less militant—in practice if not in preachment—than the Truman Administration. The world does not seem aware of this, the American people are manifestly unaware of it" (Richard Rovere, *Affairs of State: The Eisenhower Years* [New York, 1956], p. 268). James Reston also noted the decline of liberation: "The tendency of this Administration is to do less than their public statements imply, and this is particularly true when Eisenhower is in charge of the 'doing' and Dulles in charge of the talking. . . . There is now in Washington less emphasis on . . . 'liberation of the satellites' . . . [and] on psychological gimmicks" (Reston, *loc. cit.*, p. 61).

64. Conant, *op. cit.*, p. 603.

65. See Royal Institute of International Affairs, *Documents on International Affairs, 1954* (London, 1957), p. 75.

66. Harold Macmillan, *Tides of Fortune, 1945-1955* (London, 1969), p. 529.

67. *Soviet News*, February 17, 1955.

68. For details of these negotiations, see Robert L. Ferring, "The Austrian State Treaty of 1955 and the Cold War," *Western Political Quarterly*, 21, no. 4 (1968): 651-67; and Sven Allard, *Russia and the Austrian State Treaty* (University Park, Pa., 1970).

69. For the text of the treaty, see Robert H. McNeal, ed., *International Relations among Communists* (Englewood Cliffs, N.J., 1967), pp. 80-83.

70. *New York Times*, May 19, 1955.

71. See Robert Bass and Elizabeth Marbury, eds., *The Soviet-Yugoslav Controversy, 1948-58: A Documentary Record* (New York, 1959), pp. 55-60.

72. Macmillan, *op. cit.*, pp. 606-7.

73. See Paul C. Davis, "The New Diplomacy: The 1955 Geneva Summit Meeting," in *Foreign Policy in the Sixties*, ed. Roger Hilsman and Robert C. Good (Baltimore, 1965), pp. 165-68; Sherman Adams, *Firsthand Report* (New York, 1961), p. 151; and Drummond and Coblentz, *op. cit.*, p. 134.

74. Dwight D. Eisenhower, *Mandate for Change* (New York, 1963), p. 507.

75. U.S., Department of State, *The Geneva Conference of Heads of Government* (Washington, D.C., 1955), p. 8 (hereinafter cited as *The Geneva Conference*).

76. U.S., Congress, House, Committee on Appropriations, *Mutual Security Appropriations for 1956: Hearings*, 84th Cong., 1st sess., 1955, p. 1.

77. Soviet press communiqué, June 14, 1955; cf. Davis, *loc. cit.*, pp. 170-71.

78. U.S., Congress, Senate, Committee on Foreign Relations, *Hearings on S. Res. 116 favoring Discussion at the Coming Geneva Conference on the Status of Nations under Communist Control*, 84th Cong., 1st sess., June 21, 1955, pp. 4-25.

79. Memorandum dated June 18, 1955, Dulles Papers.

80. *New York Times*, June 30, 1955.

81. Memorandum for the record by Douglas MacArthur II, June 17,1955, Dulles Papers.

82. Adams, *op. cit.*, p. 176.

83. "Papers on Geneva Conference Goals," July 7, 1955, Dulles Papers.

84. Macmillan, *op. cit.*, p. 615.

85. *The Geneva Conference*, pp. 20, 41. See also Eisenhower, *op. cit.*, p. 508.

86. John R. Beal, *John Foster Dulles, 1888-1959* (New York, 1959), p. 302.

87. Post-mortem paper on Geneva for White House bipartisan congressional leaders' meeting, July 25, 1955, Dulles Papers.

88. Quoted in Drummond and Coblentz, *op. cit.*, pp. 140-41.

89. "United States Post Geneva Policy," August 15, 1955, Dulles Papers.

90. Council on Foreign Relations, *Documents on American Foreign Relations, 1955* (New York, 1956), p. 230 (hereinafter cited as *Documents on American Foreign Relations, 1955*).

91. *New York Times*, August 25, 1955.

92. *Current Digest of the Soviet Press*, pp. 7, 29, 13-20.

93. Macmillan, *op. cit.*, p. 650.

94. Drummond and Coblentz, *op. cit.*, p. 155; correspondence drafts dated November 11, 1955, Dulles Papers.

95. *New York Times*, May 23, 1955; Royal Institute of International Affairs, *Documents on International Affairs, 1955* (London, 1958), p. 271.

96. *Documents on American Foreign Relations, 1955*, p. 165.

97. Quoted in Richard Goold-Adams, *A Time of Power* (London, 1962), p. 206.

98. Deputy Undersecretary of State Robert D. Murphy, quoted in Drummond and Coblentz, *op. cit.*, p. 141.

99. "Estimate of Soviet Policy" and "Statement by Secretary Dulles in Connection with Agenda Item II: 'Review of the International Situation,' " NATO meeting, Paris, December 13-18, 1955, Dulles Papers.

100. See *Department of State Bulletin*, December 26, 1955, pp. 1067-73.

101. *Ibid.*, January 16, 1956, p. 85; *New York Times*, December 31, 1955.

102. *New York Times*, December 31, 1955.

103. John W. Spanier, *American Foreign Policy Since World War II* (New York, 1968), p. 156.

104. Quoted in Council on Foreign Relations, *The United States in World Affairs, 1956* (New York, 1957), p. 11 (hereinafter cited as *The United States in World Affairs, 1956*).

105. Council on Foreign Relations, *Documents on American Foreign Relations, 1956* (New York, 1957), p. 1 (hereinafter cited as *Documents on American Foreign Relations, 1956*).

106. *Ibid.*, p. 198.

107. David Lawrence in the *New York Herald Tribune*, January 7, 1956.

108. *New York Times*, April 17, 1956.

109. *Documents on American Foreign Relations, 1956*, p. 202.

110. *New York Times*, April 25, 1956; cf. Philip E. Mosely, "Soviet Foreign Policy: New Goals or New Manners?" *Foreign Affairs*, 34, no. 4 (1956): 553.

111. *Documents on American Foreign Relations, 1956*, p. 205.

112. Notes for a Foreign Relations Committee appearance, June 26, 1956, Dulles Papers.

113. *The New Leader*, June 18, 1956.

114. See *Documents on American Foreign Relations, 1956*, pp. 268-70.

115. *New York Herald Tribune*, February 18, 1956.

116. Holt and Van de Welde, *op. cit.*, pp. 230-32.

117. Quoted by C. L. Sulzberger in the *New York Times*, May 14, 1956.

118. *New York Times*, June 2, 1956.

119. *Ibid.*, May 30, 1956.

120. State Department statement of June 29, 1956, Dulles Papers.

121. *New York Times*, July 12, 1956.

122. See U.S., Congress, *Congressional Record*, 84th Cong., 2nd sess., 1956, 102: 11339, 11355–67. The State Department objected to the Douglas Amendment on the grounds that it would invite Soviet attacks, impair the public image of the organizations in question, and impinge upon the ongoing activities of government agencies and private groups (*ibid.*, p. 11359).

123. *Documents on American Foreign Relations, 1956*, p. 212.

124. *The United States in World Affairs, 1956*, pp. 181–82.

125. *New York Times*, August 16, 1956.

126. *Ibid.*, June 9, 1956.

127. *Ibid.*, August 22, 1956.

128. Republican party platform, draft no. 2, July 20, 1956, Dulles Papers. Presumably this line was felt to be overly encouraging to the East Europeans.

129. See, for instance, his Hartford, Conn., speech, *New York Herald Tribune*, October 3, 1956.

130. For an account of the Polish October, see Frank Gibney, *The Frozen Revolution* (New York, 1959).

131. Quoted in *ibid.*, p. 11.

132. Transcript of the CBS program "Face the Nation," October 21, 1956, Dulles Papers.

133. Memorandum of conversation, October 22, 1956, *ibid.*

134. U.S., Congress, House, Committee on Foreign Affairs, *Hearings on Foreign Policy and Mutual Security*, 84th Cong., 2nd sess., October–November, 1956. p. 191.

CHAPTER V

1. See Imre Nagy, *On Communism: In Defence of the New Course* (London, 1957).

2. *The Truth about the Nagy Affair* (London, 1959), p. 129.

3. Paul E. Zinner, *Revolution in Hungary* (New York, 1962), p. 195. For an account of the role played by the intellectuals, see Tamás Aczél and Tibor Méray, *The Revolt of the Mind* (London, 1960).

4. Ferenc A. Váli, *Rift and Revolt in Hungary* (Cambridge, Mass., 1961), p. 234.

5. Paul E. Zinner, ed., *National Communism and Popular Revolt in Eastern Europe* (New York, 1956), p. 341.

6. John MacCormac in the *New York Times*, May 7, 1956.

7. *Ibid.*, October 6, 1956.

8. Zinner, *National Communism*, pp. 390ff.

9. *Ibid.*, pp. 402–7.

10. *New York Herald Tribune*, October 25, 1956.

11. Herman Finer, *Dulles over Suez* (Chicago, 1964), p. 338.

12. Robert D. Murphy, *Diplomat among Warriors* (New York, 1964), p. 428.

13. Columbia Broadcasting System, November 23, 1961, "Eisenhower on the Presidency, Part II," published in *Hungarian Quarterly*, January 1962, pp. 49–50.

14. Quoted in Finer, *op. cit.*, p. 343.

15. *New York Times*, October 25, 1956. The "truth squad," led by Senator Karl Mundt, was trailing Democratic candidate Adlai Stevenson across the country and

holding press conferences after his public addresses.

16. Dwight D. Eisenhower, *Waging Peace* (New York, 1964), p. 63.

17. James Reston in the *New York Times*, October 25, 1956; *Washington Post*, October 26, 1956.

18. Zinner, *National Communism*, p. 409.

19. *Ibid.*, pp. 419-21.

20. *New York Times*, October 25, 1956.

21. Dulles Papers.

22. Council on Foreign Relations, *Documents on American Foreign Relations, 1956* (New York, 1957), pp. 255-56 (hereinafter cited as *Documents on American Foreign Relations, 1956*).

23. Murphy, *op. cit.*, p. 429; quoted in C. L. Sulzberger, *The Last of the Giants* (New York, 1970), p. 336.

24. Dulles Papers and *New York Times*, October 26, 1956; cf. Finer, *op. cit.*, p. 347.

25. *Christian Science Monitor*, October 27, 1956.

26. *New York Times*, October 27, 1956.

27. *New York Herald Tribune*, October 26, 1956. Stevenson later argued privately that the United States had been under a moral obligation to send aid, including troops, to Hungary and moreover would have got away with it (Sulzberger, *op. cit.*, p. 407).

28. Imre Kovács, ed., *Facts about Hungary: The Fight for Freedom* (New York, 1966), pp. 307-8.

29. Eisenhower, *op. cit.*, pp. 67-68.

30. *Documents on American Foreign Relations, 1956*, pp. 45-46.

31. Murphy, *op. cit.*, p. 428.

32. Zinner, *National Communism*, pp. 428-32.

33. *Ibid.*, p. 433.

34. *Ibid.*, pp. 435-41; Melvin J. Lasky, ed., *The Hungarian Revolution* (New York, 1957), p. 76. Observed a Yugoslav commentator after the revolution: "What took place was really the struggle of the entire population against Rákosi's variety of Stalinism, their demand for socialist democracy was independence, for socialist development, for socialism based on the broadest possible participation of the people in the country's government, and for relations with the Soviet Union on the principles of independence, equality, and non-interference in one another's affairs" (Duka Julius, "Hungary after Its Tragedy," *Review of International Affairs* [Belgrade], December 16, 1956, p. 9).

35. Lasky, *op. cit.*, p. 133.

36. *Ibid.*, pp. 133-34.

37. Finer, *op. cit.*, p. 349. There is evidence that the British and the Russians knew of Israel's plans at least as early as October 25. See Finer, *op. cit.*, p. 347; and J. M. Mackintosh, *Strategy and Tactics of Soviet Foreign Policy* (London, 1962), p. 177.

38. Finer, *op. cit.*, p. 353.

39. United States Information Agency, *Hungary: American Statements and Actions* (London, n.d.), p. 4 (hereinafter cited as USIA, *Hungary*); E. H. Cookridge, *Gehlen: Spy of the Century* (New York, 1972), pp. 304-5.

40. Dulles Papers; *New York Times*, November 1, 1956.

41. Finer, *op. cit.*, p. 6; on p. 370 the author claims that Eisenhower and Dulles "momentarily lost their heads."

42. *New York Times* and *New York Herald Tribune*, November 1, 1956.

43. Philip Deane in *The Scotsman* (syndicated column), October 31, 1956.

44. *New York Herald Tribune*, October 31, 1956.

45. See the curiously distorted account of the uprising in Nikita Khrushchev, *K[h]rushchev Remembers*, ed. Strobe Talbott (Boston, 1970), pp. 416–29. Another, and even more questionable, source claims that the Soviet General Staff also argued against intervention (Oleg Penkovskiy, *The Penkovskiy Papers* [New York, 1965], p. 212). Cf. Giuseppe Boffa, *Inside the Khrushchev Era* (New York, 1959), p. 105.

46. Zinner, *National Communism*, pp. 487–89.

47. U.S., Congress, House, Committee on Un-American Activities, *International Communism (Revolt in the Satellites)*, 84th Cong., 2nd sess., 1957, p. 24 (hereinafter cited as Committee on Un-American Activities, *International Communism*); cf. Tibor Méray, *Thirteen Days That Shook the Kremlin* (London, 1959), pp. 164–65.

48. See David J. Dallin, *Soviet Foreign Policy after Stalin* (Philadelphia, 1961), p. 373; and Z. K. Brzezinski and S. P. Huntington, *Political Power: USA/USSR* (New York, 1964), pp. 376–77.

49. Zinner, *National Communism*, pp. 462–64.

50. *Ibid.*, pp. 464–67. It is interesting to note that in the East Berlin press the name of János Kádár had been crossed off the list of Hungarian ministers by November 3, a full day before his puppet regime came into being on the heels of the second Soviet intervention (Lasky, *op. cit.*, p. 219).

51. Eisenhower, *op. cit.*, p. 79.

52. Emmet John Hughes, *The Ordeal of Power*, (New York, 1963), p. 220.

53. *Documents on American Foreign Relations, 1956*, p. 50.

54. Murphy, *op. cit.*, p. 428; and personal communication, Robert D. Murphy to the author.

55. See Finer, *op. cit.*, p. 1; and Philip Deane in *The Scotsman*, November 7, 1956.

56. Murphy, *op. cit.*, pp. 429–30.

57. See Committee on Un-American Activities, *International Communism*, hearings of November 1, 1956.

58. Murphy, *op. cit.*, p. 430.

59. Edmond Taylor, "The Lessons of Hungary," *The Reporter*, December 27, 1956, pp. 18, 21.

60. Eisenhower, *op. cit.*, p. 82.

61. *New York Times*, November 3 and 5, 1956.

62. Roscoe Drummond and Gaston Coblentz, *Duel at the Brink* (London, 1961), pp. 180–81, 176–77.

63. Christian Pineau, quoted in the *New York Times*, October 27, 1956.

64. CBS, "Eisenhower on the Presidency, Part II."

65. Eisenhower, *op. cit.*, p. 88.

66. Quoted by Philip Deane in *The Observer*, November 11, 1956 (syndicated column).

67. United Nations, General Assembly, *Report of the Special Committee on the Problem of Hungary*, 11th sess., 1957, p. 100 (hereinafter cited as *Report of the Special Committee on Hungary*).

68. Quoted in Un-American Activities Committee, *International Communism*, p. 13.

69. Lasky, *op. cit.*, p. 228.

70. Zinner, *National Communism*, pp. 473–78. The special committee later concluded that Kádár "cannot be considered to have substantiated his own claim to have

called, in the name of the Government, for Soviet help. In any event, there is abundant evidence that Soviet preparations for a further intervention, including the movement of troops and armour from abroad, had been under way since the last days of October" (*Report of the Special Committee on Hungary*, p. 138).

71. USIA, *Hungary*, p. 32.

72. *Ibid.*, p. 34.

73. Quoted in Hughes, *op. cit.*, p. 223; cf. Finer, *op. cit.*, pp. 417-18.

74. USIA, *Hungary*, p. 34.

75. *Documents on American Foreign Relations, 1956*, p. 260.

76. Eisenhower, *op. cit.*, p. 95.

77. Quoted by Philip Deane in *The Scotsman*, November 7, 1956.

78. *Le Monde*, November 3, 1956.

79. *Soviet News*, December 14, 1956; and *New York Herald Tribune*, December 23, 1956.

80. *Christian Science Monitor* and *New York Times*, November 6, 1956; see also Herbert A. Philbrick's account of American reactions in the *New York Herald Tribune*, November 25, 1956.

81. Representative Wayne L. Hays (D., Ohio), quoted in the *New York Herald Tribune*, November 14, 1956.

82. *Ibid.*, November 11, 1956.

83. *Ibid.*, December 15, 1956; Joseph C. Harsch in the *Christian Science Monitor*, December 14, 1956.

84. Quoted in DeWitt Copp and Marshall Peck, *Betrayal at the UN* (New York, 1961), p. 80.

85. *New York Times*, October 26, 1956.

86. *New York Herald Tribune*, October 28, 1956.

87. UN Document S/3690. Article 34 reads: "The Security Council may investigate any dispute, or any situation which might lead to international friction or give rise to a dispute, in order to determine whether the continuance of the dispute or situation is likely to endanger the maintenance of international peace and security."

88. *New York Times*, October 28, 1956.

89. UN Document S/3691.

90. United Nations, Security Council, *Official Records*, 746th meeting, October 28, 1956, pp. 1-8.

91. *Ibid.*, pp. 9-11, 14, 24-31; Richard I. Miller, *Dag Hammarskjold and Crisis Diplomacy* (New York, 1961), p. 134.

92. UN Documents S/3692 (Italy), S/3693 (Argentina), S/3695 (Spain), S/3696 (Turkey), S/3697 (Austria), S/3698 (Thailand), and S/3699 (Ireland).

93. Quoted in J. P. Lash, *Dag Hammarskjold* (London, 1962), p. 92.

94. Anthony Eden, *Full Circle* (London, 1960), p. 545.

95. Much of this account is based on Gordon Gaskill's "Timetable of a Failure," *The Virginia Quarterly Review*, 34, no. 2 (Spring 1958): 162-90.

96. UN Document A/3251.

97. Copp and Peck, *op. cit.*, p. 83.

98. *Ibid.*, p. 84.

99. Quoted in Gaskill, *loc. cit.*, p. 170.

100. Quoted in *ibid.*, pp. 172-73.

101. Quoted in Lash, *op. cit.*, p. 93.

102. United Nations, General Assembly, *Official Records*, 561st meeting (first emer-

gency special session).

103. *Ibid.*, 562nd meeting, pp. 35, 39. Commented an unnamed UN delegate: "There is a real urgency with real pressure. This is the kind you Americans used about Suez, about Korea, the kind you use to keep Communist China out of the UN, against the real wishes of the majority. Then there is a kind of paper urgency, which Dulles used that night, only for the galleries and the headlines" (Quoted in Gaskill, *loc. cit.*, pp. 176-77.)

104. UN Document S/3723.

105. United Nations, Security Council, *Official Records*, 752nd meeting, pp. 2-3.

106. *Ibid.*, pp. 9, 11.

107. *Ibid.*, p. 23.

108. UN Document S/3726.

109. *New York Times*, November 4, 1956.

110. United Nations, Security Council, *Official Records*, 753rd meeting.

111. UN Document S/3730.

112. United Nations, Security Council, *Official Records*, 753rd meeting, pp. 3,11, 17.

113. Kovács, *op. cit.*, p. 209.

114. United Nations, General Assembly, *Official Records*, 563rd meeting (first emergency special session), pp. 69, 71.

115. United Nations, Security Council, *Official Records*, 754th meeting, pp. 1-3, 10-13.

116. United Nations, General Assembly, *Official Records*, 564th meeting (second emergency special session), p. 7.

117. UN Document A/3286.

118. Khrishna Menon abstained on behalf of India, apparently without instructions from New Delhi; see James J. Berna, "India's UN Vote on Hungary," *America*, December 22, 1956, p. 350.

119. UN Document A/3311.

120. *Report of the Special Committee on Hungary*, p. 59.

121. *New York Times*, November 5, 1956.

122. Quoted in Miller, *op. cit.*, p. 139.

123. *New York Times*, November 8, 1956.

124. United Nations, General Assembly, *Official Records*, 569th meeting (second emergency special session), pp. 41-42.

125. *Ibid.*, 570th meeting (second emergency special session), p. 47.

126. *Ibid.*, p. 56. The five-power resolution—UN General Assembly Resolution 1005 (ES-II)—requested the withdrawal of Soviet troops without further delay, asked for free and supervised elections, and requested the secretary-general to "continue to investigate, through representatives named by him, the situation caused by foreign intervention in Hungary and to report at the earliest possible moment to the General Assembly." (India voted with the Soviet bloc against this resolution, for Prime Minister Nehru had objected to the reference to supervised elections, viewed the entire resolution as a propaganda device, and claimed to lack sufficient information about the Hungarian crisis.) The other two resolutions were the American-sponsored one, UN General Assembly Resolution 1006 (ES-II), and that introduced by Austria, UN General Assembly Resolution 1007 (ES-II).

127. UN General Assembly Resolution 1008 (ES-II).

128. United Nations, General Assembly, *Official Records*, 573rd meeting (second emergency special session), p. 88.

129. *New York Times*, November 12 and 13, 1956.

130. Quoted in Lash, *op. cit.*, p. 92.

131. *New York Herald Tribune*, November 13, 1956. For an account of Hammarskjold's attempts to carry out his mandate, see Leon Gordenker, *The UN Secretary-General and the Maintenance of Peace* (New York, 1967), pp. 203-10.

132. Copp and Peck, *op. cit.*, p. 97. The same source claims that a member of Nagy's entourage had heard the premier telephone Mrs. Kéthly in Vienna to appoint her as Hungary's representative to the United Nations and testified to this effect before the special committee, but the report makes no mention of the episode (*ibid.*, pp. 174-75).

133. *New York Times*, November 13, 1956.

134. *Ibid.*, November 14, 16, 21, and 30, 1956.

135. *Ibid.* December 1, 7, 8, 10, 12, and 23, 1956.

136. See Rosalyn Higgins, *The Development of International Law through the Political Organs of the United Nations* (London, 1963), pp. 158-59.

137. UN Document A/3357.

138. *New York Times*, November 17 and 19, 1956.

139. UN General Assembly Resolutions 1127 (XI), approved by a vote of 55 to 10, with 14 abstentions, including those of India and Indonesia; 1128 (XI), approved by a vote of 57 to 8, with 14 abstentions, including that of Poland; and 1129 (XI), approved by a vote of 69 to 2 (Hungary and Rumania), with 8 abstentions.

140. *New York Times*, November 27 and 30 and December 1 and 7, 1956.

141. *Ibid.*, December 4, 1956.

142. *Ibid.*, December 5 and 6, 1956.

143. UN General Assembly Resolution 1130 (XI), approved by a vote of 54 to 10, with 14 abstentions.

144. UN General Assembly Resolution 1131 (XI), adopted by a vote of 55 to 8, with 13 abstentions.

145. UN General Assembly Resolution 1132 (XI); the vote was 59 to 8, with 10 abstentions (India and Egypt, among others).

146. On February 5, Hungary's representative informed the secretary-general that, in the opinion of his government, the committee violated the Charter and would therefore not be admitted to Hungary (*Report of the Special Committee on Hungary*, p. 3).

147. UN General Assembly Resolution 1133 (XI), approved by a vote of 60 to 10, with 10 abstentions. Subsequently, numerous other studies upheld the conclusions of the special committee. See Ferenc A. Váli, *The Hungarian Revolution and International Law* (New York, 1959); International Commission of Jurists, *The Hungarian Situation and the Rule of Law* (The Hague, 1957); and J. A. Szikszoy, *The Legal Aspects of the Hungarian Question* (Geneva, 1963).

148. For details of the Bang-Jensen affair, which aroused wide controversy in the United States, see Copp and Peck, *op. cit.*; and U.S., Congress, Senate, Committee on the Judiciary, *The Bang-Jensen Case*, 87th Cong., 1st sess., 1961.

149. Lincoln P. Bloomfield, *The United Nations and U.S. Foreign Policy* (Boston, 1960), p. 131.

150. Miller, *op. cit.*, pp. 150-51.

151. *Report of the Special Committee on Hungary*, p. 57.

152. Quoted in Copp and Peck, *op. cit.*, p. 111.

153. *Ibid.*, p. 95.

154. Ernest A. Gross, in *The United States and the United Nations*, ed. F. O.

Wilcox and H. F. Haviland (Baltimore, 1961), pp. 89-90.

155. Sir Harold Caccia, "Anglo-American Relations" (speech delivered in New York on December 18, 1956), *Vital Speeches of the Day*, 23: 168. See also "Le fonctionnement de l'Organisation des Nations Unies à la lumière des questions égyptienne et hongroise," *Chronique de Politique Etrangère* (Brussels), May 1957, pp. 270-77.

156. Dag Hammarskjold, *The Servant of Peace: A Selection of the Speeches and Statements of Dag Hammarskjold* (London, 1962), pp. 142-43.

157. Eisenhower, *op. cit.*, p. 89.

158. Robert T. Holt and Robert Van De Welde, *Strategic Psychological Operations and American Foreign Policy* (Chicago, 1960), p. 36.

159. *New York Herald Tribune*, December 1, 1956.

160. *New York Times*, December 30, 1956.

161. Robert T. Holt, *Radio Free Europe* (Minneapolis, 1958), pp. 167-68, 177, 188-94.

162. John MacCormac in the *New York Times*, November 25, 1956; *Report of the Special Committee on Hungary*, p. 18.

163. *New York Times*, November 20, 1956; *Christian Science Monitor*, November 30, 1956.

164. See Holt, *op. cit.*, pp. 194, 198; *Le Monde*, November 22, 1956; Allan A. Michie, *Voices through the Iron Curtain: The Radio Free Europe Story* (New York, 1963), pp. 255-57, 266-67.

165. Holt and Van De Welde, *op. cit.*, p. 36.

166. Walter Ridder, "Our Propaganda in Hungary," *The New Republic*, December 17, 1956, p. 12.

167. Michie, *op. cit.*, pp. 265-66.

168. Quoted in Kovács, *op. cit.*, pp. 159-61.

169. *New York Times*, November 15, 1956.

170. *Documents on American Foreign Relations, 1956*, pp. 57-58.

171. *New York Times*, December 3, 1956.

172. *Ibid.*, December 7 and 18, 1956.

173. See James Reston's account in *ibid.*, December 18, 1956, and *Le Monde*, December 12, 1956.

174. Letter from Hans J. Morgenthau published in the *New York Times*, November 13, 1956.

175. U.S., Congress, *Congressional Record*, 85th Cong., 1st sess., March 18, 1957, pp. 3867-68.

176. U.S., Congress, House, Committee on Foreign Affairs, *Report of the Special Study Mission to Europe on Policy toward the Satellite Nations*, 85th Cong., 1st sess., June 4, 1957, H. Rept. 531, pp. 4, 7.

177. U.S., Congress, *Congressional Record*, 85th Cong., 1st sess., January 7, 1957, pp. 307-8, 318-19.

178. U.S., Congress, House, Committee on Foreign Affairs, *Hearings on Foreign Policy and Mutual Security*, 84th Cong., 2nd sess., October-November 1956, p. 223. Recalled one Soviet intelligence officer: "We in Moscow felt as if we were sitting on a powderkeg. Everyone in the General Staff was against the 'Khrushchev adventure.' It was better to lose Hungary, as they said, than to lose everything. But what did the West do? Nothing. It was asleep. This gave Khrushchev confidence, and after Hungary he began to scream: 'I was right!' After the Hungarian incident he dismissed many

generals who had spoken out against him. If the West had slapped Khrushchev down hard then, he would not be in power today and all of Eastern Europe could be free" (Penkovskiy, *op. cit.*, pp. 212–13).

179. U.S., Department of State, *American Foreign Policy: Current Documents, 1957* (Washington, D.C., 1961), p. 662.

180. Hans J. Morgenthau, *Politics in the 20th Century*, vol. 2 (Chicago, 1962), p. 41.

181. Quoted in R. A. Moore, ed., *The United Nations Reconsidered* (Columbia, S.C., 1963), p. 103.

182. For details of a petition sent by a group of congressmen to the president, see U.S., Congress, *Congressional Record*, 85th Cong., 1st sess., January 7, 1957, p. 316. See also *ibid.*, March 18, 1957, pp. 3861–65; Senator Knowland's statement reported in the *Christian Science Monitor*, February 26, 1957; and the editorial in *Life*, March 18, 1957.

183. *Department of State Bulletin*, August 12, 1957, p. 274; and Andrew H. Berding, *Dulles on Diplomacy* (Princeton, 1965), p. 111. The Suez crisis, writes Robert Murphy, "could not have been timed more advantageously for the Russians" (*op. cit.*, p. 430).

184. Eisenhower, *op. cit.*, pp. 98–99.

185. Richard Löwenthal, "Hungary—Were We Helpless?" *The New Republic*, November 26, 1956, p. 14.

186. See Hugh Seton-Watson, "Hungary and Europe," *Spectator*, November 9, 1956, pp. 638–39; and Kingsley Martin in the *New Statesman*, February 9, 1957, p. 161.

187. At the height of the revolution, the East Berlin press published tentative proposals for a mutual dissolution of NATO and the Warsaw Pact (*New York Times*, November 2, 1956).

188. *Department of State Bulletin*, November 26, 1956, p. 839.

189. *Ibid.*, January 7, 1957, pp. 3–9. The military commander of NATO, General Norstad, also was opposed to disengagement, on strategic grounds.

190. CBS, "Eisenhower on the Presidency, Part II."

191. Ernest Lefever, *Ethics and United States Foreign Policy* (New York, 1958), p. 151.

192. Murphy, *op. cit.*, p. 431.

193. Press release, December 14, 1957, Dulles Papers.

CHAPTER VI

1. U.S., Congress, House, Committee on Foreign Affairs, *Report of the Special Study Mission to Europe on Policy toward the Satellite Nations*, 85th Cong., 1st sess., 1957, pp. 6–7, 14–16.

2. U.S., Congress, House, Committee on Foreign Affairs, *Report on Foreign Policy and Mutual Security*, 85th Cong., 1st sess., June 11, 1957, p. 76.

3. *New York Times*, January 30, 1957; U.S., Congress, Senate, *A Review of United States Foreign Policy and Operations*, prepared by Senator Allen J. Ellender, 85th Cong., 2nd sess., February 13, 1958, pp. 228, 232–33. Mansfield's subsequent suggestion that the secretary of state visit East-Central Europe to seek an improvement in relations was rejected by Dulles as inopportune (*New York Times*, July 17, 1957).

4. See Edward Weintal and Charles Bartlett, *Facing the Brink* (New York, 1967), pp. 210–11.

5. "White House Leadership Meeting, January 1, 1957, General Presentation to Congressional Leaders," Dulles Papers.

6. Council on Foreign Relations, *Documents on American Foreign Relations, 1957* (New York, 1958), p. 41 (hereinafter cited as *Documents on American Foreign Relations, 1957*). See also Russell Baker, "Dulles Looks at Dulles' Policy," *New York Times*, April 28, 1957.

7. *New York Times*, July 3, 1957.

8. *Department of State Bulletin*, July 20, 1959, p. 78.

9. Chester Bowles, "Our Objective in Europe—and Russia's," *New York Times Magazine*, May 12, 1957, pp. 9, 62–66.

10. See *Department of State Bulletin*, May 19, 1958, pp. 822–23; and Eugene Hinterhoff, *Disengagement* (London, 1959), pp. 402–7.

11. *New York Times*, December 18, 1956, and January 19, 1957; Hinterhoff, *op. cit.*, pp. 205–6. Dean Acheson deplored this "new isolationism," observing: "I cannot for the life of me see how the movement toward a greater degree of national identity in Eastern Europe is furthered by removing from the continent the only power capable of opposing the Soviet Union" ("The Illusion of Disengagement," *Foreign Affairs*, 36, no. 3 [1958]: 378). See also George Kennan, *Russia, the Atom, and the West* (London, 1958); Kennan's reply to Acheson, "Disengagement Revisited," *Foreign Affairs*, 37, no. 2 (1959): 187–210, and Zbigniew Brzezinski, "U.S. Foreign Policy in East Central Europe: A Study in Contradiction," *Journal of International Affairs*, 11, no. 1 (1957): 60–71.

12. Hugh Gaitskell, "Disengagement: Why? How?" *Foreign Affairs*, 36, no. 4 (1958): 539–56. See also *idem*, *The Challenge of Coexistence* (Cambridge, Mass., 1958); and Denis Healey, *A Neutral Belt in Europe?* (London, 1958).

13. U.S., Congress, Senate, Committee on Foreign Relations, *Control and Reduction of Armaments: Final Report*, Staff Study no. 8, 85th Cong., 1st sess., June 6, 1957.

14. Royal Institute of International Affairs, *Documents on International Affairs, 1957* (London, 1960), pp. 97–99 (hereinafter cited as *Documents on International Affairs, 1957*).

15. U.S., Department of State, *American Foreign Policy: Current Documents, 1957* (Washington, D.C., 1961), pp. 673–78; *New York Times*, May 11, 1957.

16. *Documents on International Affairs, 1957*, pp. 34–41.

17. *Department of State Bulletin*, January 27, 1958, pp. 122–27.

18. Quoted in Arnold Wolfers, ed., *Alliance Policy in the Cold War* (Baltimore, 1959), pp. 156–57.

19. *Department of State Bulletin*, March 24, 1958, pp. 459–61.

20. *New York Times*, March 6 and 20, 1958.

21. *Soviet News*, November 11, 1958.

22. Richard M. Nixon, *Six Crises* (London, 1962), p. 242.

23. U.S. Senate Joint Resolution 111, 86th Cong. 1st sess.; *Department of State Bulletin*, August 10, 1959, p. 200. A noted American scholar would subsequently argue that it "seems impossible to reconcile the approval by Congress and the Proclamation by the President of 'Captive Nations Week' with the international obligation of the United States to respect the independence of other states" (Quincy Wright, "Subversive Intervention," *American Journal of International Law*, 54, no. 3 [1960]: 533).

24. Nixon, *op. cit.*, pp. 247, 251-52.

25. *New York Times*, July 18, 1959; Council on Foreign Relations, *Documents on American Foreign Relations, 1959* (New York, 1960), pp. 210-13.

26. Imre Kovács, ed., *Facts about Hungary: The Fight for Freedom* (New York, 1966), p. 311.

27. *New York Times*, August 26, 1959.

28. *Department of State Bulletin*, November 2, 1959, pp. 627, 629.

29. *New York Times*, March 13, 1957.

30. See U.S., Congress, *Congressional Record*, 85th Cong., 1st sess., January 7, 1957, pp. 325-26, and March 18, 1957, pp. 3865, 3869-70; Stephen D. Kertész, "A Political Solution for Hungary," *Current History*, 33, no. 191 (July 1957): 7-15; and *Department of State Bulletin*, January 7, 1957, p. 8. On the deterioration of U.S.-Hungarian relations, see János Radványi, *Hungary and the Superpowers* (Stanford, 1972), pp. 30-34.

31. UN Document A/3849, July 14, 1958.

32. *Department of State Bulletin*, December 8, 1958, pp. 910-12; UN General Assembly Resolution 1312(XIII). See also Radványi, *op. cit.*, pp. 37-51.

33. *Department of State Bulletin*, December 14, 1959, p. 876.

34. UN General Assembly Resolution 1454(XIV), December 9, 1959.

35. *Department of State Bulletin*, July 20, 1959, pp. 99-100; *New York Times*, July 7 and 8, 1959.

36. *Department of State Bulletin*, June 24, 1957, pp. 1003-9, and September 9, 1957, p. 44.

37. *New York Times*, June 18, 1958.

38. *Department of State Bulletin*, June 29, 1959, pp. 959-61, and November 30, 1959, pp. 789-90.

39. *Ibid.*, August 8, 1960, pp. 226-28.

40. *Ibid.*, December 5, 1960, pp. 863-64. Poland's most-favored-nation status had been revoked by the United States in 1951 (*ibid.*, December 3, 1951, pp. 913-14).

41. *Ibid.*, November 5, 1956, p. 722.

42. *Ibid.*, October 29, 1956, pp. 664-65.

43. *Ibid.*, June 10, 1957, pp. 939-40.

44. Quoted in Milorad M. Drachkovitch, *United States Aid to Yugoslavia and Poland: Analysis of a Controversy* (Washington, D.C., 1963), p. 11.

45. *Department of State Bulletin*, April 13, 1959, p. 512; April 26, 1960, pp. 670-73; and December 26, 1960, pp. 968-72.

46. *Ibid.*, August 8, 1960, p. 219; *New York Times*, October 1, 1960; *Department of State Bulletin*, October 17, 1960, p. 600.

47. *New York Times*, October 2 and 28, 1960.

48. John F. Kennedy, *The Strategy of Peace* (New York, 1960), pp. 82-98.

49. *Ibid.*, p. 18.

50. *New York Times*, January 31, 1961.

51. *Ibid.*, February 18, 1963.

52. Zbigniew Brzezinski and William E. Griffith, "Peaceful Engagement in Eastern Europe," *Foreign Affairs*, 39, no. 4 (1961): 642-54.

53. Quoted in Donald Brandon, *American Foreign Policy* (New York, 1966), p. 148.

54. U.S., Department of State, *American Foreign Policy: Current Documents, 1961*, (Washington, D.C., 1965), pp. 584-86.

55. See Theodore C. Sorensen, *Kennedy* (New York, 1965), chap. 21.

56. *New York Times*, July 26, 1961.

57. Arthur M. Schlesinger, Jr., *A Thousand Days* (New York, 1965), p. 331. See also Jean Edward Smith, *The Defense of Berlin* (Baltimore, 1963), p. 256; Philip Windsor, *City on Leave* (New York, 1963), pp. 236-37; and Hans Speier, *Divided Berlin* (New York, 1961), pp. 140-41.

58. Schlesinger, *op. cit.*, p. 331.

59. U.S., Department of State, *Berlin: 1961*, European and British Commonwealth Series, no. 64 (Washington, D.C., 1961), pp. 41-42 (hereinafter cited as *Berlin: 1961*). In fact, Rusk was advancing a spurious argument, for the 1949 four-power agreement referred to communications between the Western zones of Germany, on the one hand, and Berlin and the Eastern zone, on the other, not to communications between the four sectors of Berlin.

60. Sorensen, *op. cit.*, p. 594; *New York Times*, January 16, 1962.

61. The U.S. note of August 17 formally challenged East Germany's right to move its armed forces into the Soviet sector and held the Soviet government responsible for the whole affair (*Berlin: 1961*, p. 42). See also Schlesinger, *op. cit.*, p. 332; and Weintal and Bartlett, *op. cit.*, p. 211.

62. Smith, *The Defense of Berlin*, p. 303.

63. *Ibid.*, pp. 293-96.

64. See *ibid.*, pp. 313-35.

65. U.S., Congress, House, Committee on Foreign Affairs, Subcommittee on Europe, *Captive European Nations: Hearings*, 87th Cong., 2nd sess., 1962, pp. 303-7 (hereinafter cited as *Captive European Nations: Hearings*).

66. U.S., Congress, House, Committee on Foreign Affairs, Subcommittee on Europe, *Report on Hearings on Captive European Nations*, 88th Cong., 1st sess., April 29, 1963, pp. 13-17 (hereinafter cited as *Report on Hearings on Captive European Nations*).

67. U.S., Congress, House, *Report of the Special Study Mission to Poland*, prepared by Congressman Clement J. Zablocki, 87th Cong., 1st sess., July 12, 1961.

68. See, for instance, the editorial in the June 1, 1962, issue of *Life*, "It is High Time to Blow the Whistle on Tito." Between July 1, 1945, and June 30, 1962, the United States provided economic aid (grants, credits, etc.) in the amount of $2,304 million to Yugoslavia and $878 million to Poland (Drachkovitch, *op. cit.*, p. 8). Khrushchev reportedly told a meeting of satellite leaders in 1961: "Comrade Gomulka is wise. He takes the wheat from the Americans without giving anything in exchange. Follow his example" (*Le Monde*, September 19, 1962, cited in *ibid.*, p. 117).

69. *Ibid.*, p. 84.

70. Dean Rusk, *The Winds of Freedom* (Boston, 1963), pp. 244-46; *Department of State Bulletin*, July 2, 1962, p. 25.

71. See Drachkovitch, *op. cit.*, pp. 25ff.

72. *Ibid.*, p. 38.

73. *New York Times*, 25 January 1963; Council on Foreign Relations, *Documents on American Foreign Relations, 1963* (New York, 1964), p. 52; *Department of State Bulletin*, February 25, 1963, pp. 303-5.

74. *Department of State Bulletin*, October 28, 1963, p. 661.

75. See Lyndon B. Johnson, *The Vantage Point: Perspectives of the Presidency, 1963-1969* (New York, 1971), pp. 39-40.

76. See Jozef Wilczynski, *The Economics and Politics of East-West Trade* (London, 1969), pp. 272-76.

77. Radványi, *op. cit.*, pp. xv–xvi. For details of the lengthy negotiations and for illuminating insights into the Hungarian power structure, see *ibid.*, pp. 84–120, 140–50. The author was Hungarian chargé d'affaires in Washington during the later phase of the negotiations and subsequently defected to the West.

78. *Department of State Bulletin*, January 14, 1963, p. 75. The outcome was the UN General Assembly Resolution 1857 (XVII), of December 20, 1962.

79. *Ibid.*, July 1, 1963, p. 32. See also U.S., Congress, *Congressional Record*, 88th Cong., 1st sess., May 15, 1963, p. 8646, "Report on the Changing Situation in Hungary."

80. *Department of State Bulletin*, December 2, 1963, pp. 860–61.

81. *Ibid.*, April 2, 1963, pp. 661–63, and July 2, 1963, pp. 138–41.

82. Assembly of Captive European Nations, *Resolutions, Reports, Organization*, 9th sess., 1962–63 (New York, 1963), p. 115 (hereinafter cited as ACEN, 9th sess.).

83. *Ibid.*, p. 116.

84. *Ibid.*, p. 29.

85. *Ibid.*, pp. 106, 111–13. See also *Captive European Nations: Hearings*, pp. 242–43, for the testimony of the secretary-general of ACEN, Brutus Coste.

86. See ACEN, 9th sess., pp. 12, 118–120; and *New York Times*, February 18, 1963.

87. *New York Times*, October 15, 1962.

88. *Department of State Bulletin*, October 28, 1963, pp. 656–57.

89. See Schlesinger, *op. cit.*, pp. 763–65.

90. See U.S., Congress, Joint Economic Committee, *New Directions in the Soviet Economy*, pt. 4, Maurice Ernst, "Postwar Economic Growth in Eastern Europe: A Comparison with Western Europe," 89th Cong., 2nd sess., 1966.

91. This is born out by the reports on public opinion in the satellites compiled by the Audience Research Department of Radio Free Europe.

92. *Department of State Bulletin*, March 16, 1964, pp. 390–96.

93. *Ibid.*, October 5, 1964, p. 465.

94. George F. Kennan, *On Dealing with the Communist World* (New York, 1964), pp. viii, 6, 19, 29, 33–36, 44–51. Cf. Marshall D. Shulman, *Beyond the Cold War* (New Haven, 1966), *passim*; and Herbert von Borch, "Amerika und der Europäische Status Quo," *Aussenpolitik*, 15, no. 2 (1964): 81–91.

95. Hans J. Morgenthau, "Peace in Our Time?" *Commentary*, 37, no. 3 (1964): 66.

96. U.S., Congress, House, Committee on Foreign Affairs, Subcommittee on Europe, *Recent Developments in the Soviet Bloc: Hearings*, 88th Cong., 2nd sess., 1964, pp. 348–72.

97. U.S., Congress, House, Committee on Foreign Affairs, *Recent Developments in the Soviet Bloc: Report on Hearings*, 88th Cong., 2nd sess., 1964, pp. 12–19.

98. *New York Times*, March 26, 1964. See J. William Fulbright, *Old Myths and New Realities* (New York, 1964).

99. *Department of State Bulletin*, June 15, 1964, p. 923.

100. *New York Times*, January 5, 1965.

101. Under the U.S. Tariff Act of 1930, states that did not enjoy most-favored-nation treatment were subject to rates of duty almost four times higher.

102. U.S., Department of State, *Report to the President of the Special Committee on U.S. Trade Relations with East European Countries and the Soviet Union*, presented at the White House on April 29, 1965 (Washington, D.C., 1966).

103. *Department of State Bulletin*, May 30, 1966, pp. 843–44.

104. *Ibid.*, pp. 839–40.

105. *New York Times*, May 13, 1966.

106. U.S., Congress, Senate, Committee on Foreign Relations, *East-West Trade: Hearings*, 88th Cong., 2nd sess., 1964, pp. 25, 31-32.

107. Fulbright, *op. cit.*, p. 14.

108. See *Department of State Bulletin*, November 8, 1965, p. 742, and May 1, 1967, pp. 697-99; U.S., Department of State, *The Battle Act Report, 1967* (Washington, D.C., 1968), pp. 11-12.

109. U.S., Department of State, *The Battle Act Report, 1967*, p. 13; cf. Johnson, *op. cit.*, pp. 472-73.

110. *New York Times*, July 25, 1965.

111. See Wilczynski, *op. cit.*, pp. 126-27n.

112. *Department of State Bulletin*, November 1, 1965, pp. 700-701.

113. *Ibid.*, October 24, 1966, pp. 624-25; cf. Johnson, *op. cit.*, pp. 474-75.

114. See U.S., Department of State, *Building Bridges to Eastern Europe*, European and British Commonwealth Series, no. 70 (Washington, D.C., 1967).

115. *Department of State Bulletin*, October 2, 1966, p. 434.

116. See Wilczynski, *op. cit.*, pp. 287-88.

117. *Department of State Bulletin*, January 10, 1966, pp. 62-64.

118. See Wilczynski, *op. cit.*, pp. 272, 283-93.

119. See *Department of State Bulletin*, October 25, 1965, pp. 665-71; and L. A. D. Dellin, "Political Factors in East-West Trade," *East Europe*, 18, no. 10 (1969): 29.

120. *Captive European Nations: Hearings*, p. 24.

121. *Report on Hearings on Captive European Nations*, p. 13.

122. U.S., Congress, House, Committee on Foreign Affairs, *Winning the Cold War: The U.S. Ideological Offensive* (hearings before the Subcommittee on International Organizations and Movements), 88th Cong., 1st and 2nd sess., 1965, pp. 37-38 (hereinafter cited as *Winning the Cold War*).

123. *Britannica Book of the Year 1968: Events of 1967* (Chicago, 1968), p. 647.

124. See the testimony of the Committee for a Free Europe's president, John Richardson, Jr., in *Winning the Cold War*, pp. 599-652.

125. See Free Europe, Inc., *Radio Free Europe and East Europe* (New York, 1969); and Claude Angeli's article in *Le Nouvel Observateur*, January 12, 1970.

126. See the Evans-Novak column in the *New York Herald Tribune* (International ed.), December 14-15, 1968.

127. *Department of State Bulletin*, December 21, 1964, p. 867.

128. Quoted in Weintal and Bartlett, *op. cit.*, p. 164.

129. *Department of State Bulletin*, June 15, 1964, pp. 924-26.

130. J. F. Brown, *The New Eastern Europe* (New York, 1966), pp. 226-28.

131. Council on Foreign Relations, *Documents on American Foreign Relations, 1966* (New York, 1967), pp. 53-57.

132. *New York Times*, June 2, 1967. The Mindszenty impasse was finally resolved in 1971, when an agreement between Budapest and the Vatican impelled the cardinal to go into exile.

133. Arguments for a "European solution" to the problem of the satellites, which would leave it up to the West Europeans to work toward a reintegration of their Eastern neighbors into a European community, were advanced by Edmund Stillman and William Pfaff in their critique of U.S. foreign policy, *Power and Impotence* (New York, 1966).

134. See Zbigniew Brzezinski, "Russia and Europe," *Foreign Affairs*, 42, no. 3 (1964): 428-44.

135. See Laszlo Gorgey, "New Consensus in Germany's Eastern European Policy," *Western Political Quarterly*, 21, no. 4 (1968): 681-97.

136. This fear of popular reconciliation made Gomulka countermand an invitation sent by Polish bishops to their West German colleagues in November 1965.

137. Zbigniew K. Brzezinski, "The United States and Eastern Europe" (Address delivered at Carleton University, Ottawa, on January 20, 1967).

138. *New York Times*, December 18, 1967.

139. See Philip Windsor and Adam Roberts, *Czechoslovakia, 1968* (London, 1969).

140. See Zdenek Suda, *The Czechoslovak Socialist Republic* (Baltimore, 1969), pp. 117ff.

141. Windsor and Roberts, *op. cit.*, pp. 27-28.

142. Quoted in *ibid.*, p. 41.

143. The exchange of letters is reprinted in *ibid.*, pp. 150-68.

144. See *ibid.*, pp. 62ff.

145. Richard Löwenthal, "The Sparrow in the Cage (II)," *Encounter*, 32, no. 2 (1969): 85.

146. Windsor and Roberts, *op. cit.*, pp. 174-75.

147. *New York Times*, May 2, 1968.

148. *Ibid.*, May 26 and 27, 1968.

149. *Department of State Bulletin*, July 22, 1968, p. 91.

150. *New York Times*, July 14, 1968.

151. See John C. Campbell, "Czechoslovakia: American Choices, Past and Future," *Canadian Slavonic Papers*, 11, no. 1 (1969): 13-14. Apparently, West German intelligence learned as early as March of the Kremlin's determination to crush Dubček, but General Gehlen's warnings met with skepticism in Bonn and at NATO headquarters (E. H. Cookridge, *Gehlen* [New York, 1972], p. 361).

152. *Department of State Bulletin*, August 19, 1968, pp. 186-87.

153. Johnson, *op. cit.*, p. 486.

154. *New York Times*, June 20, 1968; *Department of State Bulletin*, July 15, 1968, pp. 75-77.

155. Johnson, *op. cit.*, pp. 487-88. See also David Wise, "The Twilight of a President," *New York Times Magazine*, November 3, 1968, p. 122.

156. Lewis Chester et al., *An American Melodrama* (New York, 1969), p. 532.

157. *Department of State Bulletin*, September 9, 1968, p. 261.

158. See the account of Harlan Cleveland, "NATO after the Invasion," *Foreign Affairs*, 47, no. 2 (1969): 251-65.

159. A. G. Mezerik, *Invasion and Occupation of Czechoslovakia and the UN* (New York, 1968), *passim*; and *Department of State Bulletin*, September 9, 1968, pp. 263-74.

160. *Department of State Bulletin*, December 9, 1968, p. 600.

161. *Ibid.*, September 9, 1968, p. 263.

162. *New York Times*, September 22, 1968. See also Campbell, *loc. cit.*, pp. 17-19.

163. See the French president's communiqué in *Le Monde*, August 22, 1968.

164. *Department of State Bulletin*, October 7, 1968, pp. 350-51.

165. *Ibid.*, September 23, 1968, p. 310.

166. *Ibid.*, December 23, 1968, pp. 647–48.
167. *Ibid.*, September 16, 1968, p. 296.
168. *New York Times*, September 21, 1968.
169. *Ibid.*, September 18, 1968.
170. *Department of State Bulletin*, September 30, 1968, p. 337. See also R. Rockingham Gill, "Europe's Military Balance after Czechoslovakia," *East Europe*, 17, no. 10 (1968): 19–20.
171. *New York Times*, August 22, 1968.
172. *Department of State Bulletin*, November 11, 1968, p. 489.
173. *Ibid.*, November 4, 1968, p. 476.
174. Observed Kennan: "The suggestion of such a meeting at this time smacks of one of the worst phenomena of American diplomacy in earlier years, namely: the abuse of external relations of our people as a whole for the domestic-political advantage of a single faction or party" (*New York Times*, September 22, 1968).
175. See Chester *et al.*, *op. cit.*, p. 532.
176. Joe McGinniss, "The Selling of the President 1968," *Harper's Magazine*, August, 1969, p. 185.
177. Quoted by Peter Grose (New York Times Service) in the *Globe and Mail* (Toronto), August 5, 1969.
178. *Department of State Bulletin*, February 26, 1968, p. 284.
179. *Ibid.*, March 25, 1968, p. 422.
180. U.S., Congress, Senate, Banking and Currency Committee, Subcommittee on International Finance, *East-West Trade: Hearings on Senate Joint Resolution 169*, 90th Cong., 2nd sess., 1968; and *Department of State Bulletin*, July 1, 1968, pp. 29–31.
181. See Peter Schrag, "America's Other Radicals," *Harper's Magazine*, August 1970, p. 39.
182. See U.S., Department of Commerce, *Export Control*, 84th quarterly report, August 14, 1968; the report noted that, in the period covered, $44.1 million worth of license applications had been approved and $5 million worth rejected.
183. *Department of State Bulletin*, September 9, 1968, p. 262.
184. *Ibid.*, September 30, 1968, pp. 341–42.
185. Quoted by Frank Hardy in *The Sunday Times* (London), November 3, 1968.
186. Mezerik, *op. cit.*, p. 5.
187. Gromyko reportedly assured Rusk in October that the invasion did not imply any threat to West Berlin (*New York Times*, October 16, 1968).
188. *Ibid.*, January 15, 1969.

CHAPTER VII

1. Donald Brandon, *American Foreign Policy* (New York, 1966), p. 134.
2. See Hans J. Morgenthau's review article, "Historical Justice and the Cold War," *The New York Review*, July 10, 1969, pp. 10–17.
3. See U.S., Congress, House, *Forward-looking Addresses in the House of Representatives together with Documents on the Captive Nations Week Movement*, 91st Cong., 1st sess., 1969, H. Doc. 91-184.
4. See *New York Times*, March 12, 1972; and Henry Kamm, "The Station That Fulbright Wants to Shut Down," *New York Times Magazine*, March 26, 1972, pp. 36–37 and 112–15.

5. "U.S. Foreign Policy for the 1970's: A New Strategy for Peace," report by President Nixon to Congress, February 18, 1970.

6. "U.S. Foreign Policy for the 1970's: The Emerging Structure of Peace," report of President Nixon to Congress, February 9, 1972.

7. Henry A. Kissinger, *American Foreign Policy* (New York, 1969), pp. 76-77.

8. For a recent account of *Ostpolitik*, see Lawrence L. Whetten, *Germany's Ostpolitik: Relations between the Federal Republic and the Warsaw Pact Countries* (London, 1971).

9. Cf. Zbigniew Brzezinski, "East-West Relations after Czechoslovakia," *East Europe*, 18, no. 11-12 (1969): 2-10.

10. *New York Times*, December 2, 1971.

11. George W. Ball, "Slogans and Realities," *Foreign Affairs*, 47, no. 4 (1969):624-25.

SELECTED
BIBLIOGRAPHY

PUBLIC DOCUMENTS

Adám, Magda; Juhász, Gyula; and Kerekes, Lajos, eds. *Magyarország és a második világháború: Titkos diplomáciai okmányok a háború előzményeihez és történetéhez*. Budapest: Kossuth, 1959.

Assembly of Captive European Nations. *Organization, Resolutions, Reports, Debate.* 1st sess., September 20, 1954–February 11, 1955. New York, 1955.

——. *Resolutions, Reports, Organization.* 9th sess., 1962–1963. New York, 1963.

Bass, Robert, and Marbury, Elizabeth, eds. *The Soviet-Yugoslav Controversy, 1948–58: A Documentary Record.* New York: Prospect, 1959.

Columbia University, Russian Institute. *The Anti-Stalin Campaign and International Communism: A Selection of Documents.* New York: Columbia University Press, 1956.

Council on Foreign Relations. *Documents on American Foreign Relations, 1952–1966.* 15 vols. New York: Harper, 1953–67.

General Sikorski Historical Institute. *Documents on Polish-Soviet Relations, 1939–*

1945. 2 vols. London: Heinemann, 1967.

Great Britain, Parliament. *All-Party Delegation to Hungary: Unanimous Report on Hungary.* London, 1946.

_____ . *Parliamentary Papers.* "Report of Proceedings, Inter-Allied Meeting Held in London at St. James's Palace on September 24, 1941." Cmd. 6315. 1941.

Hungary, Ministry of Foreign Affairs. *Documents on the Hostile Activity of the United States Government against the Hungarian People's Republic.* Budapest, 1951.

_____ . *La Hongrie et la Conférence de Paris.* Vols. 1, 2, and 4. Budapest, 1947.

_____ . *Le problème de la minorité hongroise de Slovaquie.* Budapest, 1946.

_____ . *Le problème hongrois par rapport à la Roumanie.* Budapest, 1946.

_____ . *Le problème hongrois par rapport à la Tchécoslovaquie.* Budapest, 1946.

_____ . Ministry of Information. *Fehér Könyv: A magyar köztársaság és a demokrácia elleni összeesküvés.* Budapest, 1947.

_____ . *Hungarian-American Relations, 1918–1960.* Budapest, 1960.

International Commission of Jurists. *The Hungarian Situation and the Rule of Law.* The Hague, 1957.

Osteuropa Bibliothek. *Refusal of a Compromise: Document concerning the Indian Attempts to Mediate in Hungary.* Bern, 1956.

Republican National Committee. *Official Report of the Proceedings of the Twenty-fifth Republican National Convention, 1952.* N.p., n.d.

Royal Institute of International Affairs. *Documents on International Affairs.* Volumes covering the years 1939–62. London: Oxford University Press, 1951–71.

United Nations, General Assembly and Security Council. *Official Records.*

_____ . *Report of the Special Committee on the Problem of Hungary.* New York, 1957.

U.S., Congress. *Congressional Record.*

U.S., Congress, House. *Forward-looking Addresses in the House of Representatives together with Documents on the Captive Nations Week Movement.* 91st Cong., 1st sess., 1969, H. Doc. 91-184.

_____ . *Hearings before the Select Committee to Conduct an Investigation of the Facts, Evidence, and Circumstances of the Katyn Forest Massacre.* 82nd Cong., 2nd sess., 1952.

_____ . *Report of the Special Study Mission to Poland.* Prepared by Congressman Clement J. Zablocki. 87th Cong., 1st sess., 1961.

_____ . *Report on the Yalta Conference.* 79th Cong., 1st sess., 1945.

_____ , Committee on Appropriations. *Mutual Security Appropriations for 1956: Hearings.* 84th Cong., 1st sess., 1955.

_____ , Committee on Foreign Affairs. *Captive European Nations: Hearings.* 87th Cong., 2nd sess., 1962.

_____ . *Hearings on Foreign Policy and Mutual Security.* 84th Cong., 2nd sess., 1956.

_____ . *Hearings on House Joint Resolution 200: Joining with the President of the United States in a Declaration regarding the Subjugation of Free Peoples by the Soviet Union.* 83rd Cong., 1st sess., 1953.

_____ . *The Mutual Security Program: Hearings.* 82nd Cong., 1st sess., 1951.

_____ . *Recent Developments in the Soviet Bloc: Hearings.* 88th Cong., 2nd sess., 1964.

_____ . *Report of the Special Study Mission to Europe: Conditions behind the Iron Curtain and in Selected Countries of Western Europe.* 88th Cong., 1st sess., 1963.

_____ . *Report of the Special Study Mission to Europe on Policy toward the Satellite Nations.* 85th Cong., 1st sess., 1957.

———. *Report on Foreign Policy and Mutual Security.* 85th Cong., 1st sess., 1957.

———. *Report on Hearings on Captive European Nations.* 88th Cong., 1st sess., 1963.

———. *The Strategy and Tactics of World Communism.* 80th Cong., 2nd sess., 1948.

———. *Winning the Cold War: The U.S. Ideological Offensive.* 88th Cong., 1st and 2nd sess., 1965.

———. *World War II International Agreements and Understandings: Entered into during Secret Conferences concerning Other People.* 83rd Cong., 1st sess., 1953.

———, Committee on Un-American Activities. *The Crimes of Khrushchev.* 86th Cong., 1st sess., 1959.

———. *International Communism: Revolt in the Satellites.* 84th Cong., 2nd sess., 1957.

U.S., Congress, Joint Economic Committee. *New Directions in the Soviet Economy.* 89th Cong., 2nd sess., 1966.

U.S., Congress, Senate. *A Review of United States Foreign Policy and Operations.* Prepared by Senator Allen J. Ellender. 85th Cong., 2nd sess., 1958.

———, Banking and Currency Committee, Subcommittee on International Finance. *East-West Trade: Hearings on Senate Joint Resolution 169.* 90th Cong., 2nd sess., 1968.

———, Committee on Foreign Relations. *Control and Reduction of Armaments: Final Report.* Staff Study no. 8. 85th Cong., 1st sess., 1957.

———. *Documents on Germany, 1944–1959.* 86th Cong., 1st sess., 1959.

———. *East-West Trade: Hearings.* 88th Cong., 2nd sess., 1964.

———. *Hearing on Senate Resolution 116 favoring Discussion at the Coming Geneva Conference on the Status of Nations under Communist Control.* 84th Cong., 1st sess., 1955.

———. *Hearings on the Mutual Security Act of 1952.* 82nd Cong., 2nd sess., 1952.

———. *Hearings on the Treaties of Peace with Italy, Rumania, Bulgaria, and Hungary.* 80th Cong., 1st sess., 1947.

———. *The Mutual Security Act of 1953: Report.* 83rd Cong., 1st sess., 1953.

———. *Nomination of John Foster Dulles: Hearings.* 83rd Cong., 1st sess., 1953.

———. *Overseas Information Programs of the United States: Report.* 83rd Cong., 1st sess., 1953.

———. *Tensions within the Soviet Captive Countries.* 84th Cong., 1st sess., 1955.

———. *U.S. Foreign Policy: U.S.S.R. and Eastern Europe.* 86th Cong., 2nd sess., 1960.

———. *World War II International Agreements and Understandings.* 83rd Cong., 1st sess., 1953.

and Department of State. *A Decade of American Foreign Policy: Basic Documents, 1941–1949.* Washington, D.C., 1950.

———, Committee on the Judiciary. *The Bang-Jensen Case.* 87th Cong., 1st sess., 1961.

———. *UN Reports and Documents dealing with the Hungarian Revolution.* 85th Cong., 1st sess., 1957.

U.S., Department of Commerce. *Export Control.* 84th quarterly report. August 14, 1968.

U.S., Department of State. *American Foreign Policy: Current Documents, 1956.* Washington, D.C., 1959.

———. *American Foreign Policy: Current Documents, 1957.* Washington, D.C., 1961.

———. *American Foreign Policy: Current Documents, 1961.* Washington, D.C., 1965.

———. *American Foreign Policy, 1950–1955.* Washington, D.C., 1957.

———. *The Battle Act Report, 1967.* Washington, D.C., 1968.

_____ . *Berlin: 1961.* European and British Commonwealth Series, no. 64. Washington, D.C., 1961.

_____ . *Building Bridges to Eastern Europe.* European and British Commonwealth Series, no. 70. Washington, D.C., 1967.

_____ . *Department of State Bulletin.*

_____ . *Foreign Relations of the United States: Diplomatic Papers, 1941.* Vol. 1. Washington, D.C., 1958.

_____ . *Foreign Relations of the United States: Diplomatic Papers, 1943.* Vol. 3. Washington, D.C., 1963.

_____ . *Foreign Relations of the United States: Diplomatic Papers, 1944.* Vols. 3 and 4. Washington, D.C., 1965–66.

_____ . *Foreign Relations of the United States: Diplomatic Papers, 1945.* Vol. 4 and 5. Washington, D.C., 1967–1968.

_____ . *Foreign Relations of the United States: Diplomatic Papers, 1946.* Vol. 6. Washington, D.C., 1969.

_____ . *Foreign Relations of the United States, 1945: The Conference of Berlin.* Vols. 1 and 2. Washington, D.C., 1960.

_____ . *Foreign Relations of the United States, 1945: The Conferences at Malta and Yalta.* Washington, D.C., 1955.

_____ . *Foreign Relations of the United States, 1946: The Paris Peace Conference.* Vols. 3 and 4. Washington, D.C., 1970.

_____ . *The Geneva Conference of Heads of Government.* Washington, D.C., 1955.

_____ . *Making the Peace Treaties.* Washington, D.C., 1947.

_____ . *Paris Peace Conference, 1946: Selected documents.* Washington, D.C., 1947.

_____ . *Postwar Foreign Policy Preparation, 1939–1945.* Washington, D.C., 1949.

_____ . *Program Test of Voice of America's New York and Munich Output in Hungarian.* Prepared by the Institute of Communications Research, Inc. Washington, D.C., 1953.

_____ . *Report to the President of the Special Committee on U.S. Trade Relations with East European Countries and the Soviet Union.* Washington, D.C., 1966.

_____ . *Strengthening the Forces of Freedom: Selected Speeches and Statements of Secretary of State Acheson.* Washington, D.C., 1950.

_____ . International Cooperation Administration. *The Strategic Trade Control System, 1948–1956.* Washington, D.C., 1957.

U.S., Foreign Operations Administration. *Handbook of Mutual Security Legislation.* Washington, D.C., 1954.

_____ . *The Revision of Strategic Trade Controls.* Washington, D.C., 1954.

_____ . *World-wide Enforcement of Strategic Trade Controls.* Washington, D.C., 1953.

United States Information Agency. *Hungary: American Statements and Actions.* London, n.d.

U.S.S.R., Ministry of Foreign Affairs. *Correspondence between the Chairman of the Council of Ministers of the U.S.S.R. and the Presidents of the U.S.A. and the Prime Ministers of Great Britain during the Great Patriotic War of 1941–1945.* 2 vols. Moscow: Foreign Languages Publishing House, 1957.

World Peace Foundation. *Documents on American Foreign Relations, 1944–1951.* 7 vols. Princeton: Princeton University Press, 1947–53.

Yugoslavia, Ministry of Foreign Affairs. *Conférence Danubienne, Beograd, 1948: Recueil des Documents.* Belgrade, 1949.

Zinner, Paul E., ed. *National Communism and Popular Revolt in Eastern Europe.* New York: Columbia University Press, 1956.

MEMOIRS, SPEECHES, PAPERS

Acheson, Dean. *Present at the Creation.* New York: Norton, 1969.

Adams, Sherman. *Firsthand Report.* New York: Harper, 1961.

Adenauer, Konrad. *Erinnerungen, 1953-1955.* Stuttgart: Deutsche Verlags-Anstalt, 1966.

_____. *Memoirs, 1945-53.* London: Weidenfeld & Nicolson, 1965.

Alexander of Tunis, Earl. *The Alexander Memoirs, 1940-1945.* London: Cassell, 1962.

Beneš, Eduard. *Memoirs.* London: Allen & Unwin, 1954.

Bundy, McGeorge, ed. *The Pattern of Responsibility: Speeches of Dean Acheson.* Boston: Houghton Mifflin, 1952.

Byrnes, James. *Speaking Frankly.* New York: Harper, 1947.

Cadogan, Sir Alexander. *The Diaries of Sir Alexander Cadogan, 1938-1945.* Edited by D. Dilks. London: Cassell, 1971.

Churchill, Winston. *Europe Unite: Speeches, 1947 and 1948.* London: Cassell, 1950.

_____. *The Second World War.* 6 vols. Boston: Houghton Mifflin, 1948-53.

Ciechanowski, Jan. *Defeat in Victory.* Garden City, N.Y.: Doubleday, 1947.

Clark, Mark. *Calculated Risk.* London: Harrap, 1951.

Conant, James B. *My Several Lives.* New York: Harper & Row, 1970.

Djilas, Milovan. *Conversations with Stalin.* New York: Harcourt, Brace & World, 1962.

Duke, Florimond, with Charles M. Swaart. *Name, Rank, and Serial Number.* New York: Meredith, 1969.

Dulles, John Foster. The Private and Personal Papers of John Foster Dulles, Princeton University Library, Princeton, N.J.

Eden, Anthony. *Full Circle.* London: Cassell, 1960.

_____. *The Reckoning.* London: Cassell, 1965.

Eisenhower, Dwight D. *Mandate For Change.* Garden City, N.Y.: Doubleday, 1963.

_____. *Waging Peace.* Garden City, N.Y.: Doubleday, 1964.

Forrestal, James. *The Forrestal Diaries.* Edited by Walter Millis. New York: Viking, 1951.

Hammarskjold, Dag. *The Servant of Peace: A Selection of the Speeches and Statements of Dag Hammarskjold.* London: Bodley Head, 1962.

Horthy, Nicholas. *The Confidential Papers of Admiral Horthy.* Budapest: Corvina, 1965.

_____. *Memoirs.* London: Hutchinson, 1956.

Hull, Cordell. *The Memoirs of Cordell Hull.* New York: Hodder & Stoughton, 1948.

Johnson, Lyndon Baines. *The Vantage Point: Perspectives of the Presidency, 1963-1969.* New York: Holt, Rinehart & Winston, 1971.

Kállay, Nicholas. *Hungarian Premier.* London: Oxford University Press, 1954.

Kennan, George F. *Memoirs, 1925-1950.* Boston: Little, Brown & Co.: Atlantic Monthly Press, 1967.

Khrushchev, Nikita. *K[h]rushchev Remembers.* Edited by Strobe Talbott. Boston: Little, Brown & Co., 1970.

Kővágó, József. *You Are All Alone.* New York: Praeger, 1959.

Krock, Arthur. *Memoirs.* New York: Funk & Wagnalls, 1968.
Lane, Arthur Bliss. *I Saw Poland Betrayed.* Indianapolis: Bobbs-Merrill, 1948.
Leahy, William D. *I Was There.* New York: McGraw-Hill, 1950.
Macmillan, Harold. *The Blast of War, 1939-1945.* London: Macmillan, 1967.
_____. *Tides of Fortune, 1945-1955.* London: Macmillan, 1969.
Mikolajczyk, Stanislaw. *The Rape of Poland: Pattern of Soviet Aggression.* New York: McGraw-Hill, 1948.
Murphy, Robert D. *Diplomat among Warriors.* Garden City, N.Y.: Doubleday, 1964.
Nagy, Ferenc. *The Struggle behind the Iron Curtain.* New York: Macmillan, 1948.
Nagy, Imre. *On Communism: In Defence of the New Course.* London: Thames & Hudson, 1957.
Nixon, Richard M. *Six Crises.* Garden City, N.Y.: Doubleday, 1962.
Penkovskiy, Oleg. *The Penkovskiy Papers.* Garden City, N.Y.: Doubleday, 1965.
Philby, Kim. *My Silent War.* New York: Grove Press, 1968.
Pope, Maurice A. *Soldiers and Politicians.* Toronto: University of Toronto Press, 1962.
Rusk, Dean. *The Winds of Freedom.* Boston: Beacon Press, 1963.
Smith, Walter Bedell. *My Three Years in Moscow.* Philadelphia: Lippincott, 1950.
Stevenson, Adalai. *Major Campaign Speeches, 1952.* New York: Random House, 1953.
Stimson, Henry L. *On Active Service in Peace and War.* New York: Harper, 1948.
Sulzberger, C. L. *The Last of the Giants.* New York: Macmillan, 1970.
_____. *A Long Row of Candles.* New York: Macmillan, 1969.
Taylor, Maxwell D. *The Uncertain Trumpet.* London: Stevens, 1960.
Truman, Harry S. *Memoirs by Harry S. Truman*: vol. 1, *Years of Decisions*; vol. 2, *Years of Trial and Hope.* Garden City, N.Y.: Doubleday, 1955-56.
Vandenberg, Arthur H. *The Private Papers of Senator Vandenberg.* Edited by Arthur H. Vandenberg, Jr. London: Gollancz, 1953.

BOOKS

Aczél, Tamás, and Méray, Tibor. *The Revolt of the Mind.* London: Thames & Hudson, 1960.
Allard, Sven. *Russia and the Austrian State Treaty.* University Park: Pennsylvania State University Press, 1970.
Alperowitz, Gar. *Atomic Diplomacy: Hiroshima and Potsdam.* New York: Simon & Schuster, 1965.
American Assembly. *The United States and Eastern Europe.* Edited by Robert F. Byrnes. Englewood Cliffs, N.J.: Prentice-Hall, 1967.
American Friends of the Captive Nations and the Assembly of Captive European Nations. *Hungary under Soviet Rule.* Vols. 1-7. New York, 1957-64.
Anderson, George L., ed. *Issues and Conflicts: Studies in Twentieth Century American Diplomacy.* Lawrence: The University Press of Kansas, 1959.
Baldwin, Hanson W. *Great Mistakes of the War.* London: Redman, 1950.
_____. *The Price of Power.* New York: Harper, 1948.
Baring, Arnulf. *Der 17. Juni 1953.* Bonn: Deutsche Bundesverlag, 1958.
Barraclough, G. *Survey of International Affairs, 1956-1958.* London: Oxford University Press, 1962.
Beal, John R. *John Foster Dulles, 1888-1959.* New York: Harper, 1959.
Bell, Coral. *Negotiation from Strength.* New York: Knopf, 1963.
Beloff, Max. *The United States and the Unity of Europe.* Washington, D.C.: The Brookings Institution, 1963.

Berding, Andrew H. *Dulles on Diplomacy.* Princeton: Van Nostrand, 1965.

Betts, R. R., ed. *Central and South East Europe, 1945-1948.* London: Royal Institute of International Affairs, 1950.

Bloomfield, Lincoln P. *The United Nations and U.S. Foreign Policy.* Boston: Little, Brown & Co., 1960.

Boffa, Giuseppe. *Inside the Khrushchev Era.* New York: Marzani & Munsell, 1959.

Borsody, Stephen. *The Triumph of Tyranny.* London: Cape, 1960.

Brandon, Donald. *American Foreign Policy.* New York: Appleton-Century-Crofts, 1966.

Brandt, Willy. *A Peace Policy for Europe.* New York: Holt, Rinehart & Winston, 1969.

Brant, Stefan [pseud.]. *The East German Rising.* London: Thames & Hudson, 1955.

Bromke, Adam, and Wren, Philip E., eds. *The Communist States and the West.* New York: Praeger, 1967.

The Brookings Institution. *Major Problems of United States Foreign Policy, 1949-1950.* Washington, D.C., 1949.

Brown, J. F. *The New Eastern Europe.* New York: Praeger, 1966.

Brown, Seyom. *The Faces of Power.* New York: Columbia University Press, 1968.

Brzezinski, Zbigniew K. *Alternative to Partition.* New York: McGraw-Hill, 1965.

———. *The Soviet Bloc.* Cambridge, Mass.: Harvard University Press, 1960.

Brzezinski, Zbigniew K., and Huntington, S. P. *Political Power: USA/USSR.* New York: Viking, 1964.

Burks, R. V. *The Dynamics of Communism in Eastern Europe.* Princeton: Princeton University Press, 1961.

Burnham, James. *Containment or Liberation.* New York: John Day, 1953.

Burns, James MacGregor. *Roosevelt: The Soldier of Freedom.* New York: Harcourt, Brace & Jovanovich, 1970.

Calvocoressi, Peter. *Survey of International Affairs, 1947-1948.* London: Oxford University Press, 1952.

Champaigne, Jameson G. *American Might and Soviet Myth.* Chicago: Regnery, 1960.

Campbell, John C. *American Policy toward Communist Eastern Europe: The Choices Ahead.* Minneapolis: University of Minnesota Press, 1965.

———. *Tito's Separate Road: America and Yugoslavia in World Politics.* New York: Harper & Row, 1967.

Carleton, William G. *The Revolution in American Foreign Policy.* New York: Random House, 1963.

Chamberlin, William Henry. *Beyond Containment.* Chicago: Regnery, 1953.

Chester, Lewis; Hodgson, Godfrey; and Page, Bruce. *An American Melodrama: The Presidential Campaign of 1968.* New York: Viking, 1969.

Clark, Alan. *Barbarossa: The Russian-German Conflict, 1941-45.* New York: Morrow, 1965.

Clemens, Diane Shaver. *Yalta.* New York: Oxford University Press, 1970.

Collier, David S., and Glaser, Kurt, eds. *Berlin and the Future of Eastern Europe.* Chicago: Regnery, 1963.

———. *The Conditions for Peace in Europe.* Washington, D.C.: Public Affairs Press, 1969.

———. *Western Integration and the Future of Eastern Europe.* Chicago: Regnery, 1964.

———. *Western Policy and Eastern Europe.* Chicago: Regnery, 1966.

Cook, Thomas I., and Moos, Malcolm. *Power through Purpose: The Realism of Ideal-*

ism as a Basis for Foreign Policy. Baltimore: The Johns Hopkins Press, 1954.

Cookridge, E. H. *Gehlen: Spy of the Century.* New York: Random House, 1972.

Copp, DeWitt, and Peck, Marshall. *Betrayal at the UN.* New York: Devin-Adair, 1961.

Council on Foreign Relations. *Diplomacy and the Communist Challenge: A Report on the Views of Leading Citizens in Twenty-five Cities.* Edited by Joseph Barber. New York, 1954.

Crabb, Cecil V., Jr. *American Foreign Policy in the Nuclear Age.* Evanston, Ill.: Row, Peterson, 1960.

_____ . *Bipartisan Foreign Policy: Myth or Reality?* Evanston, Ill.: Row, Peterson, 1957.

Craig, Gordon A. *War, Politics, and Diplomacy.* New York: Praeger, 1966.

Crankshaw, Edward. *The New Cold War: Moscow v. Peking.* London: Penguin, 1963.

Crocker, George N. *Roosevelt's Road to Russia.* Chicago: Regnery, 1959.

Dallin, Alexander. *The Soviet Union at the UN.* New York: Praeger, 1962.

Dallin, David J. *Soviet Foreign Policy after Stalin.* Philadelphia: Lippincott, 1961.

_____ . *Soviet Russia's Foreign Policy, 1939-1942.* New Haven: Yale University Press, 1942.

Daniel, Hawthorne. *The Ordeal of the Captive Nations.* Garden City, N.Y.: Doubleday, 1958.

Daugherty, William E., ed. *A Psychological Warfare Casebook.* Baltimore: The Johns Hopkins Press, 1958.

Davidson, Eugene. *The Death and Life of Germany.* New York: Knopf, 1959.

Dean, Vera M. *The United States and Russia.* London: Oxford University Press, 1948.

Deane, John R. *The Strange Alliance.* New York: Viking, 1947.

Dedijer, Vladimir. *Tito.* New York: Simon & Schuster, 1953.

Dennett, Raymond, and Johnson, Joseph E., eds. *Negotiating with the Russians.* Boston: World Peace Foundation, 1951.

Deutscher, Isaac. *Stalin: A Political Biography.* London: Oxford University Press, 1949.

Divine, Robert A. *Roosevelt and World War Two.* Baltimore: The Johns Hopkins Press, 1969.

Donovan, Robert J. *Eisenhower: The Inside Story.* New York: Harper, 1956.

Drachkovitch, Milorad M. *United States Aid to Yugoslavia and Poland: Analysis of a Controversy.* Washington, D.C.: American Enterprise Institute for Public Policy Research, 1963.

Drummond, Roscoe, and Coblentz, Gaston. *Duel at the Brink.* London: Doubleday, 1961.

Dulles, John Foster. *War or Peace.* New York: Macmillan, 1950.

Ehrman, John. *Grand Strategy.* Vol. 5. London: Her Majesty's Stationery Office, 1956.

Feis, Herbert. *Churchill, Roosevelt, Stalin: The War They Waged and The Peace They Sought.* Princeton: Princeton University Press, 1957.

Fejtő, François. *Behind the Rape of Hungary.* New York: McKay, 1957.

Felix, Christopher [pseud.] . *A Short Course in the Secret War.* New York: Dutton, 1963.

Finer, Herman. *Dulles over Suez.* Chicago: Quadrangle, 1964.

Finletter, Thomas K. *Power and Policy.* New York: Harcourt, Brace, 1954.

Fleming, D. F. *The Cold War and Its Origins, 1917-1960.* London: Allen & Unwin, 1961.

Fulbright, J. William. *Old Myths and New Realities.* New York: Random House, 1964.

Gaitskell, Hugh. *The Challenge of Coexistence.* Cambridge, Mass.: Harvard University Press, 1958.

Gannon, Robert I. *The Cardinal Spellman Story.* Garden City, N.Y.: Doubleday, 1962.

Gerson, Louis L. *The Hyphenate in Recent American Politics and Diplomacy.* Lawrence: The University Press of Kansas, 1964.

———. *John Foster Dulles.* New York: Cooper Square, 1967.

Gibney, Frank. *The Frozen Revolution.* New York: Farrar, Straus, 1959.

Goodrich, Leland M. *The United Nations.* New York: Crowell, 1959.

Goodwin, G. L. *Britain and the UN.* New York: Manhattan, 1957.

Goold-Adams, Richard. *A Time of Power.* London: Weidenfeld & Nicolson, 1962.

Gordenker, Leon. *The UN Secretary-General and the Maintenance of Peace.* New York: Columbia University Press, 1967.

Graber, D. A. *Crisis Diplomacy.* Washington, D.C.: Public Affairs Press, 1959.

Graebner, Norman A. *Cold War Diplomacy, 1945 –1960.* Princeton: Van Nostrand, 1962.

———. *The New Isolationism.* New York: Ronald, 1956.

———, ed. *An Uncertain Tradition: American Secretaries of State in the Twentieth Century.* New York: McGraw-Hill, 1961.

Gross, Ernest A.; Wilcox, F. O.; and Haviland, H. F., eds. *The United States and the United Nations.* Baltimore: The Johns Hopkins Press, 1961.

Halle, Louis J. *The Cold War as History.* New York: Harper & Row, 1967.

Haviland, H. F., Jr. *The Formulation and Administration of United States Foreign Policy.* Washington, D.C.: The Brookings Institution, 1960.

Healey, Denis. *A Neutral Belt in Europe?* London: Fabian Society, 1958.

Herz, Martin F. *Beginnings of the Cold War.* New York: McGraw-Hill, 1969.

Higgins, Rosalyn. *The Development of International Law through the Political Organs of the United Nations.* London: Oxford University Press, 1963.

Hilsman, Roger, and Good, Robert C., eds. *Foreign Policy in the Sixties.* Baltimore: The Johns Hopkins Press, 1965.

Hinterhoff, Eugene. *Disengagement.* London: Stevens, 1959.

Hoffmann, Stanley. *Gulliver's Troubles: Or the Setting of American Foreign Policy.* New York: McGraw-Hill, 1968.

Hogye, Michael. *The Paris Peace Conference of 1946: Role of the Hungarian Communists and of the Soviet Union.* New York: Mid-European Studies Center, 1954.

Holt, Robert T. *Radio Free Europe.* Minneapolis: University of Minnesota Press, 1958.

Holt, Robert T., and Van De Welde, Robert W. *Strategic Psychological Operations and American Foreign Policy.* Chicago: University of Chicago Press, 1960.

Horowitz, David. *The Free World Colossus.* New York: Hill & Wang, 1965.

Hovet, T. *Bloc Politics in the UN.* Cambridge, Mass.: Harvard University Press, 1960.

Howard, Michael. *The Mediterranean Strategy in the Second World War.* London: Weidenfeld & Nicolson, 1968.

Hughes, Emmet John. *The Ordeal of Power.* New York: Atheneum, 1963.

Hyde, L. K. *The United States and the United Nations.* New York: Manhattan, 1960.

International Research Associates, Inc. *Hungary and the 1956 Uprising.* New York, 1957.

Kecskemeti, Paul. *The Unexpected Revolution: Social Forces in the Hungarian Uprising.* Stanford: Stanford University Press, 1961.

Keller, John W. *Germany, The Wall, and Berlin.* New York: Vantage, 1964.

Kennan, George F. *American Diplomacy, 1900-1950.* New York: New American Library, Mentor Books, 1963.

_____ . *On Dealing with the Communist World.* New York: Harper & Row, 1964.

_____ . *Russia, the Atom, and the West.* London: Oxford University Press, 1958.

Kennedy, John F. *The Strategy of Peace.* New York: Harper, 1960.

Kertész, Stephen D. *Diplomacy in a Whirlpool.* Notre Dame, Ind.: University of Notre Dame Press, 1953.

_____ . ed. *American Diplomacy in a New Era.* Notre Dame, Ind.: University of Notre Dame Press, 1961.

_____ . *East Central Europe and the World: Developments in the Post-Stalin Era.* Notre Dame, Ind.: University of Notre Dame Press, 1962.

_____ . *The Fate of East Central Europe.* Notre Dame, Ind.: University of Notre Dame Press, 1956.

Kissinger, Henry A. *American Foreign Policy.* New York: Norton, 1969.

Kolko, Gabriel. *The Politics of War.* New York: Random House, 1968.

Komorowski, Tadeusz. *The Secret Army.* New York: Macmillan, 1951.

Korbel, Josef. *The Communist Subversion of Czechoslovakia, 1938-1948.* Princeton: Princeton University Press, 1959.

Kovács, Imre, ed. *Facts about Hungary: The Fight for Freedom.* New York: Hungarian Committee, 1966.

Kracauer, S., and Berkman, P. L. *Satellite Mentality.* New York: Praeger, 1956.

Kulski, Wladyslaw W. *Peaceful Co-existence: An Analysis of Soviet Foreign Policy.* Chicago: Regnery, 1959.

LaFeber, Walter. *America, Russia, and the Cold War, 1945-1966.* New York: Wiley, 1967.

Lash, Joseph P. *Dag Hammarskjold.* London: Cassell, 1962.

Lasky, Melvin J., ed. *The Hungarian Revolution.* London: Secker & Warburg, 1957.

Lefever, Ernest. *Ethics and United States Foreign Policy.* New York: World Publishing Co., Meridian Books, 1958.

Leiss, Amelia C., ed. *European Peace Treaties after World War II.* Boston: World Peace Foundation, 1954.

Lerche, Charles O. *Foreign Policy of the American People.* Englewood Cliffs, N.J.: Prentice-Hall, 1967.

Lippmann, Walter. *The Cold War.* New York: Harper, 1947.

Liska, George. *Imperial America.* Baltimore: The Johns Hopkins Press, 1967.

Luard, Evan, ed. *The Cold War.* London: Thames & Hudson, 1964.

Lukacs, John A. *The Great Powers & Eastern Europe.* New York: American Book Co., 1953.

_____ . *A History of the Cold War.* New York: Doubleday, 1961.

McCloy, John J. *The Challenge to American Foreign Policy.* Cambridge, Mass.: Harvard University Press, 1953.

Mackintosh, J. M. *Strategy and Tactics of Soviet Foreign Policy.* London: Oxford University Press, 1962.

Markel, Lester, *et al. Public Opinion and Foreign Policy.* New York: Harper, for the Council on Foreign Relations, 1949.

Martin, L. W., ed. *Neutralism and Non-alignment.* New York: Praeger, 1961.

McNeal, Robert H., ed. *International Relations among Communists.* Englewood Cliffs, N.J.: Prentice-Hall, 1967.

Méray, Tibor. *Thirteen Days That Shook the Kremlin.* London: Thames & Hudson, 1959.

Mezerik, A. G. *Invasion and Occupation of Czechoslovakia and the UN.* New York: International Review Service, 1968.

Michie, Allan A. *Voices through the Iron Curtain: The Radio Free Europe Story.* New York: Dodd, Mead & Co., 1963.

Mikes, George. *The Hungarian Revolution.* London: Deutsch, 1957.

Miller, Richard I. *Dag Hammarskjold and Crisis Diplomacy.* New York: Oceana, 1961.

Molnár, Miklós, and Nagy, László. *Imre Nagy: Réformateur ou Révolutionnaire?* Geneva: Droz, 1959.

Montgomery, John F. *Hungary: The Unwilling Satellite.* New York: Devin-Adair, 1947.

Moore, R. A., ed. *The United Nations Reconsidered.* Columbia: University of South Carolina Press, 1963.

Moran, Lord. *Churchill.* London: Constable, 1966.

Morgenthau, Hans J. *American Foreign Policy: In Defense of the National Interest.* London: Methuen, 1952.

———. *Politics in the 20th Century.* 3 vols. Chicago: University of Chicago Press, 1962.

———. *The Purpose of American Politics.* New York: Knopf, 1960.

Mosely, Philip E. *Face to Face with Russia.* Washington, D.C.: Foreign Policy Assoc., 1948.

Mowrer, Edgar Ansel. *An End to Make-Believe.* New York: Duell, Sloan & Pearce, 1961.

Nitze, Paul H. *U.S. Foreign Policy, 1945-1955.* Washington, D.C.: Foreign Policy Assoc., 1956.

Northedge, F. S. *British Foreign Policy.* London: Allen & Unwin, 1962.

Novak, Bogdan C. *Trieste, 1941-1954.* Chicago: University of Chicago Press, 1970.

O'Conor, John F. *Cold War and Liberation.* New York: Vantage, 1961.

Opie, Redvers, *et al. The Search for Peace Settlements.* Washington, D.C.: The Brookings Institution, 1951.

Osgood, Robert E. *Ideals and Self-Interest in America's Foreign Relations.* Chicago: University of Chicago Press, 1953.

Page, Bruce; Leitch, David; and Knightley, Philip. *The Philby Conspiracy.* Garden City, N.Y.: Doubleday, 1968.

Palmer, Alan. *The Lands Between.* London: Weidenfeld & Nicolson, 1970.

Payne, Robert. *General Marshall.* London: Heinemann, 1952.

Perkins, Dexter. *The American Approach to Foreign Policy.* London: Oxford University Press, 1962.

Phillips, Cabell. *The Truman Presidency.* New York: Macmillan, 1966.

Planck, Charles R. *The Changing Status of German Reunification in Western Diplomacy: 1955-66.* Baltimore: The Johns Hopkins Press, 1967.

Price, Harry B. *The Marshall Plan and Its Meaning.* Ithaca, N.Y.: Cornell University Press, 1955.

Radványi, János. *Hungary and the Superpowers.* Stanford: Hoover Institution Press, 1972.

Rees, David. *The Age of Containment: The Cold War, 1945-1965.* New York: St. Martin's, 1967.

Reitzel, William; Kaplan, Morton A.; and Coblentz, Constance G. *U.S. Foreign Policy, 1945-1955.* Washington, D.C.: The Brookings Institution, 1956.

Rieselbach, Leroy N. *The Roots of Isolationism.* Indianapolis: Bobbs-Merrill, 1966.

Riggs, Robert E. *Politics in the United Nations: A Study of United States Influence in the General Assembly.* Urbana: University of Illinois Press, 1958.

Ripka, Hubert. *Le coup de Prague*. Paris: Plon, 1949.

_____ . *Eastern Europe in the Post-War World*. London: Methuen, 1961.

Roberts, Henry L. *Rumania*. New Haven: Yale University Press, 1951.

_____ . *Russia and America: Dangers and Prospects*. New York: Harper, for the Council on Foreign Relations, 1956.

Rockefeller Brothers Special Studies Project. *The Mid-Century Challenge to U.S. Foreign Policy*. Garden City, N.Y.: Doubleday, 1959.

Roosevelt, Elliott. *As He Saw It*. New York: Duell, Sloan & Pearce, 1946.

Rostow, Walt W. *The United States in the World Arena*. New York: Harper, 1960.

Rovere, Richard. *Affairs of State: The Eisenhower Years*. New York: Farrar, Straus, 1956.

Royal Institute of International Affairs. *Survey of International Affairs, 1939-1946*. Edited by Arnold Toynbee and Veronica M. Toynbee. Vol. 6. London: Oxford University Press, 1955.

Rozek, Edward J. *Allied Wartime Diplomacy: A Pattern in Poland*. New York: Wiley, 1958.

Rubinstein, Alvin Z. *The Foreign Policy of the Soviet Union*. New York: Random House, 1960.

Schlesinger, Arthur M., Jr. *A Thousand Days*. Boston: Houghton Mifflin, 1965.

_____ . *The Vital Center*. Boston: Houghton Mifflin, 1949.

Schmidt, Dana Adams. *Anatomy of a Satellite*. Boston: Little, Brown & Co., 1952.

Schramm, W. L., ed. *One Day in the World's Press*. Stanford: Stanford University Press, 1959.

Scott, John. *Political Warfare*. New York: John Day, 1955.

Seton-Watson, Hugh. *The East European Revolution*. New York: Praeger, 1956.

_____ . *Neither War Nor Peace*. London: Methuen, 1960.

Shepherd, Gordon. *Russia's Danubian Empire*. London: Heinemann, 1954.

Sherwood, Robert E. *Roosevelt and Hopkins*. New York: Harper, 1948.

_____ , ed. *The White House Papers of Harry L. Hopkins*. 2 vols. London: Eyre & Spottiswoode, 1948-49.

Shulman, Marshall D. *Beyond the Cold War*. New Haven: Yale University Press, 1966.

Smith, Gaddis. *American Diplomacy during the Second World War*. New York: Wiley, 1965.

Smith, Jean Edward. *The Defense of Berlin*. Baltimore: The Johns Hopkins Press, 1963.

_____ . *Germany beyond the Wall*. Boston: Little, Brown & Co., 1969.

Smith, R. Harris. *OSS: The Secret History of America's First Central Intelligence Agency*. Berkeley and Los Angeles: University of California Press, 1972.

Snell, John L., ed. *The Meaning of Yalta*. Baton Rouge: Louisiana State University Press, 1956.

Sorensen, Theodore C. *Kennedy*. New York: Harper & Row, 1965.

Spanier, John W. *American Foreign Policy since World War II*, 3rd rev. ed. New York: Praeger, 1968.

Speier, Hans. *Divided Berlin*. New York: Praeger, 1961.

Staar, Richard F. *Poland, 1944-1962*. Baton Rouge: Louisiana State University Press, 1962.

Steel, Ronald. *Pax Americana*. New York: Viking, 1967.

Stettinius, Edward R., Jr. *Roosevelt and the Russians: The Yalta Conference*. Garden City, N.Y.: Doubleday, 1950.

Stillman, Edmund, and Pfaff, William. *Power and Impotence*. New York: Random

House, 1966.

Strausz-Hupé, Robert; Kintner, William R.; Dougherty, James E.; and Cottrell, Alvin J. *Protracted Conflict.* New York: Harper, 1959.

Suda, Zdenek. *The Czechoslovak Socialist Republic.* Baltimore: The Johns Hopkins Press, 1969.

Szikszoy, J. A. *The Legal Aspects of the Hungarian Question.* Geneva, 1963.

Taft, Robert A. *A Foreign Policy for Americans.* Garden City, N.Y.: Doubleday, 1951.

Theoharis, Athan G. *The Yalta Myths: An Issue In U.S. Politics, 1945-1955.* Columbia: University of Missouri Press, 1970.

The Truth about the Nagy Affair: Facts, Documents, Comments. London: Secker & Warburg, 1959.

Ulam, Adam B. *Expansion and Coexistence.* New York: Praeger, 1968.

Urban, George. *The Nineteen Days.* London: Heinemann, 1957.

Váli, Ferenc A. *The Hungarian Revolution and International Law.* New York, 1959.

_____ . *Rift and Revolt in Hungary.* Cambridge, Mass.: Harvard University Press, 1961.

Warburg, J. P. *How to Co-exist without Playing the Kremlin's Game.* Boston: Beacon, 1952.

Watt, D. C. *Survey of International Affairs, 1961.* London: Oxford University Press, 1965.

Weintal, Edward, and Bartlett, Charles. *Facing the Brink.* New York: Scribner's, 1967.

Welles, Sumner. *Seven Decisions That Shaped History.* New York: Harper, 1951.

Westerfield, H. Bradford. *Foreign Policy and Party Politics.* New Haven, Yale University Press, 1955.

Whetten, Lawrence L. *Germany's Ostpolitik.* London: Oxford University Press, 1971.

Wilczynski, Jozef. *The Economics and Politics of East-West Trade.* London: Macmillan, 1969.

Williams, William Appleman. *The Tragedy of American Diplomacy.* New York: Delta, 1962.

Wilmot, Chester. *The Struggle for Europe.* London: Collins, 1952.

Wilson, Theodore A. *The First Summit: Roosevelt and Churchill at Placentia Bay, 1941.* Boston: Houghton Mifflin, 1969.

Windsor, Philip. *City on Leave.* New York: Praeger, 1963.

Windsor, Philip, and Roberts, Adam. *Czechoslovakia, 1968.* London: Chatto & Windus, 1969.

Wolfe, Thomas W. *Soviet Power and Europe, 1945-1970.* Baltimore: The Johns Hopkins Press, 1970.

Wolfers, Arnold. *Discord and Collaboration.* Baltimore: The Johns Hopkins Press, 1962.

_____ , ed. *Alliance Policy in the Cold War.* Baltimore: The Johns Hopkins Press, 1959.

_____ . *Changing East-West Relations and the Unity of the West.* Baltimore: The Johns Hopkins Press, 1964.

Woodward, Sir Llewellyn. *British Foreign Policy in the Second World War.* London: Her Majesty's Stationery Office, 1962.

Wright, Quincy, ed. *A Foreign Policy for the United States.* Chicago: University of Chicago Press, 1947.

Zawodny, J. K. *Death in the Forest.* Notre Dame, Ind.: University of Notre Dame Press, 1962.

Zinner, Paul E. *Communist Strategy and Tactics in Czechoslovakia, 1918-1948.* New York: Praeger, 1963.

_____ . *Revolution in Hungary.* New York: Columbia University Press, 1962.

INDEX

ACEN. *See* Assembly of Captive European Nations

Acheson, Dean, 77, 326; and Berlin crisis of 1961, 239, 241; criticized on containment, 86, 101-2, 108; and FEC, 94; and German reunification, 83, 84; and Hungarian coup, 74-75; and Kersten Amendment, 105; in 1952 campaign, 116-17; on U.S. policies toward East-Central Europe, 89-90, 93, 103

Adams, Sherman, 121, 122, 124

Adenauer, Konrad, 84, 85, 248, 253, 266; and Berlin crisis of 1958, 229; and Berlin crisis of 1961, 241; and disengagement, 156; and East German uprising, 135, 136, 314; negotiates with Soviet Union, 161; and West German rearmament, 128, 138

AFL-CIO, 193, 257

Albania, 60, 96, 104, 270; admitted to UN, 163; Titoists purged in, 92; Western intervention in, 96-98, 102

Albanian National Committee, 97

Alexander, Harold, 10-11

Algeria, 174

Allen, George V., 92

Allied Control Commission. *See under individual countries*

Alphand, Hervé, 184

American Assembly, 256

American Legion, 257

Andropov, Yuri, 190, 197

Antonescu, Ion, 2, 21

Arciszewski, Thomas, 25, 27, 34, 39

Argentina, 208

Aron, Raymond, 107

Assembly of Captive European Nations, 144, 247; founded, 141-43; and Hungarian revolution, 194; and Hungary's credentials, 246; and UN admissions, 163

Atlantic Charter, 6, 8, 12, 27, 28, 31, 32, 33, 34, 35, 46, 61, 116, 138, 296; Anglo-American negotiations on, 4-5; and Soviet Union, 5, 7, 9

Attlee, Clement, 51

Australia, 69, 87; and Hungarian revolution, 196, 201-3, 209

Austria, 7, 66, 89, 107, 233, 268, 280, 298, 299; disposal of German assets in, 53; and Hungarian revolution, 187, 189, 193, 205, 209, 218; negotiations on, 67, 72, 73, 77, 88, 128, 136, 138, 154-56, 308; 1945 elections in, 55, 57; occupation policy for, 26-27, 48, 50, 54-55; and peace treaties of 1920, 287; recognized by U.S., 55; State Treaty for, 155-56, 164; Yugoslav territorial claims on, 88

Austro-Hungarian empire, 287

Baldwin, Hanson W., 11

Balkan Pact, 147-48, 236

Ball, George, 256-57, 277, 295-96

Baltic states, 8, 29, 53, 141, 247, 299

Bang-Jensen, Povl, 209

Bankers Association for Foreign Trade, 256

Barnes, Maynard, 59

Barnes, Spencer, 179

Beam, Jacob D., 274

Belgium, 40, 93, 201, 208, 227, 302

Belgrade conference (1948), 88, 91

"Belgrade Declaration" (1955), 155

Beneš, Edvard, 3; and communist coup, 82; and postwar government, 61, 62, 81, 305; recog-

349